# Praise

"New Jersey money manager Bruce I. Jacobs writes in the *Financial Analysts Journal* that when financial products sold as risk reducers become big hits with investors, the institutions offering them become more prone to risk that they themselves cannot diversify away or hedge. This risk then could rear up and bite deeply during periods of extreme economic volatility. 'The end result can be catastrophic,' Jacobs warns."

**—William P. Barrett,**
in "Weapons of Mass Panic," *Forbes*, March 15, 2004

"What a great time for Bruce Jacobs to bring us *Too Smart for Our Own Good: Ingenious Investment Strategies, Illusions of Safety, and Market Crashes.* We are in the middle of yet another behaviorally driven market cycle and can use his sage advice and keen observations to help us navigate through it. Jacobs argues that investment products have the potential to interact in damaging ways with investor psychology. He also discusses the classic behavioral error of trend-following trading. The lessons learned from the past can be applied to today's trend-following themes: disruptive innovation, machine learning and crypto-currency. This is a timeless book that arrives just in time."

**—Brian Bruce,**
Editor, *The Journal of Behavioral Finance*

"Bruce Jacobs has the knowledge, experience, energy, and enthusiasm to draw keen insights from financial market disruptions such as the 1987 market crash and the 2007–2008 credit crisis. *Too Smart for Our Own Good* finds the common threads among the investment strategies and products that were supposed to be risk reducing, but instead gave rise to these and other market crises."

**—Barry Burr,**
former Editorial Page Editor, *Pensions & Investments*

"*Too Smart for Our Own Good* covers most of the financial disasters in the last part of the 20th century and the beginning of the 21st century. Bruce Jacobs was there and knows what he is talking about. The coverage is thorough and isolates the critical issues. There are several threads that link these disasters together such as liquidity squeezes/freezes, complexity and obscurity of investment instruments, leverage, nifty math, and a lot of hubris. Which leaves the reader asking how could so many talented investors make such huge mistakes? The answer, of course, is complicated, and this book will help you understand what happened and why."

**—Jon A. Christopherson,**
Research Fellow Emeritus, Russell Investments

"Bruce Jacobs explains when a crash is likely: It's when the economy is strong and risks appear to be low. Buy this book today and be forewarned."

**—Elroy Dimson,**
Professor of Finance, University of Cambridge, Judge Business School, and Emeritus Professor, London Business School

"Bruce Jacobs's insightful analyses of financial crises will alert readers to how some financial instruments and strategies can mask investment risk and lead to excessive leverage. The end result can be forced selling to meet margin calls and a collapse of liquidity and prices. One remedy suggested by Jacobs is to incorporate investors' natural aversion to leverage risk into portfolio decision making. Investors and financial institutions would do well to heed the warnings in this book."

**—Frank J. Fabozzi,**
Professor of Finance, EDHEC Business School, and Editor, *The Journal of Portfolio Management*

"Bruce Jacobs takes a close look at financial blowups over four decades and finds a common element: risk management and investment strategies that appear benign at the micro level but pose dire systemic risks at the macro level. This is an important lesson as memories of the global financial crisis start to fade."

**—Greg Feldberg,**
Director of Research, Financial Crisis Inquiry Commission, United States of America

"*Too Smart for Our Own Good* is a remarkable combination of decades of hands-on wisdom from a great investor with astute analytical insight born of detailed research—on a topic that is vital not only to the world of finance, but also to the world at large."

**—Geoffrey Garrett,**
Dean, The Wharton School of the University of Pennsylvania

"A central theme of Bruce Jacobs's new book is the importance of understanding the relationship between the actions of those in the financial marketplace—financial institutions, financial advisers, regulators, and investors—and their consequences. The increasing frequency of market crashes is a clarion call for a thorough investigation of the causes of market fragility. *Too Smart for Our Own Good* offers a critical analysis that is of paramount importance for all of us."

**—Michael Gibbons,**
Deputy Dean, I. W. Burnham Professor of Investment Banking,
The Wharton School of the University of Pennsylvania

"Wall Street's equivalent of the movie *Nightmare on Elm Street – Part 10.* Portfolio insurance/dynamic hedging, the Freddy Krueger of the 1987 stock market crash, is back again with the recent growth of options and swaps. Jacobs builds the case for how portfolio insurance and dynamic hedging exacerbated the 1987 crash and points out that dynamic hedging has played a similar role in recent periods of market volatility. And he draws unsettling parallels to the market turbulence surrounding the collapse of Long-Term Capital Management: the forced selling of overleveraged arbitrage positions, the 'illusion' of market liquidity, and the frontrunning by competing traders."

**—Robert Glauber,**
Executive Director, Brady Commission and former Under
Secretary of the Treasury, endorsement for Jacobs's earlier work,
*Capital Ideas and Market Realities: Option Replication,*
*Investor Behavior, and Stock Market Crashes*

"Bruce Jacobs, a prescient, early critic of portfolio insurance, has turned his attention to the series of financial market disasters since the crash of 1987. He identifies the flaws in a variety of strategies and instruments intended to increase returns and reduce risks that have perversely increased the fragility of the financial system. Jacobs combines an expert practitioner's understanding of complex financial instruments with insights from analytic and behavioral finance to provide lucid explanations of the logical flaws in these approaches. This is a highly readable account of a series of innovations that proved too clever by half."

**—Richard J. Herring,**
Jacob Safra Professor of International Banking, and Director, Wharton Financial Institutions Center, The Wharton School of the University of Pennsylvania

"Bruce Jacobs demonstrates effectively that trend-following strategies like portfolio insurance are fair-weather techniques that may add to, rather than minimize, troubles when a major crash occurs."

**—Charles P. Kindleberger,**
author of *Manias, Panics, and Crashes: A History of Financial Crises*, endorsement for Jacobs's earlier work, *Capital Ideas and Market Realities: Option Replication, Investor Behavior, and Stock Market Crashes*

"It has been said that history is the sum total of things that could have been avoided. That statement has never been truer than when applied to the history of financial crises. Too often, financial innovation, marketed by Wall Street firms as a means to reduce or control risk, actually creates or exacerbates other, unforeseen risks. Bruce Jacobs has produced an important and timely book that explains the common themes that underlie these disruptive events and offers the possibility of avoiding them in the future. It will be of inestimable, and equal, value to practitioners, regulators, and the academic community."

**—Richard Lindsey,**
former Director of Market Regulation and Chief Economist of the Securities and Exchange Commission

"Bruce Jacobs, an investment manager who predicted before the 1987 crash that portfolio insurance would trigger chain-reaction selling, recently forecast that option-strategies ('the sons of portfolio insurance') would play a similar, though more muted, role in a future debacle. Monday [October 27, 1997] provided damning evidence."

**—Roger Lowenstein,**
in *The Wall Street Journal*, November 6, 1997

"This is the book investors should read today to be prepared for the next crash, which is certain to come."

**—Edward M. Miller,**
former Professor of Economics and Finance,
University of New Orleans

"In *Too Smart for Our Own Good*, Bruce Jacobs brings his extensive experience and expertise as a financial analyst and commentator to bear on the increasingly important, and frequent, problem of financial crises. He weaves together stories of various crises since the 1980s and explains in clear and often gripping ways how leverage, opacity, and complex investment strategies contributed to market meltdowns. He also shines a light on the often-neglected conflicts of interest among market professionals and in academia. Anyone who wants markets to be safer and more stable should harken to Jacobs's words of wisdom."

**—Frank Partnoy,**
Author of *F.I.A.S.C.O.* and *Infectious Greed*, and
Professor of Law, University of California, Berkeley

"Black Swan events seem to be occurring all too frequently in markets. Have we forgotten that market returns are not normally distributed but instead reflect the fat tails we read about but never quite take into consideration? I heartily recommend carefully reading this latest book by Bruce Jacobs. Doing so will make you better able to understand and anticipate market crashes. Every one of Jacobs's publications has offered the reader excellent documentation and reasoning as to what happened, why it happened, and the likelihood of it happening again."

**—Robert F. Ploder,**
former Senior Investment Manager, IBM Retirement Funds

"Bruce Jacobs makes a strong case for admitting that financial crises are created by activities within financial markets, not by external factors, nor by a confluence of bad luck. His main message can be paraphrased using the words from a well-known 1970 Earth Day poster, namely, 'we have met the enemy and he is us.' Jacobs does a splendid job of connecting the dots of the causes of crises and suggests how we can think about the daunting task of 'taming the tempest.' "

**—Hersh Shefrin,**
Mario L. Belotti Professor of Finance,
Leavey School of Business, Santa Clara University

"Every fiduciary should read this book. Investors have too often been taken in by promotions appealing to their basic human instincts of fear and greed. Bruce Jacobs shows how supposedly low-risk, seemingly infallible investment strategies can backfire. His views on portfolio insurance helped steer our profit-sharing fund away from that craze in 1987. Today, especially in light of the Long-Term Capital Management fiasco, investors should know what Jacobs has to say about derivatives trading strategies and market crashes."

**—John E. Stettler,**
Vice President–Benefit Investments, Georgia-Pacific Corporation, endorsement for Jacobs's earlier work, *Capital Ideas and Market Realities: Option Replication, Investor Behavior, and Stock Market Crashes*

"In this very thoughtful and comprehensive book, Bruce Jacobs takes the reader on a tour of the financial markets and the market crises we have lived through. One key piece of advice is to be wary of so-called experts, no matter how smart they are. I highly recommend this well researched and written book."

**—William T. Ziemba,**
Professor Emeritus, University of British Columbia

# TOO SMART FOR OUR OWN GOOD

Dear Alan,

I hope you find of interest my new book on market crises.

Best,

Bruce

# TOO SMART FOR OUR OWN GOOD

## Ingenious Investment Strategies, Illusions of Safety, and Market Crashes

BRUCE I. JACOBS

New York Chicago San Francisco Athens London Madrid
Mexico City Milan New Delhi Singapore Sydney Toronto

1 2 3 4 5 6 7 8 9 LCR 23 22 21 20 19 18

ISBN: 978-1-260-44054-6
MHID: 1-260-44054-0

e-ISBN: 978-1-260-44055-3
e-MHID: 1-260-44055-9



Library of Congress Cataloging-in-Publication Data

Names: Jacobs, Bruce I., author.
Title: Too smart for our own good : ingenious investment strategies, illusions of safety, and market crashes / Bruce I. Jacobs.
Description: 1 Edition. | New York : McGraw-Hill Education, 2018.
Identifiers: LCCN 2018027535 | ISBN 9781260440546 (hardback) | ISBN 1260440540
Subjects: LCSH: Investments. | Portfolio management. | Financial crises. | BISAC: BUSINESS & ECONOMICS / Finance.
Classification: LCC HG4521 .J2523 2018 | DDC 332.6--dc23 LC record available at https://lccn.loc.gov/2018027535

*To Ilene, Lauren, Julie, Sam, and Erica*
*for their love, patience, and support.*

# CONTENTS

# EXHIBITS

# ACKNOWLEDGMENTS

Writing this book has been for me a calling, as you will see in the Introduction, but one which I could not have accomplished without assistance and support.

Thanks to my partner at Jacobs Levy Equity Management, Ken Levy, for his advice and encouragement.

I am also appreciative to others at Jacobs Levy for their contributions. Judith Kimball and David Landis provided valuable editorial advice, research, and support for this book over the years. Special thanks to our project management team, Catherine Spinella, Herminia Carvalheira, Anamika Panchoo, and Melissa Weresow for their joint efforts creating what has ultimately become this book. Thanks also to the Portfolio Engineering and Trading Departments for data validation, and members of the Research and Client Service Departments for helpful comments.

Thank you to Donya Dickerson, editorial director, and Cheryl Ringer, editor, at McGraw-Hill, who have shepherded the book through the publication process.

Readers may send comments or questions via email to jacobslevy@jlem.com or find more information about the book at www.jacobslevy.com.

INTRODUCTION

# Creating Financial Storms

*". . . such is the storm*
*that comes against me manifestly from Zeus*
*to work its terrors. O Holy mother mine,*
*O Sky that circling brings the light to all,*
*you see me, how I suffer, how unjustly."*

**—Aeschylus**[1]

Why do today's financial markets fall apart with such seeming regularity? Are these turbulent episodes merely "perfect storms," fatal but unavoidable coincidences of bad luck? Or is it possible to discern the hand of something other than fate darkening the skies? Are there elements common to each of these crises that could, perhaps, allow us to anticipate the next one?

On Monday, October 19, 1987, the US stock market crashed, suffering its worst daily percentage loss ever and setting off declines in equity markets around the world. On a single day, the Dow Jones Industrial Average (DJIA) plummeted 508 points, losing 22.6 percent of its value. This was an even greater loss than occurred during the Great Crash of 1929, when the market took two days to give up a little over 23 percent of its value. (Appendix A provides a more detailed look at that crash and its aftermath.) Futures contracts on equity indexes fared even worse than stocks in the 1987 crash, declining as much as 28.6 percent. In a matter of hours, stock investors lost over $1 trillion. Even though the stock market had fallen substantially in the previous week, no events appeared significant enough to explain these losses.

In August 1998, almost 11 years later, the US stock market suffered a bout of volatility reminiscent of the 1987 crash. The Russian government essentially devalued the ruble on August 17 and announced a 90-day moratorium on repayment of $40 billion in corporate and bank debt. Currency markets went into a tailspin, and investors pulled money out of Russia and other commodity-producing countries and placed it in US dollar-denominated assets. This "flight to quality" soon spread to stocks, with international investors dumping emerging market stocks first. It also wreaked havoc on Long-Term Capital Management (LTCM), one of the world's largest hedge funds at the time. Expectations that the fund would be forced to liquidate its massive positions in global equity and bond markets created more turmoil, which lasted throughout the fall.

In the summer of 2007, as a housing bubble in the United States neared its peak, hedge funds that invested in mortgage-linked securities faced liquidity problems similar to those that confronted LTCM in 1998. Like LTCM, many of them liquidated positions, leading to a substantial decline in US stock prices on August 9, 2007. This time, unlike in 1998, the underlying problems lingered and festered. Large numbers of mortgage defaults led to sharp losses at major commercial and investment banks in the United States and Europe. Liquidity in credit markets dried up by the end of 2008, with severe repercussions for the real economies of the United States and Europe.

Crises such as those that occurred in 1987, 1998, and 2007–2008 generate innumerable books and government inquiries, and inspire nearly purple-prosed descriptions in the press. In the 10 years following the most recent global financial crisis, countless authors have attempted to explain its root causes. Why add one more book to the pile? Perhaps because we are not well-served by explanations that portray financial crises as either unforeseeable, inexplicable, or unavoidable acts of God or inherent characteristics of capital markets.

According to University of Chicago Professor Eugene F. Fama, one of the earliest and most prominent proponents of the theory that market prices always reflect all available information, changes in underlying fundamentals were behind the steep drop in stock prices on October 19, 1987. The stock market, he wrote, "moved with breathtaking quickness to its new equilibrium [reflecting changes in underlying fundamentals], and its performance during this period of hyperactive trading is to be applauded."[2] In 1988, University of California Professor Mark E. Rubinstein, co-creator of an investment strategy that came to be known as portfolio insurance, cited

12 fundamental factors that caused the 1987 crash, including increasing interest rates and rising budget deficits,[3] but later concluded that an explanation based totally on fundamentals was inadequate.[4]

Journalist Michael Lewis described the 1998 stock market crisis along these lines:[5]

> Alan Greenspan and Robert Rubin said they had never seen such a crisis and neither had anyone else. It was one thing for the average stock-market investor to panic. It was another for the world's biggest financial firms to panic. The world's finance institutions created a bank run on a huge, global scale.

Myron S. Scholes, co-creator of the Black-Scholes-Merton option pricing formula and a partner at LTCM, thought "maybe part of the blame for the flight to liquidity [in August 1998] lies with the International Monetary Fund," which had declined to bail out Russian debtholders.[6]

James E. (Jimmy) Cayne, chief executive of Bear Stearns from 1993 until its collapse in 2008, gave the following eulogy for the late, legendary firm: "Life goes on. This company achieved lofty heights for sure. But we ran into a hurricane."[7] Richard S. Fuld Jr., former head of the now defunct Lehman Brothers, looking back on the events of 2008, opined: "It's not just one single thing. It's all those things taken together. I refer to it as the perfect storm."[8]

In effect, these crises are viewed by many as perfect storms. But, as scientists are beginning to discover, perfect storms are the result not only of God and nature, but of man. The same holds true for financial storms.

For example, a number of "flash crashes"—sudden, sharp, and seemingly inexplicable price movements—have been blamed on market manipulation, investor error, and computer trading algorithms responding mechanistically to price changes. Perhaps the best known incident occurred on May 6, 2010, when the DJIA dropped 1,000 points in a matter of minutes (a decline of roughly 9% from its high point of the day), but quickly recovered. More recently, on February 5, 2018, the DJIA fell 900 points in 15 minutes and ended the day down 1,600 points. This disruption has been attributed to the effects of trend-following trading strategies tied to the VIX—the Chicago Board Options Exchange Volatility Index. Stock markets in the US and elsewhere, as well as commodity and currency markets, have experienced similar incidents at other times. Luckily, losses have generally been reversed as quickly as they occurred.

The lengthy deflation of the dot-com bubble, which began in March 2000, presents a more subtle example of investor-induced crises. The 1990s were the era of the "new economy," when pundits claimed that old yardsticks such as price/earnings (P/E) ratios, dividend yields, and cash flow could be thrown away in favor of faith in the unlimited future of the Internet. Internet companies had grown from basically nothing to account for 6 percent of market capitalization in the 10 years ending in early 2000. Between March 10 and April 14, 2000, however, the Nasdaq Composite Index fell by 34.2 percent, and it continued to decline over the next two years, ending down 78 percent from its March 10 peak. The rise and fall of the dot-coms can be attributed at least in part to an investment strategy—momentum trading.[9] Momentum trading calls for buying stocks as their prices rise, with the intention of selling these same stocks as their prices fall.

This book challenges the notion that financial crises are merely the result of happenstance, bad luck, or the markets' natural proclivities. Rather, they grow out of certain types of financial strategies and products that have the potential to interact in damaging ways with investor psychology. These strategies and products are intended to reduce the risk of investing. They rely on state-of-the-art computer engineering and sophisticated mathematics as well as marketing campaigns designed to overcome any doubt with extravagant claims and "guarantees" of favorable results. Yet, ironically, despite their purported safety, they have actually increased risk for all investors by creating conditions that give rise to financial storms.

Of particular interest are portfolio insurance in the 1980s, arbitrage strategies pursued by LTCM in the 1990s, and the mortgage-linked securities at the center of the 2007–2008 credit crisis. All these strategies and products seemed to offer a free lunch—the potential to reduce risk while increasing return. When they attracted large numbers of followers, however, they channeled individual investors' hopes and fears in a way that created market instability. They magnified steep increases in market values, to the point where prices became unsustainable. Investor pessimism then set in, suddenly turning gains into losses.

While the particular strategies and instruments that are offered change over time, they share certain commonalities. These commonalities include opacity and complexity, which make it difficult to anticipate the effects of the strategies and products and to discern the relationships they forge between different market participants. They also include leverage, facilitated by derivatives and borrowing, which increases their impact on security prices, markets, and the economy. And they include the underlying, option-like nature of the strategies and products, which can make markets behave in nonlinear ways, with prices bubbling up or crashing down.

Risk-reducing strategies and products that share these characteristics can create an illusion of liquidity, a misperception of underlying risks, a flood of capital into the strategies and products, and a magnification of their effects on underlying markets and financial institutions. Consequent feedback loops between the strategies and market behavior further increase market fragility. Investors aware of the common threads between all of these market upsets can avoid repeating the mistakes of the past and contribute to a more stable financial future.

## ABOUT THE BOOK

Part I of this book provides a brief explanation of the relationship between risk and return in the investment world, and the ways in which investors have attempted to mitigate risk. To a large extent, the crises that have unfolded in US financial markets are the result of products and strategies that obscure the relationship between risk and return. Readers already familiar with basic risk-management strategies such as diversification and hedging may want to skip ahead to Part II. Others may want to pay close attention to the mechanics of short selling, as described in Chapter 1, "Reducing Risk." Short selling is a strategy for profiting from a security's price decline. Several hedge funds famously earned billions of dollars for their investors by astutely betting against mortgage securities before the market for them collapsed in 2008.[10] While there are no guarantees that such riches will result, the insights from this book should leave readers better prepared to diagnose, and potentially profit from, the next financial meltdown.

Part II begins with a description of the stock market crash of October 1987 and then goes on to examine portfolio insurance and the role it played in the crash. Portfolio insurance grew out of the options pricing model developed by the late Fischer Black and Nobel laureates Myron S.

Scholes and Robert C. Merton. This model allowed the creators of portfolio insurance to design a stock trading strategy that replicated the effects of protecting a portfolio with a put option in order to limit losses. Widely used by investors, the strategy essentially shifts risks from "insured" portfolios to the market by mandating mechanistic selling as stock prices decline and buying as stock prices rise. When a large enough number of investors engage in this type of trend-following trading, they can sweep markets along with them, elevating stock prices at some times and causing dramatic price drops at other times.

Marketed to large institutional investors as a "free lunch" in the mid 1980s, portfolio insurance grew into a $100 billion industry by the fall of 1987. Its increasing popularity helped propel markets ever upward through the middle of the decade. Emboldened by assurances they were protected from a downturn, insured investors maintained or increased their equity positions. When equity markets began to decline in mid October 1987, however, the strategy called for mechanistic selling. The volume of sales by portfolio insurers set off a stampede out of the market on Monday, October 19.

While the use of portfolio insurance declined to negligible levels after the 1987 stock market crash, the theory behind it lives on in several similar strategies that seem to offer high returns at low risk. These include trillions of dollars in option-based financial derivatives used to hedge the risk of investing in stocks and bonds. These strategies employ the same sort of option-replication trading used by portfolio insurance, and Part II looks at their role in a series of market disruptions—"mini market breaks"—in the 1990s.

Part III concentrates on the demise of LTCM in 1998 and its effects on US stock and bond markets. The kinds of strategies pursued by LTCM can pressure markets in the same way that option replication does, especially when the strategies rely heavily on borrowing money. As LTCM's supposedly low-risk strategies became more and more risky in the summer of 1998, losses mounted and the fund was forced to sell, mechanistically, into declining markets, resulting in precipitous drops in wealth for many investors.

Part IV examines the credit crisis of 2007–2008 and shows how the growth and collapse of the US housing bubble was enabled by subprime mortgage loans, which were marketed to homebuyers with checkered credit histories. These loans, in turn, gave rise to a handful of investment products, known by their various acronyms as MBS, CDO, and CDS. These were used to shift risk from one party to another, lender to financial intermediary, financial intermediary to investor. Each party felt its own risk was reduced, to the point that many lost sight of the real risks of the underlying loans. This sense of safety, in turn, encouraged more lending, more securitized products, and more borrowing to buy mortgages and mortgage-based products.

But when house price appreciation slowed in many areas of the country, and then reversed, a large number of borrowers, especially subprime borrowers, began to default on their mortgages. This created a chain reaction of losses and consequences. The value of collateralized debt obligations (CDOs) based on securities backed by subprime loans fell. At the same time, insurance companies, hedge funds, and others that had sold credit default swaps (CDS), which insured against the defaults of such CDOs, faced rising obligations. As financial pressures mounted, the willingness of banks to lend to each other and to other customers dried up, and the evaporation of credit soon led to major problems for the real global economy. These products, designed to reduce risks for participating investors, ended up creating a broader type of risk—systemic risk—with the potential to impact the global financial system.

Part V looks at how the ongoing European debt crisis emerged from the US credit crisis and examines the differences and similarities between the seemingly disparate financial debacles discussed in this book. At first glance, the crises, emerging roughly every 10 years, appear quite different from one another. In 1987, the problems were created by institutional investors, and the damage was largely confined to the stock market, although it spread from the United States to overseas markets. In 1998, a single large hedge fund, LTCM, roiled equity and fixed-income markets, primarily in the United States. In both these cases, the crises did not have long-lasting effects. The turmoil of 2007–2008, by contrast, was a credit crisis. The paralysis that prevented US banks from extending credit to each other, to businesses, and to consumers spread globally and posed long-term problems. While each crisis was unique, however, all had a common denominator. In 1987, in the mini market breaks of the 1990s, in the LTCM failure in 1998, and in the 2007–2008 crisis, instability was magnified by strategies or instruments that were supposed to reduce risk while improving returns.

## A WATCHFUL EYE ON FINANCIAL CRISES

As a co-founder and co-principal of an equity management firm specializing in quantitative management of long and long-short portfolios for institutional clients, I have a professional as well as personal interest in the stability of financial markets. The seeds of my interest were first planted in the 1980s, when I joined the Prudential Insurance Company of America. Asked to assess a new dynamic hedging strategy that came to be known as portfolio insurance, I engaged in some heated debates with Hayne E. Leland, Mark Rubinstein, and John W. O'Brien, founding partners of Leland O'Brien Rubinstein Associates (LOR). Leland and Rubinstein, also professors at the University of California, Berkeley, had devised portfolio insurance based on the Black-Scholes-Merton option pricing formula.

Although the strategy seemed appealing on its surface, I warned that it contained its own self-destruct mechanism. In a memorandum to my higher-ups and the client service and sales forces at Prudential, I asserted that the strategy's automatic, trend-following trading could destabilize markets, which would, in turn, cause the insurance to fail.[11] Prudential followed my advice, and avoided portfolio insurance. In the short term, it missed out on the management fees associated with a burgeoning portfolio insurance industry, but in the longer term its client service force avoided the difficult discussions after the strategy failed—when it was needed most—during the 1987 crash.

Prior to the 1987 stock market crash, I engaged in several public debates with LOR and wrote a series of articles revealing the real costs of portfolio insurance.[12] My insight was later recognized by *Pensions & Investments*, which noted that I was "one of the first to warn that portfolio insurance . . . probably would be destabilizing,"[13] and in the *Wall Street Journal*, where Roger Lowenstein said that I had "predicted before the 1987 crash that portfolio insurance would trigger chain-reaction selling."[14] Rubinstein later wrote of my "prescience in forecasting the Achilles' heel of the portfolio insurance strategy."[15]

I subsequently wrote about how the mechanistic trading of portfolio insurance contributed to the crash of October 19, 1987, in "Viewpoint on Portfolio Insurance: It's Prone to Failure," "The Darker Side of Option Pricing Theory," "Option Pricing Theory and Its Unintended

Consequences," and "Option Replication and the Market's Fragility."[16] The culmination of these efforts came in 1999, with the publication of my book, *Capital Ideas and Market Realities: Option Replication, Investor Behavior, and Stock Market Crashes*.[17]

*Capital Ideas and Market Realities*, which includes a foreword by Nobel laureate Harry Markowitz, provides a detailed inquiry into portfolio insurance—whether it is a desirable investment strategy and the role it played in the 1987 stock market crash.[18] It goes on to discuss later strategies that pose similar problems for market stability. These include over-the-counter (OTC) options (bilateral agreements not subject to the rules of an exchange) and the type of highly leveraged arbitrage trading done by hedge funds such as LTCM. When such trades fall apart, the need to unwind arbitrage positions creates the same trading patterns as portfolio insurance—selling into down markets. I expanded upon this in "Long-Term Capital's Short-Term Memory," "When Seemingly Infallible Arbitrage Strategies Fail," and "A Tale of Two Hedge Funds."[19]

In a 2004 *Financial Analysts Journal* article, "Risk Avoidance and Market Fragility," I discussed the essential differences between risk sharing and risk shifting.[20] Risk sharing can reduce risk, as diversification of the risks of the individual securities within a portfolio reduces overall risk. But risk shifting (as occurs with portfolio insurance, certain arbitrage strategies, and, most recently, residential mortgage-backed securities, CDOs, and CDS) merely moves risk from one party to another. Risk shifting reduces individual investors' perceptions of the risks they are incurring, thereby encouraging more risk taking. Overall risk in the system, however, remains, and in fact increases, as investors are encouraged to take on more risk. At some point, markets become fragile and susceptible to even small shocks. As I pointed out in that article, when markets become fragile and when firms are deemed "too big to fail," the government may become "the risk bearer of last resort."[21]

My article "Tumbling Tower of Babel: Subprime Securitization and the Credit Crisis" discussed how instruments such as CDOs and CDS contributed to the 2007–2008 crisis.[22] I later became a member of the Committee to Establish the National Institute of Finance. This committee was instrumental in convincing Congress to include in its reform of financial regulation a council of financial regulators, the Financial Stability Oversight Council, charged with identifying within the financial system risks that could destabilize the US economy, and the Office of Financial Research, to support that council. This book represents the culmination of more than 35 years of effort advocating for more transparency and disclosure.

# PART I

CHAPTER 1

# Reducing Risk

*"Most of academic finance is teaching that you can't earn 40 percent a year without some risk of losing a lot of money."*

**—William F. Sharpe[1]**

Historically, stocks have offered higher investment returns than bonds. That is no accident. Stocks are riskier. Therefore, investors require an incentive, such as a bigger anticipated payoff, to choose stocks over bonds. This illustrates a simple concept: *Increased risk brings greater expected reward, and greater expected reward comes with increased risk.* This relationship applies to virtually any type of investment, from stocks and bonds to commodities and currencies.

What is risk? Statistically, risk is defined by volatility, a measure of the magnitude of price changes over a period of time. But a simpler and more cogent definition is this: Risk is the likelihood of losing some, or all, of the value of your investment. The higher the risk, the greater is the chance of loss. Risk can come from a variety of sources, including changes in economic conditions (for example, inflation risk), a company's financial health (for example, credit risk), or transaction issues (for example, liquidity risk). Appendix B provides a brief primer on how the sources of risk differ between bonds, stocks, and derivatives, and how the differences affect the returns on these financial instruments.

While risk and reward are inextricably linked, investors have long sought strategies designed to maximize the latter while minimizing the former. This can be attempted through a variety of techniques, ranging from simple to complex. But even the simplest risk-management strategies outlined below have their drawbacks.

## DIVERSIFICATION

In a portfolio, risk can be controlled via diversification, which is accomplished by holding a number of securities that are expected to react differently to events.[2] A rise in oil prices, for example, might adversely impact an airline while providing a boost to oil companies or energy exploration firms. So a portfolio that holds a mix of these stocks can be somewhat immunized against oil price shocks.

Of course, diversification protects only against company-specific risk; it does not shield against systematic risk, a generalized decline in stock prices. Systematic risk itself can be diversified to an extent by holding assets that have offsetting exposures to sources of risk. For example, bond prices tend to be hard hit when inflation rises unexpectedly, whereas stock prices hold up better as the companies issuing the stocks may be able to pass inflationary cost increases on to customers. Thus holding both bonds and stocks can help to mitigate the effects of increases in inflation.

But while diversifying across asset classes—stocks, bonds, commodities, etc.—can cushion the impact of a decline in any particular asset class, the benefits are limited. In particular, during market crises, there are often simultaneous declines in numerous asset classes. During the 1998 crisis, for example, both stock and bond investments lost value.

Diversification also can be of limited value when a portfolio is leveraged, that is, when some of its holdings are purchased with borrowed funds. Leverage can magnify losses (and gains), and this can occur even in a well-diversified portfolio. In fact, the process prescribed by finance theory for constructing a diversified portfolio with the optimal balance of risk and return assumes that investors have no aversion to (or put another way, an infinite tolerance for) the unique risks of leverage.

To the extent that leverage increases a portfolio's volatility, this widely used process, known as mean-variance optimization, recognizes some of the risks posed by leverage. But it recognizes none of the unique risks of leverage, which include potential margin calls that may force the sale of assets under adverse market conditions, the possibility of incurring losses beyond the capital invested, and the risks and costs of bankruptcy. Thus, investors may hold risky, highly leveraged portfolios that are, nonetheless, considered "optimal."

An alternative method of constructing portfolios, mean-variance-leverage optimization, explicitly considers the level of leverage risk in a portfolio and allows investors to determine optimal levels of leverage based on their degrees of leverage aversion. In this way, investors can trade off portfolio expected return against portfolio volatility risk *and* leverage risk.[3]

## PROTECTIVE STRATEGIES

One of the simplest risk-control techniques is a predefined selling strategy. Rebalancing, for example, calls for restoring a portfolio's target allocation at regular intervals by selling securities that have appreciated in value and investing the proceeds in securities that have not risen as much or have fallen. This simple process is easy to implement and requires no particular insight about the market or individual securities. It is by design a program to buy low and sell high, the most basic strategy for investing success.

Rebalancing is not foolproof, however. Purchases and sales can be untimely. Stocks might be sold when they have further room to rise, resulting in forgone gains. Or stocks may be purchased while they are still falling, leading to increased losses. Because the strategy merely rebalances as losses are incurred, it cannot limit portfolio losses to a specific target.

A stop-loss order is designed to limit losses to a specific amount. It is an order placed with a broker that calls for selling a stock once its price falls below a specified level. The order can take several forms. A stop-loss market order calls for selling the stock at the best available price once it falls below the specified threshold. A stop-loss limit order calls for selling the stock at a specific price at or below the specified threshold.

There are a number of potential costs to this strategy, however. In a volatile market characterized by "whipsaw" movements, a sudden drop in price can trigger a stop-loss sale just before the stock makes a significant upward move. In such a case, the stop-loss order would provide the expected downside protection, but at the cost of a large potential gain.

There are other cases in which the stop-loss order may not provide the expected price protection. In a fast-moving market, a stock's price could drop well below the specified threshold before a broker is able to fill the sell order. Losses could thus be greater than anticipated. This situation may be addressed through the use of a stop-loss limit order, which requires that the stock be sold at the specified price or not at all. But in a fast-moving market the broker might be unable to execute the order as specified, which also could lead to greater-than-expected losses. Thus, the user of a stop order must decide whether to take on greater price risk (with a market order) in order to ensure the order is executed, or greater execution risk (with a limit order) in exchange for greater control over the sale price.

## Portfolio Insurance

Part II of this book will discuss portfolio insurance, which is a formal stock-selling strategy that attempts to replicate the loss-limiting features of a put option. Like a put option, portfolio insurance is designed to set a minimum floor value for a portfolio, but like a stop-loss order, it doesn't always accomplish its objective.

A portfolio insurance strategy moves assets between stocks and risk-free US Treasury bills or cash according to option-based formulas and market conditions. In general, the strategy requires the sale of stocks when stock prices are falling and the purchase of stocks when they are rising. The goal is to reduce the portfolio's participation in the market when the market is declining and to increase participation when the market is on the upswing.

Portfolio insurance can perform as advertised under normal market conditions, but it can suffer during periods of unexpected turbulence, as we will see in Chapter 5, "Portfolio Insurance and the Crash." Furthermore, when portfolio insurance is wildly popular and widely employed, it can destabilize market prices, creating the very conditions that cause it to fail. When stocks are rising, the strategy requires buying, which can push prices up further. When stocks are falling, widespread selling mandated by the strategy has the potential to overwhelm available buyers, triggering liquidity risk concerns. Also, selling by portfolio insurers can cause further selling by market participants who are unaware that the surge in sales results from programmatic selling rather than a change in fundamentals. Extreme price dislocations can result, as they did during the stock market crash of 1987, severely undermining the strategy's claim to limit potential losses.

## Guarantees

Portfolio insurance really isn't insurance, despite its name. Traditional insurance requires an upfront premium payment to an independent insurer, which then takes on the risk of an unforeseen event. With portfolio insurance there are no premiums paid and no independent party to assume the risk. The portfolio insurer is essentially self-insured, giving up return in exchange for theoretical safety.

Nevertheless, investment insurance does legitimately exist in a variety of forms. Some investment products incorporate insurance-like features, such as a guaranteed return of principal. They are known by a variety of names, including guaranteed equity, equity-linked notes, and principal-protected notes. For example, a bank or broker-dealer may issue an exchange-traded note that promises to pay upon maturity the principal plus gains equal to the return of a stock index above a certain threshold.

These products can also suffer from numerous shortcomings. As with portfolio insurance, the price of protection on the downside is paid for by truncated gains on the upside. The returns of a product such as the one described above can be cheaply replicated through the combination of a Treasury security with a value equal to the principal of the note combined with a call option on a stock index. But because of numerous fees built into the structure, the retail cost of the note can be excessive. In addition, some versions of these products can have complex structures behind their relatively simple principal guarantees and suffer from transparency risk. The secondary market for these securities is thin, adding liquidity risk to a list of concerns. Even though buyers may hedge their market risk with these products, they also expose themselves to the risk that the seller of the product may default.

Perhaps the best-known type of investment insurance is that provided by the Federal Deposit Insurance Corporation (FDIC), which insures up to $250,000 per account in individual bank deposits and pays off in the event of a bank failure. Although deposit insurance has virtually eliminated the retail bank panics that occurred periodically in the United States until the 1930s, it is not without drawbacks. "Moral hazard" can arise when banks act recklessly with depositors' money, knowing any losses will be reimbursed by the government. For example, soon after deposit protection was extended to savings-and-loan depositors in the early 1980s, losses from widespread fraudulent lending cost taxpayers more than $100 billion.

Government-sponsored enterprises can also provide a form of insurance. The Federal National Mortgage Association (Fannie Mae) and the Federal Home Loan Mortgage Corporation (Freddie Mac) guarantee the timely payment of interest and principal by the mortgage-backed securities they issue. These guarantees have attracted vast amounts of capital to the mortgage market, helping to reduce the cost of home ownership. But many would say that expanded home ownership came at an eventual price, as we will see in Part IV.

Another common form of insurance is provided to issuers of municipal bonds by a specialized group of insurers known as monolines. This insurance, which guarantees the timely repayment of principal and interest in the case of default, allows state and local governments to issue debt at lower interest rates than would otherwise be possible. Monolines offered similar insurance on mortgage-backed products such as collateralized debt obligations (CDOs). The insurance served as an additional guarantee for securities that carried a low-risk AAA or similar rating from the credit rating agencies. However, losses on insured CDOs soared during the 2007–2008 credit crisis, depleting monolines' reserves and compromising their municipal bond guarantees.

## Hedging

Hedging is a strategy to limit losses from a security by owning or selling short another security with expected price movements that will offset some of the price movements of the first security. An investor might buy shares of exporting and importing companies to mitigate the impact of fluctuations in currency exchange rates.

Hedging is also widely used as a means of controlling business risk. Farmers hedge against a fall in crop prices. Manufacturers hedge against the rising cost of raw materials. Companies with international sales hedge against adverse fluctuations in foreign currency exchange rates.

A key component of most hedging strategies is the ability to sell an asset short. Short selling, or shorting, is a technique for profiting from a decline in the price of an asset. Shorting a stock involves selling shares that have been borrowed from a broker and receiving the proceeds. Later, the shares are repurchased and returned to the broker. If the shares have fallen in price, as the short seller expected, the short seller makes a profit from the difference between the price at which the shares were sold and the lower price at which they were repurchased. If the shares have risen in price, the short seller will have to repurchase them at a higher price, incurring a loss.

Consider, for example, an investment manager who holds a large position in Amazon stock. Even if the manager expects the Amazon stock to outperform the stocks of other retail companies, he or she may want to reduce, or hedge, the risk of the large exposure to the retail industry. This could be done by selling, for example, an equal dollar amount of Sears shares short. If the prices of both stocks rise, the manager will earn a profit if, as expected, Amazon outperforms Sears. The profit will equal the gain on the Amazon shares less the smaller loss on the shorted Sears shares. But even if the prices of both stocks fall, the manager will profit as long as the Amazon stock falls less than the Sears stock. In that case, the manager will take a loss on the Amazon shares but will make a larger gain on the shorted Sears shares. If the Amazon stock rises while the Sears stock falls, the profit will equal the gain on the Amazon shares plus the gain from being able to buy (and return) the borrowed Sears shares at a price lower than the price at which they were sold short.

Of course, if Sears ends up outperforming Amazon, contrary to the manager's expectations, there will be a loss whether both stocks rise in price, both stocks fall in price, or the Sears stock rises while the Amazon stock falls. In the case of both stocks falling, the gain on the shorted Sears shares will offset some of the loss on the long Amazon position, so the risk of the Amazon position is hedged to some extent. In the other scenarios, however, the hedge may actually increase the loss the manager would have sustained with an unhedged position in Amazon shares. If the Amazon stock falls while the Sears stock rises, the loss will equal the loss on the Amazon shares plus the loss on the shorted Sears shares. Hedging via shorting (or other means) has the potential to increase the risk of loss when outcomes differ from expectations.

Shorting also entails costs. The short seller must pay fees to the broker for borrowing the shares and must replace any dividends paid while the shares are on loan. The short seller must also place collateral with the stock lenders to secure the loan and will have to add to the collateral if the borrowed shares increase in price (while receiving collateral back if the price declines).

In addition to these concerns, an investor considering short selling should keep in mind that the broker may require the short seller to return the stock earlier than expected. In that case, the short seller will need to find a replacement or close out the position, perhaps at a price that represents a loss. It may also be difficult to establish short positions in stocks for which the supply of lendable shares is limited.[4] Finally, it should be kept in mind that short sales are essentially leveraged positions, as investment exposure is increased via borrowing. As noted above, leverage amplifies risk along with exposure.

Some investors might prefer to sell futures contracts to establish short positions. A short futures position can be used to bet that the price of an underlying security or index will fall. Because futures markets are typically liquid, it might be easier and less costly to establish a short futures position than to borrow shares of a security to sell short. When using index futures to hedge an underlying index, however, the investor runs the risk that the price of the futures contract and the price of the index do not move in lockstep. Divergence may lead to an unexpected gain or loss when the positions are closed out; this is known as basis risk.

Hedging strategies may also use put options or swaps to limit losses on securities to specified floor values. The purchase of a put option on a security gives the option buyer the right to sell the security back to the put seller at a price (the strike price) specified in the contract. The put buyer is thus assured of getting at least that value, less the cost of the option (the premium) at the end of the period specified in the contract.

With a swap, an investor enters into an agreement with a counterparty to exchange one stream of cash flows for another. One party, for example, may agree to pay a fixed rate of interest on a designated value of assets in exchange for receiving from the other party a floating rate of interest on the same amount. The receiver of the fixed rate eliminates the risk that rates will change over the period, while the receiver of the floating rate obtains the potential to profit should the rate increase over the period of the contract.

Counterparty credit risk has been a perennial problem in the swaps market. Prior to the 2007–2008 credit crisis, most swaps were traded over the counter, hence both parties were exposed to counterparty risk. By contrast, buyers of exchange-traded options are shielded from counterparty risk by the requirement that all parties post margin (cash equal to a portion of the value of the trade) and the exchange's promise to guarantee the transaction with its own assets, if necessary. Since the crisis, regulators have attempted to mitigate counterparty credit risk for swap users by mandating measures such as central clearing through facilities that would provide a backstop in the event of defaults and, in the absence of central clearing, minimum collateralization and capital requirements.

Hedge funds often employ some combination of swaps, options, and shorting in order to establish a desired degree of hedging. The overall fund may be net long, holding a larger long position, or net short, holding a larger short position. If both long and short positions are approximately equal in value and in sensitivity to broad market movements, the portfolio is referred to as market neutral. For a market-neutral portfolio, movements of the broad market cancel out; the portfolio has little or no systematic risk exposure. Its returns will reflect the relative performance of the specific securities held long and sold short.

## ARBITRAGE

While hedging is used to control risk with price movements expected to be offsetting, a similar strategy—arbitrage—is used to earn a low-risk profit from the price movements of two related assets. Arbitrage is based on the concept that similar assets should be priced similarly. A stock trading for different prices on two different exchanges, for example, would be an arbitrage opportunity.

When an arbitrageur finds an identical asset trading at two different prices, the path to profit is clear: Sell short the asset that is priced higher and buy the asset that is priced lower. In the case of a stock trading on two exchanges, the difference in price between the two securities, minus trading costs and any adjustment for exchange rates (if multiple currencies are involved), would represent an arbitrage profit.

Given the highly competitive nature of markets, pure arbitrage opportunities such as the one described above are rare. Most arbitrage opportunities take the form of a relative-value trade, where long and short positions are taken in securities that are related but not identical. For example, a company's stock price may reflect optimistic expectations about future prospects, while the price of a different company in the same industry reflects a pessimistic outlook. An arbitrageur could capture this difference in perceived value by going long one security and short the other. (Which is the long and which is the short? It depends on the arbitrageur's own outlook for these two companies.)

Most relative-value trades involve small differences in prices, and thus have thin profits. Profit levels can be boosted with leverage (i.e., borrowing and investing the proceeds), although at the cost of increased volatility risk and leverage risk. Many investors perceive relative-value trades as being so low in risk (after all, they involve price movements that should offset or converge) that they can safely apply a large amount of leverage. What is often overlooked is that these trades involve two different bets (one long, one short) and that it's possible to lose on both of them. In that case, what appeared to be a path to a low-risk profit will instead produce a loss, which will be magnified by leverage. Part III of the book describes the use of arbitrage by one well known hedge fund, Long-Term Capital Management (LTCM), and how leverage contributed to the fund's failure.

## SHARING RISK VS. SHIFTING RISK

Like medieval alchemists who claimed they could turn base metals into gold, some modern-day financial alchemists believe they can create investment securities that offer rich rewards with little or no risk. In fact, the high-return, low-risk securities and strategies they created were as much of an illusion as the precious metals cooked up in the alchemy labs of yore.

Strategies designed to maximize risk-adjusted return do so either through risk sharing or risk shifting. *Risk-sharing* strategies, such as diversification, combine risks so that they are offsetting. But risk sharing mitigates only specific risks. Systematic risk remains. *Risk-shifting* products, such as portfolio insurance, assume that systematic risk can be transferred from one party that is unwilling to bear it to other parties that accept it. In neither case has risk been eliminated from the system as a whole.

Just as the by-products of alchemy were often volatile chemical concoctions, modern-day finance can result in combustible products that blow up markets. In the coming chapters we will examine a number of incidents in which risk-management techniques were misused or misunderstood and wound up increasing risk rather than reducing it. In the stock market crash of October 19, 1987, portfolio insurance contributed materially to the extraordinary 508-point (22.6%) drop in the Dow Jones Industrial Average. We'll also see how hedge fund LTCM used derivatives and extreme leverage to engage in an ill-fated, multi-billion-dollar relative-value strategy that threatened the stability of global markets when it failed. Finally, we'll see how risk-shifting products, such as CDOs and credit default swaps, were at the root of the global credit crisis of 2007–2008.

# PART II

CHAPTER 2

# Black Monday 1987

*"October: This is one of the peculiarly dangerous months to speculate in stocks. The others are July, January, September, April, November, May, March, June, December, August, and February."*

**—Mark Twain**[1]

By October 1987, the US economy had been expanding for 59 straight months. Between August 12, 1982 and August 25, 1987, the Dow Jones Industrial Average (DJIA) climbed from 777 to 2,722. In 1987 alone, from the beginning of the year to the August 25 peak, the DJIA rose by 826 points, or 43.6 percent. Then came October 1987.

During the week of October 5, the DJIA declined by 6 percent. The 159-point decline was its biggest weekly point drop ever. This included a record one-day drop of 92 points on Tuesday, October 6, on heavy New York Stock Exchange (NYSE) trading volume of 176 million shares. The slide intensified during the week of October 12. On Wednesday, October 14, the DJIA dropped a record 95 points, or 3.8 percent; on Thursday, October 15, the DJIA dropped 58 points, or 2.4 percent; and on Friday, October 16, the DJIA set a new record by dropping 108 points, or 4.6 percent. From Wednesday through Friday, the DJIA had dropped a stunning 10.4 percent. These declines occurred as trading volume continued to increase. On Wednesday through Friday, respectively, 210 million, 266 million, and a record 344 million shares changed hands. At its close on Friday, October 16, the DJIA stood at 2,247, down almost 500 points, or 17.5 percent, from its August peak. (See Exhibit 2.1.)

On Monday, October 19, the market suffered its worst daily percentage decline in history. On this day, the DJIA plummeted 508 points to 1,739, a

**EXHIBIT 2.1**

The Dow Jones Industrial Average (DJIA) in the 1987 Stock Market Crash

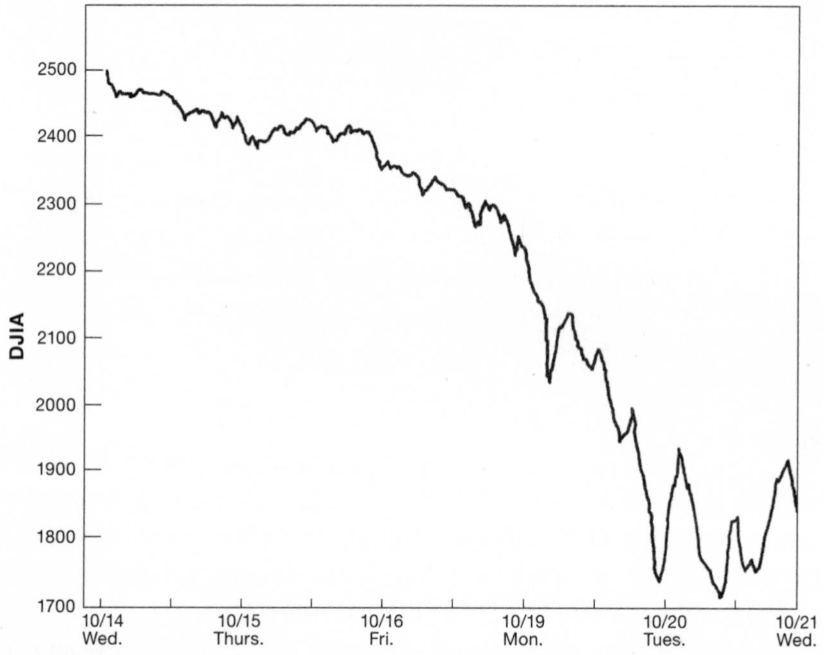


Source: Brady Commission, *Report of the Presidential Task Force on Market Mechanisms* (Washington, DC: Government Printing Office, 1988).

decline of 22.6 percent. Other stock market indexes experienced declines of similar magnitude. New York Stock Exchange (NYSE) volume skyrocketed to a record 604 million shares, worth just under $21 billion.

The market for futures contracts fared even worse. Futures contracts on the benchmark Standard & Poor's 500 (S&P 500) fell 28.6 percent, with 162,000 contracts representing some $20 billion of underlying stock changing hands. Throughout the day on Monday, futures contracts traded at substantial discounts to the stock market; that is, the prices of futures contracts on individual stocks and stock indexes fell short of what would be expected, given the prices of the underlying securities.

The *New York Times* reported the next day that "the losses were so great they sent shock waves to markets around the world." The London market, whose trading day overlaps with the US trading day, fell 10 percent on October 19 and 11.4 percent on October 20. The Tokyo market, where the trading day ends before the New York market opens, fell a record 14.9 percent on October 20.

On Tuesday morning, before the markets opened, the Federal Reserve Board released a statement from Chairman Alan Greenspan, saying that the Fed stood ready to provide liquidity to support the financial system. (Backing up Greenspan's words, the Fed infused over $11 billion in new reserves to money center banks in the week of and the week following the crash.) The DJIA started off the day with an ascent, climbing almost 200 points in the morning. It then plummeted to new depths. Trading in many stocks and on most futures exchanges simply broke down.

After hitting an intraday low of 1,709, however, the DJIA began to recover, propelled in part by massive efforts by corporations to buy back their own stock. The DJIA closed the day at 1,841, a record daily gain of 102 points (5.9%) on record volume of 614 million shares.

From its intra-day high of 2,747 on August 25 to the intra-day low of 1,709 on October 20, the DJIA declined by over 1,000 points, or by more than one-third. Over a trillion dollars in investment value evaporated. Investors were understandably upset and worried about the future.

In the two weeks leading up to and including the 1987 crash, New York State pension portfolios lost 32 percent of their value. In Chicago, pawnbrokers harvested a bumper crop of Rolexes from investors and commodities traders. At the Pacific Stock Exchange, the falling ticker quickened the rumor that exchange officials had posted a suicide watch at the Golden Gate Bridge in San Francisco. The specter of recession raised its fearsome head. Democrats began blaming Republicans, and Republicans began blaming Democrats.

New York City real estate tycoon and casino magnate (and now president) Donald Trump advised: "I'm not going back to the market, and I suggest the little guys just sit on the sidelines. Instead of playing the market, they should go to Atlantic City."[2] Many of the "little guys" took at least the first part of this advice. Although most mutual fund holders weathered the brunt of the turmoil on Monday and Tuesday, they began pulling out serious money in the following weeks. Mutual fund redemptions outpaced investment in 15 of the 17 weeks following the crash.

The crash put a crimp in many business plans. Two brokerage houses that had planned to expand in Stamford, Connecticut, pulled out. Many proposed mergers and acquisitions, including Carl Icahn's offer for Trans World Airlines (TWA), fell through. Actress Mary Tyler Moore had to postpone an offering for her MTM Enterprises. Hollywood, however, read the crash as "bullish" for its forthcoming film of unbridled greed and unbounded egos, *Wall Street.*

Soon after the crash, a *New York Times* telephone poll conducted between October 18 and October 22, 1987 found that US investors were still largely optimistic.[3] Many wealthier-than-average investors were complacent, if not happy. Walmart founder Sam Walton, whose family reportedly lost half a billion dollars in the crash, dismissed it as merely a paper loss.[4] As it turned out, the future would prove these investors right.

Ten years after the crash, Robert R. Glauber, executive director of the presidential task force that had examined the crash, looked back with some resignation: "It's ironic that we concluded that markets nearly fell apart in 1987, and just ten years later people treat it like ancient history."[5] Floyd Norris, financial columnist at the *New York Times*, noted: "In 1987, the crash traumatized investment bankers and small investors alike. A decade later it has produced something that no one could have forecast: complacency."[6]

## ECONOMIC THEORIES OF CRASHES

Crashes are a frequently occurring feature of market economies. During the twentieth century, the United States suffered 15 major stock market crashes; a stock market crash is defined as a short-term loss of 20 percent or more in market value.[7] Globally, there have been 18 bank-centered financial crises (generally accompanied by large declines in asset prices) since 1945.[8] Yet there is surprisingly little consensus about what causes them.

The development of a broad economic theory of crashes has long been hindered by an unresolved question of a more fundamental nature: Do bubbles and crashes even exist? According to the efficient market hypothesis (EMH), security prices instantaneously incorporate all available information. If so, a precipitous increase in asset values is not a bubble; and a subsequent rapid decline is not a crash. Rather, rising prices reflect optimistic, but rational, expectations about future returns, and a crash is merely a downward adjustment of those expectations, most likely in response to new information. To EMH advocate and University of Chicago economist Eugene F. Fama, the 508-point (22.6%) drop of the DJIA on October 19, 1987, was a highly efficient response to "a change in fundamental values."[9]

This idealized view of markets is rooted in neoclassical economics, which holds that transactions among rational, wealth-maximizing individuals naturally guide prices, markets, and economies toward a stable equilibrium where supply and demand are balanced. It is difficult, however, to reconcile this best-of-all-possible-worlds description with a history of frequent market upheavals.

More flexible interpretations of market equilibrium hold that markets are largely efficient, but they also allow that bubbles and crashes can be caused by external forces. Joseph A. Schumpeter, for example, saw technology as a disruptive force, though a positive one that brought progress through "creative destruction."[10] Friedrich A. Hayek and Milton Friedman championed the idea that misguided government policies could wreak havoc on economies.[11] Hayek argued that government regulation interfered with an economy's natural price-setting mechanisms.[12] Friedman blamed the Great Depression on Federal Reserve actions that allowed the amount of money in circulation to fall by a third between 1929 and 1933.[13]

Common to all of these outlooks is the belief that, in a market system, individual actions must in aggregate be rational because market forces neutralize or marginalize irrational behavior. But a countervailing view holds that people are anything but coolly rational and calculating, and that markets can amplify, rather than neutralize, human imperfections. Irving Fisher believed economic instability stemmed from people's inability to understand the effects of inflation and deflation on the price of goods, which led to inconsistent spending and saving habits.[14] John Maynard Keynes famously attributed market instability to behavior that arises from "a spontaneous optimism rather than mathematical expectations."[15] Amos Tversky and Daniel Kahneman, pioneers in behavioral finance, have documented that people often fall back on simple rules of thumb or arbitrary reference points when confronted with complex situations, and thus may overreact or underreact to economic events.[16] Other behavioral research has found evidence of herding; that is, investors take comfort in following the crowd, even when doing so may conflict with their own beliefs.[17] Robert J. Shiller has shown that a variety of factors—including peer pressure, herding, perceptions shaped by the media, and emotions such as regret and envy—can combine to form a psychological feedback loop that drives prices higher in a bubble and lower when the bubble bursts.[18]

Hyman P. Minsky took direct aim at efficient-market theorists with his wryly named financial instability hypothesis, which asserts that boundaries on prices are undermined, not maintained, by market forces.[19] In this view, prolonged periods of prosperity and rising asset prices tend to produce complacent bankers who underestimate risk and lend with increasingly smaller margins of safety. Financing progresses in ever-riskier stages ranging from "hedge" (fully collateralized) to "Ponzi" (repayment depends on continually rising asset prices). Ultimately, a change in public perception, dubbed a "Minsky moment" by the economist's admirers, brings about a collapse of asset values.

Tracing market instability back to its source is not merely an academic exercise. The causes of crashes, if pinned down, could point toward ways to head them off. For example, if crashes often follow periods of unbridled financial liberalization, effective regulation might be a reasonable focus. At the other extreme, if, as Hayek believed, slumps are a necessary phase of the business cycle during which the proper balance between saving and investment is restored, a hands-off approach would be in order.

CHAPTER 3

# Replicating Options

*"I looked at this thing, and I realized that if you did . . . dynamic trading . . . if you actually [traded] literally continuously, then in fact, yeah, you could get rid of the risk, but not just the systematic risk, all the risk."*

—**Robert C. Merton**[1]

The market crash of October 19, 1987, is one example of what can happen when sophisticated, often mathematically based products and strategies designed to reduce the risk of investing meet the messy realities of investors acting the way humans tend to act. Markets, of course, have always been driven by fear and greed, aversion to loss, and desire for gain. But advances in the mathematics of finance and computer power often seemed to be on the verge of taming the beast. Before the crash, the solution to risk seemed to be options and a strategy derived from option pricing, which came to be known as portfolio insurance.

## A BRIEF HISTORY OF OPTIONS

Options have been around for a long time. The Romans and Phoenicians optioned the cargoes transported on their ships. For example, a Roman citizen might purchase wine in Rome for shipment and sale at a much higher price in Egypt or Syria. That nice potential profit would be at risk, however; the ship carrying the wine might sink, or the wine might spoil along the way, or it might sell at a lower price than expected. Some or all of that investment might be lost.

Suppose that, for a mere percentage of what it would cost to buy a direct investment in the cargo, the citizen purchased an option that effectively provided the right to purchase a portion of the cargo at a predetermined price (say, the current cost of that portion in Rome) at some time in the future (presumably after the ship is expected to land). This kind of contract is known as a call option. If the wine arrives safely, in good condition, and is sold at a price above the price specified in the contract, the citizen would "exercise" the call option, collecting the difference between the wine's sale price and the lower price specified in the contract.

Of course, any profit on the option would be reduced by the amount paid for the option—the option premium. The option buyer would thus not be as well off as an investor who had purchased a share of the cargo outright, assuming the wine was sold at a profit. The option buyer would do better than the simple investor, however, if the wine ended up at the bottom of the sea, or as vinegar, or if it had to be sold at a loss. In that case, the option buyer would be out the amount paid for the option, but would avoid the larger loss suffered by the investor who purchased the wine outright.

A citizen that invested in a share of the cargo could, however, purchase a put option on that investment. A put option would allow the sale of the investor's share of the cargo at a specified price (say, again, the current price of the wine in Rome) at some future date. If the wine sells at a profit, the put option would not be exercised and the investor would receive the profit from the sale, less the price paid for the option. If the cargo is lost, spoiled, or sells for less than the specified price, the investor could exercise the put option, receiving the specified price, which would be reduced by the option premium paid.

Either a put option or a call option gives its buyer the opportunity to participate in any profit from the underlying asset. That profit is reduced by the cost of the option premium. At the same time, however, the option has limited the buyer's potential loss to the cost of the option premium.

The option seller assumes the risk from the option buyer. A put option seller (also known as the writer of the option) is obliged to buy the underlying asset, in this case the wine, at the price specified in the contract, even if the asset is worth less than that price. The call writer is obliged to sell the asset at the price specified in the contract, even if the asset is worth more than that price. The option premium represents the price sellers charge buyers for taking on this risk.

Options reemerged in Europe after the Middle Ages. With the collapse of Dutch tulip bulb prices in the 1630s, however, owners of put options on bulbs were left with near-worthless investments when put sellers reneged on their obligations (a harbinger of modern-day counterparty risk).[2] Their image deeply tarnished, options were driven underground, to reappear only sporadically.

In the United States, options began trading in the late eighteenth century. They were commonly used to provide agricultural and manufacturing concerns with a means of reducing their risks by locking in product prices. Options on financial securities were less well known and more suspect. At least some of the stock market's rise before the 1929 crash can be traced to price manipulators using financial options. The securities laws passed in the 1930s, in the wake of that crash, eliminated many of these types of abuses.

It wasn't until 1973 that financial options really took off in the United States. That watershed year saw the establishment of the first centralized exchange for option trading—the Chicago Board Options Exchange (CBOE)—to be followed within a few years by the American, Pacific, and Philadelphia exchanges. These exchanges offered centralized clearing. An individual or individual company that wanted to buy a put or a call option could take their orders to a centralized exchange, and buy and sell orders would be matched or repriced until orders cleared. Options could thus be traded more readily than ever before.[3]

## Pricing Options

The establishment of centralized exchanges for option trading coincided with the development of a model for determining the value of an option. In 1973, Fischer Black, Myron S. Scholes, and Robert C. Merton published their solutions to the option pricing problem, a feat for which Scholes and Merton received the Nobel Prize in Economic Sciences in 1997.[4] It was a problem that, despite promising breakthroughs dating back to the turn of the century, had stymied investors and researchers. Black, Scholes, and Merton solved it by examining the theoretically risk-free nature of a hedged option position.

An option position combined with some continuously adjusted offsetting position in the risky asset underlying the option will yield a return approximating the riskless rate available from a short-term Treasury bill. The price movements of the risky asset offset, or hedge, the price movements of the option. Consider, for example, a call option on a stock. That option becomes more valuable as the stock's price rises because the likelihood of the investor being able to exercise the option at a profit increases; the option becomes less valuable, however, as the stock's price falls and profitable exercise of the option becomes less likely. The holder of this call option could offset its movements by selling the underlying stock as its price rises and buying as its price falls. In effect, the combined position of the call plus the continuously adjusted stock holding will behave like cash, neither rising nor falling as the underlying stock price changes.

It follows that if an option can be hedged by dynamically adjusted positions in the underlying stock, the option can also be replicated by dynamically adjusting positions in the underlying stock and cash-equivalents. That is, rather than purchase a call option on a stock, an investor can hold a portfolio of the underlying stock plus cash; by purchasing more stock as its price rises and selling the stock as its price declines, the investor can reproduce the behavior of a call option that offers increasing upside participation in the underlying stock's movement as the price increases and declining participation (nearly all in cash) as the price falls.

A formal solution for pricing options lent tremendous impetus to the options market. According to Burton R. Rissman, a former counsel to the CBOE:[5]

> Black-Scholes was really what enabled the exchange to thrive. . . . It gave a lot of legitimacy to the whole notions of hedging and efficient pricing, whereas we were faced in the late 60s–early 70s with the issue of gambling.

Furthermore, the essential insight about the equivalence of an option and a portfolio that combined the underlying risky asset and cash can be generalized to many other assets and financial contracts with option-like characteristics, allowing for their pricing also. Many new products, not just options, owe their viability to Black, Scholes, and Merton.

### BLACK, SCHOLES, AND MERTON

In 1973, Fischer Black and Myron S. Scholes published "The Pricing of Options and Corporate Liabilities" and Robert C. Merton published "Theory of Rational Option Pricing." Together, these works constituted the first valid analytical formulation for valuing options. Black, Scholes, and Merton took ad hoc valuation techniques and replaced them with a formula that allows investors to solve for the value of an option analytically.

Black and Scholes modeled a call option and the stock underlying it in a way that allowed them to build a formula for deriving a "fair" option value from the current price of the stock, its price volatility, the risk-free interest rate, the strike price of the option, and its time to expiration. Merton generalized the Black-Scholes formula for stocks paying a continuous dividend.

The Royal Swedish Academy of Sciences recognized the contributions of Black, Scholes, and Merton in 1997 by awarding Merton and Scholes the Nobel Prize in Economics, known officially as the Bank of Sweden Prize in Economic Sciences in Memory of Alfred Nobel. (Unfortunately, Black had died, at 57, in 1995.) The Academy noted:

> Black, Merton and Scholes... laid the foundation for the rapid growth of markets for derivatives in the last ten years. Their method had more general applicability, however, and has created new areas of research—inside as well as outside of financial economics. A similar method may be used to value insurance contracts and guarantees, or the flexibility of physical investment projects [such as investment in plant and equipment].

## SYNTHESIZING OPTIONS: PORTFOLIO INSURANCE

Option-pricing theory fostered the development of a product that would take the markets by storm in the 1980s—portfolio insurance. Portfolio insurance is essentially a real-life version of the hypothetical dynamic portfolio assumed by Black, Scholes, and Merton to be equivalent to an option. By taking and trading positions in the security underlying an option and positions in risk-free Treasury bills or cash, an investor can in theory replicate the behavior of any desired option.

In the case of portfolio insurance, the option being replicated is a protective put—that is, a put option combined with an underlying portfolio. In a real protective-put strategy, the stock position affords an investor the opportunity to benefit from increases in the stock's price, while the put option provides the ability to sell the stock to the put writer at a specified price, the so-called strike price, so the investor is assured of a minimum price. The investor expects to achieve, at the cost of the put premium, participation in upside gains and protection from downside losses.

Like a protective put, portfolio insurance aims to maximize an investment portfolio's stock exposure while limiting portfolio losses to a specified amount. Computerized rules based on the Black, Scholes, and Merton option-pricing model call for moving portfolio assets between stock and cash to replicate the behavior of a stock portfolio protected by an actual put option.

Option-pricing theory demonstrates that put- or call-option replication requires buying stock as the market rises and selling stock as it falls. The concept of buying as prices rise and selling as they fall may seem counterintuitive, but it makes sense within the context of portfolio insurance. Intuitively, a decline in the price of the stock component of the insured portfolio lowers the portfolio's return, jeopardizing the goal of achieving a required minimum return. Reducing the portfolio's commitment to stock, a risky asset, and increasing its commitment to cash, a riskless asset, firms up the portfolio's return. Conversely, an increase in the price of the stock component of the portfolio lowers the probability that the portfolio will fall below the assured minimum. The portfolio's commitment to equity can thus be increased, thereby increasing participation in any market advance.

Although portfolio insurance via option replication is theoretically equivalent to a put option on the underlying portfolio or to an actual insurance policy, in reality portfolio insurance differs from both options and insurance in a number of critical aspects. A put option, for example, provides a minimum floor value for a portfolio of risky assets. This value is pegged to the strike price specified in the option contract. The investor pays an explicit price for this protection—the option premium.

A portfolio insurance strategy replicating a protective put also promises a minimum floor value. However, the investor does not have to pay an explicit premium to an option writer. This does not mean that portfolio insurance is without cost. In fact, its costs may be incurred not only by the investor insuring the portfolio, but also by the market as a whole.[6]

## Cost of Portfolio Insurance

The protection supposedly offered by portfolio insurance is for a specific investment horizon; this is analogous to the time to expiration of an actual option or to the term of an insurance policy. The overall performance of the portfolio insurance program must be measured over this investment horizon. If the market declines during this period, the portfolio insurance program is supposed to provide a minimum floor value by reallocating portfolio assets from the risky asset to cash. If the market rises, the insured portfolio is supposed to participate in the gain by reallocating portfolio assets from cash to stock.

Reductions in risk, however, usually cannot be accomplished without cost; in the investment world, cost often comes in the form of reduced return. For portfolio insurance, cost is incurred through a reduction in achievable return in periods when stock returns exceed cash returns. In such periods, the insured portfolio's return will fall short of the return to a portfolio fully invested in stock because of the insured portfolio's allocation to cash. The difference between the insured portfolio's return over the horizon and the fully invested portfolio's return is called the shortfall.

The shortfall is likely to be larger the riskier the stocks. Higher risk will, other things equal, necessitate a larger allocation to cash to ensure a given minimum return. The premium for an option on a stock will be higher the more volatile the stock. The higher the portfolio's allocation to cash, the lower its allocation to stocks, hence the lower its expected return.

The bigger the potential loss the investor is willing to assume the smaller the shortfall is likely to be. An investor willing to accept a loss of 10 percent will be able to allocate a relatively larger percentage of an insured portfolio to stock than someone who will tolerate a maximum loss of only 5 percent. This investor will thus be positioned to capture more of any upside market moves.

The difference between an insured portfolio's initial value and the investor's maximum tolerable loss or, equivalently, the assured minimum portfolio floor, is comparable to the deductible in an insurance policy, or to the difference between the initial value of the underlying stock and the option's strike price. The smaller the deductible, the higher the expected cost of the program in terms of potential profit sacrificed.

The cost of portfolio insurance, then, depends importantly on the percentage of the portfolio allocated to cash rather than stock. This constitutes a major difference between portfolio insurance and insurance with an actual option or traditional insurance, where the cost of insurance is explicit in the premium and paid up front. With portfolio insurance, the cost is implicit and is incurred not at the start of the insurance program, but over its life; the cost of portfolio insurance is thus obscured.

## Not Real Insurance

The eventual cost of a portfolio insurance program will be largely determined by the volatility of the underlying portfolio returns over the course of the program's horizon. If experienced volatility is in line with expectations at the outset of the portfolio insurance program, the actual cost will turn out to be roughly equal to the anticipated cost. If volatility turns out to be higher than expected, the cost of the portfolio insurance program will be higher than anticipated. This is because higher-than-anticipated volatility will necessitate more frequent or larger adjustments of the cash and stock positions.

Higher volatility increases the likelihood of whipsaw price movements, whereby sudden stock price increases are followed by declines, which are in turn followed by increases. As portfolio insurance calls for buying when prices rise and selling when prices fall, it can put the investor on the unprofitable side of trades when a market is whipsawing. More frequent selling before price rises and buying before price declines will erode portfolio return. Of course, if volatility turns out to be lower than expected, the actual cost of portfolio insurance will be lower than the anticipated cost.

Compare this with traditional insurance. With traditional insurance, numerous insured parties each pay an explicit, predetermined premium to an insurance company, which accepts the independent risks of such unforeseeable events as theft or fire. The traditional insurer pools the risks of these participants and draws on these premiums and accumulated reserves, as necessary, to reimburse losses. With actual options, too, the buyer pays a known, up-front premium and the option seller takes on the risk of unforeseeable market moves.

With portfolio insurance, there is no up-front cost. The eventual real cost of the insurance is unknown. Perhaps most importantly, portfolio insurance, unlike either traditional insurance or options, is essentially self-insurance. The investors who "buy" the insurance take on the risk. They give up some degree of portfolio return in exchange for the theoretical assurance of receiving no less than a chosen minimum return. They are not able to draw upon the premiums of many thousands of other investors in the event of catastrophe. They rely upon the ability to get into or out of the market as needed, hence upon the willingness of other investors to take the offsetting sides of the trades required by portfolio insurance programs.

## POTENTIAL EFFECTS ON MARKETS

The behavior of portfolio insurers may discourage the emergence of counterparties willing to trade with their insured portfolios. This is because the trend-following behavior of portfolio insurers—buying as markets rise and selling as markets fall—has the potential to create volatility when there is a substantial amount of portfolio insurance trading. Furthermore, the extent of this type of trading is unknown to other investors, or even to other portfolio insurers; as portfolio insurance is self-insurance, there is no public exchange or publication of prices or volumes to indicate what the cost of or demand for the strategy might be.

Investors, even insured investors, will generally not know what portion of volatility reflects the mechanistic responses of insured portfolios to market movements. They may interpret such selling as reflective of new information. They may thus be more inclined to sell declining stocks, or buy rising stocks, than to take the other sides of portfolio insurers' trades. Portfolio insurers' trend-following trades can have a snowball effect.[7]

In fact, the trading demands of portfolio insurers may overwhelm other investors' ability or willingness to meet their needs. In the face of concentrated selling by portfolio insurers, market prices can gap down; rather than moving smoothly on the way from one price to a lower one, prices may skip over intermediate prices. In the presence of such price discontinuities, portfolio insurers may not be able to execute their trades at the required prices, and the strategy may fail to provide the desired protection.

Volatility and price discontinuities motivated by portfolio insurance trading can lead to market instability or even a crash. In that case, it is not merely portfolio insurers who must bear the risk of their insurance, but all market participants.

CHAPTER 4

# Portfolio Insurance and Futures Markets

*"Institutions employing portfolio insurance strategies . . . assumed that it would be infeasible to sell huge volumes of stock on the exchange in short periods of time with only a small price impact. These institutions came to believe that the futures market offered a separate haven of liquidity sufficient to allow them to liquidate huge positions over short periods of time with minimal price displacement."*

—**Brady Commission**[1]

At the advent of portfolio insurance, the programs were implemented by buying and selling stocks to alter a portfolio's allocations to equity. In the early 1980s, futures contracts on stock market indexes began trading on US exchanges. Most portfolio insurance programs started to use futures contracts on stock market indexes in place of the underlying shares.

A stock index futures contract is an exchange-traded agreement to buy or sell the stock market index on a specified future date (the expiration date). If at expiration the index has increased above the purchase price of the contract, the buyer makes a profit; if the index has declined, the buyer incurs a loss. Alternatively, an investor can sell a futures contract. In this case, if at expiration the index has declined below the sale price, the seller makes a profit; if the index has increased, the seller incurs a loss.[2]

Futures, like options, are derivatives. That is, their values are contingent on the values of real underlying assets. In the case of stock index futures, the underlying asset is a stock index such as the Standard & Poor's 500 (S&P 500). Unlike options, which convey a right to buy or sell, futures are an obligation to buy or sell. The buyer of a futures contract cannot cancel it if, at the expiration date, the underlying asset is worth less than the purchase price of the contract. The buyer can, however, sell the contract before its expiration date at prevailing prices, just as a seller of a futures contract can close out (cover) the position by purchasing the contract at prevailing prices.

A long futures position offers exposure to the underlying asset and will move in concert with the underlying asset. A short futures position will hedge exposure to the underlying asset; it will move in the opposite direction to that of the underlying asset. A short futures position combined with the underlying asset creates "synthetic cash"; the combined position has (theoretically at least) no risk and offers no return premium over the risk-free rate of return (a cash return).

With a portfolio insurance program for an underlying stock portfolio, a short stock index futures position can offset much of the risk of the underlying stock portfolio; covering the short futures position (buying futures) increases exposure to the underlying stock portfolio. As the portfolio's value falls toward its assured minimum floor, selling futures hedges by creating synthetic cash. As the underlying portfolio's value rises, covering short futures positions substitutes equity exposure for synthetic cash and restores the portfolio's upside potential.

## INDEX ARBITRAGE

Compared with the underlying market, the futures market has lower margin requirements and fewer restrictions on short sales. The futures market is also commonly perceived as having lower transaction costs (although this is not always the case). For these reasons, the equity futures market soon surpassed the underlying market (the "spot market" or "cash market") in volume and liquidity. Futures quickly became the primary trading vehicle for implementing portfolio allocation changes.

With the rapid growth of trading volume in futures markets, some market observers began to fear for the stability of the underlying stock market. In particular, many market observers, including the Securities and Exchange Commission (SEC), feared that volatility in the heavily traded futures market would be transmitted to the underlying, less heavily traded stock market via the mechanism of index arbitrage.

Index arbitrageurs are investors who take advantage of price discrepancies between different markets—in this case, the market for stock index futures and the underlying stocks constituting the index. Arbitrageurs buy (sell) futures contracts and sell (buy) the underlying stocks when futures are underpriced (overpriced) relative to the stocks. The purchases and sales of the stocks are likely to be executed through program trades—trades that use computers to execute many stock transactions at the same time.

If trading in futures is motivated by the arrival of new information, any resulting increase in volatility that is transmitted to the underlying spot market should not be destabilizing. In this case, index arbitrage is merely transferring the new information from the futures market to the stock market; it is just that the more liquid futures market is incorporating the information first, and faster. Price changes in either market should reflect the movement necessary to restore both futures contracts and share prices to a range of values consistent with the new information. Arbitrageurs are thus actually increasing price efficiency and enhancing stock market liquidity.

According to traditional financial theory, trading is undertaken in response to changes in fundamental conditions underlying security prices, whether in the broad economy, a market sector, an industry, or a specific stock. But in reality, trading also reflects investors' overreaction or underreaction to news, misinterpretation of news, and made-up news (rumors), as well as investor liquidity needs and investor strategies not based on fundamental information about the stock. If index arbitrageurs' futures trading reflects noise rather than new fundamental information, it may prove destabilizing to the underlying stock market. Noise can obscure fundamental value.

Futures trading may be noisier than trading in the underlying stocks if the perceived ease and cheapness of trading in the futures market encourages more noisy trading than would occur in the absence of such a market. Investors might take advantage of the lower margin requirements and transaction costs in the futures market to undertake larger or more frequent trades than they would in the underlying stock market. Portfolio insurers can potentially increase noise in security pricing because their trading decisions are not based on underlying fundamentals, but rather on price changes, and because the extent of their trading activity may not be known.

## NOISE

*Noise* represents price movements that do not reflect fundamentals.[3] Noise can be the result of simple errors by investors genuinely attempting to interpret information or to extrapolate its implications. Theoretically, such errors will cancel out over large numbers of investors. For example, for every individual who is too optimistic about a stock's price there may be another individual who is too pessimistic.

Research undertaken in the decades since the 1987 stock market crash suggests, however, that investors may tend to err in the same direction when it comes to certain aspects of investing. This can happen if investors are driven not merely by fundamentals but by common behavior. Behavioral finance, which examines the role of psychology in stock pricing, suggests that individuals and individual investors share certain cognitive biases. For example, they tend to see the future as a continuation of the past and to favor information that substantiates this view over information that suggests a change in course may be coming.

Investors also tend to be overly optimistic. For many reasons, forecasts of company earnings, and hence forecasts of stock prices, may tend to be overoptimistic. Companies are often loath to publicize bad news; they may thus delay its release or attempt to disguise it via window dressing (or, sometimes, commit outright fraud). Brokers tend to issue more "buy" than "sell" recommendations. Publishing negative opinions about a company can jeopardize investment banking relationships. It also may threaten the job security of the analyst issuing the negative recommendation. Buy recommendations generally elicit more commissions than sells, as all customers are potential purchasers, whereas commissions from sales are primarily limited to those customers who already own the stock.

More short selling activity could encourage more sell recommendations, put a check on overly optimistic prices, and allow investor pessimism to be reflected; but short selling is often limited by institutional restrictions and investor lack of familiarity.[4] When, for example, a large number of investors share a bias toward optimism, irrespective of actual information, their trading can create upwardly biased noise in security pricing.

Noise may also be introduced by investors who use share prices and price changes, rather than fundamental factors, to determine their trading decisions. For example, investors caught up in a fad or speculators participating in a bubble tend to use recent price changes as a guide to trading. Such trading may cause prices to deviate from prices based only on fundamentals about a company or the economy.

When traders buy as a stock's price rises and sell as a stock's price falls, their trades can cause prices to rise even more or fall even more. The incremental increase or decrease in price can encourage more purchases or more sales, leading to further price changes. Such trading is called positive feedback trading. To the extent that feedback trading amplifies price changes, it amplifies any noise present in prices. Furthermore, to the extent that feedback trading does not reflect any change in fundamental information, it can itself create noise, which is amplified by the feedback mechanism.

Certain trading strategies depend upon price movements to the virtual exclusion of other information. Market technicians, for example, base their decisions primarily or solely on price patterns. Their trading may not consistently amplify noise, however, because they do not always buy into rising markets or sell into falling markets.

Other price-dependent trading strategies, however, lead to feedback trading that has the potential to amplify noise and destabilize markets. Momentum traders, for example, buy as prices continue upward and sell as prices decline. Portfolio insurers are essentially large-scale momentum traders. They will consistently amplify market movements, buying as prices rise and selling as prices decline.

Arbitrage-related futures trading may also pose problems for the underlying market if it places too much demand on that market's liquidity. A given amount of capital can support a much larger equity exposure in the futures market than in the spot market, given the difference in margin requirements. In the years leading up to the 1987 stock market crash, the volume of underlying shares represented by the average daily trading in all equity index futures contracts was 1.5 to 2.0 times the volume on the New York Stock Exchange (NYSE), yet the spot market seemed able to digest without major incident any associated increase in the trading demand for futures contracts.[5] However, as Chapter 5, "Portfolio Insurance and the Crash" will detail, futures trading during the crash period itself outpaced the above multiple many times over.

## A CASCADE OF SELLING

The trading demands of portfolio insurance can interact with index arbitrage in such a way as to devour market liquidity. If equity prices fall, portfolio insurers will sell futures. If they sell in sufficient volume, their sales may drive futures prices down to the extent that arbitrageurs view the futures contracts as cheap relative to the underlying stock. Arbitrageurs will then be motivated to buy the (cheap) futures contracts and sell the (expensive) stock.

With the sale of stock by arbitrageurs, stock prices will continue falling, and portfolio insurers will require more sales of futures contracts. If there is more portfolio insurance selling than arbitrage buying, futures prices may decline further, inciting more arbitrage and more sales of the underlying equity. The interplay between portfolio insurance and index arbitrage (see Exhibit 4.1) can lead to a downward spiral for both futures and underlying spot markets.

Several incidents prior to the 1987 stock market crash indicated that the stock market did not possess sufficient liquidity to accommodate the trading needs of insurers. On September 11, 1986, the Dow Jones Industrial Average (DJIA) fell 87 points (4.6%), the largest point drop to that date. Over September 11 and 12, the index fell 121 points (6.4%) on then record trading volume. Futures prices fell even more, with contracts on the S&P 500 stock index selling at an unprecedented discount to stock prices.

The anomalous behavior of equity and futures markets on September 11 and 12, 1986, was dismissed by many as merely a response to economic fundamentals. But on January 23, 1987, the market again experienced extreme price volatility. In about one hour, the DJIA fell 115 points on, again, record trading volume, and again, the futures discount was extreme. Some market commentators at the time posited that these incidents may have resulted from the portfolio insurance-index arbitrage interaction, which created a "cascade scenario" that drove both stock and futures prices lower.

The SEC asserted that the likelihood of such a cascade would depend on the "design of portfolio insurance programs, the incidence of the 'trigger points' at which the programs generate sell orders [and] the amount of capital subject to these programs."[6] The SEC interviewed several market

**EXHIBIT 4.1**

## Index Arbitrage-Portfolio Insurance Cascade

Source: *New York Times*, December 15, 1987: D6.

participants and echoed their view that the possibility of a cascade scenario was remote.

The surmise at the time was that portfolio insurance strategies covered a broad enough range, with different minimum ending values and insurance horizons, and that any impact it had on prices would be "distributed over a wider range of trading sessions rather than focused at a particular point in time."[7] But this argument ignores the fact that *all* insurance programs buy as prices rise and sell as they fall, and a large enough market move either up or down will trigger *all* portfolio insurance programs to trade at the same time.

Even so, many argued, market forces should be able to resolve such a trading imbalance. As prices decline, value investors, who look for bargain-priced stocks, should step in to buy, thus stabilizing prices. Value-based investors tend to buy as the market falls and sell as it rises, hence they are natural trading partners for portfolio insurers. But the ability of value-based investors to offset the effects of portfolio insurance traders depends on several factors, including the amount of portfolio insurance trading versus value trading overall and the likelihood that value traders will quickly respond to changes in stock prices.[8]

Portfolio insurers are much more sensitive to price movements than value investors. The Presidential task force that investigated the stock market crash of 1987—called the Brady Commission after its chairman Nicholas F. Brady—estimated that a 1 percent market price change would induce portfolio insurers to trade about 2 percent of their portfolios.[9] For value-based investors, on the other hand, a 15 percent to 20 percent discount to their estimated "fair value" of a security may be required to induce them to trade.[10] Furthermore, portfolio insurers often react to market moves within a matter of minutes, whereas value investors may take a number of days to decide whether to trade.[11] Trading by portfolio insurers is thus likely to be far more intensive than that of their potential trading partners.

CHAPTER 5

# Portfolio Insurance and the Crash

*"If options on a particular stock or on a portfolio do not exist, we can create them by using the appropriate strategy for the underlying asset and cash. . . . Such an investment strategy would be tantamount to insuring the equity portfolio against losses by paying a fixed premium to an insurance company."*

**—Mark Rubinstein and Hayne E. Leland[1]**

Portfolio insurance was popularized by Los Angeles-based Leland O'Brien Rubinstein Associates (LOR) in the 1980s. LOR was founded by Hayne E. Leland and Mark E. Rubinstein, professors of finance at the University of California, Berkeley, and John W. O'Brien, who had been an investment consultant at his own firm, O'Brien Associates, and at Chicago-based investment bank A.G. Becker & Co. By 1987, almost every major asset management firm offered some form of portfolio insurance—LOR and its licensees Aetna, Wells Fargo, First Chicago, Kidder Peabody, and BEA Associates, as well as J. P. Morgan, Bankers Trust, Chase Manhattan, Travelers, MassMutual, and Mellon Capital Management.[2]

The growing popularity of the strategy was not surprising. For one thing, despite the emergence of option exchanges and the development and dissemination of the option pricing formula, large institutional investors faced substantial hurdles when it came to using options. Regulations at the time restricted the number of option positions an entity could hold to well below the amounts suitable for large-scale investors. Also, the options available on the exchanges had relatively short time horizons, whereas many institutional investors (for example, pension funds) had quite long horizons. Portfolio insurance offered a way around these restrictions.

LOR and other purveyors of the strategy marketed it aggressively. Portfolio insurance, it was asserted, could insure equity portfolios against market declines while allowing participation in any market advances over the horizon of the insurance program. In fact, LOR's advertising suggested that portfolio insurance would allow investors to increase their equity allocations, and thus their expected returns.[3] Portfolio insurance appealed to the two most basic human instincts—fear and greed.

In 1984, at a Berkeley Program in Finance Conference, LOR partner and chairman Leland distributed a memorandum the day after my debate with LOR partner O'Brien.[4] The memorandum was a response to my 1983 article, "The Portfolio Insurance Puzzle."[5] In the memorandum, Leland went so far as to suggest that those using portfolio insurance could beat the market "by levering an index fund, or using index futures." (For some background, see the sidebar "A Debate on Portfolio Insurance.") The memorandum noted that an index fund based on the Standard & Poor's 500 (S&P 500) would have had an annual compound growth rate of 8.8 percent over the 1928–1983 period, so that $1 invested at the beginning of the period would have grown to $105.50 by the end. According to LOR's simulation, over the same period, investment in a leveraged S&P 500 index fund with a beta of 1.5 (having 150 percent of the risk and volatility of the S&P 500 index), insured for a maximum loss of 10 percent below the Treasury-bill rate, would have had an annual compound growth rate of 9.8 percent, after assumed 1 percent transaction costs.[6] This simulation showed that $1 invested in the insured, leveraged S&P 500 index fund in January 1928 would have grown to $171.10 by 1983. Furthermore, using S&P 500 index futures (instead of an S&P 500 index fund), with assumed transaction costs of 0.25 percent, the insured, leveraged portfolio with a beta of 1.5 would have had an annual compound growth rate of 10.2 percent, for an ending value of $209. According to Leland, "these figures . . . show conclusively that portfolio protection programs can be used to increase return, while limiting downside risks."[7]

Yet the promise portfolio insurance vendors were selling was as unachievable as life in the fictional town of Lake Wobegon, "where all the women are strong, all the men are good looking, and all the children are above average."[8] Everyone can't be above average, and every investor can't beat the market because the market is a composite of everyone. The promise of above-average returns for all, and with limited downside risk, is unattainable; it is a pipe dream.

## A DEBATE ON PORTFOLIO INSURANCE

In 1982, I had recently joined the Pension Asset Management Group at Prudential Asset Management Company, a part of Prudential Insurance Company of America. James (Jim) Gately, who headed the Pension Asset Management Group and had hired me, asked me to attend Leland O'Brien Rubinstein Associates' (LOR's) public introduction of what was variously called "portfolio insulation," "portfolio insurance," or "dynamic asset allocation." John W. O'Brien and Hayne E. Leland hosted the seminar, called "Dynamic Asset Allocation Laboratory," at The Pierre hotel in New York City on May 26. One of the sessions, titled "A Year in the Life of a Dynamic Strategy," supposedly demonstrated that the strategy was foolproof.[9]

The seminar attracted major interest in the institutional investment community. Among the 42 distinguished guests were corporate pension officers from Exxon and General Motors, government pension officers from the World Bank and the Virginia Retirement System, bank officers from Manufacturers Hanover Trust and Citibank, Wall Street representatives from Merrill Lynch and Salomon Brothers, investment managers from Pacific Investment Management Company and Scudder, Stevens & Clark, and journalists from *Fortune* and *Institutional Investor*.

Despite the enthusiastic reception accorded portfolio insurance, I was troubled by several characteristics of the new strategy. My critique, in the form of a Prudential memorandum issued January 17, 1983, noted several potential pitfalls.[10] This memorandum (see Appendix C) would become Prudential's accepted view and would allow it to dodge the disasters that portfolio insurance inflicted on so many other firms.

In the memorandum, I remarked that, although the simulation results LOR presented showed favorable performance over the most recent 10 years that ended in 1981, this was not a representative period because stocks performed relatively poorly while short-term interest rates were unusually high.[11] In such an environment, a strategy that required some portion of a portfolio to be invested in Treasury bills was thus almost bound to outperform a strategy requiring a full investment in stocks. I noted that the put option premium in a dynamic option replication (synthetic) strategy is paid implicitly and is represented by the opportunity cost of the hedge position in cash equivalents.

Among the other concerns I discussed was that portfolio insurance clients generally chose protection over one calendar year at a time, regardless of the longer-term duration of pension plan liabilities. Also, the transaction costs associated with a dynamic strategy, including both commissions and market impact, would be higher than those for a more traditional approach not required to trade merely because underlying prices changed. Furthermore, trades would not necessarily execute at the trigger prices required by put option replication, leading to the possibility that portfolio value could fall below the insurance program's floor. In addition, if volatility turned out to be higher than assumed at the outset of the insurance program, the cost of the implicit premium on the put option replication would be higher than expected and the technique could even fail. I concluded that:

> If a large number of investors utilized the portfolio insulation technique, price movements would tend to snowball. Price rises (falls) would be followed by purchases (sales), which would lead to further price appreciation (depreciation).

I subsequently analyzed the performance of a portfolio insulation strategy versus alternative strategies over the 1928–1982 period and published the results in "The Portfolio Insurance Puzzle" (see Appendix C).[12] My basic finding was that, over this period, $1 invested in a portfolio insulation strategy consisting of the S&P 500 and Treasury bills and designed to sustain a loss of no more than 5 percent in each year would have ended 1982 with a value of $52.63. By contrast, $1 invested in a strategy of buying and holding the S&P 500 over the same period would have ended with a value of $104.25. Both performances excluded trading costs and investment management fees.

"The Portfolio Insurance Puzzle" also compared the insulated portfolio strategy with a portfolio rebalanced yearly to maintain a static mix of 61.75 percent in the S&P 500 and 38.25 percent in Treasury bills. This mix was chosen so that the two portfolios would have had the same volatility (measured statistically by standard deviation). Again, over the 1928–1982 period, the uninsulated strategy outperformed the insulated strategy.[13] Granted, there were calendar years when the uninsulated strategy experienced larger losses than the insulated strategy; the largest loss was

26.5 percent. The relevant question for institutional investors with long horizons and portfolios diversified across many asset classes is whether such losses on a portion of the overall portfolio, while not desirable, would be manageable.

Considering my deep concerns with the strategy, my higher-ups at Prudential declined to license LOR's portfolio insurance products. LOR's O'Brien told me at the time that he would have preferred Prudential Insurance over Aetna, because Prudential had a retail arm, Prudential-Bache Securities, LLC. LOR went on to form an exclusive insurance-company relationship with Aetna, which offered "Guaranteed Equity Management" (GEM).[14]

As a result of my analysis, I was invited by Polly Shouse of MCM to join her in debating O'Brien at a conference on portfolio insurance sponsored by the University of California, Berkeley Program in Finance, held in Monterey, California, September 16–19, 1984. As this was a late invitation to participate, I am not listed on the conference agenda. There, Shouse and I debated O'Brien on the merits of a buy-and-hold strategy (a static mix of stocks and cash) versus a dynamic portfolio insurance strategy. It was at this conference, following the debate, that Leland distributed an LOR memorandum he wrote, "Portfolio Insurance Performance, 1928–1983."[15] The memorandum (see Appendix C) was a response to "The Portfolio Insurance Puzzle," which, in Leland's words, "questions whether portfolio insurance offers the advantages which have been heralded."

In his memorandum, Leland states that: "Dynamic strategies or 'portfolio insurance' can substantially raise expected portfolio returns, when contrasted with static investment strategies offering comparable protection against downside risk.... We shall show that his [Jacobs's] conclusions are wrong. In fact, we shall show that 55 years of empirical experience fully supports the contention that portfolio insurance offers significant gains over static risk-equivalent alternatives." Leland claimed that I made "two fundamental errors:

(i.) a failure to make appropriate risk comparisons, and
(ii.) a failure to use optimal portfolio insurance strategies."

I subsequently requested access to their portfolio insurance simulator to test their proposition that their simulator was better, but they denied access.

As to appropriate risk comparisons, Leland calculated (based on historical returns) what static mix of stock and cash equivalents would have produced no calendar-year losses exceeding 5 percent. This would have required a very conservative stock/cash mix of 14 percent stock and 86 percent cash equivalents. He also addressed the static mix that would lead to a 95 percent confidence level that calendar-year losses would not exceed 5 percent, that is, losses would be greater than 5 percent in only 5 percent of the calendar years. This approach allowed for a slightly more aggressive stock/cash mix of 35 percent stock/65 percent cash, still conservative for a long-term investor. Not emphasized in the memorandum is that the return on the portfolio insurance strategy fell substantially short of the return from buying and holding the S&P 500; the strategy underperformed the market over this longer time span, as opposed to the outperformance over the 10-year period highlighted in their initial promotions, which happened to be a time of low stock returns.

My empirical analyses were not based on the static-mix strategy that would provide the same level of downside protection as the insured strategy. Rather, they were based on the static-mix strategy that would provide the same dispersion of returns (measured by standard deviation) as the insured strategy. While it is interesting to examine results from a static mix that provides the same level of downside protection as an insured strategy, the time horizon for protection (as mentioned earlier) was a calendar year, which bears no relationship to the duration of retirement-plan liabilities. I felt return dispersion to be a more appropriate measure of risk from the perspective of a long-term investor. Moreover, retirement plans have portfolios that are diversified across many asset types, so protecting one asset—equities—against loss may not be necessary and may cost the investor in terms of forgone returns. Alternatively, the entire plan's portfolio could be protected, but that again would entail costs that would reduce returns.

Furthermore, my analyses highlighted another problem with portfolio insurance: The insulated strategy could require that the stock portion of the portfolio be fully liquidated if stock prices fall so precipitously that the portfolio could not recover enough to meet the maximum-loss goal by the end of the protection period. If the market subsequently rises after such a "stop-out," the investor is shut out of these market gains. I found stop-outs in two years.[16] In 1933, the S&P 500 fell 17 percent by the end of February, causing the insured portfolio to be fully invested in cash and thus miss the 85.5 percent market rise during the rest of the year. In 1938, the insured strategy stopped out by March, after an 18.6 percent decline; the S&P 500 subsequently rallied by 61.1 percent. In 1987, real portfolio insurance programs would be stopped out on October 19, 1987; their clients would be stuck at their maximum-loss limitations (or at a greater loss, because for many the floor of protection was pierced), unless they terminated their insurance programs and reinvested in the market.

In his memorandum, Leland compared the "superior LOR insurance technique" with my "suboptimal implementation" and denied that any stop-outs occurred. Yet one of his LOR colleagues later reported stop-outs in the same two years, 1933 and 1938, with no upside capture for the insured portfolio (although he subsequently dismisses these results as products of a hedging strategy that was too simple).[17] After the 1987 crash, however, LOR partner Mark E. Rubinstein admitted that stop-outs were "virtually impossible to prevent."[18]

In the year before the 1987 stock market crash, the Institute for International Research, a conference organization, held "Innovative Portfolio Insurance Techniques: The Latest Developments in 'Dynamic Hedging,'" at the Omni Park Central Hotel in New York City on June 10–11, 1986. It attracted a huge crowd of about 500 participants. O'Brien and I faced off in the session "A Public Debate on Dynamic Hedging." O'Brien introduced me to conference attendees as "the dark side," and said toward the end of the debate that I was not just an "agent of darkness," I was the "prince of darkness."[19] Yet it was not darkness but thorough analysis that motivated my skepticism; the crash that occurred in the following year proved that my skepticism was warranted.

As the US equity market rose virtually without interruption from 1982 into 1987, many investors, concerned with elevated stock price levels and anxious to preserve the investment gains already under their belts, turned to portfolio insurance as a safety net.[20] Rather than retrenching and reducing their stock allocations, these investors retained or even increased their equity exposures, placing even more upward pressure on stock prices. And, of course, as equity prices rose more, "insured" portfolios bought more stock, causing prices to rise even higher.

## PORTFOLIO INSURANCE AS A FAD

By the time of the crash, the heavy promotion of portfolio insurance had fueled a fad. It had attracted up to $100 billion in assets (about 3 percent of the market value of all domestic stocks). Based on a survey taken after the crash, Yale economist Robert J. Shiller concluded that before the crash 10.2 percent of institutional investors had some form of stop-loss policy in place—a kind of directive that calls for selling shares if their prices drop by predetermined amounts.[21] This figure includes the 5.5 percent of institutional investors using portfolio insurance. In addition, 10.1 percent of wealthy individuals were employing stop-loss rules. Shiller suggested that "stop-loss behavior increased as a result of the publicity that portfolio insurance had received, and of the publicity campaign launched by entrepreneurs who found a new way, by selling portfolio insurance, to profit from such stop-loss behavior."[22]

The task force that investigated the 1987 crash—the Brady Commission—found that:[23]

> The rapid rise in the popularity of portfolio insurance strategies . . . contributed to the market's rise. Pension fund managers adopting these strategies typically increased the fund's risk exposure by investing more heavily in common stock during this rising market. The rationale was that portfolio insurance would cushion the impact of a market break by allowing them to shift quickly out of stocks.

It seems highly likely that portfolio insurance, by increasing demand for equities, accelerated the market's rise prior to the crash. Portfolio insurance also encouraged investors to maintain levels of equity exposure that otherwise would have been reduced. The availability of portfolio insurance increased investors' willingness to bear risk. Insured investors were willing to hold more risky assets than they would have held had they not been insured. Furthermore, their greater tolerance for risk led them to buy still more risky assets as the prices of those assets, and hence the insured investors' wealth, appreciated.

According to a Securities and Exchange Commission (SEC) survey, investors maintained relatively high equity exposures in part because of the risk-reduction capability of portfolio insurance.[24] The SEC found that institutional investors using portfolio insurance had an average equity commitment of 56 percent, compared with 46 percent for those not insured. A study undertaken for the New York Stock Exchange (NYSE) concluded that portfolio insurance served to "encourage institutional investors to remain with a higher percentage of equity longer than might, in view of market fundamentals, seem prudent."[25] According to a study from the General Accounting Office, now known as the Government Accountability Office (GAO), portfolio insurance "gave institutional investors a false sense of security, thereby encouraging overinvestment in the stock market."[26]

Portfolio insurance may be seen to encourage somewhat paradoxical investment behavior. In the normal course of events, as prices increase and investors become wary of a possible market setback, one would expect them to reduce their equity exposure. With portfolio insurance, however, the opposite happens. As market uncertainty increases, the demand for insurance increases. But as long as prices continue to climb, portfolio insurance will call for increased equity exposure. The contradiction between the anxiety of insured investors and their actions—buying more stock—set the stage for a destabilization of the market.[27]

## LEAD-UP TO OCTOBER 19, 1987

In the weeks before October 19, 1987, an increase in the prime rate, a large trade deficit, and fears of a weakening dollar depressed prices in both the stock and futures markets. In February 1987, the United States and its major trading partners (Japan, West Germany, the United Kingdom, France, and Canada) had agreed to prop up the US dollar, which was under heavy selling pressure because of an ever-widening US trade deficit. In the months following the so-called Louvre Accord, however, Japan and West Germany proceeded to raise their interest rates, in seeming contradiction to their February promises. To keep the dollar in line with Louvre standards, the United States had to increase its interest rates.

Higher interest rates could depress stock prices for several reasons. First, they might draw money away from equity into fixed-income investments. Second, they could increase the discount rate used to translate future expected income streams into present values; this would lead to a decline in current equity prices. Third, higher rates would raise borrowing costs, which could put a damper on the then-hot leveraged buyout market. (Leveraged buyouts, in which companies are taken over by private partnerships funded by heavy borrowing, had helped feed the merger-and-acquisition activity that had burgeoned like the market in the mid-1980s.)

But there was nothing new about rising rates. Although rates had fallen through much of 1986, the Federal Reserve had switched to a tighter monetary regime in early 1987, and the market had continued to rise through most of August, with merger-and-acquisition activity proceeding apace.

There was a political factor that may have kicked in right around the time of the crash. A bill before the US Congress in October would have severely limited tax deductions for the interest paid on debt used to finance corporate takeovers. Some feel that this bill was a specific trigger for the October 19 stock market crash.[28] Indeed, acquisition candidates seem to have been especially heavily hit on several days leading up to the crash, particularly on October 16. Nevertheless, the market fell along a broad front during the week of October 12, and all stocks fell, and fell hard, on October 19, not just takeover targets. Furthermore, President Ronald Reagan was expected to veto the tax bill if it did pass Congress.[29]

Perhaps the stock price declines reflected the US economy in general. On October 14, US trade figures for August were released. At $15.7 billion, the trade deficit had shrunk from the previous record level but it remained huge. The *New York Times* reported that US Treasury Secretary James A. Baker III was raising the possibility of allowing the dollar to weaken in the face of the general lack of support from foreign central banks.[30] A weaker dollar could help the US trade deficit by encouraging more exports. A weaker dollar would also customarily imply lower interest rates, as had been the case in 1985 and 1986.

Lower interest rates could be good for the economy, but not if they brought higher inflation. There may have been some justification to fear such an outcome. A stubborn US budget deficit persisted despite the generally healthy economy and strong equity market, and many political observers doubted President Reagan's ability or resolve to make the necessary compromises with Congress to raise taxes and/or cut spending. At the same time, Iranian threats to shipping in the Persian Gulf were generating fears of rising oil prices.

Preliminary reports on the US budget deficit, published on the Tuesday preceding the crash, showed that it remained substantial. It was, however, down at least $70 billion from the previous year's record of $221 billion. Although oil prices had increased considerably (throughout the year, not merely since the market's peak in August), inflation seemed under control. Thus, although there are plenty of fundamentals that could serve as likely candidates for the cause of the 1987 stock market crash, it is difficult to intuit how or even in what direction such fundamentals could have moved the market.

## The Eve of the Crash

The stock market experienced particularly sharp losses on the Wednesday, Thursday, and Friday immediately preceding the October 19 crash, with the Dow Jones Industrial Average (DJIA) falling 3.8 percent, 2.4 percent, and 4.6 percent, respectively. The *Wall Street Journal* noted that futures traders in Chicago believed the late-day decline on Thursday was set off by portfolio insurers selling, perhaps in response to the market's sharp decline the day before.[31]

These declines called for substantial selling by insured investors. In fact, portfolio insurers sold futures equivalent to $530 million, $965 million, and $2.1 billion in stock on that Wednesday, Thursday, and Friday.[32] A typical portfolio insurance program would require selling about 20 percent of stocks held in response to a 10-percent decline—and from Wednesday through Sunday, the DJIA had fallen 10.4 percent. Even at a conservative estimate of $60 billion of insured equities, a decline of that size would have required sales of about $12 billion. Yet less than $4 billion in sales had been completed by the end of the week.

According to the Brady Commission's postmortem on the crash:[33]

> [There was a] huge overhang of selling pressure—enough to crush the equity markets in the following week. This overhang was concentrated within two categories of reactive sellers, portfolio insurers and a few mutual fund groups, and exacerbated by the actions of a number of aggressive trading-oriented institutions selling in anticipation of further declines. . . . These traders could well understand the strategies of the portfolio insurers and mutual funds. They could anticipate the selling those institutions would have to do in reaction to the market's decline.

> They could also see those institutions falling behind in their selling programs. The situation presented an opportunity for these traders to sell in anticipation of the forced selling by portfolio insurers and mutual funds, with the prospect of repurchasing at lower prices.

But only a small number of speculators knew enough to anticipate the huge overhang of portfolio insurance selling pressure. A careful inspection of the *Wall Street Journal* and other publications reveals that the insurance overhang was not common knowledge just prior to the crash. Stock specialists, futures traders, institutional investors, and the public at large had, at best, only partial information and could not distinguish portfolio insurance trades from trades that may have been motivated by new information.

## BLACK MONDAY, OCTOBER 19, 1987

An avalanche of sell orders overwhelmed both the stock and futures markets at their openings on October 19, 1987. In one extreme case, a portfolio insurance client was instructed, based on the stock market's close on Friday, October 16, to sell 70 percent of its remaining stocks on Monday—even though the client had been selling throughout the prior week. Mutual funds also faced selling pressure on that Monday; telephone redemptions made it easy for customers to retreat from equity funds, and on Friday alone net redemptions (the difference between the amount investors took out of their mutual funds and the amount of new investment in the funds) exceeded $750 million, with more selling demand coming over the weekend.[34]

Insurers' direct sell programs in stocks amounted to $250 million at the opening; sell programs by index arbitrageurs amounted to another $250 million in stock. A small number of mutual fund companies also placed large sell orders for individual issues. One (Fidelity Investments) sold about $500 million during the first hour. Exhibit 5.1 shows that portfolio insurance and index arbitrage dominated program selling on the NYSE.[35]

Exhibit 5.2 shows portfolio insurance trading in futures during the day and the discount on futures prices relative to stock prices. In the first half hour of trading on Monday, a few portfolio insurers sold futures equivalent to about $400 million in stock. That represented 28 percent of

**EXHIBIT 5.1**

Program Selling on the New York Stock Exchange (NYSE), October 19, 1987

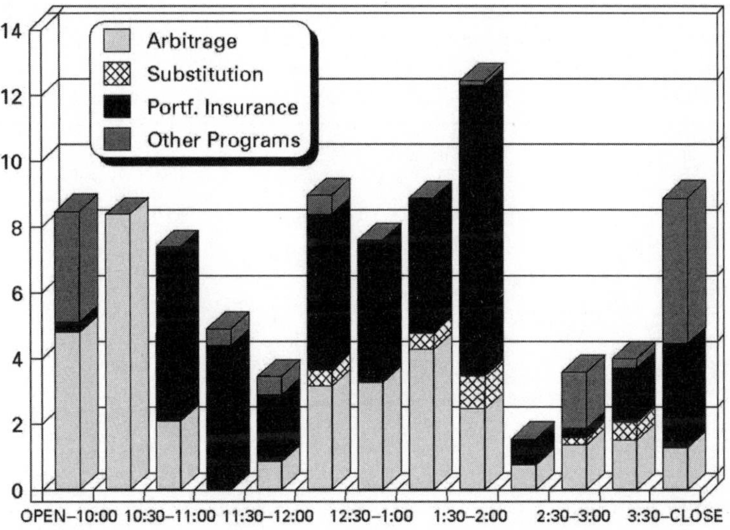


Source: Securities and Exchange Commission, "The October 1987 Market Break" (Washington, DC: Division of Market Regulation, SEC, 1988).

the public futures volume (that is, the volume exclusive of local market makers' volume). Futures sales by portfolio insurers picked up throughout the morning. Between 11:40 a.m. and 2:00 p.m., portfolio insurers sold about $1.3 billion in futures, representing about 41 percent of the public futures volume.[36]

In addition, portfolio insurers sold approximately $900 million in NYSE stocks. In stocks and futures combined, portfolio insurers had contributed over $3.7 billion in selling pressure by early afternoon. Program selling pressure from portfolio insurers and arbitrageurs often hit the NYSE simultaneously. For example, total program selling constituted 61 percent of trading volume from 1:10 p.m. to 1:20 p.m., and over 60 percent in two intervals from 1:30 p.m. to 2:00 p.m.[37]

According to the post-crash report from the Commodity Futures Trading Commission (CFTC), the interaction of index arbitrage and portfolio insurance could not explain the market decline on October 19.[38] The CFTC's analysis of trading during the day showed instances when the stock market temporarily reacted to arbitrage selling (see Exhibit 5.3), but

**EXHIBIT 5.2**

S&P 500 Futures Discounts and Portfolio Insurance Trading, October 19, 1987

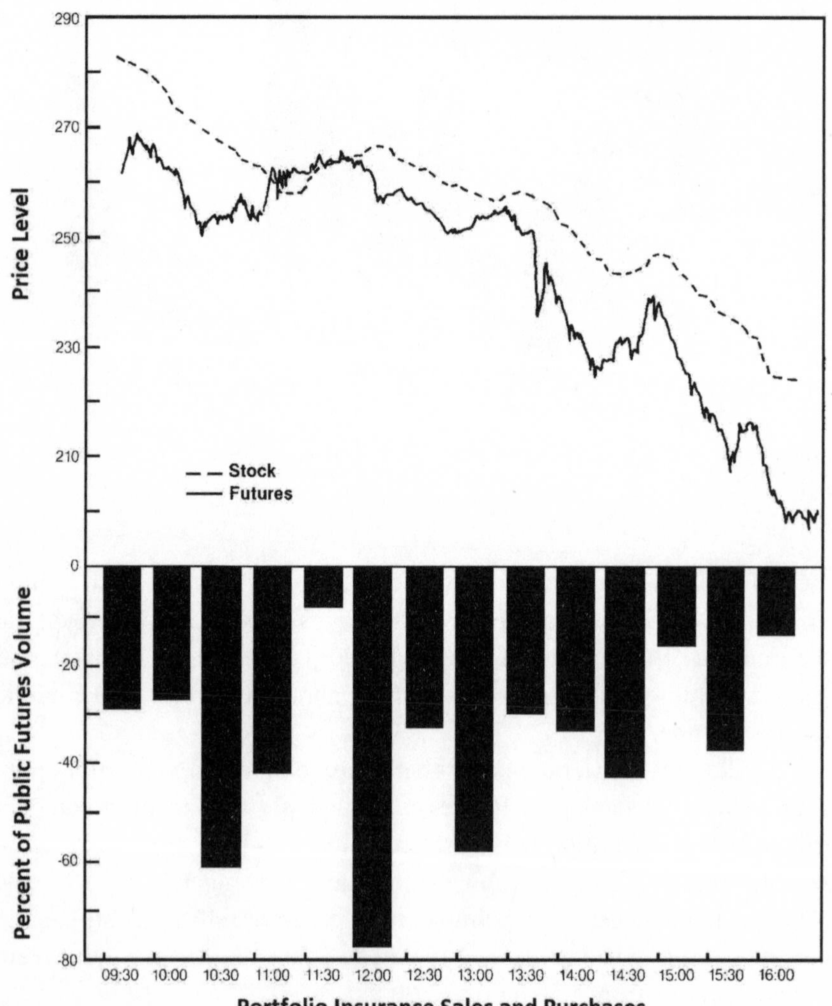


Source: Brady Commission, *Report of the Presidential Task Force on Market Mechanisms* (Washington, DC: Government Printing Office, 1988).

the report concluded that because futures prices were also declining, these instances were a sign of "general weakness" in the markets rather than evidence of any portfolio insurance-index arbitrage cascade. Perhaps a

**EXHIBIT 5.3**

The Dow Jones Industrial Average (DJIA) and Index Arbitrage, October 19, 1987

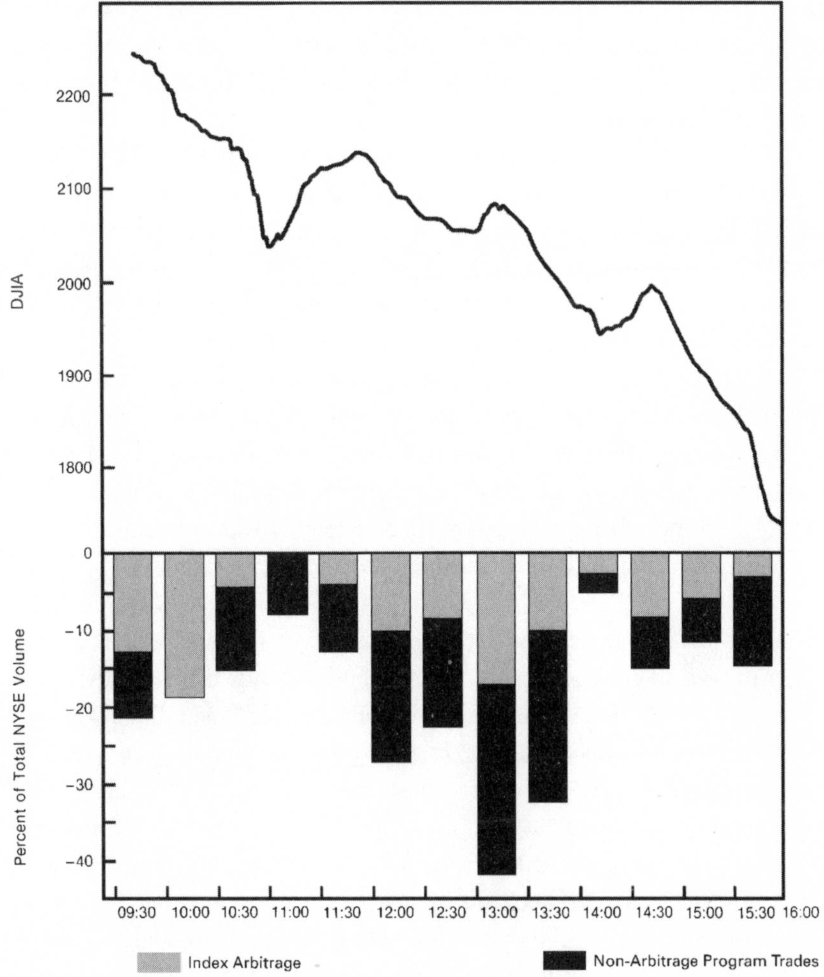


Source: Brady Commission, *Report of the Presidential Task Force on Market Mechanisms* (Washington, DC: Government Printing Office, 1988).

more likely explanation is that futures sales by portfolio insurers overwhelmed futures purchases by arbitrageurs, sending the futures market, as well as the stock market, down.

By 2:00 p.m., in any case, order execution problems in the spot market had slowed index arbitrage, while futures sales by portfolio insurers remained heavy. Despite the heavy sales, portfolio insurers "remained far behind the hedge ratios dictated by their computer programs."[39] The SEC later concluded that this large portfolio insurance overhang had a significant psychological impact on the markets on that Monday, depressing any potential enthusiasm for purchasing futures or stocks and perpetuating a large futures discount that further discouraged institutional buyers and even market makers.[40]

In the last hour and a half of trading on October 19, insurers sold $660 million in futures. With index arbitrageurs largely absent from the market, futures fell to a discount of 20 points relative to stock market.[41] Portfolio insurers also continued to sell stock directly in program trades. The DJIA sank almost 300 points in the last hour and a quarter of trading on its way to a decline of 508 points (22.6%) for the day.

By the end of trading on Monday, portfolio insurers had sold 39 million shares and index arbitrageurs sold another 38 million shares.[42] Futures sales by portfolio insurers on October 19 amounted to 21 percent of the total futures volume and 43 percent of the public futures volume.[43]

Much of the selling activity on Black Monday was concentrated in the hands of surprisingly few institutional investors:[44]

> Out of total NYSE sales of just under $21 billion, sell programs by three portfolio insurers made up just under $2 billion. Block sales of individual stocks by a few mutual funds accounted for another $900 million. About 90 percent of these sales were executed by one mutual fund group. In the futures market, portfolio insurer sales amounted to the equivalent of $4 billion of stock, or 34,500 contracts, equal to over 40 percent of futures volume, exclusive of locals' transactions; $2.8 billion was done by only three insurers. In the stock and futures markets together, one portfolio insurer sold stock and futures with underlying values totaling $1.7 billion. Huge as this selling pressure from portfolio insurers was, it was a small fraction of the sales dictated by the formulas of their models.

Exhibits 5.4 and 5.5 provide breakdowns of selling and buying for stocks and futures, respectively, by various investor groups during the crash period. Notably, portfolio insurers were by far the largest net sellers (sells minus buys) of stock and futures on October 19. One examination of portfolio insurance sales over the October 14–20 period suggests that such sales may have contributed to a decline in market price of almost 17 percent.[45]

**EXHIBIT 5.4**

## Stock Sales and Purchases on the New York Stock Exchange (NYSE) (millions of dollars)*

| | October 15 | October 16 | October 19 | October 20 |
|---|---|---|---|---|
| SELL | | | | |
| Portfolio insurers | $257 | $566 | $1,748 | $698 |
| Other pension | 190 | 794 | 875 | 334 |
| Trading-oriented investors | 1,156 | 1,446 | 1,751 | 1,740 |
| Mutual funds | 1,419 | 1,339 | 2,168 | 1,726 |
| Other financial | 516 | 959 | 1,416 | 1,579 |
| Total | 3,538 | 5,104 | 7,598 | 6,077 |
| Index arbitrage (included in above) | 717 | 1,592 | 1,774 | 128 |

| | October 15 | October 16 | October 19 | October 20 |
|---|---|---|---|---|
| BUY | | | | |
| Portfolio insurers | $201 | $161 | $449 | $863 |
| Other pension | 368 | 773 | 1,481 | 920 |
| Trading-oriented investors | 1,026 | 1,081 | 1,316 | 1,495 |
| Mutual funds | 998 | 1,485 | 1,947 | 1,858 |
| Other financial | 798 | 1,221 | 2,691 | 2,154 |
| Total | 3,391 | 4,721 | 7,884 | 7,290 |
| Index arbitrage (included in above) | 407 | 394 | 110 | 32 |

* Sample does not include: (1) individual investors, (2) institutional accounts with purchases and sales less than $10 million per day and (3) certain sizable broker/dealer trades.

Source: Brady Commission, *Report of the Presidential Task Force on Market Mechanisms* (Washington, DC: Government Printing Office, 1988).

**EXHIBIT 5.5**

## Futures Sales and Purchases on the Chicago Mercantile Exchange (CME) (millions of dollars)

| SELL | October 14 | October 15 | October 16 | October 19 | October 20 |
|---|---|---|---|---|---|
| Portfolio insurers | $534 | $968 | $2,123 | $4,037 | $2,818 |
| Arbitrageurs | $108 | $407 | $392 | $129 | $31 |
| Options | $554 | $998 | $1,399 | $898 | $635 |
| Locals | $7,325 | $7,509 | $7,088 | $5,479 | $2,718 |
| Other pension | $37 | $169 | $234 | $631 | $514 |
| Trading-oriented investors | $1,993 | $2,050 | $3,373 | $2,590 | $2,765 |
| Foreign | $398 | $442 | $479 | $494 | $329 |
| Mutual funds | $46 | $3 | $11 | $19 | $40 |
| Other financial | $49 | $109 | $247 | $525 | $303 |
| Published total | $16,949 | $18,830 | $19,640 | $18,987 | $13,641 |
| Volume accounted for | $11,045 | $12,655 | $15,347 | $14,801 | $10,152 |
| Percent accounted for | 65.2 | 67.2 | 78.1 | 78.0 | 74.4 |
| Portfolio insurance: Percent of publicly accounted for volume | 14.37 | 18.80 | 25.70 | 43.30 | 37.91 |

| BUY | October 14 | October 15 | October 16 | October 19 | October 20 |
|---|---|---|---|---|---|
| Portfolio insurers | $71 | $171 | $109 | $113 | $505 |
| Arbitrageurs | $1,313 | $717 | $1,705 | $1,582 | $119 |
| Options | $594 | $864 | $1,254 | $915 | $544 |
| Locals | $7,301 | $7,530 | $7,125 | $5,682 | $2,689 |
| Other pension | $90 | $76 | $294 | $447 | $1,070 |
| Trading-oriented investors | $1,494 | $2,236 | $3,634 | $4,510 | $4,004 |
| Foreign | $240 | $298 | $443 | $609 | $418 |
| Mutual funds | $0 | $27 | $73 | $143 | $51 |
| Other financial | $155 | $57 | $126 | $320 | $517 |
| Published total | $16,949 | $18,830 | $19,640 | $18,987 | $13,641 |
| Volume accounted for | $11,259 | $11,976 | $14,763 | $14,320 | $9,915 |
| Percent accounted for | 66.4 | 63.6 | 75.2 | 75.4 | 72.7 |
| Portfolio insurance: Percent of publicly accounted for volume | 1.80 | 3.86 | 1.43 | 1.31 | 6.98 |

Source: Brady Commission, *Report of the Presidential Task Force on Market Mechanisms* (Washington, DC: Government Printing Office, 1988).

## BOUNCE-BACK TUESDAY

Volume on Tuesday, October 20, 1987, remained high and price movements resembled a roller coaster ride. S&P 500 futures opened at a substantial premium to fair value as the market surged upward, but that premium reversed to a slight discount by approximately 10 a.m. During this period, portfolio insurance selling accounted for 26 percent of S&P 500 futures volume.[46]

This volume of portfolio insurance trading appears to have been a substantial factor behind futures discounts at several points during the day. Insurance strategies accounted for 25 percent of futures volume between 10:00 a.m. and 10:30 a.m., as the discount widened to 16 points, and for more than 34 percent of futures volume during the next hour, as the markets plunged.[47]

The S&P 500 futures contract moved to a discount as wide as 40 points as the market plummeted 27 percent between 10:00 a.m. and 12:15 p.m.[48] At its lowest point, the futures price implied a DJIA level of about 1,400.[49] When futures reached this level, the Chicago Board Options Exchange

(CBOE) and the Chicago Mercantile Exchange (CME) halted trading in the contracts.

The SEC's investigation found that sales dictated by portfolio insurance significantly dampened price recoveries in both the futures and stock markets on October 20.[50] By the afternoon of that Tuesday, however, several factors converged to offset insurance selling and produce a market rally. These factors included news of pending corporate buybacks of stock, assurances of sources of liquidity for NYSE specialists, the ebbing of stock sales volume, and the availability of bargain prices. The DJIA ended up closing at 1,841, for a gain of 102 points on the day, or 5.9 percent. The volume of 614 million shares for that day set a record, surpassing even the previous day's volume of 604 million shares.

## FAILURE OF PORTFOLIO INSURANCE

In the wake of the crash, portfolio insurance vendors blamed the failures of the strategy on higher than expected market volatility, discontinuities or gaps in stock prices, and substantial futures discounts—everything but the strategy itself.[51] Yet, the strategy itself may have caused that turbulent market behavior. Portfolio insurance failed to live up to its claim to be equivalent to a traditional insurance policy.[52]

However, as we have noted, portfolio insurance even in theory differs markedly from traditional insurance because portfolio insurance is essentially self-insurance. The insurance "coverage" is "purchased" by selling stock as stock prices decline. The cost of such a purchase can explode when the volatility of stock prices increases. Furthermore, sales by insured portfolios contribute to this volatility, dramatically increasing the likelihood of gaps in market prices. When stock prices fall discontinuously, as they did during the crash, the very viability of portfolio insurance is compromised. Sales simply cannot be made at the levels necessary to provide the desired protection.

Some of the hourly stock price moves on October 19 and 20, 1987, were comparable in magnitude to the previous daily record fall of 12.8 percent on Black Tuesday, October 29, 1929. These large, discontinuous price moves, and the resulting chaotic conditions, created major problems for all portfolio insurers. Portfolio insurers that had the flexibility to sell in the stock market as well as the futures market generally fared somewhat better than those confined to the futures market alone.[53] Even these insurers, however, found it difficult to hedge properly. According to the SEC, General Motors was able to sell less than half the amount it needed to attain full insurance coverage.[54]

The available evidence indicates that portfolio insurance performed poorly during the crash. Many if not most insurance programs breached their floors. Furthermore, even those that hit their floors or fell only slightly below found themselves stopped out. That is, these insurance programs were forced out of stock completely and into all-cash positions to assure that the downside protection would be met at the end of the insurance horizon. As the market recovered after the crash, stopped-out insured portfolios incurred substantial opportunity costs by being shut out of the market rise. Ironically, portfolio insurance, touted as a vehicle for locking in bull market gains,[55] ended up locking many insurance clients out of subsequent market gains and into maximum loss limitations.

After the crash, many portfolio insurance vendors and users (including Aetna, BEA Associates, San Diego Gas and Electric, Duke University, and Bayer USA) got out of the strategy altogether. The Brady Commission reported that of the 13 insured pension funds that responded to their survey, two had dropped portfolio insurance prior to October 19, 1987, and seven more had eliminated their insurance programs after the crash.[56] Another survey of 14 vendors indicated that their portfolio insurance assets dropped by two-thirds between September 30, 1987 and December 31, 1987, from $37 billion to $12.6 billion.[57] The amount of insured assets managed by LOR fell from $54 billion in early 1987 to $8.4 billion in early 1988 to $154 million in early 1989.[58]

The decline in portfolio insurance assets was reflected in a simultaneous decline in the volume of futures contracts on the S&P 500. Beginning with the advent of exchange-traded futures in 1982, the average daily volume of futures trading had grown steadily, doubling between year-end 1985 and early October 1987. The volume dropped off by about half after the crash. At the same time, demand for actual exchange-traded options soared.

Portfolio insurance did not live up to its name. Rather, it proved that it is *not* insurance under the generally accepted meaning of the term. There is no pool of assets an insurance provider can draw on to reimburse client losses; in fact, there is no insurance provider to bear the risk of loss. The insured investors themselves bear that risk, relying on the ability to get into or out of stocks in a timely and cost-effective manner. Whether they can do so depends upon the willingness of other investors to accept the downside risk that insured investors want to lay off.

In the 1987 crash, portfolio insurance failed just when it was most needed. That did not, however, deter investors and investment advisers from continuing to seek the Holy Grail of no-risk reward.

## THE INTERNATIONAL CRASH

Some market observers have argued that portfolio insurance could not have been a major contributor to the crash of October 19, 1987, because portfolio insurance strategies were pretty much unique to the United States, whereas markets around the world crashed along with the US market. This line of reasoning was most extensively developed by Richard Roll when he was a professor of finance at the UCLA Anderson School of Management.

Roll maintained that "most of the other markets around the world displayed dramatic declines on their October 19, foreshadowing the crash in North America."[59] But the US decline of 10.4 percent from Wednesday, October 14 through Friday, October 16 was a significant decline. It was, in fact, the sharpest drop over such a short period since the fall of Europe in World War II. Furthermore, a chronological review of worldwide market returns reveals that non-US markets crashed after, not before, the US market. From October 1 through October 16, the last trading day before the big crash, the US market had slipped about 12 percent, much more than any non-US market.

On Monday, October 19, the Asian markets, among the first to trade each day, opened to significantly bad news. Friday's sharp sell-off on Wall Street, which came on the heels of two prior down days, had occurred after the Asian markets had closed. Furthermore, military hostilities between the United States and Iran were escalating, and US Treasury Secretary James A. Baker III was threatening to let the dollar decline in order to combat tightening German interest rates. It is not surprising that the Asian markets were down on October 19. Even so, the average Asian market decline from October 1 through October 19 was less than the US market decline through its close on October 16.

The European markets were the next to trade on October 19, and they fell sharply, especially London, down 10 percent for the day. But London had been effectively closed on the previous Friday because of extreme weather, so much of the decline in London on October 19 may be attributable to the previous Friday's decline in the United States. Also, US institutional investors, wishing to get a jump on New York's Monday opening, sold in European markets early in the day. By the end of the day in Europe, of course, markets there were feeling the effects of the US crash in New York. Even so, the average European market decline from October 1 through Monday October 19 was less than the US market's decline through the Friday preceding the crash.

The US crash in the DJIA of 22.6 percent on October 19 in turn triggered crashes around the globe. The Asian markets were devastated on October 20. The Tokyo exchange closed down a record 14.9 percent that Tuesday, despite delayed openings in half its listed stocks. The markets in Australia and New Zealand were also off sharply. The European markets, which had witnessed the start of the US crash on the previous Monday afternoon, were hit hard on Tuesday, with the London market off by 11.4 percent. The US market, always the last to trade, rose on October 20, and closed up 5.9 percent. All major international markets rose on Wednesday, October 21.

To market observers at the time, the epicenter of the crash certainly seemed to be New York. In London, then Chancellor of the Exchequer Nigel Lawson noted: "This began on Wall Street."[60] Rüdiger von Rosen, executive vice chairman of West Germany's stock exchanges, blamed the German market crash on a "significant dependence on Wall Street."[61] Peter J. Morgan, chief economist for Barclays de Zoete Wedd, Tokyo, attributed the Japanese market's collapse to Wall Street: "It's a reaction to New York. It's just coming out of the clear blue sky. There's nothing domestically that would lead to this."[62] The SEC concluded that the US market led Japan and the United Kingdom.[63] The International Stock Exchange concurred, noting that by Tuesday, October 20, "perceptions had changed due largely to the dramatic 509-point [22.6%] fall in the DJIA Index on the NYSE overnight."[64]

CHAPTER 6

# After the 1987 Crash—Options

*"Derivatives have value only in an environment of volatility; their proliferation is a commentary on our times."*

**—Peter L. Bernstein**[1]

The 1987 stock market crash highlighted two major problems with portfolio insurance. First, it showed that the strategy of self-insurance upon which portfolio insurance relied is not insurance in the true sense of the word; market participants were not willing to step in as buyers to guarantee insured portfolio values. Second, the crash made manifest the latent danger large amounts of insured assets pose for market liquidity and market stability. By 1989, the amount of assets covered by portfolio insurance programs had declined by 60 percent to 90 percent from the peak reached just before the 1987 stock market crash.[2]

But the market crash had increased investors' awareness of the potential fragility of the market, and their consequent desire for protection. This desire was only heightened by the rise in market levels in the years following the crash. By 1989, institutions had realized substantial market gains, which they wanted to protect without having to liquidate their equity portfolios.

The decade following the crash witnessed the emergence of a cornucopia of products designed to protect investors from market downturns. These included an expanded list of exchange-traded options, privately contracted over-the-counter (OTC) options, swaps geared to institutional investors, and, for retail investors, hybrid products that offered stock participation with a bond-like guarantee of principal. These largely option-based or option-like products had in common with the old portfolio insurance strategy more than just a similar investment objective. They relied ultimately on the same option-replicating trading that destabilized stock and futures markets in 1987.

## REPLACING PORTFOLIO INSURANCE

Publicly traded options offer numerous advantages over portfolio insurance when it comes to providing protection. They do not require selling stock into a falling market, as portfolio insurance does. Put options are thus not in danger of failing to perform because of volatile or discontinuous markets.

Publicly traded options offer another advantage over portfolio insurance: Trading intentions are not obscured. The number of outstanding options contracts and the prices of exchange-traded options are publicly available. These data provide an indication of the demand for protection and the expectation for market volatility. Exchange-traded options are, therefore, less destabilizing than portfolio insurance.

Portfolio insurance had been motivated in part by the substantial obstacles to the use of option markets by institutional investors. Before the crash, exchange-traded options were only available for certain standardized strike prices and expiration dates, and their time horizons were fixed and generally quite short. While an investor could have used a series of publicly traded short-term options to provide protection over a longer horizon, the cost would not be known in advance, as it would depend on market volatility at the time the options expired. Furthermore, the Securities and Exchange Commission (SEC) had imposed maximum position limits on option holdings, making publicly traded options more or less useless to institutional investors with sizable portfolios.

Following the crash, options exchanges began to offer instruments that were more suitable to institutional investors' needs. In early November 1987, the Chicago Board Options Exchange (CBOE) began trading in Standard & Poor's 500 (S&P 500) index options with two-year maturities. October 1990 saw the birth of Long-term Equity AnticiPation Securities (LEAPS)—two-year puts and calls on individual securities and on the Standard & Poor's 100 (S&P 100) and S&P 500 indexes, as well as the Major Market Index. LEAPS had maturities of up to six years and covered market sectors such as oil and biotechnology as well as broader-based indexes. FLexible EXchange (FLEX) options, introduced in 1996, allowed customers to choose the underlying index (e.g., S&P 100 or S&P 500), the expiration date (up to five years), the strike price, the exercise style (e.g., American or European), and settlement value (based on the expiration-day opening, closing, or average price). Position limits on FLEX options were eliminated at the end of 1997.

## OTC Options

Institutional investors who did not see what they needed on the menu of exchange-traded products could turn to the over-the-counter market to achieve, for a price, just about any desired payoff pattern. The OTC option, a privately negotiated contract between two parties—the *option writer,* or *seller* (usually an investment bank, bank subsidiary, or broker-dealer), and the *option buyer* (typically a large institutional investor)—can be tailored to meet particular exposure and protection requirements, without being confined by the horizons or maximum positions that may limit exchange-traded options.

A so-called plain-vanilla OTC option may offer customization in the amount or nature of the underlying assets (stock, stock portfolio, or index), the option's strike price, the option's maturity, and the exercise style. Numerous elaborations on the plain vanilla are provided by so-called exotic options, which offer a wide variety of payout patterns.

OTC options suffer from several disadvantages relative to listed options. Given their specialized natures, OTC options largely lack a secondary market, so they are substantially illiquid, hence more difficult to value. As customized instruments, they are also generally more expensive than listed options, whose prices are determined by competing buyers and sellers. Finally, in the absence of a clearinghouse providing a financial guarantee, holders of OTC options face greater risk of counterparty default.

## Swaps

Swaps are contracts between two counterparties to exchange a series of cash flows. A simple example might be an issuer that swaps the fixed-rate interest payments on a new bond issue for floating-rate payments, or dollar-denominated bonds for bonds in other currencies.

With equity swaps, one of the cash flows is linked to the performance of an established equity index or basket of stocks. The investor generally exchanges a fixed or floating interest rate for the dividend and capital appreciation on the underlying equity index. An investor with a stock portfolio, however, can combine it with an equity swap, paying out the dividends and any capital gains on the stocks and receiving a fixed rate of return.

## Guaranteed Equity

The early 1980s saw the emergence of "90:10" funds aimed primarily at individual, rather than institutional, investors. The fund would invest 90 percent of its capital in certificates of deposit and the remaining 10 percent in a call option on a stock index. Investors were guaranteed the return of at least 90 percent of their initial investment, while the call option offered participation in any stock market advance. Interest in these types of funds languished in the market environment that prevailed until the 1987 crash, as investors were placated by low volatility and rising equity returns.

Nevertheless, some banks began offering similar instruments in the mid 1980s. With Chase Manhattan's Market Index Investment, first offered in March 1987, depositors received a guarantee of 100 percent of their initial deposit for accounts up to $100,000, backed by the Federal Deposit Insurance Corporation (FDIC). In place of the usual interest rate on bank deposits (averaging 5.4 percent at the time), depositors could choose to receive 75 percent of any gain in the S&P 500; 60 percent of the index's gain or a 2 percent return, whichever was higher; or the higher of 40 percent of the index return or a 4 percent return. In exchange for the give-up in interest, the depositor received the opportunity to participate in any stock market rise.

The 1987 crash brought an end to many of these products because their issuers lost so much money. Nevertheless, as noted, the crash instilled in investors a renewed appreciation for protection of portfolio value. In the spring of 1993, Citigroup began marketing a "stock index insured account" that offered "Stock market returns. Zero risk to principal." Other banks followed Chase Manhattan's example, offering equity-linked certificates of deposit that paid little or no interest but gave back at maturity the original deposit plus a return linked to the performance of a given equity index. Broker-dealers and others offered a variety of similar instruments named: Equity Participation Notes, Stock Upside Notes,

Structured Upside Participation Notes, Structured Upside Participating Equity Receipts, and Synthetic High-Income Equity Linked Securities.

For all these, the basic underlying framework is a certificate of deposit or bond plus a call option on an underlying index. Purchase of the call option is essentially funded by the interest forgone by the investor or depositor or, perhaps, by the sale of an out-of-the-money call option. Such instruments offer investors participation in equity returns at a bond-like level of risk, although with a reduced or zero interest rate.

Such guaranteed-equity products really took off in Europe, where they also offered investors tax breaks. Estimated sales there totaled $40 billion to $100 billion by the end of the 1990s. Sales lagged in the United States, where investors seemed to feel more comfortable with stock mutual funds or direct stock investment. In the United States, the notional value of guaranteed equity by 1997 amounted to only $3 billion to $5 billion.[3]

Although the ultimate users of guaranteed equity may be primarily retail investors, the issuers of the products are generally financial intermediaries that rely on options to provide equity participation. The writers of these options must, just like put option sellers, manage their risk exposures.

## HEDGING OPTION RISK

With portfolio insurance, sudden plunges in stock prices on and around October 19, 1987, made it difficult for insurance programs to execute the trades required to provide the programs' minimum floors. The programs generally failed to provide the protection they had promised. This is generally not a problem with options. Once the buyer has purchased a put option, for example, the option most likely will provide the level of protection anticipated even if the underlying market prices gap down.

The option buyer is also protected against unexpected changes in volatility over the life of the option. An option's potential value, hence its price, generally increases as the volatility of the underlying asset increases, and decreases as the underlying asset's volatility decreases. This occurs because higher (lower) volatility brings a higher (lower) probability of the option ending in the money.

A change in the underlying asset's volatility after the option is purchased, however, has no impact on the option buyer. The option buyer will not have to pay more if volatility increases; nor will the buyer receive a refund if volatility declines. Furthermore, the option buyer will not have to trade more options in order to maintain the original level of protection or participation. The major risk the option buyer is exposed to is the risk that the option writer will default on its obligations. The use of options exchanges, which provide backup in case of member defaults, greatly reduces this type of credit exposure.

What is true for option buyers, however, is not necessarily true for option sellers. The option writer is exposed to substantial risk. If the value of the underlying asset declines below a put's strike price, the option is exercised; the writer pays the option holder the exercise price and receives, in return, an asset that is worth less. If the value of the underlying asset rises above a call's strike price, the option is exercised; the writer receives the exercise price from the option holder and provides, in return, an asset that is worth more. The writer of either a put or a call will presumably have incorporated this risk exposure into the premium charged the option buyer. Nevertheless, the risk remains that the asset's price move will be adverse to the option writer and larger than the option premium received, resulting in a loss for the writer.

Dealers and market makers that write options are generally not speculators. They do not wish to remain exposed to the risk that an option will be exercised against them. They will, therefore, try to lay off the risk that their short positions expose them to. There are several ways to do this.

Dealers and market makers do not have to hedge every single option position they hold. Their various positions will offset each other to a large extent. That is, they will have long put positions as well as short put positions, and also offsetting call positions. Netting the cash flows from all their transactions leaves only a residual amount that must be hedged.

Ideally, dealers and market makers will be able to hedge by finding appropriate exchange-traded options. The ability of exchange-traded options to offset the risks undertaken by option sellers, however, may be limited. The option positions used must be changed over time as the exposure of the option writer changes. Short-term options, for example, must be rolled over as time passes. The need for discrete rebalancing introduces the near certainty of hedging errors, leaving the option writer open to the same dangers of market gaps and hidden costs that threaten strategies that, like portfolio insurance, rely on dynamic hedging.

Furthermore, the demand for options, particularly as vehicles for portfolio protection, can exceed the natural supply of sellers. This may be more likely the case for equity options than for other types of derivatives. Either side of a currency or interest rate swap, for instance, may be used to reduce risk, depending upon the nature of the user's cash inflows and outflows. A company in the United Kingdom exporting to the United States and a company in the United States exporting to the United Kingdom might be natural counterparties in a swap of US dollars for pounds sterling. There is thus likely to be a natural interest in either side of the swap from companies seeking to hedge their particular market exposures. For a swap dealer, payments to one counterparty are mirrored by payments from the other; the dealer's own exposure is eliminated through offsetting positions.

Equity options are more problematic. The option writer is essentially speculating, taking on the risk of uncertain market volatility in the expectation either that volatility will move the market in a direction that will prove profitable or that volatility will remain within a range where exercise of the option is unprofitable for the buyer. Furthermore, equities tend to be more volatile than interest rate and currency derivatives. It may thus be harder to find counterparties willing to take on short equity option positions.

When option dealers or market makers cannot buy options to hedge the exposures from the options they have sold, they may have to replicate long option positions synthetically. Replicating long option positions requires selling stock (or shorting stock futures contracts) as the market falls and buying stock (or covering short stock futures positions) as the market rises. In other words, it requires the same trend-following trading that portfolio insurance relied upon.

## Portfolio Insurance Redux

As with synthetic insurance, using listed and OTC options for equity risk protection may encourage making higher-than-warranted commitments to stock. As demand for stock pushes prices away from fair valuations, prices become more susceptible to correction. This may lead to more demand for protection via options. Demand for options may increase the need for option writers to hedge dynamically in the underlying stock market. As this requires purchasing stocks as long as their prices are rising, this dynamic hedging will add further upward pressure to stock prices. When overpriced stocks eventually suffer a correction, the option writers' hedging demands will require selling into declining markets, which may push prices down further and encourage selling by other investors. This positive-feedback dynamic may be exaggerated by growth in demand for put option protection in a market that is already declining.

The price transparency of exchange-traded options may help to reduce the effects of option writers' dynamic hedging by revealing that the selling reflects only hedging needs, not fundamental information. By contrast, when the source of selling by hedgers is obscured, as may be the case with OTC options, other investors may decline to buy the offered stock, or sell along with hedgers in the mistaken belief that their trades are motivated by information rather than hedging needs.

A series of episodes beginning soon after the 1987 crash signaled cause for concern about option-related volatility. Specifically, in 1989, 1991, and 1997, episodes arose in which dealers that had sold put options were forced to hedge their positions by selling futures. Futures sales in turn accentuated declines in the underlying equity market.

## PUT OPTIONS IN 1989

After the 1987 crash, the US economy continued to grow. The stock market remained stable throughout 1988 and rose substantially in 1989, setting a record high on October 9, with the Dow Jones Industrial Average (DJIA) closing at 2,791. Over the next three days, however, the DJIA lost about 30 points. On Friday, October 13, 1989, the DJIA plunged 191 points, or 6.9 percent.

As Exhibit 6.1 shows, before 2:30 p.m. on October 13, the DJIA fell by about 25 points, possibly because of economic indicators released by the government before the opening. Specifically, a rising producer price index and an increase in retail sales were viewed as negative factors for stocks because they implied a delay in any lowering of interest rates by the Federal Reserve.

The steep fall-off in stock prices occurred later that day, triggered by corporate events. At 2:40 p.m., the New York Stock Exchange (NYSE) specialist in United Airlines (UAL) stock received permission to halt trading pending significant news. By 2:55 p.m., newswires were carrying

**EXHIBIT 6.1**

The Dow Jones Industrial Average (DJIA) on October 13, 1989

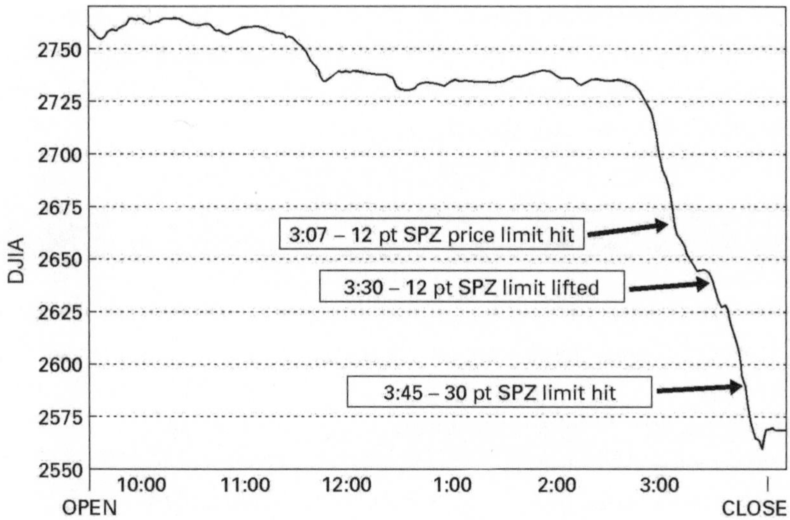


Source: Securities and Exchange Commission, "Trading Analysis of October 13 and 16, 1989" (Washington, DC: Division of Market Regulation, SEC, 1990).

the announcement that financing for the planned takeover of the company was in doubt.[4] In addition, the media began reporting that the US Congress had rejected a proposal to cut the capital gains tax rate.[5] In the context of an already weakened market for high-yield bonds,[6] the UAL news seemed extremely bearish for actual and rumored takeover targets, as well as for stocks in general.[7]

Prices on both the NYSE and the Chicago Mercantile Exchange (CME) immediately began to fall sharply. By 3:07 p.m., the S&P 500 December futures contract (SPZ), the most actively traded stock index futures contract, hit its 12-point price limit. This was part of a system of circuit breakers introduced after the 1987 crash, designed to slow trading during severe market declines or steep advances.

These 12 points were equivalent to a 92-point drop in the DJIA (which itself was 84 points off the previous day's close) and triggered NYSE sidecars (other circuit breakers) that paused program trades for five minutes. Unrestricted trading in the CME's S&P 500 futures contract resumed at

3:30 p.m. and prices proceeded to fall fairly steadily until the 30-point limit was hit at about 3:45 p.m. The index futures contract had fallen an equivalent of 230 DJIA points, although the DJIA itself was down by only 150 points.[8] Stock index futures on other exchanges also hit their limits during this period. The American Stock Exchange (AMEX) and CBOE both halted trading in their index option futures after 3:16 p.m. and effectively remained closed for the rest of the day.[9]

## CIRCUIT BREAKERS

The various government reports on the 1987 crash suggested structural changes that might help to prevent future crashes. These recommendations resulted in, among other things, the establishment of a system of circuit breakers designed to restore order to markets in free fall.

In October 1988, the US stock exchanges set price limits that would halt trading in stocks at times of unusual market stress. The initial parameters called for a one-hour halt in trading on all exchanges if the DJIA fell 250 points below the previous day's close (about a 12 percent decline given then-current index levels). A two-hour trading halt would be triggered if, upon reopening, the DJIA fell another 150 points. Later rules called for trading halts based on percentage price drops, with one- and two-hour halts for 10 percent and 20 percent drops, respectively, that occurred before 2:00 p.m., and market closure for a 30 percent drop. Currently, halts are linked to price changes in the S&P 500 and call for 15-minute breaks after drops of 7 percent or 13 percent, until 3:25 p.m., after which the limits do not apply; after a 20 percent price drop, trading is suspended for the rest of the day.

The futures exchanges instituted their own price limits, which were coordinated with those on the stock exchanges. All the futures exchanges initially called for a trading halt if their index futures contracts fell more than the equivalent of 250 DJIA points; most called for a halt at 100 DJIA-equivalent points. On the CME, for example, trading in the S&P 500 futures contract would be suspended for 30 minutes if the contract fell 12 points below the previous day's close. At 30 points down, trading would be halted for one hour or, if the DJIA had fallen more than 250 points, until at least half the stocks in the S&P 500 index had begun trading again. If the DJIA fell more than 400 points, trading in the futures contract would halt for two hours. In addition, the contract was subjected to a daily limit of 50 points up or down, and to a 5-point limit, up or down, on its opening price. Current halts are synched to stock exchange rules and based on S&P 500 prices.

The exchanges also passed rules to limit program trading during periods of significant market volatility. These rules, triggered by point or percentage drops in S&P 500 futures, the DJIA, or another index, variously shunted program trading from automated systems, halted program trading for set periods or until prices recovered to preset levels, or required that any sales be made on upticks in prices (or purchases on downticks). Program trading "breakers" were eliminated in 2007.

By the time the NYSE closed at 4:00 p.m., the DJIA had fallen 191 points (6.9%) to 2,569. This was the market's second-largest point decline to date. Trading in American Airlines (AA), UAL, and two other airline stocks had stopped; neither AA nor UAL had reopened by the end of the day. An excess of sell over buy orders had halted trading in six additional stocks, only one of which had reopened by the end of the day.[10]

About 87 percent of the DJIA's drop on October 13, 1989, occurred in the last 90 minutes before the close, on extraordinarily heavy volume. During the last hour alone, 112 million shares were traded on the NYSE, a level approaching the 116.6 million shares traded during the busiest hour of the stock market crash of October 19, 1987.[11]

On Monday morning, October 16, 1989, a backlog of sell orders suggested that Friday's market decline would continue. The S&P 500 December stock index futures contract opened 5 points below Friday's close, triggering the CME's opening price limit. However, the price rebounded immediately, and the limit was lifted after just one minute of trading.[12] On the NYSE, an excess of sell orders delayed opening in 151 stocks, representing nearly 20 percent of the DJIA's price weighting and 11 percent of the capitalization of the S&P 500. By the time UAL opened at 11:08 a.m., the share price dropped $55, or 20 percent, since Friday afternoon.[13]

Heavy selling and delayed openings drove the DJIA down more than 60 points in the first hour of trading. After that, however, prices recovered dramatically, following the lead of the stock index futures market.[14] The recovery maintained its momentum throughout the day, and the DJIA ended 88 points above its close on Friday. NYSE trading volume on October 16 was 421.5 million shares, the fourth heaviest on record at the time, exceeded only by October 19, 20, and 21, 1987.[15] More than 225 million shares traded during the first two hours on that day, setting a record for the NYSE.[16]

On Tuesday of the following week, October 24, 1989, the DJIA fell 80 points in the first hour of trading. The S&P 500 December futures contract briefly hit the 12-point limit at 10:33 a.m., but recovered almost immediately. Stocks reversed their decline just as rapidly, regaining 40 points in the next half hour and ending the day off just 4 points on total volume of about 239 million shares. The initial sell-off may have been triggered by news after Monday's close that UAL's board wanted to keep the airline independent, once again dashing prospects of a buyout.[17]

## Effects of Put Options

While OTC equity options were not actively used before 1988, the dollar amount of assets in equity portfolios covered by put options had grown substantially by October 1989. At least three major broker-dealers had written put coverage for eight institutional money managers. The aggregate value of institutional portfolios protected in this manner was approximately $2 billion.[18]

While seemingly small compared with the $60 billion to $100 billion covered by portfolio insurance in 1987, portfolio puts nevertheless contributed significantly, albeit indirectly, to market behavior on the afternoon of October 13, 1989, and at the opening of the market on October 16, 1989. The institutions using portfolio puts as insurance were able to avoid selling in the stock and futures markets. For the broker-dealers that had written the puts, however, it was a different story. In order to insulate themselves from the risk their put sales exposed them to, they had to sell as the market fell.

On October 13, 1989, selling pressure on the CME depressed S&P 500 index futures contracts until they were selling at a discount to the underlying spot index. This created an opportunity for index arbitrageurs to profit by buying the futures contracts and selling the underlying index. Selling pressure was thus transferred to the stock market. However, futures continued to sell at a discount. Many broker-dealers that had written puts were unable to sell futures at prices that would fully hedge their exposures. They turned to the stock market, using program trades to sell at the end of the day.[19]

At 3:49 p.m. on October 13, 1989, just before the DJIA reached its low, nearly 200 points down, three firms hit the floor of the NYSE with program sell orders for 2.5 million shares. All three later told the SEC that the sales were hedging transactions. Two, accounting for 83 percent of the program volume, attributed the selling directly to portfolio put strategies.[20]

In sum, OTC options did not so much reduce the need to sell into declining markets as they shifted this need from institutional investors to broker-dealers (replacing portfolio insurance). Just as portfolio insurers had earlier in the decade, these broker-dealers trusted that the liquidity of the futures market would allow them to hedge their own proprietary risk exposures as needed. Also, just as portfolio insurers learned in 1987, the broker-dealers found that a hedge that depends on selling during market downturns can be a hazardous proposition.

We have noted that, before the markets opened on Monday, October 16, 1989, accumulated sell orders indicated that Friday's price declines would continue. Some broker-dealers that were net sellers at the opening told the SEC that those transactions were a continuation of the hedging they had begun late Friday afternoon. There was also concentrated arbitrage-related selling. When that abated, prices on the NYSE began to recover.

On October 19, 1987, arbitrage sell programs had been joined by portfolio insurance sell programs, and the market's partial recovery from a morning sell-off was reversed as the market continued plummeting. On October 16, 1989, without those portfolio insurance programs, buy programs were able to maintain enough momentum to support the recovery.[21] Portfolio puts seem to have had less effect on market prices in October 1989 than portfolio insurance had in October 1987. But the difference can be attributed to the comparative sizes of put coverage in 1989 ($2 billion) and portfolio insurance in 1987 ($60 billion to $100 billion).

## DOUBLE-WITCHING HOUR IN 1991

On Friday, November 15, 1991, another severe market decline piqued regulators' interest in program trading and in investment strategies designed to protect portfolio values. On that day, the S&P 500 fell 14.5 points (3.7%) and the DJIA fell 120 points (3.9%) (see Exhibit 6.2). Again, much of the decline came in the afternoon and, again, futures contracts at times overshot the underlying spot market declines by considerable margins.

Unlike Friday, October 13, 1989, Friday, November 15, 1991 was a "double-witching hour." That is, it was a day on which both equity index options and index futures contracts expired. On such Friday expirations, NYSE member firms must enter expiration-related market-on-close (MOC) orders one hour before the 4:00 p.m. close of trading.

By just after 2:00 p.m. on November 15, the DJIA had fallen 50 points (1.6%) below its previous day's close. This triggered the NYSE's collar rule limiting index arbitrage program trading. The DJIA and the S&P 500 held fairly steady over the next hour, with the DJIA actually gaining a little ground. When unexpectedly large sell-order imbalances became

**EXHIBIT 6.2**

The Dow Jones Industrial Average (DJIA) on November 15, 1991

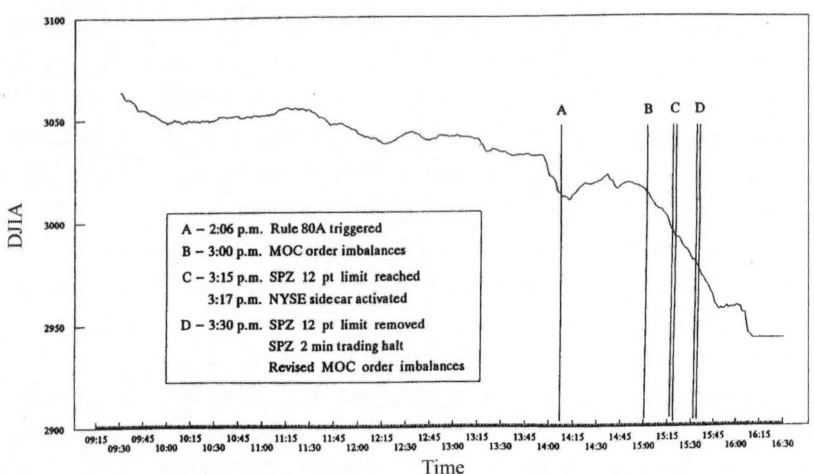


Source: Securities and Exchange Commission, "Market Decline on November 15, 1991" (memorandum from William H. Hayman, Director, Division of Market Regulation, to SEC Chairman Breeden), Division of Market Regulation, SEC, December 24, 1991.

apparent after 3:00 p.m., however, both indexes began to decline sharply. Down 1.6 percent at 3:00 p.m., the DJIA was down a full 2.7 percent by 3:30 p.m. The S&P 500 also fell, but not by as much as the futures contracts on the index.

The CME's December S&P 500 futures contract had started gapping down relative to the underlying spot index before 3:00 p.m. That is, its price fell in large steps, without hitting intermediate prices. It hit its first 12-point limit at 3:15 p.m. Despite the imposed breather, the contract continued to gap down, falling to a low for the day, down 4.7 percent, between 3:15 p.m. and 3:30 p.m. After a two-minute trading halt at 3:30 p.m., the contract regained substantial ground by 3:45 p.m. and ended the day down just 3.6 percent. The S&P 500 spot index stabilized briefly with the recovery in futures prices at 3:45 p.m. but continued its sell-off afterward. An SEC staff report found that the majority of trades after 4:00 p.m. (82%) reflected market-on-close sell orders related to futures and options expirations.[22]

The potential for large expiration-related selling appears to have pressured market prices during the day. The SEC virtually dismissed a number of macroeconomic factors that were offered as possible triggers, including negative economic news released that morning, a proposal in Congress to limit the interest rates that could be imposed on credit card balances, and rumors of unrest in the Soviet Union. The SEC did, however, point a finger at certain investor behavior and investment strategies:[23]

> The market decline on November 15, 1991, at least on its face, appears similar to the declines in October 1989 and, to a lessor [sic] extent, October 1987. In all of these instances, it appears that institutional money managers had grown concerned over protecting year-to-date gains in their stock portfolios. . . . In some of our preliminary telephone interviews with traders, it was discovered that some firms may have engaged in dynamically hedging (in options and futures) risks assumed in OTC puts negotiated with institutional money managers.

## THE ASIAN FLU IN 1997

On Monday, October 27, 1997, the DJIA fell 7.2 percent, or 554 points—a record point drop (see Exhibit 6.3). NYSE volume of over 685 million shares also set a record, even though it was a shortened trading day.

**EXHIBIT 6.3**

The Dow Jones Industrial Average (DJIA) on October 27, 1997

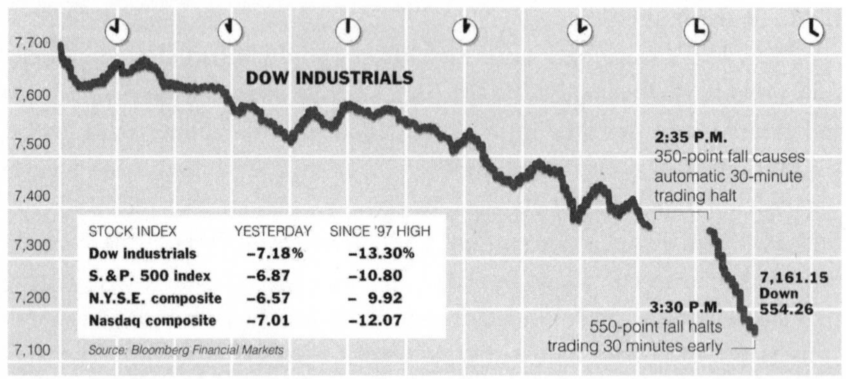


Source: *New York Times*, October 28, 1997: A1.

Trading on the NYSE was first halted at 2:35 p.m. when the 350-point limit was hit. Although trading resumed at 3:05 p.m., it didn't last long. The threat of the second price limit appeared to act like a black hole, sucking prices down. It took less than half an hour for the average to fall another 200 points. The 550-point limit was hit at 3:30 p.m., and trading was halted for the day, half an hour before the exchange's usual close.

On Tuesday, October 28, the market rallied. The DJIA rose 4.7 percent, its biggest percentage gain in more than a decade. Volume, at 1.2 billion shares, was more than twice the volume seen on October 19, 1987. So, near the tenth anniversary of the 1987 crash, the market appeared to be repeating the same pattern—a steep decline on a Monday followed by a strong rebound on the following day. Were the causes the same?

Superficially, October 1997 appears to have little in common with October 1987. Unlike 1987, neither interest rates nor inflation rates were rising or even expected to rise. Furthermore, the US budget deficit was at its lowest since the early 1970s. US economic fundamentals were strong.

But several Asian currencies, particularly Thailand's and Hong Kong's, were under attack, and the Asian economic miracle seemed to be coming to a close. Booms in Thailand and Indonesia were imploding, Hong Kong was shaky, and the Japanese economy and stock market continued to drag on in a sickly state. Fears that depression in Asia would affect US businesses may have had something to do with the US market's dive on October 27, 1997. However, it is difficult to construe the quick bounce back on the following day as reflecting an overnight change in fundamentals.

## THE ASIAN CRISIS

On July 2, 1997, Thailand abandoned efforts to peg the value of its currency, the baht, to the US dollar, effectively devaluing it. Indonesia, Malaysia, and the Philippines soon followed suit. The speed with which Thailand's troubles spread to neighboring countries seemed to catch the world by surprise.

During the early 1990s, foreign capital poured into these newly industrialized Asian economies, attracted by their strong growth and healthy fiscal situations. Thailand's economy grew by more than 7 percent annually between 1992 and 1995.[24] Asian growth rates, interest rates, and dividend yields appeared particularly attractive when compared with those of industrialized nations, many of which were coping with weak economies. The region also benefited from the rising popularity of emerging market mutual funds, which catered to retail investors' desire for higher returns and new sources of portfolio diversification.

But the influx of foreign capital posed dangers to these up-and-coming economies. Much of it was made up of short-term lending from foreign banks, money that could depart as quickly as it arrived. Surging foreign investment also stoked inflationary pressures and exposed weaknesses in the regulation of these Asian economies' domestic banks, many of which loaned money imprudently during the boom.

When export growth began to slow in 1996, the region's many vulnerabilities—large current account deficits, high short-term foreign debt, and bubble-like real estate prices—came into focus. A reduction in foreign capital inflows, combined with rising US interest rates beginning in early 1997, began to weigh on Thailand's currency. In order to maintain the baht's peg to the dollar, the Bank of Thailand was forced to purchase large amounts of its currency. Hedge funds and other speculators began betting against the baht, calculating that Thailand's efforts to support the baht would eventually exhaust the country's foreign currency reserves.

Thailand's decision in July to abandon its currency's dollar peg set off a domino effect among other exchange rates in the region. On July 11, the Philippines allowed the peso, which had been unofficially pegged to the dollar, to float in value. Malaysia soon adopted a similar strategy for the ringgit. On August 14, Indonesia allowed the rupiah to float. By mid-October, the baht and the rupiah had fallen by 30 percent against the dollar and the ringgit and peso by 20 percent.[25] Spillover effects of the crisis weakened currencies in Hong Kong, Singapore, and Taiwan, and pushed up interest rates in South Korea. Equity markets throughout Asia turned down in August 1997 and bond prices fell.

Stocks fell 23.3 percent over four consecutive days in Hong Kong, culminating in a 10.4 percent plunge on October 23. In the United States, the DJIA fell 554 points (7%) on October 27. Russian stocks plummeted by 21 percent the next day. Investors began fleeing to the safety of developed countries' bond and equity markets, especially those of the United States.

Some anecdotal evidence suggests that, again, hedging related to portfolio puts was a factor. The US dealer community was increasingly short options by the fall of 1997. Investor demand for option protection had risen through the year as the US stock market's continuing rise and Asia's increasing problems had investors torn between greed and fear.[26] Hedging a net short position would have required dynamic trading in the stock and futures markets. When the economic woes in Asia finally came to a head in October, a US stock market downturn would have triggered a wave of selling by option dealers.

The *New York Times* noted on October 28, 1997, that the previous day's sell-off had been characterized by substantial program selling, which "may indicate use of some strategies known as 'dynamic hedging,' which call for traders to limit losses by selling as prices fall." Large, institutional-size trades continued to add to sales on Tuesday, October 28, even as retail investors drove the market up.

# PART III

CHAPTER 7

# Options, Hedge Funds, and the Volatility of 1998

*"Of the maxims of orthodox finance, none, surely, is more antisocial than the fetish of liquidity. . . . It forgets that there is no such thing as liquidity of investment for the community as a whole."*

**—John Maynard Keynes[1]**

On April 20, 1998, the *Wall Street Journal* noted that "Friday's record closes leave large stocks trading at or beyond history's most extreme limits of valuation." Interest rates were low. Inflation remained contained. For the first time in 30 years, the United States faced a healthy budget surplus. Investors still seemed to be riding high on the profits of the electronic revolution. The rewards of the new era of unfettered global markets and permanent sustainable economic growth seemed to be at hand. But investors had yet to meet the summer of their discontent.

On July 17, 1998, the Dow Jones Industrial Average (DJIA) reached 9,337.97. This would turn out to be a peak. On July 23, the DJIA fell 2.15 percent—over 195 points—after Federal Reserve Board Chairman Alan Greenspan warned Congress that stock price levels were too high. (See Exhibit 7.1.) The average fell below 9,000 for the first time since June 30. On July 30, the *Wall Street Journal* announced that "the bear market is here," noting that through July 28, the average New York Stock Exchange (NYSE) share was down over 24 percent from its 52-week high, and the average share on the Nasdaq was down even more, by 35 percent.

On August 4, the DJIA closed down nearly 300 points (3.4%) amid investors' fears of slower US economic growth, reflecting the impacts on

EXHIBIT 7.1

The Dow Jones Industrial Average (DJIA) in 1998

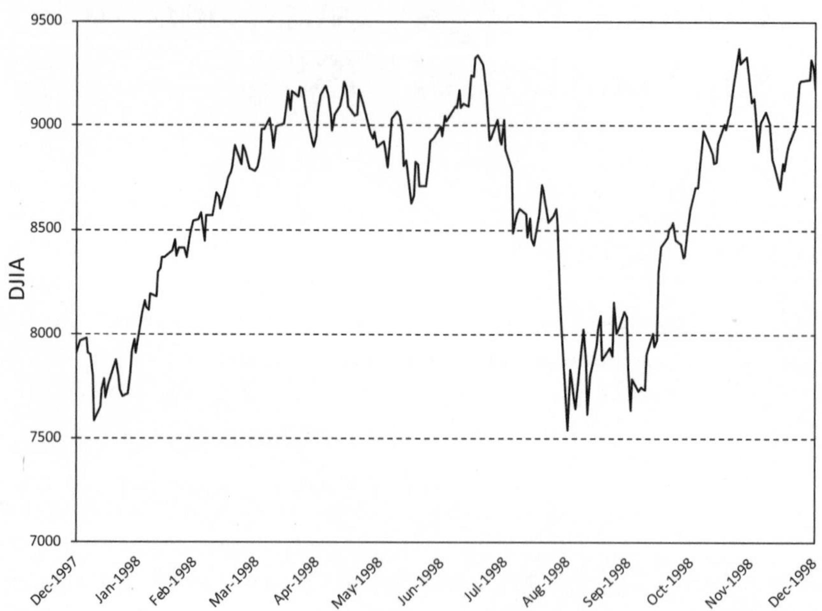


US exports of the economic slump in Asia and the strength of the US dollar.[2] Also weighing on the market were concerns about continuing weakness in Asia, particularly Japan, which overwhelmed the salubrious effects of a US environment characterized by low interest and inflation rates, high employment, and steady, though somewhat slower, growth.[3] Fear continued to pervade the market as the DJIA fell over 1 percent on both August 11 and August 13.

On August 17, 1998, another kind of bear raised its head. Russia announced a de facto devaluation of the ruble and a 90-day moratorium on repayment of $40 billion in corporate and bank debt to foreign creditors. These events crystallized a more free-floating anxiety over economic malaise in Asia generally. The seeming unwillingness of the Japanese government to come to terms with its own leadership role in the area, and its resistance, in the face of huge budget deficits, to underwriting some form of fiscal stimulus, had darkened hopes for an economic recovery in the region. By mid-August, the markets of Hong

Kong, Malaysia, and Singapore had fallen by 33 percent to 45 percent for the year.

Continuing weakness in Asia had meant lower demand for the commodity exports that were vital to many emerging economies. The effects had been most pronounced in Russia, whose market had fallen over 70 percent from the beginning of the year to the time of the ruble devaluation. However, Mexico, down 32 percent, and Argentina, down 30 percent, had also been affected.

World currency markets were sent into a spin by the Russian default. Funds were sucked out of Russia and other commodity-producing countries, including Canada, Mexico, Brazil, and Venezuela, as well as Japan and Hong Kong, and plunked down on the US dollar. The flight to safety soon spread to equity markets, with international investors dumping emerging market stocks first. The real shock wave hit the major markets on August 27: the DJIA fell nearly 4.2 percent; Tokyo fell 3 percent to a six-year low; and London was off by 3 percent.

The US economy had appeared to be fairly well insulated from the immediate effects of much of the global turmoil. Interest rates were holding steady at a relatively low level. Inflation was well contained. Corporate earnings growth, although slowing, was continuing to rise on average. Russia accounted for only 1 percent of US exports. Even US bank loans to emerging markets were small, compared with the emerging-market exposure of European banks. The bank loans totaled just $117 billion, or 1.5 percent of the US gross domestic product (GDP), compared with the $426 billion lent by European banks, which represented 7 percent of European GDP.[4] US markets had provided a refuge for international investors fleeing Asian markets. In the last half of 1997, non-US investors had been putting their money into US equities at an annual rate of about $100 billion, quadruple previous rates. By the first quarter of 1998, the influx had risen to $125 billion.[5]

Discernible within the US stock market, however, was a faint shadow of non-US investors' flight to the safety of US stocks. One of the most notable characteristics of the US equity market in 1998 was its dual nature. The price-earnings multiples of large-company stocks were extremely high at mid-year, whereas smaller companies lagged markedly, with the small-company stock averages having peaked in April, well before the DJIA's July peak. In most of the significant market declines over the summer, the smaller-stock averages had fallen more than the large-company DJIA.

The intra-market flight to safety seems to have been driven in part by individual investors. Four of the 10 largest mutual funds experienced net outflows for August; only three enjoyed net inflows, and those were of modest size.[6] Overall, mutual fund investors pulled almost $5 billion out of funds during the month.[7]

Some larger investors sought safety in more sophisticated measures than simply selling stock. They bought options. On August 4, the day of the DJIA's 3.4 percent slide, listed index puts had been a "hot commodity."[8] There had also been a "frenzy" of index put buying on August 11.[9] On Friday, August 21, index put purchases were characterized as "extremely extreme."[10]

In the following week, however, some investors obviously felt they were not hedged enough. The volatility levels implied by options prices were higher than they had been since the October 1997 mini-crash, and index put prices were so high that some money managers were hedging with individual security options, which is generally a much more expensive proposition than using index options.[11]

With demand for index puts at record levels, writers of put options were undoubtedly hedging in stock and stock futures markets. Indeed, the *New York Times* reported that a record number of investors had bought listed put options in August, and that S&P 500 futures trading on August 27 and 28 had reached record volumes.[12] Despite skyrocketing premiums, demand for options on the Chicago Board Options Exchange (CBOE) was so great on August 28 that its computer systems began to have trouble handling the volume.[13]

On Monday, August 31, the DJIA plummeted 512 points, or 6.4 percent, leaving it 19.3 percent off its July peak and below the level at which it had started the year. The day's decline brought the average's loss for the month to 15.1 percent, the eleventh-worst month in the DJIA's history. Smaller stocks did even worse. The Nasdaq fell 8.6 percent on that Monday, with high-flyers Amazon and Yahoo off 21 percent and 17 percent, respectively. Non-US markets followed the US decline, with Mexican stocks down 5.1 percent, Canadian and Brazilian stocks down 4.1 percent, and the Hong Kong market off by 2.9 percent.

Traders noted heavy futures selling on August 31 and, during the afternoon especially, computerized program trading by institutions, including mutual funds.[14] The market's 512-point decline sent index option implied volatility to levels reminiscent of those seen in the aftermath of the 1987 crash.

On September 1, the DJIA rallied; it closed up 3.8 percent on record volume. Unfortunately, this did not signal a sustained recovery. The DJIA ended the week off by 5.1 percent. The market bounced back early the next week, only to fall 3.2 percent on September 10, with US investors selling heavily to offset losses in foreign markets and foreign investors pulling out of US equity.

The demand for options increased, raising option prices to the point where market makers trying to hedge net short option positions could not afford to do so in the options markets. They turned to dynamic hedging in the stock and stock futures markets instead. By one estimate, option market makers were net short $27 billion in stock index futures on September 11.[15]

According to one options trader, the "market gets more and more volatile because you end up trading stock against the options."[16] On September 8, as the market rose, there was a flurry of buying by investors covering short positions.[17] On September 10, as the market fell, trading in S&P 500 futures was "insane."[18] Option hedgers were getting whipsawed by a market that was rising over 3 percent and then falling over 3 percent in the same week, partly as a result of their own trading. Options traders found the environment more painful than even the 1987 crash. One trader said "this market has been likened to a long, slow bleed; 1987 was just a quick hanging."[19] Then came the Long-Term Capital Management (LTCM) crisis.

LTCM, like a number of other hedge funds and some investment banks, had built many of its trades on the assumption that higher-risk assets selling below their historical norms would increase in price while lower-risk assets selling above their historical norms would decline in price. As the flight to safety set off by the Russian default grew in force, the prices of risky assets fell as they were sold off, while the prices of low-risk assets rose. Hedge funds and investment banks that had expected the opposite sustained heavy losses.

With capital of under $5 billion at the beginning of 1998, LTCM had assets of about $12.5 billion (and exposures to over $1 trillion if its derivatives positions are included). Many of its investments were tied up in arbitrage positions based on the assumption that the difference in interest rates paid by higher- and lower-risk securities, known as the spread, would narrow over time. When those spreads instead widened, the hedge fund took losses that eroded its capital and threatened to bankrupt the fund. As other investors became aware of the extent of the sales that LTCM would have to undertake in order to close out its positions, spreads widened further, compounding LTCM's problems.

## HEDGE FUNDS

Hedge funds are investment vehicles that have substantial latitude in the kinds of investments they make. They employ a number of different types of strategies. These include arbitrage strategies, such as those used by Long-Term Capital Management (LTCM), which involve both holding assets long and selling assets short in order to capture the spread between the long and short positions, and directional strategies, such as those used by George Soros's Quantum Fund, which may use long or short positions to "bet" on the future direction of asset prices.

Hedge funds often employ the same securities and instruments as more conventional strategies, including stocks, government bonds, corporate bonds, mortgage-backed securities, and convertible bonds. Hedge funds may exploit approaches similar to those used by conventional active strategies, such as in-depth fundamental analysis, technical analysis, and/or quantitative valuation and portfolio construction techniques. But hedge funds tend to be more reliant on short positions, derivatives, and leverage and may require that investors commit funds for a certain number of years.

The type of leverage hedge funds use may reflect the nature of the strategies or instruments they employ. Short sales, for example, rely on borrowing shares to sell short, while derivatives are often inherently leveraged (for example, by posting up front a relatively small portion of the value of the exposure generated by a derivatives position). Hedge funds may also borrow via loans or repurchase agreements (repos).

The first documented hedge fund was started by Alfred Winslow (A.W.) Jones in 1949. Short sales had traditionally been undertaken by dedicated short sellers, investors who sold short particular stocks expected to decline because of situations like accounting fraud. Jones used short sales in a portfolio context, selling securities short to offset some of the market risk introduced by holding long positions. The Jones fund retained a tilt toward long positions, with short positions of a generally smaller magnitude increased or reduced depending upon whether Jones expected the broad market to decline or advance. In this sense, Jones used both a hedging and a directional strategy.

Other hedge funds are designed to be market neutral, that is, to hold short and long positions of the same amount and market sensitivity to neutralize portfolio exposure to various systematic sources of risk, including stock market and interest rate movements. Rather than seeking to profit from correctly forecasting market moves, market-neutral strategies seek to profit from detecting perceived mispricings in individual securities and constructing portfolios that deliver the excess return (and risk) associated with those securities, regardless of market moves.

Market-neutral strategies have the same basic aim as more conventional strategies—to buy low and sell high. A market-neutral investor buys "cheap" assets (or derivatives) and simultaneously sells short an offsetting amount of "rich" assets (or derivatives), with the aim of profiting if prices normalize—that is, prices of cheap assets rise and prices of rich assets fall. The assets bought and sold may be related (for example, they may be in the same industry). In any case, there is a risk that the cheap assets will become cheaper and the rich assets will become richer, resulting in a loss.

This type of arbitrage does not fall within the strict definition of classical arbitrage. In classical arbitrage, a security is purchased at one price in one market and simultaneously sold at a higher price in another market. In this case, virtually no risk is incurred. The arbitrage generally undertaken by hedge funds is not riskless, but it may be less risky than holding unhedged positions. However, leverage is often applied to amplify returns, and it also amplifies risk.

At the same time, market losses brought about change at Wall Street firms—resignations, layoffs, and losses. The chairman and several other executives at UBS were forced to resign. Merrill Lynch laid off 3,400 employees and demoted its worldwide risk manager. On October 22,

Nomura Securities announced that it had lost $1.7 billion in the first half of the year, largely owing to positions in US mortgage-backed securities. The same day, Bankers Trust reported a loss of $488 million, primarily because of its holdings of emerging-market and high-yield debt.

On October 14, Bank of America announced a 50 percent drop in earnings for the quarter, with a $370 million charge relating to its investment in the hedge fund D.E. Shaw. The hedge fund founded by David E. Shaw, a former Columbia University computer science professor, had leveraged up a $1 billion investment from Bank of America into a $20 billion portfolio. Shaw blamed his fund's losses on the price distortions caused by the asset liquidations of other distressed firms, particularly LTCM.

The effects of such losses were soon felt in credit markets. By mid-October, several Wall Street firms, including Merrill Lynch and Bankers Trust, were backing away from commitments they had made to finance pending mergers. The market for newly issued public stocks was drying up, too. By early October, the number of companies going public had declined to its lowest level in seven years. One of the victims was Goldman Sachs, which announced on September 28, 1998, that it was postponing its highly anticipated public offering.

CHAPTER 8

# Long-Term Capital Management

*"We're not just a fund. We're a financial-technology company."*

**—Myron S. Scholes**[1]

August 1998 proved a particularly tough time for hedge funds. Hedge funds, largely unregulated private investment partnerships, are typically limited to well-heeled, sophisticated investors. The popularity of these investment vehicles had grown in the 1990s as institutional investors, sovereign wealth funds, and money managers sought a larger share of the growing value of international capital markets. At the end of 1997, there were about 4,500 US domestic and offshore hedge funds with about $300 billion in capital.[2]

Many hedge funds had invested heavily in emerging markets, often leveraging their capital with borrowing. The collapse of the ruble and the Russian bond market, and the ensuing flight of investors from other emerging markets, spelled disaster for many hedge fund strategies. Tiger Management Corp. (The Tiger Fund), one of the largest such funds with about $20 billion in assets under management, lost $600 million in Russian debt investments.[3] Soros Fund Management, with about $13 billion under management, lost $2 billion on similar positions.[4] But the main hedge fund victim of the extreme volatility in equity and bond markets in the late summer and early fall of 1998 and the ensuing flight to safety was Long-Term Capital Management (LTCM), one of the world's largest hedge funds.

## SETTING UP SHOP

LTCM was founded in 1994 and was headed by John W. Meriwether, who had gained fame and fortune in the 1980s by creating a bond arbitrage operation at the storied investment bank, Salomon Brothers. Several of his former staff at Salomon Brothers had jumped ship to join LTCM. Meriwether also brought on board David W. Mullins Jr., a former vice chairman of the Federal Reserve Board, as well as Robert C. Merton and Myron S. Scholes, who were soon to win the Nobel Prize for their work on valuing options. Their option pricing theories, based on arbitrage relationships between options and their underlying stocks or bonds, had spawned not just portfolio insurance but the whole new world in which LTCM operated.

By mid 1994, Meriwether had raised over a billion dollars in capital, on top of the $100 million to $150 million anted up by the firm's general partners. LTCM's investors—institutions and a small number of wealthy individuals—were required to keep funds invested for a three-year lock-up period and to pay an annual management fee of 2 percent plus an incentive fee of 25 percent of profits earned on investors' capital.

LTCM ran a host of arbitrage strategies from its headquarters in Greenwich, Connecticut, and offices in London and Tokyo. Arbitrage strategies are theoretically low risk. Consider, for example, an investor who holds a portfolio of long bond positions. This investor has effectively placed a bet on the direction of interest-rate movements; if rates decline the portfolio will increase in value, but if rates rise the portfolio's value will fall. Now consider an investor who has both long and short bond positions—say, long positions in high-yield junk bonds and short positions in lower-yield Treasury securities. If interest rates in general either rise or fall, the response of the securities held long should be approximately offset by the response of the securities sold short. This investor's profit and risk will depend on the relative values of the two positions.

LTCM's core strategies were designed to exploit various perceived inefficiencies in interest rate and equity markets. The firm specialized in convergence trades, holding offsetting positions that were scheduled to converge in price at a given future date, and relative-value arbitrage, where convergence was expected to occur at some time in the future, but it was not certain to occur. In general, LTCM sought to hold long securities with higher yields and to sell short securities with lower yields.

For example, Treasury notes that have been on the market for a while (off-the-run Treasuries) usually sell for lower prices than comparable newly issued notes (on-the-run Treasuries), because demand for and trading in off-the-run notes are less intense. When LTCM perceived the spread between the two to be large relative to historical or theoretical norms, it would purchase off-the-run notes and sell short on-the-run notes. The offsetting long and short positions would neutralize the fund's exposure to general interest rate changes, while a convergence of the spread as the notes matured would offer a profit as the off-the-run notes held long increased in price and/or the on-the-run notes shorted declined in price.

LTCM looked for opportunities created by regulatory or structural frictions that caused prices to diverge from historical norms or perceived values. Japanese banks that engaged in yen-denominated swaps were for some time required to take the position of receiving a fixed rate and paying floating rates, regardless of their expectations for rates going forward. LTCM held long positions in Japanese government bonds and bond futures and then engaged in swaps with Japanese banks, paying them the fixed rates and receiving floating rates. The fund thus hedged underlying rate exposure while keeping a window of profitability open if interest rates rose.

Many of its strategies were quite complex. In the United Kingdom, lack of demand for government bonds caused short-term rates to rise, which in turn led UK lenders to pay fixed rates on interest rate swaps. LTCM borrowed 10-year UK government bonds (effectively a short position) and entered into 10-year interest rate swaps to pay floating rates and receive the fixed rate; at the same time, it purchased 10-year German government bonds and entered into 10-year interest rate swaps to pay the fixed rate and receive floating rates.

LTCM also engaged in convertible arbitrage, equity pairs trading, and, toward the end, risk arbitrage. Convertible arbitrage involves purchasing convertible bonds, which are bonds that can be profitably exchanged for equity shares if the price of the shares rises sufficiently; risk is hedged by shorting the equity, by buying put options on the equity and/or bond components of the convertible, or by entering into interest rate swaps. Equity pairs trading involves buying stock in a company that is expected to outperform and selling short the stock of a similar company that is expected to underperform; the offsetting long and short positions neutralize much of the underlying market risk while the investor can potentially earn a profit on the spread between the long and short positions.

Risk arbitrage is a play on forthcoming mergers. The investor generally buys the stock of the company being acquired and sells short the stock of the company doing the acquiring. Again, the offsetting long and short positions dampen the underlying market risk. At the same time, the investor expects to profit from a rise in the price of the acquired company and, possibly, a decline in the price of the acquirer.[5]

## Risk Control and Return Maximization

As befits a firm that employed two Nobel laureates in economics, LTCM relied heavily on analytical models. LTCM's complicated risk aggregator analyzed all the firm's positions on a global basis; it took into account the risks of the positions, the correlations between positions, and estimated potential losses from extreme events. Nevertheless, the fund's overall investment approach, its partners maintained, was not reliant on any black box, but based on sound market and economic fundamentals.[6]

LTCM's portfolio was structured to be market neutral with respect to interest rates, stock market risk, and currency risk; the overall fund was said to have "triple net zero" exposure to these systematic risks.[7] With these major sources of risk supposedly neutralized, the risk level of LTCM's portfolio was deemed to be very low. LTCM had informed its investors early on, in October 1994, that the probability of a loss of 20 percent or more of portfolio value was only 1 in 100.

Of course, expected return was also low, on a per trade basis, as low as a few cents on the dollar. LTCM aimed to provide high returns, while maintaining a very low risk profile. The high returns were attained via leverage. In particular, its aim was to have enough leverage to bring its low-risk positions to the point that overall portfolio risk approximated that of an unleveraged position in the US equity market.

LTCM engaged in large amounts of repo financing. "Repo" is short for repurchase agreement. With a repurchase agreement, one large company sells an asset to another large company in exchange for cash, but the selling company agrees to buy the asset back at an agreed-upon price by an agreed-upon date. A repurchase agreement is essentially a loan. For providing the cash, the buyer extracts a fee equivalent to the interest rate and charges a haircut (in the form of a deduction in the value of the assets sold) that reflects the quality of the borrower and the asset. Repo loans are generally very short term, often overnight.

## REPO FINANCING

A repurchase agreement, or repo, is a short-term, collateralized loan. The borrower, typically a large bank, sells a security to a counterparty and agrees to repurchase it later (often the next day). The price paid to reclaim the security includes a premium equivalent to the appropriate short-term interest rate. Because repo loans are very short term, with standard loan periods ranging from overnight to a year, and the securities that serve as collateral for the loan are deemed high quality, repo loans have traditionally been viewed as virtually riskless transactions.

Banks, securities dealers, investment banks, and hedge funds use repo financing to fund the purchase of loans and other assets, to cover short positions, to engage in arbitrage, and to speculate on interest rates. Repo lenders include corporations, large institutional investors, municipalities, and foreign central banks seeking extra return on portfolios or a safe place to put surplus cash to work. From the lender's perspective, the transaction is considered a "reverse repo."

The repo market exploded in size over the years leading up to 2007, as it became a ready source of funding for the purchase of portfolios of loans that could be sold for securitization. The emergence of securitization also brought about a fundamental change in the nature of the repo market. Demand for collateral for the repo market (and the rapid growth of trading in derivatives, which also require collateral) began to outpace the supply of the Treasuries typically used for this purpose. As a result, acceptable collateral expanded to include slightly higher-risk assets such as money market instruments and mortgage-backed securities (MBS) with high credit ratings. To offset the higher risk of these additional forms of collateral, lenders began to impose "haircuts." That is, the amount loaned is worth less than the face value of the securities pledged as collateral; the differential essentially serves as insurance against the possibility of a decline in the value of the collateral. A haircut is normally a nominal percentage of the asset, but the percentage can be increased in line with the lender's perception of the riskiness of the collateral and the borrower.[8]

By 2007 the repo market had become gargantuan, with loans totaling $12 trillion, roughly the size of the regulated banking sector.[9] Though this estimate may be bloated by counting repos and reverse repos separately when they are, in fact, two sides of the same loan, the market was by any measure one of the world's largest and most liquid. More importantly, repos financed roughly half the assets of the top US investment banks,[10] thereby enabling the growth of the mortgage securitization industry.

While the foundation of traditional banking was investors' equity and depositors' cash backed by government deposit insurance, a new "shadow banking" system consisting of less-regulated entities, like investment banks and hedge funds, became increasingly reliant on repo and other non-traditional sources of financing. Repo financing, in turn, encouraged even more leverage: Repo loans underwrote the purchase of assets, which were then used as collateral for more repo loans, which underwrote the purchase of more assets, etc.

Banks and dealers apparently viewed LTCM's arbitrage trades as quite low risk; they may also have been a bit starstruck by the heady reputations of LTCM's partners. In any event, they were eager to lend to the company, and to do so at terms extremely favorable to LTCM. In its early years, LTCM was often able to borrow at below-market interest rates and to pay no haircuts on repo arrangements.

Leverage is often used in the hedge fund world; however, it is limited. The Federal Reserve Board's Regulation T prevents retail investors from borrowing more than half the cost of a stock purchase, although there are several ways around this restriction. The Federal Reserve also has regulations governing commercial bank leverage in the United States. Large US banks that operate internationally are also subject to the Basel Accords of the Bank for International Settlements. Investment bank leverage is somewhat limited by the Securities and Exchange Commission (SEC). Concerns over risk should also limit leverage. Soros Fund Management and Tiger Management Corp. reportedly had fairly low borrowing levels of about four times capital,[11] perhaps because they engaged in directional trading (speculating on price movements), which is perceived as much riskier than arbitrage.

Through much of LTCM's short history, its leverage averaged about 25-to-1. This was in line with the firm's aim of attaining an overall risk level approximately equal to the risk of the US equity market. LTCM was by far the most heavily leveraged hedge fund at the time, more akin to an investment bank than a hedge fund or even a commercial bank.[12]

Moreover, LTCM held massive derivatives positions, with a notional principal value of over $1 trillion.[13] Its swap exposures at one point reportedly represented 2.4 percent of the global swaps market, and its futures exposures represented 6 percent of the US futures market.[14] These types of exposures can be attained with very little capital outlay, as an exchange-traded derivative, such as a futures contract, can be obtained with a margin payment of as little as 5 percent of the value of the underlying asset. Over-the-counter (OTC) derivatives, such as swaps, may require no initial margin. As the value of the asset changes over the life of the derivative contract, however, positions are marked to market and payments made from and to counterparties to reflect ongoing gains and losses.

Most of LTCM's derivatives positions would presumably have been offsetting, with a long position in one asset offsetting a short position in a related asset. Thus a notional principal value of $1 trillion might theoretically net to near zero. But this assumes that the hedges perform as expected—that is, the long positions rise in value and the short positions fall in value. If prices move adversely, the fund would sustain a net loss and marking to market might require the firm to make collateral payments. The larger the adverse moves, the more demand is put on the fund's capital.

LTCM apparently believed that its high leverage and huge derivative positions would not become a problem. The fund undertook value-at-risk (VaR) analyses, stress tests, and scenario analyses to ensure capital adequacy. Its leveraged positions were fully collateralized and subject to marking to market by LTCM and its counterparties. In addition, LTCM had secured lines of credit from major banks ensuring the availability of funds in case liquidity was needed.

LTCM undoubtedly also believed that safety was ultimately provided by the wide diversification of its investments. Not only had LTCM invested around the globe in bond markets and equity markets, it had also diversified across investment horizons, from short term to long term, and across investment strategies.

## FROM GLAM TO GLOOM

When LTCM launched in 1994, it was entering a bond market in turmoil. The Fed had raised rates a quarter point in early February and another quarter point in late March. Between January 28 and April 14, prices of 30-year US government bonds fell 14 percent. Elsewhere, political instability was roiling Mexico, the yen was surging against the dollar, and bond prices were falling across Europe.

These developments plagued bond investors, including Goldman Sachs, Fidelity Investments, Bankers Trust, the Soros Fund, and the hedge funds of Julian Robertson (The Tiger Fund) and Michael Steinhardt. Many of these investors were unloading their more liquid positions in order to raise capital to meet margin calls on their loans and derivative positions. For LTCM's partners, of course, liquidity was not a problem. Flush with their $1 billion-plus in new capital, they were like kids in a candy shop, eager and able to pick up the bargains, including off-the-run Treasuries and interest-rate-only collateralized mortgage obligations. LTCM ended up the year with a net return of about 20 percent, even as the average bond investor lost money.

### 1994 DEBT MARKET DEBACLE AND THE DEMISE OF ASKIN CAPITAL

A series of events in early 1994 upset expectations that a favorable environment for US bonds would continue. Japanese share prices began to rise, dashing hopes that interest rates there would be lowered. US–Japan trade talks broke down, and the dollar began to weaken against the yen and the German deutsche mark, confounding expectations. In February, the Federal Reserve instituted the first in a series of six rate hikes for the year. All of this took place against a backdrop of heightened political and economic concerns in Canada, Sweden, Italy, and Mexico. From early February through the end of March, bond yields rose between 60 and 100 basis points in France, Italy, Belgium, the Netherlands, and the United States, and by more than 100 basis points in the United Kingdom, Canada, and Sweden.[15]

A US hedge fund, Askin Capital Management (ACM), had invested in collateralized mortgage obligations (CMOs) with the objective of returning 15 percent annually "regardless of whether the bond market moves up, down or stays the same," according to its marketing materials.[16] The fund's strategy was to be market neutral in order to gain from the outperformance of individual securities in the portfolio while neutralizing the impact of up-and-down movements in the broad market. ACM said it hedged market movements by taking long positions in both undervalued bullish securities and in undervalued bearish securities.[17]

Market-neutral strategies typically consist of offsetting long and short positions, but a long-long strategy like ACM's seemed achievable given the variety of instruments available in the MBS market. Principal-only securities (POs), for example, could be expected to rise in value when interest rates decline because homeowners become more likely to refinance, accelerating principal repayment. In the same environment, interest-only securities (IOs) could be expected to lose value because homeowner refinancing curtails the expected stream of interest payments.

ACM had boosted its market-neutral gains by borrowing, investing up to 3.5 times its capital. The borrowing took place in the repo market, where ACM purchased securities and then sold them back to the broker-dealers it had bought them from on the understanding that it would repurchase them at a later date. This was, in effect, a collateralized loan on which ACM paid interest of 3 percent to 4 percent.

ACM's leveraged investments produced gross returns of 17 percent to 18 percent in 1992, its first full year, and about 20 percent in 1993. Both years were characterized by a benign interest-rate environment. But the interest-rate changes in 1994 jolted the mortgage market and proved disastrous for ACM.

ACM's net asset value declined 20 percent in February 1994, according to broker-dealer estimates. ACM, using its own estimates, initially reported a 1 percent to 2 percent decline, but admitted to the full, 20 percent drop in late March, when its troubles became public. This set off a series of margin calls by ACM's broker-dealers, who suddenly discovered the collateral posted by ACM was not enough to cover potential losses. ACM, unable to raise additional capital or sell assets (most of which were held as collateral by its creditors), filed for bankruptcy on April 4.

A bankruptcy court trustee's report later detailed the many shortcomings of the fund. Investment committee minutes showed that the managers believed the funds to be close to market neutral.[18] But more than 90 percent of the fund's investments constituted bullish securities by the end of February, when the market took a decidedly bearish turn. An expert hired by the trustee found that the fund's portfolios were, in fact, highly exposed to interest-rate movements.

The fund's missteps were amplified by the complicated nature of the securities they invested in, presaging many of the problems that would arise in the 2007–2008 financial crisis. For example, prices for securities ACM bought were not available from a readily objective source, forcing ACM and its counterparties to rely on their own valuation models. This opened the door to a host of problems, including ACM's misleading initial loss report in February.

Some of the securities ACM had purchased, with names like "super PO," "Z bond," "inverse floating rate IO," and "two-tier PAC IO," were also known in some quarters as "toxic waste." They were the speculative remains of pools of mortgages that had been meticulously sliced and diced into structured finance products. Some of the instruments had the potential to react to changes in interest rates and prepayment levels in nonlinear ways, losing or gaining a great deal of value with very small movements in underlying fundamentals. That made it difficult for ACM to estimate their future performance.

All these shortcomings, combined with the illiquidity of the portfolios and leverage, proved fatal. Given the limited market for the securities, and the lack of transparent pricing, ACM was at the mercy of the broker-dealers, not only as lenders, but also as the ultimate arbiters of the value of the assets. Even with its relatively modest leverage, ACM could not meet its lenders' margin calls.

ACM was hardly alone in the difficulties it encountered during the turbulent bond market of 1994. Many investment banks and hedge funds were forced to unload large amounts of securities in order to meet margin calls. The resulting surplus of bargain-priced securities left in the wake of the bond market rout was a boon for funds that had the wherewithal to be buyers. One such fund, launched later in 1994 and flush with $1 billion in capital, was Long-Term Capital Management. It would figure prominently in the global crisis to erupt four years later.

LTCM's net return in 1995 was a stunning 43 percent. The firm had by now more than doubled its initial investment. On the strength of this stellar performance, LTCM raised an additional $1 billion in capital. But despite the increased capital, the firm's leverage was also rising. By the spring of 1996, the firm was leveraged at about 30-to-1, with assets of $140 billion. It ended 1996 with a net return of about 41 percent.

Success breeds imitation. Some hedge funds and proprietary trading desks sought to deduce LTCM's trades, often by becoming LTCM counterparties, and duplicate the fund's strategies. Further selling of lower-yielding, overpriced assets and buying of higher-yielding, underpriced assets served to narrow the spreads on LTCM's trades. Narrowing spreads translated into profits for LTCM, which closed out long positions that had risen in price and covered short positions that had declined.

But the competition for potentially profitable arbitrage meant narrower spreads and fewer new opportunities for LTCM. In 1997, the fund's returns began to level off. The firm's leverage also dropped, at one point to below 20-to-1. At LTCM's annual meeting in July, the partners expressed concern about the reduced potential for profits in bond arbitrage.[19]

Heading for a net return of under 20 percent for 1997, less than half of what it had garnered in each of its previous two years, the LTCM general partners decided to return $2.7 billion to investors at the end of September. With fund capital reduced to under $5 billion from about $7 billion, the fund maintained assets of about $125 billion. Leverage was back in the range of 25-to-1, excluding derivatives. Apparently LTCM still believed increased leverage could compensate for reduced profit margins.

At the time, LTCM had about 100 strategies in play, with 7,600 positions and 6,700 separate contractual arrangements with 55 counterparties. Some of these represented ventures away from the fund's traditional bond arbitrage trades. LTCM had become a substantial player in merger arbitrage. By 1997, it had about $5 billion in securities involved in merger situations. It also took substantial long positions in mortgage-backed securities, hedged by interest rate swaps.[20]

LTCM got heavily involved in options. By mid-1997, troubles in Asian economies had caused a worldwide increase in equity market volatility. This resulted in more demand for options. (See Chapter 6, "After the 1987 Crash—Options.") In addition, European investors had developed a taste for products that, like portfolio insurance, offered a guaranteed minimum return plus the opportunity to participate in equity market appreciation. Issuers of these products, however, usually used options on equity indexes in order to provide the upside. This further increased the demand for options.

On October 27, 1997, heavy selling in Hong Kong spooked the US equity market, which dropped about 7 percent. Markets around the world followed suit. Increased equity market volatility spiked option demand. In Europe, implied volatility rose to 24 percent, well above the historical level of 15 percent. LTCM viewed this as a ripe profit opportunity. Through the end of 1997 and into 1998, it sold large amounts of long-dated option positions on US and European equity indexes.

This seemed like a good bet at first, as equity markets recovered strongly after October 1997 and LTCM profited as their short option positions gained ground. Government bond spreads, especially in the United States, also continued to narrow, as did the spread between corporate and government bonds. This benefited LTCM's existing positions, while it further reduced new arbitrage opportunities.

## Months of Losses

From beneath this seemingly benign surface, problems began to emerge in early 1998. Investors in mortgage-backed securities (MBS) suffered a sharp setback when lower interest rates sparked an unexpectedly heavy rush of mortgage prepayments. Some investors covered their losses by selling off profitable positions in emerging market debt. These sales seemed to reawaken investors' perception of risk in emerging markets. More money was pulled out of these markets, driving down prices and increasing the interest rates required to attract investors. Meanwhile, money poured into developed countries' relatively safe government securities, raising prices and lowering interest rates in those markets.

LTCM was hit by losses on the 16 percent of its capital that was committed to mortgage-related investments.[21] Then its arbitrage positions got hammered as interest rates on swap contracts increased unexpectedly and those on government securities declined. LTCM ended May 1998 down about 6.5 percent and June 1998 down another 10 percent. It was the first time in its history that the fund had experienced losses in two consecutive months. LTCM decided to respond by lowering its risk. The daily standard deviation of the fund's portfolio amounted to about $45 million, in line with the fund's objective of targeting the volatility of the broad equity market.[22] The partners decided to take this down to $34 million. They did so, however, by selling some of the fund's more liquid positions, retaining less liquid positions that seemed to offer higher profitability over the longer term.

LTCM ended July 1998 flat. But the omens in that month were not good. On July 7, it was announced that Salomon's US-bond arbitrage group—the very breeding ground of LTCM—would close. By this time, Salomon was no longer Salomon Brothers. Since Meriwether's departure, it had been sold to Citicorp, which had in turn merged with Travelers, and Salomon Brothers had become Salomon Smith Barney. The bond arbitrage desk was not a good fit in this new environment, and when it started losing money in early 1998, its fate was sealed.

The actual and pending liquidation of the Salomon arbitrage positions created real problems for LTCM and other funds and proprietary trading desks, which held similar positions. As July turned into August 1998, swap spreads widened considerably. The prices of LTCM's long positions continued to fall as the prices of its short positions rose.

Then came August 17, 1998, and Russia's de facto devaluation of the ruble and moratorium on repayment of debt. The impact of these announcements was compounded by several factors. First, although the safety of investments in Russia was never a sure thing, the timing of these announcements was completely unexpected; Russia had just sold $3.5 billion in new bonds less than a month before. Second, the safety nets that many investors had expected to protect them from the full impact of such an event failed to materialize. Many of the hedging arrangements, such as forward contracts, on which large investors in Russian debt had relied, fell through for various technical reasons.

Nor did the International Monetary Fund (IMF) come to the rescue. Investors had watched the IMF bail out Mexico in 1994 and South Korea in 1997. They fully expected like protection in the event of a Russian collapse. But the IMF declined to step in this time. A flight to safety engulfed emerging and developed equity and bond markets and volatility exploded.

LTCM took a triple hit. Some 8 percent of its trading book was involved with Russian debt.[23] Increasing bond spreads meant it had to pony up more collateral on its arbitrage positions. Increasing volatility translated into larger marks to market on its option positions. LTCM found itself on the hook for tens of millions of dollars. In the last week of August, with its trading positions imploding, LTCM scrambled for additional capital. It approached George Soros and Warren Buffett, as well as the investors it had cashed out in 1997. Buffett said he was not interested. Soros offered $500 million on the condition that LTCM could raise another $500 million.

But LTCM was already facing difficulties meeting the margin calls on its losing positions. Unable to raise additional capital, it was equally hamstrung by its inability to liquidate assets. It had sold off its more liquid positions following the losses in May and June. The positions it retained constituted the longer-term, more illiquid positions whose wide spreads at that time had promised the most profit potential. But the spreads had only gotten wider in the intervening months. LTCM was holding losers, both long and short. Those that might serve as the natural buyers of these trades—other hedge funds and proprietary trading desks—were hardly in a position to take more bets on; they were in the same sinking ship as LTCM.

Goldman Sachs and Chase Manhattan had suffered substantial losses in Russian bonds. Travelers and its subsidiary, Salomon Smith Barney, were racking up losses as interest rate swap spreads in Europe widened. Stocks and high-yield bonds were being sold to cover losses on leveraged positions around the world. Heavy selling of stock index futures, motivating sales by index arbitrageurs in the underlying stock market, contributed to a 6.4 percent drop in the Dow Jones Industrial Average (DJIA) on August 31.

For the month of August alone, LTCM lost $1.8 billion. Since the start of the year, it had lost about half its equity. Its leverage ratio was, involuntarily, up to 55-to-1. That figure doesn't incorporate the firm's derivative positions. At the end of August, LTCM held derivative positions, including equity and interest rate swaps and equity options, on some $1.4 trillion worth of underlying assets.[24]

At this point, transparency—both too little and too much—started to pose problems for LTCM. In order to keep its strategies proprietary, the firm had split trades up across counterparties; the long positions of a trade, for example, would be arranged with one broker, while LTCM held the short positions with another broker. Each of LTCM's counterparties was thus left with exposure it had to hedge, as well as with an incomplete picture of the offsetting positions that reduced LTCM's overall risk. As LTCM's problems increased in the late summer and early fall of 1998, the fund tried to remedy the situation and assuage the fears of its counterparties by transferring positions to make the offsetting nature of its trades more transparent. Unfortunately, its attempts were hampered by the complexity of the trades, the size of the positions, and the large number of counterparties.

On the other side of the problem, LTCM's attempts to shuffle trades and raise capital made its positions more transparent to the firms it did business with, many of which were in essence competitors. From the end of August 1998, Wall Street traders seemed to be anticipating many of LTCM's trades and trading in front of them, either in an attempt to profit from LTCM's straitened circumstances or merely to get out from under the pending liquidation of LTCM assets. The pressure increased substantially in early September, after a letter from Meriwether to LTCM investors went public via Bloomberg news.[25] According to LTCM partner Merton:[26]

> One dynamic that happened. When the problems at Long Term became known, every bank, each counterparty tells their trading desks to cut their exposures to Long Term. . . . Guess what they got back as an answer? 'We can't because we're termed out and they have a contract.' . . . and so what they began doing was marking the positions so that they got the maximum collateral that they could . . . to protect themselves . . . each side, wherever the counterparty was, they marked it. Theoretically, we could ask two competing bids and challenge the marks. But in the middle of a crisis, you can't do that. . . . It wasn't like what they talk about in crises, where all assets move together. That happens too, but this was far more concentrated—it was literally our positions.

LTCM incurred losses of over $100 million on several days in early September. Bear Stearns was threatening to cease clearing trades for the firm unless LTCM deposited more capital. In last-ditch efforts, LTCM opened its books to Goldman Sachs, hoping for a capital infusion. On September 20, Peter R. Fisher, executive vice president of the Federal Reserve Bank of New York, visited LTCM's Greenwich offices, together with officials from Goldman Sachs and J. P. Morgan, to assess the situation.

On September 21, LTCM lost over $500 million. Its equity was now below $1 billion, and its leverage, not including derivatives, was over 100-to-1. LTCM finally called on its line of credit, receiving enough at least to satisfy Bear Stearns. But, to the New York Fed at least, it appeared too little, too late.

## A Forced Marriage

According to the president of the Federal Reserve Bank of New York, William J. McDonough, the Fed determined that default by LTCM would have led LTCM's counterparties to immediately close out their positions.[27] A fire sale of billions of dollars of assets would have eventually led to losses extending beyond LTCM's counterparties and creating tremendous turmoil and uncertainty. The end result would have been extreme price moves, disruption of credit and interest rate markets, and reverberating effects that could have lifted the cost of capital to unreasonable levels.

The New York Fed thus encouraged the investment banks and brokers involved with LTCM to come up with a solution that did not require default. On September 23, 1998, senior officers of US and European banks and brokerage firms met at the Fed's headquarters in New York. At the end of the day (having rejected an interim offer from Buffett, allied with American International Group and Goldman Sachs), Meriwether and LTCM accepted the buyout offer that came from 14 of the institutions represented at the Fed's offices—$3.6 billion in exchange for 90 percent of LTCM's assets. This left the old investors with about $400 million, less than one-tenth of the value of their assets at the beginning of 1998. Effective control of the fund was turned over to a six-man oversight committee composed of managers put in place by Merrill Lynch, Salomon Smith Barney, J. P. Morgan, UBS, Morgan Stanley, and Goldman Sachs.

LTCM and its problems came as a surprise to much of the market. Like other hedge funds and private partnerships, LTCM was not subject to the extensive disclosure requirements demanded of public investment funds. The Federal Reserve admitted that it did not become aware of the full measure of LTCM's debt until September 20, when the fund's would-be rescuers first met.[28]

On Thursday, September 24, the day following the firm's bailout, the DJIA fell almost 1.9 percent. William Sullivan, Morgan Stanley Dean Witter chief money market economist, noted: "The awareness that exposure [to LTCM] was extensive, and larger than many expected, helped spark a renewed flight to quality."[29] Helping the truth sink in was the coincident announcement by UBS of a $720 million loss for the third quarter, much of it related to the bank's investment in LTCM.

Inasmuch as the bailout gave investors an idea of the amount of trading that might be required to unwind LTCM's positions, and those of other funds and institutions holding similar portfolios, it is not surprising that the bailout failed to quell the US equity market's volatility. This remained at the highest levels since the 1987 crash. In part, of course, it reflected investors' awareness of a new source of risk—the overhang of arbitrage positions that would have to be unwound. This motivated some speculators to front run arbitrage trades, and it most certainly discouraged many investors from entering the market to buy the positions arbitrageurs had to lay off, just as the overhang of portfolio insurance sell orders discouraged buyers on October 19, 1987.

Of course, LTCM itself contributed to the selling pressure. At around the time of the bailout, the firm was unwinding some of its risk-arbitrage trades. It reportedly sold half a million shares of American Bankers Insurance at prices substantially below the expected takeover price.[30] The fund had also bailed out on MCI Communications earlier in the month, only days before its acquisition by WorldCom.[31] One bank later blamed trading by LTCM, perhaps related to LTCM's option positions, for 30 percent of the volatility in the French stock index, the CAC 40, during the year.[32]

On Thursday, October 1, the DJIA fell 2.7 percent, concurrent with Merrill Lynch's announcement that it had a $1.4 billion exposure to LTCM, including derivative positions. In the following week, the DJIA moved in a 450-point trading range. Since September, the DJIA had whipsawed between 7,400 and 8,200, with intra-day swings averaging 240 points.

## AFTER THE END

LTCM continued to hemorrhage after its bailout. The fund reportedly lost $200 million to $300 million in the following two weeks,[33] partly because the dollar's plunge against the yen on October 7, 1998, had required the fund to cover short yen positions at a loss. The *Wall Street Journal* announced that LTCM was looking for more funding and laying off about

20 percent of its employees, even while rebuffing a renewed offer from Buffett to buy the fund at a deeply discounted price.[34]

The oversight committee that had taken control identified LTCM's biggest problems to be its UK swaps and its equity options. LTCM had huge positions in both strategies. The committee arranged for regular public auctions to unwind the positions gradually. It also continued to consolidate the offsetting positions of LTCM's trades by pairing up the counterparties and backing LTCM out of the trades.

By mid December 1998, LTCM was reporting a profit, although facing an SEC hearing into its August fundraising activities, particularly its disclosures to potential investors. By December 1999, some 10,000 swaps on LTCM books at the time of the bailout had been reduced to 50. For the post-bailout year ending September 28, 1999, LTCM had a positive return of 10 percent.

In January 2000, the banks that had financed the bailout were paid back in full with a final payment of $925 million, and LTCM announced that it would close down. Meriwether had already set up a new firm, JWM Partners, offering a new hedge fund, Relative Value Opportunity Fund. The stated objective of this fund was annual returns of 15 percent to 20 percent with leverage of 10-to-1.

CHAPTER 9

# Long-Term Capital Management Postmortem

*"As the result of conscious and unconscious imitation, many of LTCM's positions became 'consensus trades.' "*

**—Costas Kaplanis, Trader, Salomon Brothers[1]**

In his September 1998 letter to investors, Long-Term Capital Management (LTCM) founder John W. Meriwether sought to assign blame for the fund's losses on the Russian default: "Events surrounding the collapse in Russia caused large and dramatically increasing volatility in global markets through August." That is, an external event, beyond control of the fund, led to the fund's eventual demise.

This explanation fails to account for LTCM's own missteps—its unwarranted confidence in its arbitrage models, its overreliance on leverage, and its failure to take into consideration its own effects upon the markets in which it traded. As the result of these missteps, LTCM's trades failed, it was unable to raise additional capital, and it was toppled by its own leverage. LTCM's failure, in turn, created turmoil in financial markets. The increased volatility and uncertainty in debt markets led to a credit crisis that foreshadowed what was to come a decade later.

## ARBITRAGE GONE WRONG

Victor Haghani, one of LTCM's chief traders, stated in the aftermath of the bailout that "What we did is rely on experience . . . if you're not willing to draw any conclusions from experience, you might as well sit on your hands and do nothing."[2] Indeed, LTCM's many models analyzed reams of historical and hypothetical data to determine how various financial instruments would likely behave in various market and economic environments. The results were then stress-tested and scenario-analyzed to a fine point. Further reducing the possibility of unwanted outcomes was the vast diversification of the strategies; LTCM had invested across strategies, countries, instruments, counterparties, and investment horizons. Its positions seemed to be offsetting in terms of risk exposures and well diversified across instruments and currencies.

Yet LTCM's experience was apparently not as wide as the fund's partners assumed. In particular, LTCM seemed to have ignored the bouts of investor panic and contagion across markets that had occurred in 1997 and, most notably, in 1987, which resulted in dramatic and sudden tightening of correlations between seemingly unrelated markets.[3] Edward O. Thorp, a legendary trader and student of games of chance who had come up with his own version of an options-pricing formula before Black-Scholes-Merton (and who had declined to invest in LTCM), found that some of LTCM's models were based on only four years of data.[4] In the crucible of the Russian debt crisis, LTCM's strategies came apart as trades that appeared to be uncorrelated on a fundamental level suddenly became highly correlated.

In this environment, the diversification of LTCM's strategies failed. The prices of the long positions in virtually all its strategies fell while the prices of the short positions rose. It became evident that LTCM's portfolio was *not* diversified.

LTCM had viewed itself as a liquidity supplier. Both Myron S. Scholes and David M. Modest, LTCM partners, described LTCM as being in the business of supplying liquidity.[5] This was reflected in the firm's trades; virtually all its long positions were less liquid, and all its short positions more liquid. In a flight to safety, investors seek liquidity and shun illiquidity; the yield spreads on LTCM's positions thus widened, and the fund's losses mounted. Meriwether admitted in his September 1998 letter to investors, "Our losses across strategies were correlated after the fact."

Not only were LTCM's trades undiversified after the fact, but so was its very line of business. The fund viewed itself as a financial intermediary, similar to a major investment bank or broker-dealer. Unlike banks or brokers, however, LTCM had a single line of business—arbitrage. Banks and brokers that engage in arbitrage do so as only one part of a more diversified palette of financial activities. Their arbitrage losses may be offset by gains in other areas, such as underwriting or brokerage. LTCM could rely only on its arbitrage trades. Its book of business was *not* diversified.

## Leverage and Liquidity

Had LTCM adopted a more modest view of its ability to model financial markets, it might have made more modest bets, or withdrawn from or reduced some bets as their risk increased. Instead, LTCM took on massive amounts of leverage to multiply its exposures by up to 100 times its capital. And, rather than reducing its positions in early 1998, after it had returned almost $3 billion to investors, it maintained the positions on a smaller capital base, thereby increasing its leverage.

This high degree of leverage doomed LTCM in 1998 when, rather than supplying liquidity, it needed to access liquidity, which was not available. The losses on its arbitrage positions were, by the early fall of 1998, serious but not necessarily fatal in and of themselves. In the year following the bailout, market liquidity improved, perceived risk declined, equity volatility fell, and spreads narrowed, in line with LTCM's long-run expectations, and many of the positions were eventually unwound at a profit.

As LTCM experienced those losses in the summer and fall of 1998, however, it was only one of many firms that found themselves in equally precarious positions. Intent on maximizing its own profits, LTCM had seemingly always neglected the context in which it operated—the impact its strategies might have on other investors and, in turn, the effects those investors might have on LTCM's strategies. This neglect proved fatal.

According to Haghani, LTCM "put very little emphasis on what other leveraged players were doing . . . because I think we thought they would behave very similar to ourselves."[6] This was true in the early years of LTCM's existence, when copycat trading by other hedge funds and investment banks had served to narrow the spreads on LTCM's arbitrage trades—adding to LTCM's enormous profits while reducing the fund's potential future profits. But LTCM apparently continued to believe in mid 1998 that other arbitrageurs were going to hang onto trades as spreads widened ever further, just as LTCM had hung onto its potentially most profitable trades in July.

LTCM also apparently assumed competitors would provide LTCM with potential counterparties if it needed to liquidate positions to reduce its leverage. But hedge funds and investment banks instead chose to reduce their own risks by selling their long positions and covering their shorts. This is hardly surprising, given that the imminence of LTCM's own potential liquidation was already roiling markets and increasing losses for arbitrage strategies.

LTCM expected that investors would always be willing to buy the liquidity it was selling. But investors' fear can lead to panicked behavior, when the desire to sell overwhelms more rational interests such as long-term value. In times of panic such as August 1998, investors tend to sell across the board. One result is the spike in correlations across markets that did so much damage to LTCM's investments.

LTCM also appears to have neglected to take into consideration the extreme illiquidity of many of its own positions. In some US and non-US futures markets, for example, LTCM's trades accounted for over 10 percent of all open contracts.[7] According to one source, the notional value of LTCM's derivative positions in the UK government bond market was larger than the underlying market itself.[8] And, of course, LTCM was in the business of supplying liquidity across the board, in equity and debt markets, in Japan, Europe, and the United States. It is thus hardly surprising that when LTCM looked to markets to supply it with liquidity in the summer and fall of 1998, there were no suppliers.

As a last resort, LTCM assumed that it could turn to lenders or investors to provide new capital to underwrite its potentially profitable positions, even as losses increased. But investors' willingness to support speculative activities such as arbitrage was limited and likely to become more limited as arbitrage mispricing, and the uncertainty of profits, increased. As risk increases, investors demand higher returns. At some point, the riskiness of the investment outweighs the potential gain and capital stops flowing.[9]

Furthermore, as asset volatility increases, lenders increase borrowing rates and either mark down the value of collateral or demand safer collateral; this is just when arbitrageurs and other traders require more capital to shore up the eroding values of their positions. The level of trading and liquidity falls. This can lead to higher asset volatility, more demands from lenders for collateral, and diminished liquidity. A flight to quality may ensue.[10] Liquidity disappears when it is needed most.

LTCM was unable either to liquidate assets or to raise new capital fast enough to enable it to retain its highly leveraged positions. As losses mounted, leverage effectively stopped out LTCM's strategies, just as portfolio insurance programs stopped out in the October 19, 1987 crash (see Chapter 5, "Portfolio Insurance and the Crash"). The bailout left LTCM's remaining original investors with a vastly reduced share of the hedge fund and a commensurately reduced share in any eventual profits.

After LTCM was finally closed, and as his own new firm was being launched, Meriwether gave the final verdict. He stated, "Our whole approach was fundamentally flawed."[11]

## GHOSTS OF CRISES PAST AND FUTURE

LTCM's demise brings to mind some vivid and ironic connections to portfolio insurance and the financial crisis of 1987. Not least of the ironic connections is the presence of Scholes and Robert C. Merton. In the foreground as partners of LTCM, these two Nobel laureates played dominant background roles in portfolio insurance as the creators, with the late Fischer Black, of the option replication model that underlied the strategy. Less obvious, and more profound, links between portfolio insurance and LTCM are to be found in the way both debacles unfolded, allowing a small number of operators with substantial positions to become significant threats to the stability of global markets.

Portfolio insurance vendors, with a marketing blitz based on the seeming ability of sophisticated finance theory to remove risk from equity investing, were able to attract enough capital from institutional investors to amass a US equity market stake of as much as $100 billion. LTCM relied on complicated financial mathematics to devise strategies that also promised low-risk returns, which attracted investors and enough lenders to leverage LTCM's capital into a $100 billion portfolio. LTCM was also able to use highly leveraged derivatives contracts to magnify its theoretically low-risk positions even more.

Arbitrage is not, like portfolio insurance, trend following. In fact, it should stabilize markets to the extent that it limits divergences of assets' prices from their fair values. The unwinding of arbitrage positions, however, generally means trading *with* market trends. When these types of strategies constitute a large enough fraction of the market and are mirrored by the actions of other investors, including hedge funds and investment banks, sudden unwinding can devour market liquidity, just as portfolio insurers' selling demands (and their effects on other investors) did in 1987. Arbitrage, like portfolio insurance, can then become destabilizing.

With arbitrage positions as highly leveraged as LTCM's, even relatively minor discrepancies between expectations and actual outcomes can force unwinding and create market instability. This is because losses on leveraged positions can translate into margin calls—demands for more collateral from the broker lending cash or securities to the fund. To meet these margin calls, the fund must raise more capital from outside sources or liquidate positions.

But LTCM, like portfolio insurers, fell prey to the *illusion* of liquidity. Portfolio insurers believed investors would underwrite their insurance policies by buying stocks when portfolio insurers needed to sell stocks. The crash of 1987 disabused them of this notion. LTCM believed that lenders or investors would be available to lend it cash or act as counterparties to its increasingly risky positions. In the end, the Federal Reserve Bank of New York had to coerce LTCM's counterparties into supplying that liquidity.

## Credit Crunch

In the week following the September 23, 1998, bailout of LTCM, the yield on 30-year Treasuries fell below 5 percent for the first time in 30 years, as investors in search of safety and liquidity drove their price up.[12] At the same time, investors fearing the eventual liquidation of LTCM's huge arbitrage portfolio shunned high-yield bonds, emerging market debt, and mortgage-backed securities. From the beginning of August 1998 to mid October, the premium that investors demanded to hold high-yield, high-risk bonds jumped from 375 to 750 basis points, despite little change in actual default rates. At the same time, US commercial and investment banks were retreating from global bond markets; in the third quarter of 1998, the average emerging market bond fell over 27 percent, and there were virtually no issuances by an emerging-market government or company in August and September.

The market for US commercial mortgage-backed securities, in which LTCM held substantial positions, collapsed, foreshadowing what was to come in the next decade. The spread between 10-year commercial mortgage-backed securities and 10-year Treasuries widened from 80 to 155 basis points between June and October; this sent real estate investment trust Criimi Mae Inc., the largest US buyer of the riskiest commercial mortgage-backed bonds, into bankruptcy. Commercial mortgage lenders found it increasingly difficult to find buyers for their mortgage securitizations. As a result, these lenders upped the level of collateral they required for commercial loans from 5 percent of the loan value, which had prevailed in mid summer, to 25 percent. Commercial real estate prices fell 15 percent to 20 percent between mid August and the beginning of October, as potential buyers encountered financing difficulties.

In the two decades or so preceding the 1998 crisis, corporations had become less and less reliant on traditional banks for their funding needs and increasingly reliant on capital markets and what came to be known as the shadow banking system—investment banks, non-bank lenders, hedge funds, and other non-bank, non-depository institutions. Commercial banks, which had provided 35 percent of funds to nonfinancial borrowers in 1974, provided only 22 percent in 1994.[13] Money market funds, commercial paper, and high-yield "junk" bonds began to replace commercial bank depositors as sources of funds for lending. Bank and non-bank lenders also turned to securitization, whereby loans were packaged into securities sold to investors who took on the risk of the loans in exchange for a portion of the payments on them. These new sources of funding and methods of risk reduction, together with the increased quality and availability of financial information, made it easier for firms to raise funds and significantly reduced the edge commercial banks had held in obtaining and lending funds.

Economist Henry Kaufman observed in 1994 that this change in financial structure was compounded by the growing influence of individuals, through vehicles such as mutual funds, on market behavior; the increasing Americanization of global markets; and the emergence of high-octane portfolio managers ranging across all markets and countries. As a result, Kaufman posited, the world's economies were more susceptible to excess in both credit creation and credit withdrawal. He warned that this was likely to increase volatility in financial markets. And, with traditional sources of credit losing ground to the capital markets, "restraint [on lending] will come more from unprecedented asset price variation and less from squeezes on short-term credit availability or cost."[14]

This was precisely what was happening as the US economy entered the fourth quarter of 1998. The capital markets seized up, despite low interest rates and healthy reserves at commercial banks. Fearing the effects on the economy should such a credit crunch continue, the Federal Reserve cut interest rates by a quarter point on October 15. This cut came as a surprise to the market, as the Fed had just announced a quarter-point reduction on September 29. The Dow Jones Industrial Average (DJIA) responded with a strong rally; it closed up 4.2 percent, with financial firms' shares, which had been off as much as 50 percent to 60 percent from their peaks, leading the way. The DJIA ended October at 8,592, its highest level since August 25; it proceeded to climb back over the 9,000 mark by late November.

Had LTCM not been bailed out, the immediate liquidation of its highly leveraged bond, equity, and derivative positions may have had effects—particularly on the bond market—rivaling the effects that the forced selling by portfolio insurers had on equity markets in 1987. Given the links between LTCM and investment and commercial banks, and between LTCM's positions in different asset markets and different countries' markets, the systemic risk much talked about in connection with the growth of derivative markets may have become an unwelcome reality. As it was, LTCM's activities contributed to a panic in credit markets that threatened markets and economies worldwide.

# PART IV

CHAPTER 10

# The Credit Crisis and Recession, 2007–2009

*"What we need to understand is, one, that there are market failures; and two, that there are things like asset bubbles and irrational exuberance. There are periods of booms, bubbles, and manias. These things, if left to themselves, can lead to crashes, to busts, to panics."*

—**Nouriel Roubini**[1]

At the start of 2007, the United States seemed to be in good economic and financial shape, despite a bit of a slowdown in economic growth, from a very solid 3.8 percent of gross domestic product (GDP) in 2004 to 2.7 percent in 2006. The unemployment rate had declined since 2004. The delinquency rate on mortgages was well under 4 percent, and mortgage securitization was in full swing. According to the International Monetary Fund (IMF), in April 2006, "the dispersion of credit risk by banks to a broader and more diverse group of investors . . . has helped to make the banking and overall financial system more resilient."[2]

There were nevertheless some troubling underlying currents. The report from the US government's Financial Crisis Inquiry Commission named some individuals who foresaw the coming financial storm. According to William K. Black, former head of a Congressional commission created in 1990 to address a previous financial crisis in which more than 1,000 savings and loan banks failed, many due to risky loans and investments: "The claim that no one could have foreseen the [credit] crisis is false."[3] In fact, the index for swaps on mortgage-backed securities (the ABX) began to experience unusual perturbations as early as January 2007.[4]

Of particular concern was the marked increase in leverage. From 1997 to 2007, US private-sector debt grew at an annual rate of 9 percent, and US mortgage credit had increased by 134 percent since the start of the new millennium.[5] By the end of 2007, reports former Treasury Secretary Timothy F. Geithner, capital levels at the big US investment banks constituted just 3 percent of assets.[6] At the Federal National Mortgage Association (Fannie Mae) and the Federal Home Loan Mortgage Corporation (Freddie Mac), the government-sponsored entities (GSEs) created to spur housing by buying mortgages created in the private sector and repackaging them for sale to investors, capital levels barely covered 1 percent of the value of their assets.

Furthermore, in early 2007, the central bank of Japan raised interest rates. The yen had served for some time as the favorite borrowing vehicle for an arbitrage-type strategy known as a carry trade. In this case, investors borrowed yen at a cheap rate and used the borrowed funds to invest in other assets, expecting to profit from a higher rate of return on these investments. The borrowed yen funded investments in stock markets around the globe, in currencies, and in US mortgage-backed securities (MBS). With the Japanese central bank's action, the yen became more costly to borrow and hence the investments it funded less attractive. The Chinese market dropped 9 percent and the Dow Jones Industrial Average (DJIA) dropped 416 points (3.3%) on February 28, but both recovered fairly quickly. Problems in the market for mortgage-related securities, which had been buoyed by a 10 percent annual average increase in US home prices from 2000 to 2005, would prove more lasting.

The market for asset-backed commercial paper (ABCP) provided a harbinger of developing problems. Commercial paper is a short-term, interest-bearing note issued by banks (or by their off-balance-sheet entities), corporations, and other firms to investors such as money market funds. The proceeds are used to fund operations or make investments. In the case of ABCP, some of the proceeds were used to fund investments in longer-term, higher-yielding securities, including mortgage-backed instruments. Note purchasers essentially receive interest in return for lending short term to note sellers, who use the loans to purchase longer-term assets. Into early 2007, ABCP provided funding for about 22 percent of private-label (primarily mortgage-backed) securities.[7]

ABCP is generally assumed to be low risk because it is fully collateralized by assets with high credit ratings and because it has a very short maturity. But by mid 2007, the problems in the mortgage market began to become apparent, as delinquency rates on mortgages and foreclosures on residential property started to rise. Investors in ABCP, knowing or suspecting that some portion of the collateral underlying their loans consisted of mortgage-backed securities, became unwilling to purchase the notes. The issuers of the paper, faced with a dearth of buyers, had to fund their longer-term investments by using their own capital or by selling assets, which put more pressure on the prices of mortgage-related securities.

Hedge funds also faced turbulence. They were leveraged buyers, and in some cases issuers, of mortgage-related securities. As that market deteriorated, lenders to hedge funds demanded more collateral to compensate them for the increased risk. To raise cash, and also to reduce the riskiness of their portfolios, some hedge funds began to sell assets. A number sold their most liquid assets, including common stock. Some of these hedge funds were highly leveraged, multi-asset funds, such as Goldman Sachs's Global Equity Opportunities Fund. As they sold common stocks, they caused a "quant crisis" because other (non-leveraged) quantitative managers were pursuing similar strategies and holding the same stocks.[8] On August 9, 2007, the stock market declined substantially, subjecting equity investors to substantial losses.

Through the fall of 2007, equity market volatility remained high, while liquidity in the credit market continued to be plagued by concerns about residential mortgages. Citigroup, Bank of America, and J. P. Morgan Chase, unable to sell the ABCP notes funding some of their off-balance-sheet mortgage securities, had to bring these highly leveraged assets back onto their balance sheets. At year-end 2007, UBS announced a $10 billion write-down, largely the result of losses on mortgage-related securities.

In January 2008, Bank of America bought Countrywide Financial, once a major mortgage lender but now faced with imminent bankruptcy as a result of mounting delinquencies and defaults on its mortgages. Monoline insurance companies, which had sold swaps protecting the value of mortgage-related securities, were struggling to compensate insurance buyers. As the mortgage-related losses of monolines undermined their reputation for sterling creditworthiness, the perceived riskiness of the other main securities they insured—municipal bonds—rose to unprecedented levels.

In March 2008, less than a year after suffering near-total losses in two of its subprime-focused hedge funds, Bear Stearns came to its demise.

The investment bank faced write-downs on its substantial mortgage positions, and by the second week in March was finding it impossible to roll over some $14 billion in repurchase agreements (repos).[9] Bear Stearns' share price had fallen to around $30, down from $171 in January 2007. The prices of swaps that paid off in case of a Bear Stearns credit event soared. As Bear Stearns hovered on the brink of bankruptcy, with its customers fleeing, J. P. Morgan Chase, aided by a $29 billion guarantee from the US government, took over the firm for $10 a share (up from the $2 originally offered and accepted).

The US Federal Reserve Board opened its discount window to investment banks and offered to lend them up to $200 billion in US Treasury securities, to be collateralized by mortgage-related securities. Between August 2007 and the early spring of 2008, the US government provided nearly $1 trillion in direct and indirect support to financial institutions. Nevertheless, the banks' ability and willingness to lend became more and more limited.

By June 2008, the troubles at the monoline insurers had turned into formal downgrades of their creditworthiness. These meant immediate downgrades of all the debt they had insured. Municipalities found themselves having to pay higher rates on their bonds. The monoline insurance companies themselves, as well as many other entities that had used monoline-insured debt instruments as collateral for borrowing, had to provide more collateral to secure their borrowing.

In July, IndyMac Bank, once a major independent mortgage lender, was seized by the US government after a run by depositors. On September 6, Fannie Mae and Freddie Mac, the largest purchasers of US mortgages, were taken fully under the wing of the federal government. This meant that the once-implicit government guarantees of the securities the agencies sold were now explicit liabilities of the government.

During the following weekend, US Treasury officials met with several banking leaders in an attempt to find buyers for ailing investment bank Lehman Brothers. No buyers for Lehman emerged, but Bank of America did agree, at Treasury's urging, to buy fabled investment bank Merrill Lynch. On September 15, the same day the announcement of this purchase was made, Lehman Brothers filed for Chapter 11 bankruptcy, gaining the dubious distinction of becoming the largest bankruptcy in US history.

Lehman Brothers had been an aggressive buyer in the commercial and residential real estate markets, purchasing five mortgage lenders during the boom period of the market in order to ensure its supply of mortgages for securitization. By 2007, Lehman had become a leading player in mortgage securitization; it had continued to originate subprime loans even as housing prices dropped after mid 2006, retaining many of these loans on its books as investments. All this activity had been highly leveraged; as concerns about the quality and value of mortgages and mortgage-related assets grew in 2008, lenders had increasingly declined to do business with Lehman, or refused to accept its mortgage-related assets as collateral.[10] On September 15, 2008, no longer able to fund its operations, Lehman Brothers filed for bankruptcy.

Barclays, based in the United Kingdom, eventually bought most of Lehman Brothers' US business, but Lehman's failure wiped out the investments of thousands of German and Asian retail investors holding what they thought were very safe equity-linked notes that Lehman itself had guaranteed. Most significantly, with Lehman Brothers' collapse, the bottom of the mortgage market started to fall out.

One immediate victim was the huge US insurance company American International Group (AIG). AIG held a derivatives portfolio with a notional value of $2.7 trillion.[11] It had sold billions of dollars of protection on Lehman Brothers' debt and on mortgage-related debt held by other investors. The firm had seen its share price decline as it booked losses quarter after quarter into the fall of 2008. At the same time, the deterioration in the mortgage market had meant increasingly large collateral payments to protection buyers. By mid-September, buyers of the protection AIG had sold on Lehman's and other debt were demanding upwards of $23 billion in additional collateral from the insurer. (Notable among protection buyers was Goldman Sachs, which accounted for about 40 percent of the $80 billion of protection AIG had written on mortgage-related securities.[12])

On September 16, 2008, the day after Lehman's bankruptcy filing, the US government effectively acquired most of AIG for $85 billion. AIG eventually needed $182 billion in government aid. According to Ben S. Bernanke, chairman of the US Federal Reserve at the time, ". . . the failure of AIG would have been basically the end. It was interacting with so many different firms. It was so interconnected with both the US and the European financial systems and global banks. We were quite concerned that if AIG went bankrupt, we would not be able to control the crisis any further."[13]

September 2008 ended with the government's seizure of large mortgage lender Washington Mutual and the sale of its branches and assets to J. P. Morgan Chase. A $700 billion government rescue package for the US financial sector was voted down by the US House of Representatives on September 29, causing an 8.8 percent decline in the Standard & Poor's 500 (S&P 500) index, the largest since the crash of 1987. Despite the eventual passage of the Troubled Asset Relief Program (TARP) on October 3, 2008, the stock market ended October with the S&P 500 index down 16.9 percent—its worst monthly loss since October 1987, even after a rebound in the last week of the month.

By the end of 2008, central banks in Europe, the United States, Japan, and other countries had pumped trillions of dollars into the global banking system. The US government had rescued Citigroup, once the country's largest financial institution, offering tens of billions in loans and agreeing to backstop some $300 billion of potential losses on the bank's troubled asset portfolio. In return, the US government received preferred stock and warrants then worth $27 billion. The government had pledged more money—up to $600 billion—in support of Fannie Mae and Freddie Mac. It had expanded TARP to absorb losses on small-business and consumer loans, as well as to extend loans to two of the Big Three US automakers. Nevertheless, the US economy contracted at a sharp annual inflation-adjusted rate of 8.2 percent in the fourth quarter of 2008, while corporate profits experienced their sharpest drop since 1953 and consumer spending fell at a record rate.

The first three months of 2009 saw developed countries suffering their worst quarters since 1960, with the GDP of the Group of Twenty large developed and developing nations falling 1.5 percent compared with the previous quarter.[14] In the United States, the unemployment rate in February hit its highest level since 1983. Home prices continued to decline, with the seasonally adjusted S&P/Case-Shiller US National Home Price Index ending the quarter down about 19 percent from its February 2007 peak and the 20-city index off almost 31 percent from its April 2006 peak. Delinquencies and foreclosures on prime loans and commercial property increased, while remaining significantly below the levels for subprime loans.

In February 2009, President Barack Obama announced plans to spend up to $275 billion to aid homeowners in refinancing and modifying existing mortgages, the US Treasury proposed the Consumer and Business Lending Initiative for up to $1 trillion in new consumer and business loans, and Congress passed a fiscal stimulus bill with $787 billion in new spending and also tax cuts. The Federal Reserve announced in March that it was buying $300 billion in longer-term Treasuries, with the aim of exerting downward pressure on mortgage rates, and would extend more funds to shore up Fannie Mae and Freddie Mac. That spring, Chrysler and General Motors filed for Chapter 11 bankruptcy protection and received more funding from the government; the US Treasury became the majority shareholder of both automakers.

The DJIA fell to a 12-year low of 6,547 in early March 2009, about 54 percent below its October 2007 peak (see Exhibit 10.1). As the equity market plunged and liquidity evaporated during the credit storm, among the debris exposed were two notable Ponzi schemes, perpetrated by Bernard

**EXHIBIT 10.1**

The Dow Jones Industrial Average (DJIA) in the 2007–2009 Crisis

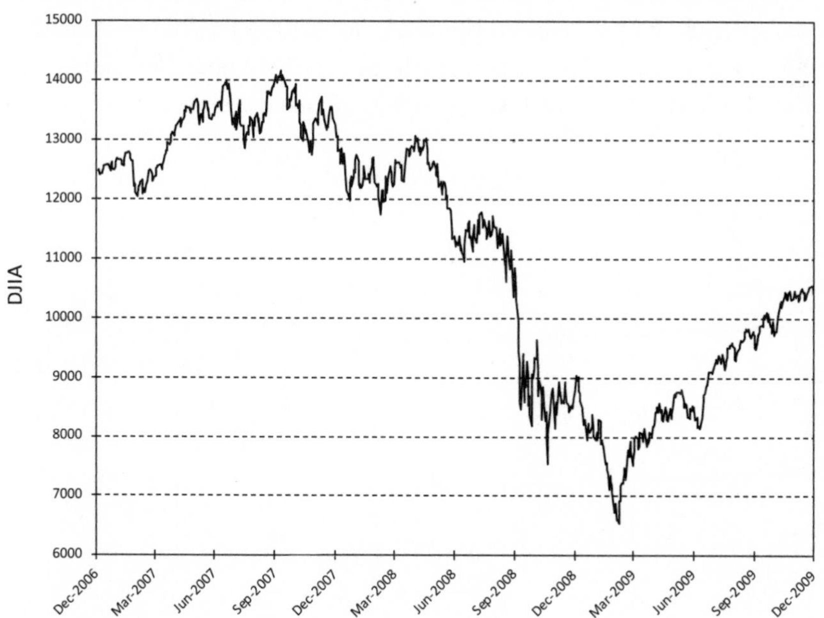

L. Madoff Investment Securities and Stanford Financial Group. Madoff's firm, which had been running a fraudulent market-maker scheme for at least two decades, cost clients some $65 billion, although all but $10 billion to $20 billion of that reflected fictional gains. Madoff was charged with securities fraud in December 2008 and sentenced to 150 years in prison in June 2009. In February 2009, Allen Stanford was charged with a $7 billion fraud; convicted in March 2012, he is currently serving a 110-year prison sentence.

The DJIA performed strongly after its March trough, rebounding 21 percent in the next three weeks and ending up 19 percent for 2009. This was the biggest annual percentage rise in six years, but it still left the index some 26 percent below its 2007 peak. For the decade 1999 to 2009, the equity market lost ground, with the DJIA down 9 percent.

Meanwhile, the economy continued to struggle. Unemployment in the United States kept rising, topping out at 10 percent in October 2009. Consumer spending for the year grew at its lowest rate in 47 years. While the S&P/Case-Shiller National Home Price Index gained ground after reaching a low in the spring of 2009, foreclosure starts reached a high in the second half of the year and remained at roughly twice their immediate pre-crisis rate through the rest of the year. Nevertheless, according to the National Bureau of Economic Research, June 2009 marked the trough of the business cycle downturn that had begun in December 2007, and hence the official end of the Great Recession. It would be a slow climb out.

CHAPTER 11

# Blowing Bubbles

*"Without calling the overall national issue a bubble, it's pretty clear that it's an unsustainable underlying pattern."*

**—Alan Greenspan**[1]

There is little disagreement that the proximate cause of the 2007–2008 credit crisis was the decline in housing prices and subsequent losses on, and write-downs of, securities and derivatives backed by residential mortgages—in particular, subprime mortgages. Beyond that, there is a range of opinions about where to place blame for the unsustainable run-up in housing prices and the destructive effects of the subsequent declines. Some of these (by no means mutually exclusive) theories are discussed below.

## DEEPER IN DEBT

Within a week of the terrorist attacks of September 11, 2001, the US Federal Reserve Board (the Fed) reduced the fed funds rate from 3.5 percent to 3 percent (it had begun the year at 6%); within three weeks, the rate was cut to 2.5 percent, and by the end of 2001 it was down to 1.75 percent. According to theory, lowering the rate at which banks can lend to each other will lead banks to lower the rates they charge for lending, which in turn will encourage businesses and individuals to borrow and invest, increasing economic activity.

By mid June 2003, the economy appeared to be recovering from the attacks of September 11 and the earlier bursting of the technology stock bubble in 2000. The stock market was up and housing prices were soaring. The fed funds rate had been lowered to 1 percent, appreciably below the prevailing inflation rate of 2 percent to 3 percent. Even after the Fed began to raise the fed funds rate in 2004, it remained below the inflation rate until the end of 2005.

## BURSTING OF THE TECH STOCK BUBBLE

The dawn of the twenty-first century marked the climax of one of the larger stock bubbles in US history. From the beginning of January 1980 to the end of August 2000, the Standard & Poor's 500 (S&P 500) index rose 1,306 percent, far surpassing the growth in company dividends (189%) and earnings (254%) over that period. At the peak of the bubble in March 2000, shares of the index were trading for an unprecedented 47.2 times earnings. The highest price/earnings (P/E) ratio seen previously was 32.6, a month before the October 1929 stock market crash.[2]

Though stock prices had been trending upward since the early 1980s, their rate of increase accelerated in the mid 1990s, driven by an insatiable demand for technology stocks, and particularly for internet companies. The Nasdaq Composite Index, which includes numerous technology and internet firms, increased more than six times from 1995 to 2000, reaching an intra-day peak of 5,132.52 on March 10, 2000. At that point, shares of internet companies, many of which hadn't existed a decade earlier, comprised 6 percent of the market capitalization of all US publicly traded companies.[3]

Even Alan Greenspan, a staunch defender of market prices as the best indicator of value and chairman of the Federal Reserve Board from 1987 to 2006, felt compelled to remark that prices had reached the point where they reflected "irrational exuberance."[4] That famous characterization came rather early in the game, on December 5, 1996, when the Nasdaq index was at 1,300 and the Dow Jones Industrial Average (DJIA) was at 6,437. Yet the indexes continued to rise inexorably for several more years.

Supporting the rise was a perception, even on the part of professionals, that a new era of investing had arrived, where old relationships between prices and earnings, risk and return, no longer mattered. A 1999 article in *The Atlantic* magazine entitled "Dow 36,000" argued: "A profound change has occurred in the attractiveness of stocks since the early 1980s, as investors have become more rational. The old 'limits' of yields and P/Es do not apply anymore—if they ever did."[5] This line of thinking was reinforced by highly visible advances in computers, cell phones, and the internet, which seemed to confirm that the economy had entered a period of unprecedented, technology-driven growth.

One of the biggest drivers of the gains was momentum trading by professional investors. The stock market's years-long upward trend was tailor-made for the strategy. Investors could buy stocks as prices rose, financing their purchases with margin debt borrowing. When prices fell, momentum traders expected to be able to limit their downside by selling stocks.[6] Provided sells could be executed quickly enough, the strategy offered a lot of upside and limited downside. What momentum traders had yet to discover was that the "fail-safe" exit strategy, selling quickly, did not work so well in a down market.

A second force propelling stocks upward was the individual investor. With the demise of traditional corporate pension plans and the accompanying rise in self-directed retirement plans, investment decision-making was shifted from professional portfolio managers to individuals. At the same time, popular media, as well as financial advisers, were herding retail investors into stocks. In his 1994 book, *Stocks for the Long Run: The Definitive Guide to Financial Market Returns & Long-Term Investment Strategies*, Wharton Business School Professor Jeremy J. Siegel demonstrated that stocks had a significant historical return advantage over bonds, a conclusion that gained widespread acceptance.[7] Stock analysts and portfolio managers were showcased on CNBC, a 24-hour financial news television network, and not surprisingly recommended buying, not selling. Between 1989 and 1998, the number of individuals owning stock rose from 42.1 million to 75.8 million.[8]

The market for initial public offerings (IPOs) of internet stocks was especially frenzied and was the most extreme manifestation of the bubble. The heated competition for IPO shares could be traced back to the public offering of Netscape, a maker of web-browsing software. The day it went public on August 9, 1995, shares of the not-yet-profitable company soared from the $28 offering price to an intra-day high of $75; the shares went on to hit $171 by year-end.

By the first quarter of 2000, at the peak of the frenzy, every other day a technology company went public and doubled in value.[9] It seemed not to matter that many of these firms had no profits, brief operating histories, and sketchy business plans.

No single event signaled the end of the bubble. But three days of losses in the Nasdaq index following its peak on March 10, 2000, may have been enough of a sign of weakness to trigger momentum traders' cut-and-run strategy. By March 15, the Nasdaq index had lost more than 9 percent; by April 14, it was off 34 percent. The precipitous fall in prices was consistent with a momentum-based selling panic, which occurs when expected gains fail to materialize and momentum traders all try to exit stocks at the same time. Declining prices also triggered margin calls for leveraged investors, which may have forced these investors to sell stocks, inducing further price declines.

Stock prices fell for more than two years. By the time they bottomed in October 2002, some $7 trillion in market value had evaporated. The Nasdaq index lost 78 percent of its value, the biggest decline in a major index since the Great Depression.[10] The DJIA and S&P 500 indexes lost 27 percent and 44 percent, respectively.

With money so cheap, banks had tremendous incentive to lend. Even at very low loan rates, they could make sizable profits. Low lending rates, in turn, attracted more borrowing. Credit to the US non-financial corporate sector increased by about two-thirds from the end of 2001 to the third quarter of 2008 ($14.7 trillion to $25.0 trillion), while credit to US households almost doubled ($7.8 trillion to $14.3 trillion).

## Global Imbalances

Total US debt had been increasing for many years before the Fed adopted its low-rate policies in the early 2000s. The nation's indebtedness as a percentage of gross domestic product (GDP) doubled between 1984 and 2006.[11] Fed Chairman Alan Greenspan asserted early in the credit crisis that low US interest rates came despite, rather than because of, Fed policy. Global economic competition following the fall of the Berlin Wall in 1989 reduced inflation and wage growth. Falling savings rates in developed countries were offset by increased savings rates in emerging markets. Euphoria rose and asset prices decoupled from short-term interest rates.[12]

According to other economists, economic growth in low-labor-cost developing countries such as China and India pushed up demand for resources, which lifted profits in commodity-exporting areas such as

Brazil, Russia, and the Middle East. This resulted in excess liquidity in the developing world. Those economies could not absorb it, given their relatively undeveloped financial markets and low domestic demand. Excess savings thus flowed to developed countries, funding borrowing and reducing the returns investors demanded to bear risk. The United States was absorbing two-thirds of the net savings of countries that had trade surpluses in 2004–2006.[13]

## Inefficient Allocation of Resources

When borrowing is cheap, borrowers may be inclined not only to borrow more and invest more, but to take more risks with the borrowed money. This can have a positive economic impact if borrowed funds are directed to investments that increase sustainable economic wealth. This may be the case, for example, if investment is directed to new projects or the improvement of old ones. These may range from a corner restaurant to biogenetic engineering. Obviously, not all new projects or processes will be successful. Many, if not most, will fail. But some, like the Apple iPhone or the company Walmart, may grow to be spectacularly successful, fueling employment and economic growth. The many failures may be a price worth paying for the few, but great, successes.

One problem, however, is that when borrowing is cheap and readily available, funds borrowed may exceed the opportunities for new productive investment; borrowed funds may instead be directed to existing assets. This puts pressure on their prices and can lead to asset price bubbles. In bubbles, asset prices rise above the value supported by underlying fundamentals and they can stay overpriced for an extended period of time.

Investment in an asset bubble can be profitable—over the short term. Furthermore, not investing in the bubble can be costly. As former Citigroup chief executive Charles Prince observed: "As long as the music is playing you've got to get up and dance."[14] Betting against a bubble, as many hedge funds found during the dot-com boom, can be fatal. Timing is everything.

If bubbles exist (and there are some theorists who refuse to acknowledge them), they may be said to come in two flavors—rational and irrational—although the dividing line is somewhat blurred. Participants in a rational bubble recognize that, in the aggregate, prices are at levels that cannot be justified by underlying fundamentals. The prices, however, are supported by speculators who may be behaving quite rationally as individuals. These speculators choose to invest in a rising market, despite their awareness that it is overpriced, with the expectation of being able to get out, at a profit, before the bubble bursts.

But bubbles may also be seen as irrational, as seems to have been the case with the tech stock bubble of the late 1990s. Humans, even bankers, are subject to exuberance, short-term myopic thinking, and what early-twentieth-century economist John Maynard Keynes termed "animal spirits."[15] Behavioral economist Robert J. Shiller viewed the run-up in stock prices preceding the 1987 market crash as a self-reinforcing fad fed by the focus on stock prices in both public media and private discourse.[16] (He viewed the housing bubble of 2002–2005 in much the same light.)

## Why Housing?

In the United States, the overinvestment enabled by cheap borrowing costs in the years preceding the credit crisis was concentrated in residential real estate. Investments in US real estate increased at a substantially higher rate than US economic growth from 2003 to 2006, at about 4 percent a year, versus 3 percent GDP growth.[17] Household mortgage debt by 2006 equaled 89 percent of GDP, whereas it had been only 54 percent in 1996.[18]

Certain developments made real estate appear to be a particularly appealing asset. The low cost incurred by banks for borrowing enabled them to offer mortgages at very attractive rates. Mortgage rates were historically low in 2002 and 2003. Low rates encouraged both more borrowing for new home purchases as well as refinancing of existing mortgages. Buying demand pushed housing prices up. Increasing prices attracted home seekers and speculators looking to "flip" houses for a profit.

From 1996 into 2006, real (inflation-adjusted) housing prices increased a cumulative 92 percent, versus a 27 percent increase from 1890 to 1996.[19] Origination of all types of mortgages started to increase markedly in 2002, but originations of subprime mortgages grew at a remarkable rate, from $231 billion in 2002 to $625 billion in 2005.[20]

Why did subprime lending emerge as the nexus of the US housing bubble? The growth in subprime lending was made possible by innovations in the way mortgages were financed. These innovations allowed mortgage originators to repackage the risks of mortgages (particularly, the relatively high risk of subprime mortgage defaults) so that the mortgages appeared less risky and more suitable for resale to a broad range of potential investors.

## PRIME, SUBPRIME, ALT-A, AND JUMBO

There is no standardized definition of a subprime mortgage, despite the fact that it played a central role in the 2007–2008 crisis. Below are descriptions of the characteristics of subprime and other types of mortgages.

**Prime:** Prime mortgage loans are offered to the most creditworthy borrowers, those with strong histories of timely loan payments and documentation of their financial capacity to repay the loans. Prime loans typically carry the lowest interest rates and most favorable terms relative to other types of mortgage loans.

Eligibility for prime loans is determined by a number of factors, most importantly a borrower's credit score. FICO scores produced by a private firm, Fair Isaac Corp. (FICO), are the de facto standard. They are based primarily on a borrower's current debt load, record of on-time loan payments, and length of credit history. Scores range from 300 to 850; the median is around 720. The minimum score to define a prime loan can vary from lender to lender, but a common cutoff figure is 620. The Federal Housing Finance Agency (FHFA), which oversees the Federal National Mortgage Association (Fannie Mae) and the Federal Home Loan Mortgage Corporation (Freddie Mac), as well as the 11 Federal Home Loan Banks, uses a cutoff of 660.

Prime mortgage loans are considered "conforming loans"; that is, they are suitable for purchase by Fannie Mae and Freddie Mac. Until fairly late in the housing bubble, these government-sponsored entities (GSEs) were not allowed to purchase subprime mortgages or jumbo mortgages. Prime borrowers are more likely than others to qualify for a traditional 30-year, fixed-interest mortgage. Two ratios are considered in the decision to extend a prime loan. The first is the loan-to-value (LTV) ratio, the ratio of the loan amount to the value of the home. The second is a borrower's debt-to-income (DTI) ratio, the ratio of the loan amount plus other debt to the borrower's income. Lower is better in both cases.

**Subprime:** Subprime loans are extended to borrowers who pose a high risk of default because of low credit scores, undocumented or uncertain income sources, or a history of late loan payments, defaults, or bankruptcy. These borrowers need to pay higher interest rates and fees to compensate for the added risk of lending to them.

There is no standard definition of a subprime loan, but there is a widespread practice of classifying loans made to borrowers with FICO scores below 620 as subprime. Other markers of a subprime loan include a down payment that is low, which results in an undesirably high LTV ratio, and a high DTI ratio. A sufficiently high down payment could, in some cases, overcome a low FICO score.

To compensate for the higher risk of subprime loans, lenders demand higher interest rates. Lenders may also seek to reduce risk and costs by requiring subprime borrowers to take out an adjustable-rate mortgage (ARM) rather than a fixed-rate mortgage. Most subprime loans are ARMs. A typical example is a 2/28 loan that offers a fixed interest rate for two years, then resets to a variable rate for the remaining 28 years. About 75 percent of subprime mortgages issued from 2003 to 2007 were 2/28 loans.[21]

**Alt-A:** Alt-A loans occupy a middle ground between prime and subprime. They are extended to borrowers who cannot qualify for a prime loan because of a problem in one of several areas. The most common is an inability to fully document assets or sources of income because the borrower is recently divorced, self-employed, or has an irregular or commission-based income. Other issues that might knock a loan down from prime to Alt-A are a high LTV ratio, a high DTI ratio, or a loan secured by a vacation home or an investment property rather than a primary residence.

Alt-A loans can require fixed or adjustable payments. Some have no principal payments for the first three to 10 years; others are "negative amortization" loans, which offer the borrower multiple payment options but add any unpaid principal and interest below a specified minimum to the loan balance. In each case, costs are deferred to future years on the expectation that rising home values will allow the loan to be refinanced before more onerous terms take effect.

The difference in interest rates between prime and alt-A loans is relatively small. Alt-A loans are typically 0.5 to 1.5 percentage points higher.

**Jumbo:** Jumbo mortgages are high-balance loans that cannot be purchased by Fannie Mae and Freddie Mac. As a result, jumbo loans pose greater risks to lenders than prime loans. Interest rates on jumbo loans are higher than for conventional loans, even for borrowers with good credit records.

Neither Fannie Mae nor Freddie Mac can own jumbo mortgages because of limits established by Congress on the size of mortgages they can purchase. Currently, the limit is $453,100, although the maximum can range up to $679,650 in certain high-cost areas.

Interest rates for jumbo loans are typically 0.25 to 0.50 percentage points higher than those for prime mortgages. Lenders may also require a higher percentage down payment for jumbo loans.

Mortgages are essentially risk-shifting instruments. In the United States, a mortgage borrower can often shift some of the risk of a decline in the value of the house to the mortgage lender. That is, if the value of a house declines below the value of the mortgage, the homebuyer can default on the loan without the lender having recourse to the homebuyer's income or assets other than the house.[22]

Subprime loan default rates are likely to be more affected than prime loan default rates by declines in underlying housing prices. Down payments relative to the value of the mortgaged house are generally smaller for subprime than for prime borrowers. For subprime mortgages issued in 2006, the average size of the loan as a percentage of the home's value (the loan-to-value ratio, or LTV ratio) was about 15 percentage points higher than the average LTV ratio for prime mortgages.[23] Having made a smaller down payment than the prime borrower, the subprime borrower has less to lose by defaulting. Moreover, in the event of default, the subprime borrower has fewer assets and less income to attach than the prime borrower, even in the relatively rare case that the lender has legal recourse to assets other than the mortgaged house.

Mortgage lenders can reduce their exposure to this default risk by lending to a large number of borrowers, a form of investment diversification. Diversification is what a traditional insurance company does to protect itself against the monetary risk of a particular home burning down; it diversifies geographically among policyholders. The likelihood of all insured houses burning at the same time is minuscule. Even if a few houses burn, the well-diversified insurance company can use the proceeds from other insurance premiums to pay off the losses. Risk is essentially shared among policyholders.

Diversification of mortgage loans can reduce a lender's exposure to default by a given homeowner when that default is the result of a specific, diversifiable event—say, the borrower's loss of a job. Risk of default resulting from housing-price declines, however, is unlikely to be that specific a risk. The value of one house rarely declines in isolation. Usually, a decline in the price of one house signals broader woes that affect the prices of surrounding houses. The risk-reducing benefits of diversification are more limited when the underlying risk is more systematic, and the risk of a decline in housing prices is more systematic than the risk of a house fire.

Mortgage lenders, however, do not have to retain this risk because much of it can be shifted to others. Mortgages can be pooled and repackaged into securities that are sold to various types of investors. This process of securitization has been used since the 1970s to reduce risk and increase the funds available for prime mortgages. The 1990s and 2000s witnessed the widespread adoption of increasingly sophisticated methods of securitization that allowed a vast expansion in lending to subprime borrowers. This expansion was abetted to a greater or lesser extent by agents such as the quasi-governmental mortgage buyers, credit rating firms, and mortgage originators themselves.

## FANNIE MAE AND FREDDIE MAC

In 1977, the US Congress passed the Community Reinvestment Act, designed to encourage lending to low-income neighborhoods that had often been "redlined" by bank loan officers. In the early 1990s, this law was strengthened so that banks had to prove that they actually made loans to low-income borrowers, not just tried to do so. According to some critics, this spurred a deterioration in bank lending practices. This was compounded, some argue, by the later actions of the US Congress regarding the government-sponsored enterprises (GSEs) that purchased the bulk of new mortgages—the Federal National Mortgage Association (Fannie Mae) and the Federal Home Loan Mortgage Corporation (Freddie Mac).

Fannie Mae and Freddie Mac were created by the US government (in 1938 and 1970, respectively), and owned by private shareholders. These GSEs support US home ownership by purchasing mortgages from private-sector mortgage lenders and creating mortgage-backed securities (MBS) for sale to the public. The corporations guarantee timely interest and principal payments on these securities. However, those guarantees were until fairly recently collateralized solely by the corporations' own capital, which came primarily from earnings on the sale of the MBS. It was not until Fannie Mae and Freddie Mac were taken into the conservatorship of the government in 2008 that their guarantees became explicit obligations of the US government.

The Federal Housing Enterprises Financial Safety and Soundness Act, passed in 1992, required that the GSEs meet certain goals for affordable housing. The law set up the Office of Federal Housing Enterprise Oversight (OFHEO) to regulate the GSEs. Nevertheless, Fannie Mae and Freddie Mac were still confined to purchasing only mortgages and mortgage securities that conformed to specified limits on loan amounts. Issuance and securitization of subprime, Alt-A, and jumbo mortgage loans were left to the private market, so-called private-label or non-agency securitizers, including banks.

Fannie Mae and Freddie Mac accounted for nearly 90 percent of the mortgage securitization market until the early 2000s. As issuance of non-conforming loans burgeoned with the housing bubble, however, the private sector began to take over a larger and larger portion of this market. By 2006, private-label securitizers made up 50 percent of the market.[24]

In 2001, Fannie Mae and Freddie Mac began to enter the subprime market via purchases of highly rated securitizations of subprime loans. According to data given to the Financial Crisis Inquiry Commission (FCIC), the GSEs purchased 10.5 percent of the subprime securities privately issued in that year and as much as 40 percent of the subprime securities issued in 2004.[25] Critics such as former Fed Chairman Greenspan have argued that the affordable housing requirements led the GSEs into the subprime market and that their purchases in turn fueled the issuance of these types of mortgages.[26]

The FCIC found that the GSEs would have met most of the affordable housing goals without needing to purchase the subprime MBS.[27] Yet the risk in the GSEs' portfolios did increase during the housing bubble and ensuing crisis, with increased commitments to subprime and Alt-A mortgages, higher average LTV ratios, and declining average credit scores.[28] In particular, as liquidity in the private market dried up in 2007 and 2008, Fannie Mae and Freddie Mac increased their mortgage portfolios. By the second half of 2007, they were purchasing about 75 percent of all new mortgages.[29] At the time, the US Congress, the New York Fed, and the marketplace all supported further easing of the capital requirements of the GSEs to allow them to purchase even more mortgages.[30]

As delinquencies and defaults on riskier mortgages increased in 2007 and, markedly, in 2008, however, losses on the GSEs' mortgage portfolios and guarantees mounted, and they found their own liquidity evaporating. Losses were particularly problematic because of the massive leverage the GSEs operated with—around 70 to 1.[31] According to the FCIC, by the third quarter of 2010 the realized and unrealized losses at Fannie Mae and Freddie Mac amounted to almost 60 percent of the capital they had held before the crisis began.[32]

The Housing and Economic Recovery Act of 2008, passed in July 2008, created a new regulator for the GSEs, the Federal Housing Finance Agency (FHFA), and gave the US Treasury the power to extend credit to the GSEs, to inject capital, and to purchase their mortgage securities. Two months later, the government placed the GSEs under conservatorship, wiping out shareholders (including not only many US financial institutions but also the central banks of China and Russia), and dismissed the executives and boards of directors of both agencies. In addition to receiving $200 billion in funding, the GSEs unloaded $220 billion of their mortgage securities onto the US Treasury and the Federal Reserve Board, while the Fed bought an additional $172 billion of GSE debt.[33]

## CREDIT RATING AGENCIES

Reliance on the ratings from US credit rating agencies (CRAs) undoubtedly contributed to the crisis by buttressing the mammoth buildup in credit instruments, particularly securities based on subprime mortgage loans. CRAs analyze the creditworthiness of debt obligations and instruments issued by corporations, financial institutions, governments, and other entities, and provide ratings based on default probabilities. The ratings range from investment-grade (high-quality, low probability of default)

EXHIBIT 11.1

Bond Ratings

Long-Term Credit Ratings

| Moody's | S&P | Fitch |
|---|---|---|
| Aaa | AAA | AAA |
| Aa1 | AA+ | AA+ |
| Aa2 | AA | AA |
| Aa3 | AA- | AA- |
| A1 | A+ | A+ |
| A2 | A | A |
| A3 | A- | A- |
| Baa1 | BBB+ | BBB+ |
| Baa2 | BBB | BBB |
| Baa3 | BBB- | BBB- |
| Ba1 | BB+ | BB+ |
| Ba2 | BB | BB |
| Ba3 | BB- | BB- |
| B1 | B+ | B+ |
| B2 | B | B |
| B3 | B- | B- |
| Caa1 | CCC+ | CCC+ |
| Caa2 | CCC | CCC |
| Caa3 | CCC- | CCC- |
| Ca | CC | CC |
| C | C | C |
|  | D | D |

Source: Moody's Investors Service, S&P Global, Fitch Ratings.

to non-investment-grade (low-quality, higher probability of default) (see Exhibit 11.1).

In general, low-quality debt commands a higher interest rate to compensate for its greater risk of default. Ratings provide an expedient measure of riskiness that potentially increases the efficiency, and lowers the cost, of lending and borrowing.

Since 2006, the Securities and Exchange Commission (SEC) has registered Nationally Recognized Statistical Rating Organizations (NRSROs), CRAs whose ratings are broadly accepted (or were accepted) as "reliable and credible." At the time of the crisis, there were 10 CRAs recognized as

NRSROs, but only three of these rated virtually all the mortgage-related securities—Standard & Poor's, Moody's Investors Service, and Fitch Ratings. NRSROs were, until 2007, basically unregulated. The Credit Rating Agency Reform Act of 2006, effective June 2007, required the CRAs to disclose information about their methodologies, but little else.[34]

CRA ratings are important for many large investors, including pension funds, mutual funds, money market funds, and insurance companies, which may be prevented by regulation from investing in securities below a given rating. Smaller and less sophisticated investors may rely on ratings because they do not have access to the data the agencies use to rate loans and/or the analytical capability to determine loan quality.

Investors in structured products seem to have relied heavily on credit ratings, rather than on their own in-depth analyses.[35] UBS, for example, in attempting to explain its massive losses on subprime-related debt instruments, admitted in a 2008 report to shareholders that it had not "looked through" the securitized instruments it had invested in to assess the risks of the underlying mortgages. It had instead relied on the high credit ratings the instruments had received.

Ratings are also used by regulators in setting leverage limits for many financial intermediaries, including commercial and investment banks and insurance companies. In general, securities with higher ratings require less capital underpinning than securities with lower ratings and allow issuers to pay lower interest rates. For counterparties in contracts such as collateralized debt obligations (CDOs), changes in ratings can trigger collateral exchanges and principal repayments.

Historically, the CRAs focused on rating corporate and municipal bond issues. For corporate bonds, this meant analyzing individual company fundamentals to determine the probability of default and the probable amount that bondholders could recover in the event of default. By 2006, however, over 40 percent of the revenues of the big three CRAs came from rating securitized instruments including MBS. This growth reflected not only the higher fees for rating securitized products—$30,000 to $40,000 for a $100 million residential mortgage-backed security (RMBS) versus $10,000 for a municipal bond[36]—but the explosive expansion in securitized products.

Securitized instruments bear the same ratings as corporate bonds. According to the Bank for International Settlements: "All ratings are ultimately mapped onto an alphanumeric scale benchmarked to the historical performance of corporate bonds."[37] There is thus a seeming similarity between the ratings for individual corporate bonds and the ratings of securitized products. During the housing bubble, the bulk of any given mortgage pool was assigned the highest rating—AAA or its equivalent—by the CRAs. Soon, there were some 64,000 AAA-rated tranches of securitizations including prime and subprime mortgages, student loans, and other credit instruments, versus about a dozen corporations that merited such a high rating.[38] Securitization thus vastly expanded the amount of assets available to investors required by regulation to hold only highly rated securities. Unfortunately, it began to become apparent by 2007 that the high ratings assigned to some subprime and some Alt-A securities were not warranted. Delinquencies and defaults rapidly increased beyond the parameters assumed by the CRAs, and massive ratings downgrades followed. The CRAs had obviously missed some important factor or factors in their analyses of mortgage securities.

## Ratings Fumbles

A 2008 SEC review found that CRAs were ill-prepared to handle the growing volume of business in the years following 2003.[39] In rating corporate bonds, the CRAs based their analyses on years of data about the performance of a company and its debt. But securitizations, such as MBS, differ considerably from corporate bonds. Each securitization involves hundreds or even thousands of underlying loans. Especially given the growth in the number of securitizations, it was impossible for the CRAs to do in-depth fundamental analysis of each loan in every securitization.

The CRAs tended to take at face value the loan-related information provided to them and to concentrate instead on modeling the diversity of the entire pool of assets. This could be done using historical data; using market price reactions to expected losses, estimated from a model; using estimated correlations across ratings changes; or using the co-movements of related, but more liquid, instruments, such as swaps on mortgage instruments.[40] The aim was to measure and ensure the diversification of the pool's risks.

While diversification may mitigate the idiosyncratic risk of a mortgage pool, it does not reduce the systematic risk of the pool. It may protect against individual defaults by a handful of borrowers, but it does not necessarily protect against risk exposures that are common to a large number of the pool's constituents. A decline in interest rates, for example, is likely to encourage a broad swath of mortgage borrowers to accelerate their loan payments or refinance their loans, constituting prepayment risk. A rise in unemployment is likely to result in an increase in defaults across the mortgages in the pool. A decline in house prices that leads to home values falling below the principal owed on their mortgages will also increase defaults.

The CRAs seem to have underestimated the occurrence of events that would have a systematic impact on the loans in a mortgage pool. This error was to some extent the result of the limited historical data. There had not been a significant nationwide housing price decline in the United States since before World War II.[41] To compound the problem, there was little appreciation of the extent of the overvaluation of house prices in the mid 2000s. A former managing director at Moody's Investors Service stated in 2005: "Moody's position was that there was not a . . . national housing bubble."[42]

Furthermore, after the onset of the 2007–2008 credit crisis, it became apparent that the ratings agencies had not considered the diversity of the originators of the loans within a pool or, in the case of securitizations from different issuers, the diversity of the issuers. In July 2007, downgrades of subprime MBS were concentrated in only four issuing firms.[43] Pools also tended to be concentrated in terms of the year of mortgage origination.[44] Thus pools of mortgages may have been diversified in terms of the geographic dispersion of the borrowers, but they were not diversified in other important respects.

The ratings agencies did consider whether the issuers retained a portion of the pools they securitized; they assumed that the issuers would police the credit quality of the pool more diligently if they had "skin in the game." The ultimate strength of this assumption, however, appears to have been undermined by the ability of the issuers to hedge the risks they retained.[45]

The CRAs did not appear to take into account possible declines in the quality of the loans underlying the securities they were rating. One former Moody's director testified before the FCIC: "Never once was it raised . . . or put in our agenda that the decline in quality that was going into the pools, the impact possibly on ratings. . . ."[46]

The crisis and the role played by the CRAs highlighted the potential conflicts of interest that arise from the relationship between CRAs and the issuers of securitized products. Of primary concern is that the issuers—the sellers of securitized products—are the ones who pay the raters for their services. Some critics argue that this led CRAs to inflate the ratings for some securitized products. While there seems to be no direct evidence for this, some researchers have found indications that the issuers did "shop" for ratings.[47]

Aside from the payment arrangement, the close relationship between the issuers and the raters has raised some critical eyebrows. CRA models are generally known to the issuers of securitized products. Furthermore, securitizers often consult with ratings agencies before finalizing a securitization. Thus, the issuers might be able to increase their profits by structuring products to meet the minimum standards required by the rating agencies, rather than to provide the best risk-return tradeoff for investors.[48] Furthermore, when the issuers rely on the raters' models, the securitization process itself, and the resulting products, will likely reflect any errors or shortcomings of the model used.

## DETERIORATION OF UNDERWRITING STANDARDS

Subprime mortgage originations went from under 10 percent of all mortgages issued in 2001 to nearly 25 percent of mortgage originations in 2006.[49] One study found that denials of loans to both prime and subprime borrowers declined as house price appreciation increased. At the same time, denial rates in the subprime market also declined as demand for loans, and as securitization of loans, increased, whereas denial rates in the prime market remained largely unchanged.[50] The expansion in subprime lending relative to total mortgage lending in itself provides evidence of a decline in lending standards as the housing boom developed.

Securitizations of subprime loans increased along with mortgage originations. The percentage of subprime loans securitized by private-label issuers went from 53 percent in 2002 to 75 percent in 2006.[51] The increase in securitization enabled the growth in subprime lending. As securitization allowed the lenders to sell the loans they made, taking them off their books, it reduced the lenders' risk. Risk reduction was especially important when it came to the relatively risky subprime sector.

Was the crisis abetted by a decline in underwriting standards above and beyond the growth in subprime lending and securitization alone? Because securitization removed loans from the lenders' books, it reduced the lenders' incentives to ensure the creditworthiness of their borrowers. At the same time, mortgage brokers received higher fees for subprime loans relative to prime or even Alt-A loans and could also profit from selling the loans to securitizers seeking their own hefty profits from the sale of subprime RMBS and CDOs. This motivated mortgage brokers to issue subprime loans, even if the loans were unsound.

One might expect that regulators would be able to enforce standards for mortgage lending. But during the housing boom, the Federal Reserve Board and other federal regulators appeared reluctant to strengthen lending standards or even enforce them. In 2000, the Fed had refused to reform the Home Ownership and Equity Protection Act to ban certain types of problematic mortgages. When some states tried to create higher standards for mortgage lending, they were quashed by the Office of the Comptroller of the Currency and the Office of Thrift Supervision.[52] During the run-up to the crisis, the Fed referred only three institutions to the Department of Justice for possible mortgage lending fraud.[53] It was not until 2007, during the crisis, that the Fed began to really examine the subprime subsidiaries of the large banks under its purview.[54]

In the absence of regulatory enforcement, types of mortgages that lent themselves to predatory lending practices proliferated. These included mortgages with low "teaser" rates that reset to much higher rates after two or three years; "liar loans" or "low-doc" loans that allowed borrowers to state false income levels or did away with income statements altogether; "NINJA" (no income, no job, no assets) loans; and negative amortization loans, by which the home buyers used a portion of the loan as the down payment on the house. These features were generally more characteristic of Alt-A and jumbo loans than of subprime loans. For example, over 80 percent of the Alt-A loans for new-home purchases reportedly required no documentation of income.[55] Although Alt-A loan delinquencies and defaults increased during the crisis, the increases were not nearly as large as those for subprime loans. Furthermore, Alt-A loans and jumbo loans constituted much smaller portions of the mortgage market, and thus much smaller percentages of the pools underlying securitized products.

Many subprime loans did require an interest rate reset at two or three years, but the initial rates on these loans were not especially low and were significantly higher than prevailing rates on prime mortgage loans.[56] Furthermore, the initial jolt of mortgage defaults occurred in subprime mortgages issued in 2006 and 2007. These experienced high delinquency rates almost immediately after issuance and defaulted well before the loan rates on them were scheduled to reset.

Some have found evidence of deterioration in underwriting standards for subprime loans between 2002 and 2007.[57] One study discovered that about 70 percent of default losses were associated with fraudulent misrepresentations on loan applications.[58] But a number of analyses using quantitative measurements of loan characteristics have found that it was the post-mortgage-origination decline in house prices, and the corresponding increase in LTV ratios, that was by far the most important factor explaining delinquencies and defaults on subprime mortgages.[59] Deterioration in the loan characteristics studied was not nearly as significant.

There is some analytical and anecdotal evidence that the quality of securitizations of subprime loans declined as the rate of increase in housing prices began to decline. For example, subordinated tranches grew to account for a larger share of the pool's value as mortgage credit risk increased from 2001 to 2005. As the housing market peaked in 2005 and 2006, however, subordinated tranches' share declined significantly.[60] According to Clayton Holdings LLC, a firm that reviews mortgage loans on behalf of investment firms intending to securitize them, the percentage of loans that met the investment firms' own underwriting standards fell from 54 percent to 47 percent between January 2006 and June 2007; the substandard mortgages were nevertheless securitized.[61]

The propensity of lenders to take shortcuts with respect to borrower quality could, of course, be ameliorated if potential buyers of the securitizations performed adequate due diligence and demanded quality of issuers. Such due diligence would help mitigate faults in the debt rating system. But due diligence is less likely to be exercised if:

(1) the initial buyer can resell the products, perhaps by incorporating them into a new product;

(2) the products are complex and lack transparency;

(3) the buyers are less sophisticated than the sellers or have less information about the underlying assets;
(4) the prevailing market environment is benign, encouraging complacency about risk; and/or
(5) the differences between the rates on riskier and less risky or riskless investments are narrowing to such an extent that investors prioritize yields at the expense of risk reduction.

Unfortunately, securitization, which made subprime mortgage lending possible, also strengthened each of these barriers to due diligence.

CHAPTER 12

# Weapons of Mass Destruction[1]

*"When I read prospectuses for CDO and CDO-squared deals, I felt as if I were reading comic books."*

**—Janet Tavakoli[2]**

As Chapter 11 discussed, the actions of the Federal Reserve Board (the Fed) and the credit raters, among other agents, contributed to the 2007–2008 credit crisis. But the nexus of the crisis was the residential housing market and, in particular, the subprime sector of the housing market. This is clear from the way in which the crisis unfolded.

The centrality of the subprime market to the crisis itself and its economic consequences is somewhat surprising. After all, residential investment represented just 6.3 percent of US gross domestic product (GDP) in the middle of the decade; the subprime portion of that was considerably less. How could such a small part of the economy create such huge problems for the whole economy? The answer lies in the way in which the risk of mortgage lending—in particular, the risk of lending to subprime borrowers—was extended and magnified via novel financial instruments. These instruments seemed to reduce the credit risk of subprime loans while offering yields above those available from similarly rated instruments. Unfortunately, these perceptions would prove to be illusory.

## MORTGAGES

With a mortgage, a homebuyer takes out a loan from a bank or other mortgage originator. The mortgage lender, rather than receiving a lump-sum payment of principal at the end of the term of the mortgage, as would be the case with a bond, receives from the homebuyer monthly payments that represent both a payment of interest for use of the money and a payment of principal that reduces the amount of the loan.

Mortgages contain embedded, or implicit, options. Assume, for instance, that a homebuyer borrows $300,000 to purchase a $350,000 house, and the house subsequently declines in value to $250,000. If the principal payments made have been less than $50,000, the borrower now owes more than the house is worth. The mortgage is said to be "underwater." Unless there is some reason to expect that the home's value will soon rise above the principal owed, the homebuyer may decide to just walk away, rather than make further payments on the property. That is, the homebuyer may default on the mortgage. The ability to default in effect gives the mortgage borrower a put option; the borrower can "put" the house back to the mortgage lender.

The mortgage borrower may also have a call option if refinancing is permitted. If the value of the house increases from $350,000 to $400,000, say, the borrower can arrange to borrow an amount larger than the original $300,000, pay off the original $300,000 mortgage, and take in cash the difference between the old and new loans. Even if the house does not increase in value, but interest rates decline, the homebuyer can refinance to obtain a mortgage at a lower mortgage rate, benefiting from the difference between the old and new, lower, monthly mortgage payments.

Mortgages have for various reasons proved to be popular ingredients for a number of financial innovations over the last 40 or so years. They have played a major role in a veritable alphabet soup of financial products—mortgage-backed securities (MBS), collateralized debt obligations (CDOs), structured investment vehicles (SIVs), asset-backed commercial paper (ABCP) conduits, credit default swaps (CDS), and synthetic CDOs.

## MBS

MBS—mortgage-backed securities—are a form of asset-backed security. An asset-backed security (ABS) is a security whose value is based on an underlying pool of assets. A bank, for example, may pool many hundreds or even thousands of loans it has made or purchased and sell to investors notes that entitle the buyer to a specified share of the payments on the loans. The loans may be credit-card loans, corporate loans, mortgage loans, student loans, car loans, and other sorts of loans.

Securitizing loans in this way has potential advantages for both borrowers and lenders. The lender receives funds that can be used for further investments, including more loans, and lays off the credit risk associated with the loans. A bank that pools, securitizes, and sells its loans receives up front the proceeds from the sale, whether or not the underlying borrowers default. The credit risk, the risk of default, is essentially passed from the lender to the buyers of the securities. Securitization may also provide a profit for the securitizing lender if the underlying assets can be sold for more than their worth or cost.

Although MBS were developed and sold in the 1970s by US banks, they were most widely used, starting in the 1980s, by entities backed or sponsored by the US government. The Federal Home Loan Mortgage Corporation (Freddie Mac) and the Federal National Mortgage Association (Fannie Mae) facilitate residential mortgage lending by purchasing from mortgage originators residential mortgages that meet certain size and quality standards. The purchases provide loan originators with more funds for further lending, and they helped to increase the percentage of home ownership in the nation from 63.5 percent to 69.2 percent over the 1985 to 2004 period.[3]

Fannie Mae and Freddie Mac purchase mortgages from private lenders, pool them, and issue securities entitling investors to principal and interest payments on the pools; they also purchase MBS from private issuers. While sponsored and overseen by the US government, they are stockholder-owned corporations with publicly traded shares. They guarantee the timely payment of interest and principal on the securities they issue, but the guarantee was not, until 2008, actually backed by US government resources. Most investors, however, assumed an implicit guarantee, so securities issued by Fannie Mae and Freddie Mac were also viewed as virtually riskless in terms of credit exposure.

The most basic form of MBS passes through to the buyers interest and principal payments on a pro rata basis. More complex structures carve up the payments on the mortgages in various ways so as to create securities with a variety of different cash flows that appeal to different investment needs. For example, payments may be divided between interest payments, principal payments, and prepayments.

## MBS via SPV

Banks and other non-government entities issuing MBS are called "private-label issuers." Private-label issuers may originate mortgages through lending or may purchase mortgages from mortgage originators, thus funding originators' loans. Issuers typically use borrowed funds to purchase at least some portion of the loans they use for securitization.

For MBS, mortgages are pooled and then usually sold to a special purpose vehicle (SPV)—a special purpose entity or a special purpose company. An SPV is a trust created by the MBS sponsor, but it is legally separate from the sponsor. Its sole purpose is to buy the loans from the sponsor and to create from them MBS to sell to investors. Exhibit 12.1 provides an illustration.

Mortgages sold to an SPV are transferred off the balance sheet of the bank or other business that made or bought the mortgage loans and sponsored their securitization. The sponsor has no responsibility for or recourse to the assets transferred, nor would its bankruptcy affect the value of the assets transferred. The assets are used as collateral for the MBS, which are sold to investors, including banks, insurance companies, mutual funds, pension funds, and hedge funds.

**EXHIBIT 12.1**

Securitization Through a Special Purpose Vehicle (SPV)

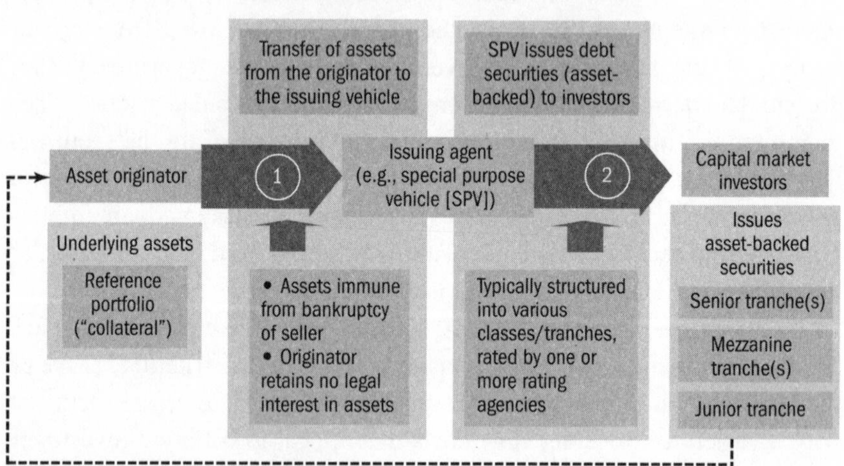


Source: Andreas Jobst, "What Is Securitization?" *Finance and Development: A Quarterly Magazine of the IMF* 45, no. 3 (2008): 48.

There are a number of motivations for securitizing mortgage loans in this manner. Securitization replaces illiquid assets, such as mortgage loans, with cash from the sale of the securities, which may be used for further investment. Securitization has historically proved to be a cheaper source of funding than alternatives, such as the issuance of corporate bonds.[4]

Furthermore, by removing assets, such as mortgages, from the sponsor's balance sheet, securitization may reduce balance sheet risk. Commercial banks are subject to regulations governing the amount of capital they must hold in relation to the value of the assets on their balance sheets. A higher ratio of assets to equity capital represents higher leverage, and more leverage is generally riskier than less leverage. Without the ability to transfer assets off the balance sheet, the bank would at some point need to either raise more capital or curtail lending and other investment activities.

Investment banks are also subject to capital requirements that limit their leverage, although these are looser than the requirements for commercial banks. Even less-regulated entities, such as hedge funds, will maintain some safety cushion of capital to protect themselves, their investors, and creditors from unexpected adverse movements in asset values.

Securitization via an SPV has the potential to increase the profitability of its sponsor. Everything else equal, transfer of loans to the SPV increases profitability as measured by return on capital, as the same amount of capital can essentially support an expansion of potential profits.

Borrowers and investors can also benefit from securitization. For borrowers, the benefit may come in the form of lower borrowing costs and expanded mortgage availability. Inasmuch as securitization increases the funds available for lending and appears to reduce the risk of lending, lenders may be willing to lend more, at lower rates, when securitization is available.

Investors in MBS benefit to the extent that securitization gives them access to investments that would otherwise be unavailable to them. Even for many institutional investors, investments in whole mortgages would be too expensive, too illiquid, and too undiversified to be suitable; these impediments are not present with MBS. The pooling of the mortgages underlying an MBS also has diversification benefits for the purchasers. The risk of default by one or a few borrowers is diluted within a pool of numerous individual loans to numerous entities, perhaps in various types of business and spread over various localities. The effects of default by one borrower are statistically likely to be mitigated by a large number of otherwise healthy loans. Pooling diversifies the specific, or idiosyncratic, risk of the individual mortgages in the MBS.

The primary risk-reducing mechanism of the MBS, however, is not risk sharing (diversification) but rather risk shifting. This is accomplished via a further step in the securitization process: tranching the cash flows from the underlying mortgage pool to create classes of MBS with different exposures to default risk. Tranching produces structured securitization.

## Tranching

Mortgage default risk is shifted via tranching (see Exhibit 12.2). With tranching, the payments on the underlying mortgage pool—and any associated losses on them—are directed to three basic categories of securities, called tranches, each of which offers a different payoff and exposure to default risk. At the top, the senior tranche offers the lowest interest rates and is the least risky because it is protected from loss by the tranches below it; it is the first to receive cash flows from the underlying mortgage pool. As such, it is the last tranche to incur losses and the first to be paid down.[5]

Cash flows not required for paying the promised interest on the senior tranche then flow to the next-most-senior tranche, and so on until all the cash flows from the mortgage pool have been distributed. Any losses are absorbed first by the bottom, or equity, tranche; if losses totally erode that tranche, further losses are directed to the next-lowest tranche, and so on. The equity tranche is the riskiest, but if the underlying assets perform well, this tranche can offer high returns. The mezzanine tranche falls between the senior tranche and the equity tranche in terms of both risk and return.

For residential mortgage-backed securities (RMBS) exposed to subprime loans, tranching is particularly important as a means of converting the inherently risky mortgage loans into tranches with top credit ratings. Most of the credit risk of the underlying assets is assumed by lower-rated tranches. The protection afforded by tranching is usually supplemented by overcollateralization and excess spread. Overcollateralization means that the security's assets exceed its liabilities; the equity tranche may be

**EXHIBIT 12.2**

Tranching Mortgage Pools

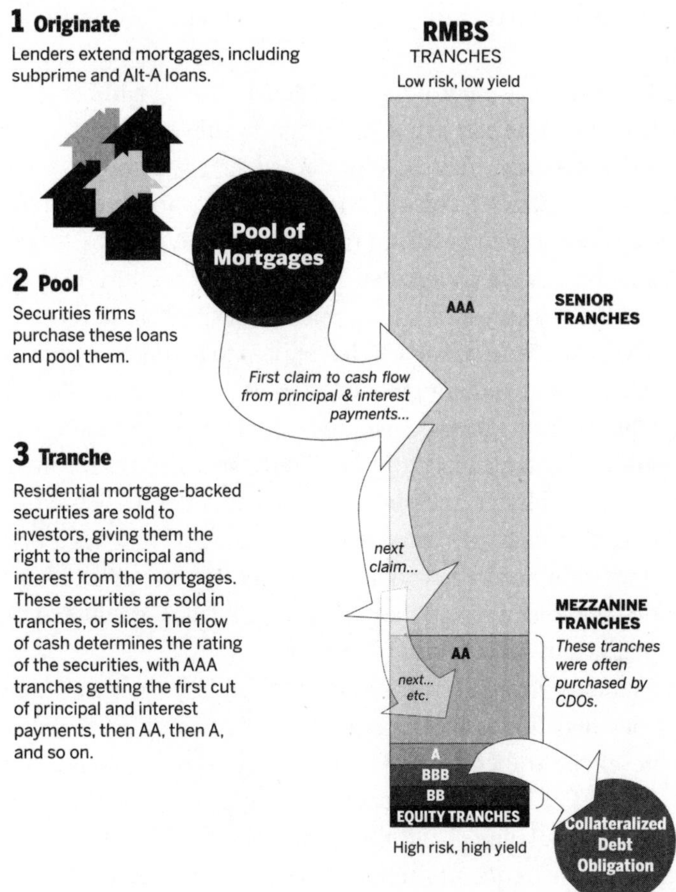


Source: Financial Crisis Inquiry Commission, *The Financial Crisis Inquiry Report: Final Report of the National Commission on the Causes of the Financial and Economic Crisis in the United States (Financial Crisis Inquiry Commission)* (New York: PublicAffairs, 2011): 73.

retained by the sponsor of the securitization to provide the overcollateralization. Excess spread means that the interest payments on the underlying mortgages are expected to exceed the payments offered to the purchasers of the tranches, as well as any anticipated expenses.

Tranching aims to create from the same pool of underlying assets a range of securities with different risk-return tradeoffs. The equity tranche, for example, may be designed to absorb up to a 2 percent loss on the underlying pool of mortgages. The mezzanine tranche may be designed to absorb a level of losses between 2 percent and 5 percent. The senior tranche may be considered safe unless pool losses rise over 5 percent.

Each basic tranche may be subdivided into any number of subdivisions. It became common after 2005, for example, to extract from the most senior tranche an even more protected super-senior tranche. Different tranches may also be designed to offer fixed or floating rates, or to absorb cash inflows or losses from mortgage prepayments.

Decisions on how to tranche an RMBS are guided by various objectives. One of the primary aims is to achieve a desired credit rating. Related concerns are to structure tranches that appeal to given investor clienteles. Some investors—for example, money market funds—can only buy assets that have the highest ratings. Insurance companies, pension funds, and certain mutual funds can usually hold only securities with investment-grade ratings (rated BBB- and above, or the equivalent). Hedge funds may be willing to take on the greater risk of the lowest tranches in exchange for more uncertain but higher yields. Demand for one or another tranche may rise or fall depending on the yields the tranches are able to offer and the risk appetites of investors.

At the same time, issuers are looking to satisfy their own needs. For example, they may not be able to sell all tranches created from a mortgage pool. Some of the tranches may be too risky; some may not offer high enough yields. The pieces that cannot be sold may have to be retained on the sponsor's balance sheet. Over the period of the real estate boom and bust, the most frequently retained tranches seemed to shift from the equity tranche to the top-rated AAA tranches. Sponsors have to consider the extra capital reserves they will have to hold to support any tranche or tranches on their balance sheets. As riskier holdings require more capital, sponsors generally aim to minimize the risk, or alternatively the size, of the tranches they expect to retain.

The sum of these considerations results in top-heavy RMBS constructions (see Exhibit 12.3). Issuers aim to put into top-rated tranches as much of the underlying value of the pool as is consistent with the standards of the credit rating agencies. Some 70 percent to 80 percent or more of a typical subprime RMBS, more for a prime, might be AAA-rated, with

**EXHIBIT 12.3**

Typical Subprime Residential Mortgage-Backed Security (RMBS) Structure

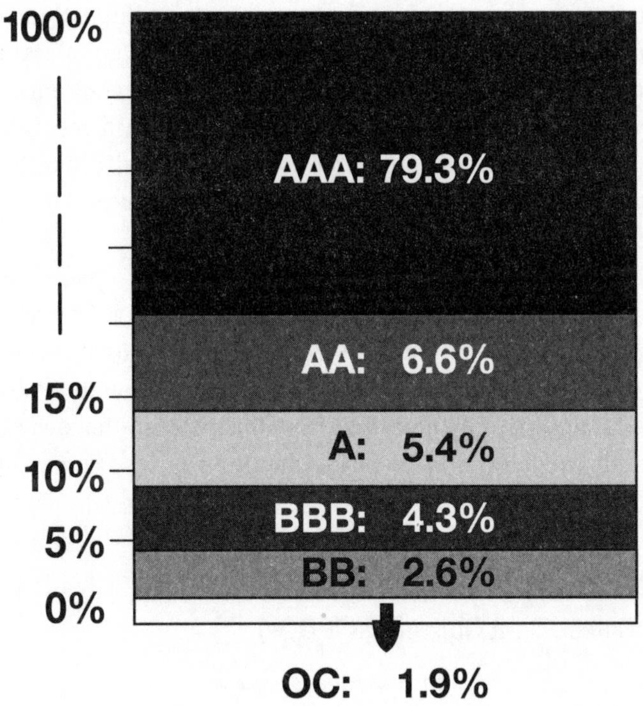


Note: OC = overcollateralization.

Source: Adam B. Ashcraft and Til Schuermann, "Understanding the Securitization of Subprime Mortgage Credit," *Foundations and Trends in Finance* 2, no. 3 (2008).

the equity tranche constituting as little as 1 percent to 2 percent of the pool's value.

Tranching shifts risk within the RMBS structure and allows for the transformation of subprime underlying mortgages into AAA-rated senior tranches and BBB-rated mezzanine tranches, with a small, unrated equity tranche supposedly bearing the brunt of the risk. The sale of the tranches shifts the risk of the underlying mortgages, particularly the risk of default, from the seller to the investor. Tranching shifts the risk from buyers of the top-rated tranches to buyers of subordinate tranches.

## CDOs

RMBS may be pooled and tranched to create collateralized debt obligations (CDOs) (see Exhibit 12.4). In the United States, CDOs that hold RMBS and other structured securitizations are technically referred to as ABS CDOs; we will simply call them CDOs. The collateral pools for CDOs may be a mixture of different kinds of securitized products backed by high-yield bonds, corporate bank loans, credit-card receivables, and car loans, as well as residential and commercial real estate loans. The RMBS in CDOs may include subprime, Alt-A, and jumbo loans, as well as prime loans.

Like RMBS, CDOs represent a pool of underlying assets carved into tranches of differing risk-return profiles. Banks, insurance companies, or asset managers such as mutual funds and hedge funds may provide the pools, which, again, are carved up and sold mostly through SPVs. As with RMBS, the risk of a CDO is shifted from the upper to the lower tranches. Also, the sale of CDOs facilitates a higher level of investment and return on equity for CDO sponsors.

EXHIBIT 12.4

Collateralized Debt Obligations (CDOs)

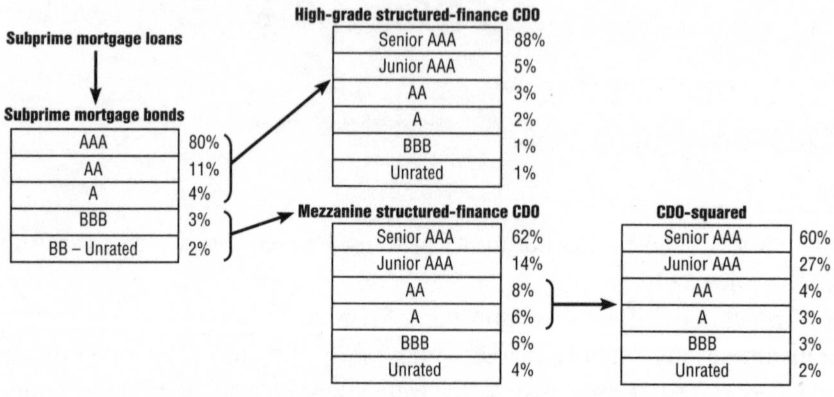


Note: CDO = collateralized debt obligation.

Source: International Monetary Fund, "Global Financial Stability Report: Containing Systemic Risks and Restoring Financial Soundness" (Washington, DC: IMF, 2008): 60. Available at http://www.imf.org/external/pubs/ft/gfsr/2008/01/index.htm.

CDOs may differ in the manner in which they operate. One of the most important distinctions is between a cash CDO and a synthetic CDO. Cash CDOs rely on actual assets that have been purchased by the sponsor; synthetic CDOs duplicate exposure to such assets by using credit derivatives. Synthetic CDOs are described in more detail below. There are also hybrid CDOs, which combine cash and synthetic assets. Some CDOs during the housing bubble also funded higher-rated tranches through the issuance of commercial paper, rather than by sales of notes.

CDOs expand upon the diversification, risk-shifting, and liquidity-enhancing powers of RMBS. Because a CDO generally combines different types of credit instruments, a CDO pool may be viewed as even more diversified, and more protected from specific credit instrument risk, than an RMBS pool. In the credit crisis, however, CDO securitization resulted in increased risk for investors.

One type of CDO that became particularly popular in the mid 2000s combined mezzanine RMBS tranches and sometimes other ABS to produce a preponderance of securities with AAA ratings. For example, a tranche representing 5 percent of the initial face value of a given RMBS collateral pool (subordinate to 70 percent to 90 percent of that pool's value) was combined with like tranches, and 70 percent to 80 percent of this new pool was turned into an AAA-rated tranche. This process of retranching can theoretically go on forever. CDOs can also pool tranches of other CDOs to create a $CDO^2$ (CDO-squared) or $CDO^3$ (CDO-cubed). Sometimes they did.

## ABCP CONDUITS AND SIVs

Asset-backed commercial paper (ABCP) conduits and structured investment vehicles (SIVs) operated by banks and other financial and commercial entities fund the purchase and retention, or warehousing, of mortgages and mortgage securitizations. ABCP conduits and SIVs sell short-term commercial paper (CP) and medium-term notes, which promise to pay holders a specified amount at a given date after issuance, generally 30 days to a year for CP and one to 10 years for medium-term notes (see Exhibit 12.5).

ABCP conduits and SIVs are unlike RMBS and CDOs in that they do not transfer credit risk to note buyers; the assets in ABCP conduits and

**EXHIBIT 12.5**

## Asset-Backed Commercial Paper (ABCP) Conduits and Structured Investment Vehicles (SIVs)

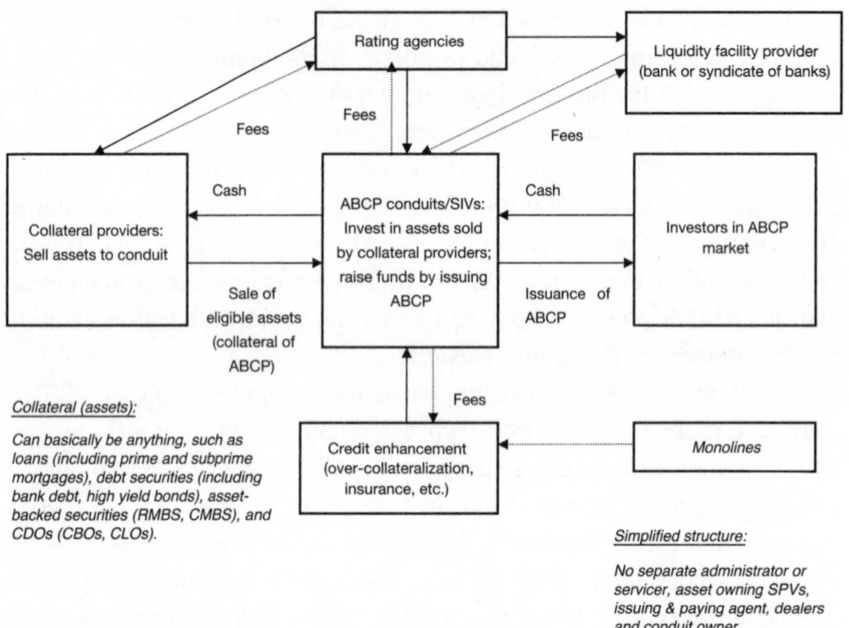


Source: Sarai Criado and Adrian Van Rixtel, "Structured Finance and the Financial Turmoil of 2007–2008: An Introductory Overview," Banco De España Occasional Paper Series 0808, September 2, 2008: 21.

SIVs are retained to serve as collateral for the notes sold. They do, however, allow for the removal of exposure to credit risk from sponsor balance sheets, and a consequent reduction in sponsor capital requirements.

The sale of commercial paper (CP) is essentially equivalent to borrowing at a short-term rate equal to the rate offered the CP buyers. Because short-term rates are generally lower than long-term rates, as risk is assumed for a shorter period of time, the short-term rates paid on CP are generally lower than the rates received on the collateral assets. The transactions are generally accomplished via an SPV, so that the assets are not on the sponsoring bank's balance sheet and do not affect the firm's capital requirements.

One risk is that the cash flow on the assets serving as collateral will unexpectedly decline, threatening payments to CP holders. In that case, existing holders may sustain losses and future payments may face cuts.

Under such conditions, demand for the CP may dry up, putting even more pressure on the collateral assets.

Several practices mitigate this risk. ABCP conduits generally purchase only investment-grade assets. Furthermore, ABCP conduits usually have explicit full or partial recourse to their sponsors' balance sheets. That is, if the cash flow from the assets is not sufficient to pay off existing CP holders, the sponsor will provide the necessary funds. Explicit guarantees appear on the sponsor's balance sheet and are subject to capital requirements. ABCP conduits may also have specified minimum values for the assets in the SPV, which, if hit, trigger liquidation of the assets and payoffs to CP holders.

SIVs are somewhat similar to ABCP conduits, but differ in some important respects. The assets they hold, including RMBS and CDOs, tend to be riskier than those in ABCP conduits. This is particularly true of SIV-lites, which emerged at the height of the housing bubble. SIV-lites were heavily invested in subprime RMBS and CDOs containing subprime RMBS, especially mezzanine-level tranches.[6]

SIVs generally do not explicitly offer full recourse to the sponsoring bank. A typical SIV liquidity backstop may cover 5 percent to 10 percent of the issued CP and notes.[7] Recourse for investors in SIV-lites is even more precarious. To offset the greater risk of their assets, SIVs typically issue medium-term notes along with shorter-term CP, which somewhat reduces the risk that they will be unable to make the payments for CP and note holders. SIV-lites, however, are more dependent on CP, although they are also generally less leveraged than SIVs, which at the time of the crisis had assets of 12 to 14.5 times capital.[8]

## CDS

Credit default swaps (CDS) are by far the most common form of credit derivatives. The seller of a CDS (aka the protection seller) agrees to "make whole" the buyer of the contract (the protection buyer) if the latter suffers because a default or other specified credit event (e.g., missed payment) causes a loss in the specified notional amount of the underlying asset referenced in the contract. For this protection, the buyer pays the seller a periodic premium equaling a certain percentage of the notional value of the reference asset, which may be a debt issue, a tranche, or an index.

The seller of a CDS is, somewhat confusingly, "the investor," as it is the party that is taking on exposure to credit risk. The seller thus has a long position, just as an investor who buys stock has a long position exposed to market risk; and the value of the position reflects the behavior of the reference asset. The protection buyer, conversely, has a short position. The typical CDS at the time of the crisis was a bilateral agreement between two parties, one usually a dealer, and hence largely unregulated.

While practices vary across contracts, it is not uncommon for CDS buyers to demand some collateral from sellers at the outset of the contract, in order to reduce the risk that the protection seller will not be able to make up or cover losses. The amount of collateral might depend upon the credit quality of the protection seller, as well as the riskiness of the reference asset. In addition, CDS contracts often require mark-to-market payments from seller to buyer, or buyer to seller, as the creditworthiness of the reference asset changes, affecting its value.

During the housing boom, monoline insurance companies (monolines) were one of the largest sellers of CDS. Monolines are so called because their business focuses on insuring debt, particularly municipal bonds. Their insurance of such bonds comes in the form of financial guarantees subject to insurance regulations and to, albeit low, capital requirements. Monolines also began to offer protection on highly rated tranches of RMBS and CDOs, often by selling CDS on these ABS. These CDS were not subject to insurance regulation or capital controls.

The purchaser of a CDS does not have to have an insurable interest in the protected asset. That is, the CDS buyer does not have to own the reference asset to purchase insurance on it. The buyer will nevertheless benefit if the creditworthiness of the reference asset declines, increasing the value of the buyer's short position and resulting in margin payments from the CDS seller, even if the buyer has experienced no actual losses. Conversely, the seller may benefit if the credit quality of the reference asset improves.

In January 2006, a group of dealers and Markit Group introduced the Markit ABX.HE index—which is really a series of indexes, with a new one introduced every six months. Each index tracks the CDS on a given basket of subprime RMBS tranches. The basket contains 20 tranches of each of six different investment-grade credit ratings. Markit shortly afterward introduced individual indexes on the variously rated tranches.

The index buyer pays the seller a monthly premium equal to a percentage of the prevailing principal of the underlying RMBS, with the seller offering protection in the form of reimbursements for write-downs and reductions in principal affecting the RMBS over the period. Banks, hedge funds, and other investors can trade CDS indexes to hedge mortgage-related positions or to speculate on the direction of the mortgage market. The indexes thus function as instruments for trading credit risk, and their prices provide an indication of investor sentiment about subprime investments.[9]

## Synthetic CDOs

Instead of using instruments like RMBS tranches, synthetic CDOs use CDS that reference specified underlying tranches of RMBS and other ABS (see Exhibit 12.6). Investors can take long or short positions on each tranche. Short investors pay the SPV premiums in exchange for credit protection on the referenced tranches they have shorted. Funded investors hold long positions; they provide the SPV cash in exchange for payments equivalent to the principal and interest payments on given referenced tranches. Of course, if these tranches do not perform well, these investors may take a loss on their investment. The SPV invests the cash received from these long investors in highly rated assets, which may be used if necessary to pay the short investors (the protection buyers). There may also be unfunded investors, who take a long position. They receive premiums from the CDO; instead of making cash payments to the SPV, however, they agree to reimburse protection buyers, if necessary. They are essentially selling protection to the SPV and, through it, to the short investors.

The synthetic CDO has several advantages over a cash CDO. It does not transfer loan assets off the sponsor's balance sheet. In fact, the sponsor may not actually own such assets; it can design a CDS structure that creates exposure to given underlying tranches, whether it owns them or not. A synthetic CDO is thus not reliant on a specific underlying asset being available for purchase.

Furthermore, a synthetic CDO does not have to be fully funded. It became common practice for sponsors to create so-called super-senior tranches for synthetic CDOs. With a super-senior tranche, the sponsor of the SPV offering the synthetic CDO retains most of the AAA tranche,

**EXHIBIT 12.6**

## Synthetic Collateralized Debt Obligations (CDOs)

*Synthetic CDOs, such as Goldman Sachs's Abacus 2004-1 deal, were complex paper transactions involving credit default swaps.*

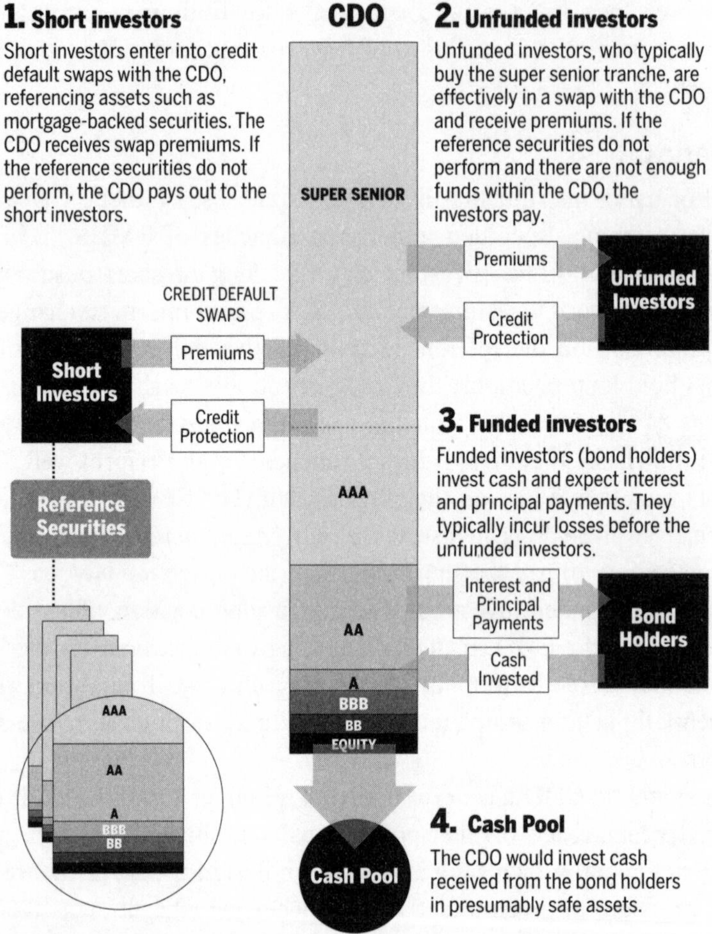


Source: Financial Crisis Inquiry Commission, *The Financial Crisis Inquiry Report: Final Report of the National Commission on the Causes of the Financial and Economic Crisis in the United States (Financial Crisis Inquiry Commission)* (New York: PublicAffairs, 2011).

together with the income from it. This super-senior retained tranche would be considered very safe, hence require little capital against its balance sheet value. The sponsor could also purchase protection in the form of a CDS. Because of the perceived safety of the tranche, the cost of the CDS would be low, often below the income expected from holding the super-senior tranche.[10]

CDS essentially provided a means for market participants to bet on the performances of existing mortgages and mortgage securities during the housing boom and bust. They did not contribute directly to the origination of new mortgages. They did, however, magnify losses when mortgage holders began defaulting. They did so because the total notional value of CDS on a given reference asset was much greater than the value of the underlying asset itself, as there could be many CDS referring to the same underlying asset. One $38 million subprime MBS created in June 2006 was included, via CDS, in more than 30 debt pools and ended up causing losses of $280 million.[11]

## SHIFTING RISKS

Instruments like RMBS, CDOs, and SIVs shifted risk from lenders to investors, while CDS appeared to provide an ultimate backstop at the end of the line—the final destination for the risk of loss resulting from defaults on mortgages. One point that seems to have been forgotten in this long chain of products, however, is that shifting risk does not eliminate risk, or even reduce it; it may actually increase risk. Many have made this mistake over the years, and some have suffered disastrous consequences. Portfolio insurance in 1987 and the unwinding of Long-Term Capital Management's arbitrage strategies in 1998 provide two salient examples. (See also Appendix D, "Derivatives Disasters in the 1990s.")

Diversification by pooling of mortgage loans may reduce the lender's, or investor's, exposure to a specific geographic area, and combining RMBS with other types of debt in a CDO may further reduce exposure to subprime loans. For the most part, however, the underlying systematic risk represented by housing-price declines was merely shifted from borrower to lender, from one tranche to another, from lender to investor, from investor to insurer. Although opaque, the risk remained, and it eventually almost brought down the banking system and the economy.

CHAPTER 13

# Securitization and the Housing Bubble

*" 'I want a clean cup,' interrupted the Hatter: 'let's all move one place on.' He moved on as he spoke, and the Dormouse followed him: the March Hare moved into the Dormouse's place, and Alice rather unwillingly took the place of the March Hare. The Hatter was the only one who got any advantage from the change; and Alice was a good deal worse off than before. . . ."*

**—Lewis Carroll**[1]

By 2001, US home prices had been increasing steadily since 1997. At this time, however, lower-priced homes began to rise at a faster rate than higher-priced homes; Exhibit 13.1 shows the pattern for Boston, which is representative of the national trends for low-, mid- and high-priced homes. Subprime originations, roughly \$190 billion in 2001, grew to \$231 billion in 2002, \$335 billion in 2003, \$540 billion in 2004, and peaked at \$625 billion in 2005.[2] As a share of all US residential mortgage originations, subprime loans grew from about 7 percent in 2001 to 20 percent in 2005.[3]

Not coincidentally, the increasing rate of subprime mortgage origination was accompanied by an increasing rate of securitization of subprime loans. Some 40 percent of the subprime loans originated in 2001 were packaged into residential mortgage-backed securities (RMBS); the rate of securitization increased to 53 percent, 58 percent, 67 percent, and 74 percent in the years 2002 through 2005.[4] The growth of subprime lending was dependent on the increasingly intensive implementation of financial innovations such as RMBS, collateralized debt obligations (CDOs),

EXHIBIT 13.1

Home Price Index by Tier in Boston Area

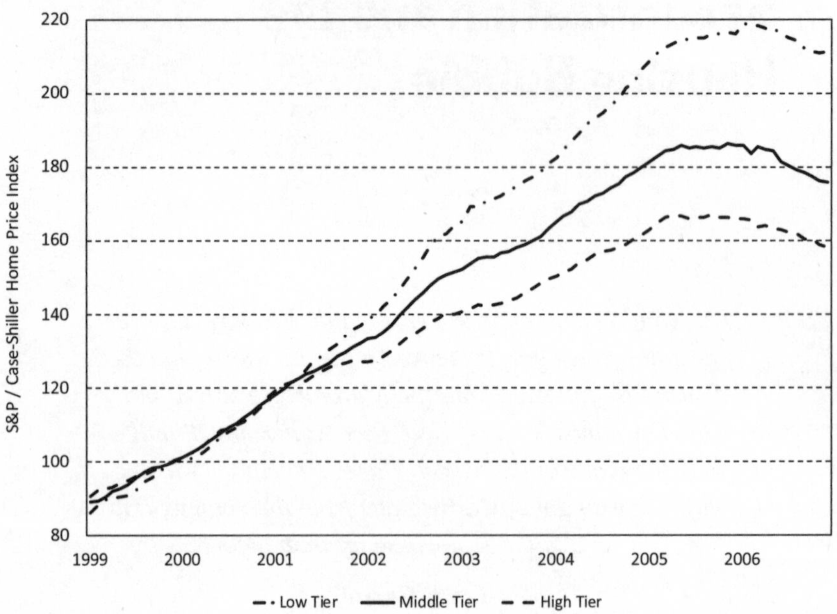


Note: Index Jan 2000 = 100

structured investment vehicles (SIVs), and credit default swaps (CDS). Much like portfolio insurance programs' sales of stock in the 1980s and the unwinding of Long-Term Capital Management's (LTCM's) highly leveraged arbitrage strategies in the 1990s, the instruments and mechanisms that manipulated the cash flows to and from mortgage loans formed a positive feedback system that magnified underlying market trends.

## A PRECURSOR

Subprime mortgage lending was enabled in the early 1980s by the passage of various US government laws that allowed mortgage lenders to charge higher rates and variable rates—the Depository Institutions Deregulation and Monetary Control Act of 1980 and the Alternative Mortgage Transaction Parity Act of 1982. As interest rates rose in 1994, mortgage lenders increasingly favored the subprime market to offset declining demand for prime loans.[5] Subprime loans were often funded by the issuance of mortgage-backed securities (MBS).

From 1995 through 1998, subprime origination grew from about $65 billion to about $150 billion, and the portion of subprime loans that were securitized rose from 28.4 percent to 55.1 percent.[6] In 1997, delinquencies and defaults on subprime loans had exceeded expectations. In addition, steep declines in emerging Asian markets created problems that developed into a full-blown flight to quality after the Russian debt default and LTCM rescue in 1998 (see Chapter 8, "Long-Term Capital Management"). Subprime loan origination continued to tick up in 1999, to $160 billion, but dropped off to $138 billion in 2000. The rate of securitization of subprime loans also dropped—to 37.4 percent in 1999 and 40.5 percent in 2000—as investors' appetite for subprime MBS declined.[7] Both origination and securitization of subprime picked up again in 2001.

The growth and decline of subprime lending in the 1990s presaged the problems that were to recur, on a much larger scale, in the following decade. Most notable, of course, was the growth and decline of mortgage securitization. Also apparent in both episodes was increasing concentration of the sources of subprime lending. The top 25 subprime originators had under 40 percent of the market in 1995, but by 2000 they controlled nearly 75 percent of the market, as many originators were bought by larger lenders that needed mortgages for their securitization businesses.[8] In 1998, as the securitization market peaked, First Union (later Wachovia) acquired the second-largest subprime lender, The Money Store, while insurance giant Conseco, Inc. purchased Green Tree Financial Group. By the end of 2001, The Money Store had closed and Conseco was bankrupt.

In the late 1990s, of course, problems in subprime lending were overshadowed, and to some extent offset, by the euphoria of the dot-com bubble. But the bursting of that bubble created the conditions that would allow the next surge in subprime lending.

## THE APPEAL OF SUBPRIME

Subprime mortgage lending is, by definition, riskier than prime lending. Borrowers generally have lower credit scores and make smaller down payments. What would induce mortgage lenders to take on this additional risk, and increase their exposure to it in the years following 2001?

Mortgage lenders may have believed that the risk of lending to subprime borrowers was declining. Defaults were relatively high for subprime mortgages issued in 2001 and 2002, and foreclosures on subprime properties in these years were two to four times their 1998 levels.[9] However, house prices were rising, and forecasts based on price indexes, at least before 2006, showed few indications of a letup.[10] As long as prices continued to increase, subprime borrowers unable to make loan payments could sell their houses for prices that would cover full repayment of the mortgages. Alternatively, lenders could foreclose on the loans and sell the houses at prices that fully reimbursed them.[11]

Mortgage lenders also charged subprime borrowers for bearing the added risks of subprime loans. Interest rates on subprime loans were, at the outset of the decade, at least two to three percentage points higher than prime rates.[12]

Lenders could also transfer the risk of default on subprime loans by selling the mortgages for securitization. Subprime loans could not generally be sold to the Federal National Mortgage Association (Fannie Mae) and the Federal Home Loan Mortgage Corporation (Freddie Mac), the major mortgage securitizers, because subprime loans did not meet the quality criteria required by these government-sponsored enterprises (GSEs). The MBS issued by the GSEs were perceived as virtually free of credit risk. This was not the case with securitizations issued by non-GSE entities, which did not enjoy the implicit backing of the US government. Securitizations backed by subprime loans would be considered especially risky, as the underlying loans were inherently riskier than prime loans. Financial products seemed to provide a solution. Subprime lenders could pool subprime loans and use structured securitization to create tranches that were considered to be virtually free of credit risk. Tranching transformed as much as 80 percent to 85 percent of a pool of subprime loans into AAA-rated notes.

The relatively higher rates paid on subprime mortgages allowed securitizers to offer AAA-rated tranches that paid investors higher rates than those available on many other similarly rated securities, including government debt and MBS collateralized primarily by higher-quality mortgages. For many investors, including banks, the combination of relatively high returns and seemingly low risk was too appealing to resist.

## Benefits of Securitization for Lenders

Financial institutions that purchased mortgage loans for securitization were often able to book a profit by reselling them to a special purpose vehicle (SPV) at a higher price. But even absent this incentive, securitization had return-enhancing and risk-reducing benefits.

As noted in the last chapter, and discussed further in the sidebar "Bank Capital Requirements," commercial banks are required to hold capital equal to a certain percentage of the assets on their balance sheets to limit their capacity to make leveraged investments. Improving a bank's capital position may require the sale of assets to pay down debt or the issuance of shares. By managing the assets on its balance sheet, a bank can minimize the capital it must retain and maximize its capacity to make leveraged investments.

Securitization allows banks to increase lending capacity. Under bank capital regulations, a bank has to hold capital equal to 4 percent of the value of a residential mortgage held on its balance sheet. However, some mortgage securities, when rated highly and hedged appropriately, might incur a capital charge of just 1.6 percent.[13] Thus holding mortgage securities, rather than mortgages themselves, requires less capital.

### BANK CAPITAL REQUIREMENTS

In 1974, the Bank for International Settlements (BIS), a coordinating body for central banks, invited representatives from 13 countries to its headquarters in Basel, Switzerland, to draw up a set of uniform standards for large, international depository institutions. The group established the Basel Committee on Banking Supervision, which adopted the Basel Capital Accord in 1988.

This agreement set an overall minimum capital requirement of 8 percent of a bank's assets, half of which was to be composed of Tier 1, or core, capital, which consists primarily of common and preferred equity and retained earnings. The agreement also created five categories of assets and allowed the capital requirement to be adjusted according to each category's risk level, as described below.

- Low-risk assets, such as cash, gold, and government-guaranteed debt of most developed nations, were given a risk weighting of zero and carried no capital charge.
- Debt issued by government-sponsored agencies, such as Fannie Mae and Freddie Mac, had a risk weighting of 20 percent. Holdings of those assets had to be backed by capital equal to 1.6 percent (20% of 8% capital charge) of the investment.
- Residential first mortgages and mortgage-backed securities had a 50 percent risk weighting and were assessed a 4 percent capital charge.
- Commercial loans had a 100 percent risk weighting and carried the full 8 percent charge.

The Basel Committee itself had no enforcement power and left it up to each participating country to adopt legislation implementing the agreement. The United States, which had begun to impose minimum capital requirements on its own in the early 1980s, signed on in 1992. Eventually, more than 100 countries adopted the accord,[14] and it was credited with helping to increase overall bank capital levels and with keeping bank failures to a minimum.

While the accord's risk-weighting scheme was a step forward from a simple one-size-fits-all rule, it still left room for banks to game the system. For example, the accord did not distinguish between AAA-rated bonds and those that were barely investment grade. By requiring the same capital charge regardless of rating, the accord inadvertently encouraged more risk taking since lower-rated bonds would be expected to yield more than higher-rated bonds. It also encouraged banks to securitize their assets and thus remove them from their balance sheets.

The accord rewarded other types of off-balance-sheet maneuvers. For example, capital charges did not apply to so-called "liquidity facilities"—loan guarantees made to off-balance-sheet entities—that involved a commitment of less than a year, so banks created renewable liquidity facilities with 364-day maturities.[15] In addition, the accord provided for no specific charges related to operational risks, such as fraud, poor accounting, or bad management, even though they can cause bank failures. Also, the accord made no attempt to account for liquidity risk.

**BASEL II**

The Basel Committee went back to work in 1998 to address concerns that the banking system had grown too large and complex to be governed by the rudimentary accords of a decade earlier, even though they had been modified a dozen times since then. The new standards, dubbed Basel II, were published in 2004.

The revised accord maintained the 8 percent baseline capital charge, but more elaborate systems for risk weighting made the new rules more subjective. The original five asset categories were expanded into a matrix of classifications that, for the first time, tied capital charges to letter-grade ratings assigned by recognized credit rating agencies. The higher an asset's rating within a category, the lower the capital charge. Basel II also permitted the largest banks to use their own internal risk models, as long as the models were approved and closely supervised by regulators. This approach was perceived as innovative at the time but later proved to be a Pandora's box.

Basel II also tightened rules on the use of liquidity facilities and required proof that "significant credit risk" had been transferred by securitization and sale to a third party before capital charges could be reduced. It included explicit capital charges for operational risks and tried to foster greater regulation by market forces through expanded public disclosure of details about the amount and type of capital held by a bank and the types of risk exposures it faced, both on and off the balance sheet.

Many countries had not yet implemented the Basel II standards by the time the 2007–2008 credit crisis erupted. Early adopters Hong Kong and Japan put the new regime in place in 2007, and the European Union (EU) followed in 2008. In the United States, fewer than a dozen of the largest banks began to phase in compliance with Basel II in 2009.

Securitization, of course, could also be used to remove relatively risky mortgage loans entirely from the balance sheet. Doing so would replace risky assets with the riskless cash proceeds from their sale. Basically, in a very simplified setting, the bank's balance sheet would be restored to what it had been before the mortgage loan was made. The bank could thus extend another mortgage loan, which it could securitize, enabling it to make another loan, and on and on. Securitization preserved the banks' ability to lend, increasing leverage in the financial system.

At the same time, securitization allowed commercial banks to control their balance-sheet leverage ratios. The balance-sheet ratio of assets to capital of US commercial banks declined slightly over the 2000–2005 period,[16] thanks to the banks' ability to remove assets, including subprime loans, from their balance sheets by selling them to SPVs. Investment banks, which didn't face capital requirements as strict as those on commercial banks, increased their leverage during this time.

Moving assets, including mortgage loans, off balance sheets also enabled banks to increase profitability measures such as return on capital. In effect, securitization increased the amount of potentially profitable investments the bank could make while leaving unchanged the amount of capital underlying those returns. Securitization thus leveraged bank profitability.

While securitization allowed commercial banks to maintain their leverage ratios by moving assets off balance sheet, it allowed investment banks to beef up their balance sheets with assets. Investment banks did not have to restrict their balance-sheet asset growth to the same extent commercial banks did, but they did need high-quality assets they could use as collateral for short-term borrowing in the repurchase (repo) market.[17] Tranches of AAA-rated securitizations filled this bill, and they could either be created by investment banks themselves or be purchased from other sponsors, including commercial banks.

Banks and other securitizers did not securitize all loans; nor did they remove from their balance sheets every part of every loan they securitized. The high-risk equity tranches of subprime securitizations, for example, were frequently retained by sponsors because it was difficult to find investors to take on these risky tranches. Even when the high-risk equity tranche had to be retained, however, securitization was usually worthwhile. It allowed for profits from the sale of the securities, relief from capital requirements, and potentially higher return on capital. Furthermore, the equity tranche typically made up a very small portion of a loan pool, from under 5 percent to perhaps as much as 10 percent, so maintaining it on the balance sheet was usually not too onerous a burden.

The banks, hedge funds, and others that performed the work of tranching and selling the tranches collected substantial fees. Citigroup, with fees of 0.4 percent to 2.5 percent on securitizations of more than $20 billion in 2005, up from $6.3 billion in 2003, reportedly made hundreds of millions of dollars in fees in 2005 alone.[18] Merrill Lynch earned fees of 1 percent to 1.5 percent of deal value, up to $15 million for a typical $1 billion deal.[19] Other securitizers, especially Lehman Brothers, Bear Stearns, and the Royal Bank of Scotland, fared similarly.[20]

Securitization was thus a lucrative business that offered risk and return benefits for sponsors, dealers, and investors. Securitization of subprime mortgages was particularly attractive. It allowed lenders and investors to take advantage of rising house prices. It provided higher interest rates than available in other mortgage sectors. Also, it faced essentially no direct competition from the mortgage-securitizing giants, Fannie Mae and Freddie Mac. See Exhibits 13.2 through 13.4, which provide a sample of the hype-filled print advertisements run by banks, mortgage brokers, and realtors—with claims such as "Bad Credit? No Problem!," "No Income, No Assets," and "No Documentation OK!"—to entice borrowers to fill the demand of securitizers for non-agency loans.

**EXHIBIT 13.2**

Bad Credit? No Problem!

EXHIBIT 13.3

No Income, No Assets

EXHIBIT 13.4

No Documentation OK!

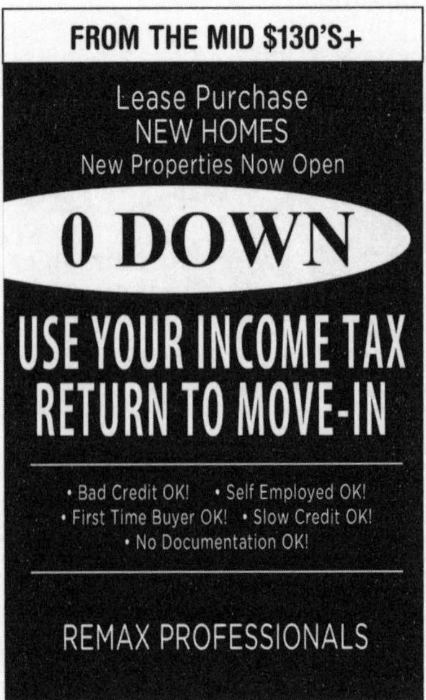

When firms such as Bank of America, HSBC, and UBS were reporting profits of $11 billion to $16 billion in 2005, largely from partnering with subprime mortgage instruments, it would have been extremely difficult for other CEOs to resist the music and tell shareholders to settle for much lower returns. In fact, UBS's postmortem of its 2007 write-down on subprime investments noted that the consultant it had retained in 2005 to hone the firm's broad business plan had recommended "that UBS selectively invest in developing certain areas of its business to close key product gaps, including in Credit, Rates, MBS Subprime and Adjustable Rate Mortgage products . . ."[21]

## SINGING IN THE RAIN

Delinquency rates on subprime mortgages during the first half of the 2000s remained, as usual, above prime delinquency rates. But subprime delinquencies declined significantly, from close to 15 percent to well under 10 percent, by 2005.[22] Meanwhile, residential housing starts rose, peaking in January 2006 at a level last seen in the early 1970s. Meeting in January 2005, the Counterparty Risk Management Policy Group II, an informal group of financial industry executives that advises on risk management issues, beheld a world of risk in check. Since 1998, the financial markets had survived, relatively intact, despite multiple shocks, including the tech stock crash that began in 2000 and the attack of September 11, 2001. Inflation and interest rates were low. Credit instruments, including CDS, were providing tremendous liquidity to lending activity.

Yet troubles in the underlying housing market were beginning to emerge. The S&P/Case-Shiller US National Home Price Index indicates that US housing prices continued to increase at a healthy 14.7 percent rate in 2005. But a look at individual markets shows that much of the increase in 2005 came from a few markets, including Miami and Phoenix. In other markets that had seen the biggest rises, including San Diego and Las Vegas, appreciation rates were down sharply in 2005. In 2006, national prices were essentially flat.

Meanwhile, delinquency rates on subprime mortgages picked up in 2005, while delinquency rates on prime mortgages rose only slightly.[23] By the end of 2006, subprime delinquency rates rose to 10 percent for variable- and fixed-rate mortgages, compared with a little over 2 percent for prime fixed-rate mortgages.[24]

Nevertheless, subprime originations continued apace, peaking in 2005 at $625 billion, followed by $600 billion in 2006. The rate of securitization of these loans also went up, rising from 67 percent in 2004 to 75 percent in 2006, respectively.[25] Furthermore, even as the delinquency rates on underlying mortgages were increasing and the quality of the loans (as indicated by loan-to-value ratios and proportions of low-documentation loans) was declining, spreads between subprime and prime mortgage rates were narrowing.[26]

One factor working to narrow spreads was an increase in demand for subprime loans to securitize.[27] As commercial banks expanded their capacities for buying, originating, and securitizing nonprime mortgages, investment banks felt themselves being shouldered out of the market. Lehman Brothers, Bear Stearns, Merrill Lynch, Morgan Stanley, and Goldman Sachs expanded their direct access to the subprime market by purchasing independent mortgage originators.[28] When they had to buy the mortgages, some Wall Street firms were paying a 3 percent premium for loans they could turn into securities.[29]

Competition among lenders put a check on the interest rates paid by mortgage borrowers. This in turn reined in the rates that could be offered on MBS tranches, particularly the already relatively low-yield AAA-rated tranches. This eventually started to reduce the tranches' appeal to investors. Also, because the vast bulk of subprime mortgage pools went into AAA-rated tranches, declining demand for these tranches threatened the viability of securitization itself. It meant that a very substantial part of a given pool of subprime mortgages could not be profitably sold and might have to be retained by sponsors at no profit or even at a loss.

Luckily, there were solutions to this problem at hand. One came from the CDO market, which grew phenomenally from 2004 to 2006. Issuance of CDOs collateralized by RMBS, commercial MBS, and other collateral totaled a little over $1 billion in 2000, but had grown to almost $85 billion by the end of 2004.[30] The market's value reached $157 billion in 2005 and $307 billion by 2006. RMBS contributed a substantial portion of the underlying collateral of such CDOs, about one-third in 2005. Moody's reported that RMBS made up just under 40 percent of the CDOs it rated in 2006, and 70 percent of that was in subprime loans and home equity loans, including subprime mortgages.[31]

RMBS were used for both high-grade CDOs and mezzanine CDOs. Mezzanine CDOs, as their name implies, incorporated BBB-rated tranches of RMBS, while high-grade CDOs incorporated tranches further up the ratings ladder. In the 2005–2007 period, high-grade CDOs had about a 50 percent exposure to subprime RMBS, whereas mezzanine CDOs had a 77 percent exposure.[32] Mezzanine CDOs provided an answer for subprime lenders and securitizers, as well as investors, squeezed by narrowing spreads.

Mezzanine CDOs could provide higher rates than high-grade CDOs because their constituent mezzanine tranches came with higher rates. However, mezzanine tranches accounted for a small percentage of the underlying mortgage pool, so there were not a lot of mezzanine tranches to be divvied up. Securitizers found a way around the too-bigness of AAA-rated tranches and the too-smallness of mezzanine tranches: synthetics.

CDOs could be created synthetically using CDS (see Chapter 12, "Weapons of Mass Destruction"). Using CDS to synthesize credit exposure, CDO sponsors could tailor issues to maximize profits. The relatively small size of mezzanine RMBS tranches was no longer a limiting factor. CDO exposure to mezzanine RMBS issuance—65 percent in 2004—grew to 160 percent in 2005 and 193 percent in 2006.[33] This growth represented the use of CDS to create synthetic tranches, which allowed multiple CDOs to reference the same single mezzanine RMBS tranche.

Sponsors also shored up their own returns by using synthetic CDOs to create "super-senior" tranches (see Chapter 12). Rather than selling an AAA-rated tranche representing 70 percent to 85 percent of the loan pool at very low or even negative profit margins, a sponsor could retain a super-senior tranche and create a synthetic CDO that sold an AAA-rated tranche representing only a very small sub-portion of the original AAA-rated tranche.

Purchasers of these AAA-rated CDO tranches were receiving the low rates commensurate with the seemingly low risk of an AAA rating, but they were holding positions that were subordinate to the claims of the super-senior tranche, which represented the largest part of the underlying collateral pool. Most investors presumably did not realize this or they would have demanded higher returns.[34] Meanwhile, the sponsor kept the payments due to the super-senior tranches it retained, which, as they were highest in repayment priority, were deemed to have extremely low risk.

The amount of capital banks had to hold against super-senior tranches was generally much lower than the amount they would have had to hold against the equivalent amount of underlying loans, as the latter would be considered riskier than the super-senior tranches created from them. Furthermore, holders of super-senior tranches often insured them, in whole or in part, by purchasing CDS. Purchase of CDS protection, much like sale of loans to an SPV, essentially moved the protected tranche off the balance sheet.

The premiums paid for CDS protection on super-senior tranches were usually low, in line with the supposedly super-safe nature of the tranches. Much of this insurance was provided by monoline insurers such as Ambac Financial Group, Inc. and MBIA, Inc. (Municipal Bond Insurance Association). But other insurers—most notably American International Group (AIG)—as well as hedge funds, banks, and other entities, sold CDS protection on super-senior and other AAA-rated tranches of CDOs and RMBS.

With the introduction in January 2006 of the ABX indexes on subprime mortgage CDS, it also became feasible to hedge subprime exposure by offsetting it with index CDS. Furthermore, long and short index positions could be taken by speculators betting on the direction of the market. By 2006, Goldman Sachs and Deutsche Bank, among others, were taking short positions against the mortgage market.

Asset-backed commercial paper (ABCP) conduits and SIVs provided other means of getting the mortgage exposure represented by super-senior tranches off balance sheets (see Chapter 12). The assets in ABCP conduits and SIVs grew rapidly in 2006 into 2007.[35] SIVs, which had a nominal value of over $400 billion in 2007,[36] had a particularly hefty exposure to residential and commercial MBS, including an 8.3 percent exposure to subprime mortgages.[37] SIVs also held large amounts of CDOs loaded up with subprime MBS. For many CDO sponsors, SIVs provided a handy parking space for super-senior and other tranches pending sale.

## FEEDING THE BEAST

The housing bubble was prolonged and enlarged, if not enabled, by the expansion of lenders into subprime lending, which in turn was driven by the demand for high-yield products—particularly subprime RMBS—on the part of CDO packagers and other investors. Just as portfolio insurance, with its trend-following purchases of stock as stock prices rose, buttressed the equity market's run-up before the 1987 crash (see Chapter 5, "Portfolio Insurance and the Crash"), the interaction between structured finance products and subprime lending helped inflate the housing bubble.

As house prices rose in the years following 2001, total mortgage loans peaked in 2003 at $3.9 trillion. Prime loans dropped off by half in the following year, but subprime lending continued to grow, with subprime originations of $335 billion in 2003 increasing to $625 billion in 2005.[38] These figures suggest that subprime lending took up some of the slack left by a decline in demand for prime loans as house prices rose and interest rates began to increase. Subprime loans enabled average home prices to continue to increase from 2003 into 2006.

Such risky loans would not have been made, at least in the volumes seen, in the absence of securitization. This is reflected in the material increase in the proportion of subprime loans that ended up being securitized. Securitization itself was driven by the demand for its products—RMBS, CDOs, and SIVs—which ended up with much of the risk and reward of subprime lending. The seeming benefits of securitization were widespread, accruing to sponsors, dealers, and investors as well as mortgage borrowers. At the same time, securitization, as was the case with portfolio insurance in the 1980s, seemed to do away with the risks.

Structured finance products were more diversified than the underlying mortgages. After all, RMBS might hold thousands of mortgages, and CDOs might hold hundreds of RMBS tranches. Risk of default for CDOs was thus spread over a broad and geographically diverse base.[39] The structured instruments also seemed to offer smoother payouts because the effects of refinancing and default were distributed over a large number of mortgages.[40] The pooling of the mortgages underlying RMBS and CDOs also afforded buyers some protection against adverse selection, whereby sellers with superior information could cherry-pick mortgages, retaining the best mortgages and securitizing the least attractive ones for sale.[41]

The tranching process transformed underlying subprime loans into AAA-rated RMBS tranches, and underlying BBB-rated RMBS tranches into AAA-rated CDO tranches (see Chapter 12). The incorporation of CDO tranches into SIVs resulted in the seemingly safest product of all, as the commercial paper issued by these entities was held by money market funds perceived by most of their investors as being impervious to default risk as well as being highly liquid.

Securitization appeared to transform illiquid assets—individual mortgage loans—into more liquid assets. This seemed true, above all, for SIVs and other ABCP conduits funded by money market funds. Many money market fund investors seem to have relied on these vehicles' ability to tap liquidity as needed. The belief that one can get out before everyone else is what helps build and sustain price bubbles, including the tech stock bubble.[42] But the most seemingly liquid markets are often the first to reflect underlying problems; when problems emerge, these markets quickly become illiquid. This was to be the case with SIVs and ABCP conduits in the subprime mortgage crisis.

CHAPTER 14

# Securitization and the Credit Crisis

*"I found a flaw."*

**—Alan Greenspan[1]**

While residential mortgage-backed securities (RMBS), collateralized debt obligations (CDOs), structured investment vehicles (SIVs), and credit default swaps (CDS) may have appeared to reduce risks for individual market participants, these instruments ended up increasing the risk of the entire financial sector and the economy. They did so by facilitating a huge increase in lending to highly risky borrowers, while obscuring the nature of that risk, who ultimately held the risk, the vast expansion of leverage in the system, and the degree of interconnection between vital market participants.

When housing prices began to level off in late 2006, the real risk of mortgage instruments started to become apparent, and the entire edifice began to collapse. At first, there were isolated incidents of losses at a handful of hedge funds heavily invested in mortgage-heavy CDOs. These soon coalesced, however, into what could be called a run on the most liquid part of the mortgage market—money market funds invested in asset-backed commercial paper (ABCP) conduits. Deterioration in this market then hit bank balance sheets and amplified concerns about the quality of CDOs.

As rating agency downgrades accumulated, CDOs continued to lose value. This pressured banks and other securitizers, which could no longer sell their products or park them in ABCP conduits. Furthermore, the repo market was becoming increasingly leery about accepting CDOs and other mortgage-related assets as collateral for loans, constraining this source of liquidity. The ultimate bulwark of protection, CDS insurance, threatened to crumble under the onslaught of mounting losses on mortgage instruments suffered by their sponsors and investors.

## DISAPPOINTMENT SETS IN

The housing bubble began to deflate in 2006, with an essentially flat average housing price for the year masking a decline late in the year. For 2007, according to the S&P/Case-Shiller US National Home Price Index, home prices ended the year off 5.4 percent. They were to decline even more steeply in 2008, down 12 percent.[2]

While some markets did better than others, the surprising factor was the scope of the decline, with markets throughout the United States affected. As with the 1987 stock market crash, it is difficult to find fundamental economic reasons for the extent of the decline.

The bubble may simply have run its course. Subprime lending had offset the slowdown in the prime mortgage business earlier in the decade, but now the capacity of the subprime market was becoming exhausted, especially as the Federal Reserve (the Fed) continued moderate interest rate hikes. Meanwhile, builders had ratcheted up construction to the point where housing supply was outdistancing demand and putting downward pressure on prices.[3]

### Exercising Options

A mortgage loan has an embedded put option (see Chapter 12, "Weapons of Mass Destruction"). The homebuyer is long this put option and can default on the loan, limiting losses if the home's price declines. The lender is short the put option; it absorbs any losses if the home cannot be sold for a price high enough to cover the principal on the mortgage.

Option values are nonlinear; small changes in underlying parameters, such as volatility or interest rates, can lead to large changes in the price of the option. As option-pricing expert Robert C. Merton has pointed out, the put options embedded in mortgage loans are no exception.[4] Even though they may not be defined in the same mathematical terms as financial puts, the puts embedded in mortgage loans may behave in a broadly similar way.[5] In particular, the value of the put will increase at an increasing rate as the price of the underlying asset approaches the strike price.

As the value of a house declines toward and then below the remaining principal on the mortgage used to finance it, the put that allows the borrower to default on the loan becomes more valuable; the borrower is, therefore, more likely to exercise the put.[6] For a given decline in average house prices, subprime borrowers are more likely than prime or Alt-A borrowers to reach the point at which the remaining principal on their mortgages exceeds the values of their homes, because their loans likely represent substantially larger percentages of the homes' purchase prices; that is, they have higher loan-to-value (LTV) ratios.

The occurrence of defaults on mortgage loans has the potential to escalate in a nonlinear manner. There are both fundamental reasons and behavioral reasons for this. As homeowners default, neighborhoods may deteriorate, causing prices of still occupied homes to fall further, and increasing the odds that their owners will default.[7] Foreclosures also increase the supply of housing, as foreclosed houses become available for resale. An increase in supply may further depress prices. Thus, an initial decline in house prices that leads some of the most heavily leveraged mortgage borrowers to default may trigger further price declines, an increase in homeowners who are "underwater" (more is owed on the home than it is worth), and more defaults and foreclosures.[8]

There are also behavioral reasons that cause defaults to beget more defaults. Individuals may avoid defaulting to the extent that it is viewed as a sign of personal failure or unethical. As people see their neighbors default on loans, however, default may be seen less as stigmatizing and more as a solution to an economic problem. At least one survey found that willingness to default increased by half if the respondent knew someone who had strategically defaulted.[9] Thus house price declines may set off an initial round of defaults, which leads to further declines in house values, which lead to more defaults and further price declines.

Foreclosures on all mortgages, including prime mortgages, traced a reverse image of falling house prices starting in 2006 (see Exhibit 14.1). Delinquencies and defaults among subprime mortgages traced a similar pattern, but at considerably higher levels. In mid 2005, 5.6 percent of subprime mortgages were seriously delinquent; by September 2008, 23 percent were. About 8 percent of subprime mortgages issued between 2000 and 2004 defaulted within three years; by mid 2008, the default rate was 14 percent for subprime mortgages originated in 2005. Many subprime

**EXHIBIT 14.1**

US House Prices and Foreclosures

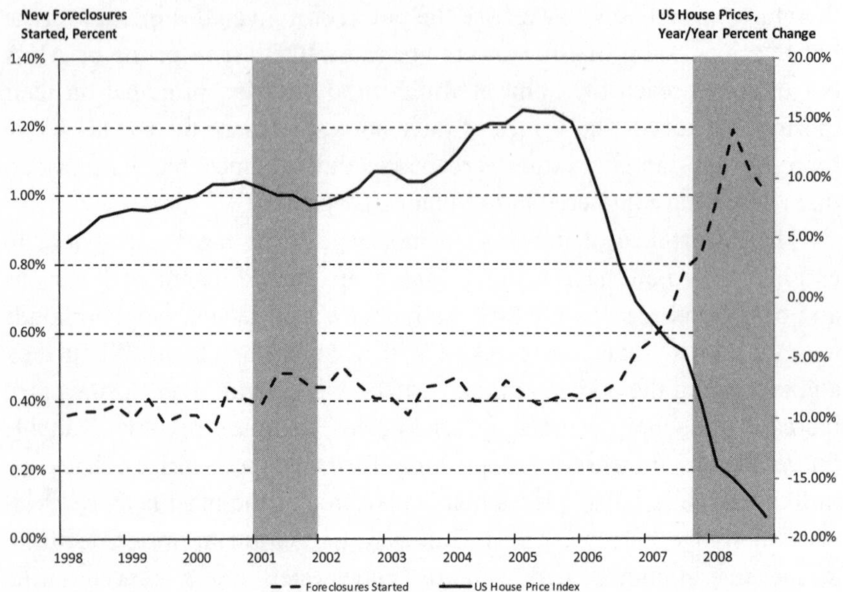


Source: James Bullard, Christopher J. Neely, and David C. Wheelock, "Systemic Risk and the Financial Crisis: A Primer." *Federal Reserve Bank of St. Louis Review* 95, no.1 (2009): 404. "US House Prices" shows the year-over-year percentage changes in the S&P/Case-Shiller National Home Price Index. Foreclosure data from Mortgage Bankers Association. Vertical gray bars indicate recessions.

mortgages were defaulting within a year of origination. From 2000 to 2004, only 1.5 percent of subprime loans defaulted within a year; in 2007, 8 percent of subprime loans defaulted within a year.[10] Subprime mortgage originations subsided dramatically and virtually disappeared in 2008.

## A Put Comes Due

Securitization had effectively passed the short put position embedded in mortgage loans on to the buyers of RMBS and CDOs and sellers of protection via CDS. Holders of subprime tranches and sellers of CDS on them were essentially short a huge put option on the subprime market. That is, they would bear the losses associated with home values falling below the mortgage principal owed.

By late 2006, defaults on subprime mortgages began to rise.[11] The defaults were not only more numerous than the rating agencies had expected, but more widespread geographically and more concentrated in time. While the United States had experienced regional declines in house prices, a nationwide decline of the sort that emerged had not occurred since the Great Depression. It was a systematic event and, as such, many of the risk-control mechanisms of structured securitization were ineffective against it.

Diversification, even the kind of geographic diversification present in CDOs, was not helpful. Diversification can help protect against the specific risks of individual mortgages. A well-designed pool of mortgages should withstand defaults by disparate home buyers if the defaults are few and don't happen all at once. But diversification is ineffective against the kind of systematic risk represented by a widespread fall in home values. It also became increasingly apparent that many RMBS and CDOs containing RMBS were not very well diversified. For example, two-thirds of Moody's downgrades involved four issuers—New Century Financial Corporation, Western Asset Mortgage Capital Corporation, Long Beach Financial Corporation, and Fremont General Corporation.[12] Furthermore, downgrades were particularly high for those mortgages originated in 2006 and 2007.

As defaults breached the levels assumed when the tranches were constructed, and the value of subordinate tranches eroded, the rating agencies were forced to reconsider the ratings on subprime-related tranches. It was becoming apparent that, had the agencies allowed for the effects of multiple, highly correlated defaults, they would probably not have assigned such high ratings to these securities. By September 2007, 17 percent of all subprime RMBS tranches had been downgraded.[13]

Ratings downgrades had significant implications for holders of mortgage-backed securities (MBS). First, the downgrades would be expected to reduce the value of the securities. Parties that had pledged the downgraded securities as collateral may have been required to make compensatory payments to their counterparties. Second, the downgrades increased the riskiness of the securities, which may have required regulated banks to increase the amount of capital they held against the downgraded securities on their books. Third, the downgrades called into question the value of the securities as collateral for repo loans or other borrowing vehicles such as SIVs. Overall, the downgrades reduced the liquidity of the financial system.

## ASSET-BACKED COMMERCIAL PAPER CONDUITS COLLAPSE

In the years following the 1987 stock market crash, financial firms greatly expanded their use of the commercial paper (CP) market. This move was seen at the time as reducing risk in the financial system, inasmuch as it diversified sources of funding and made the system overall less reliant on banks alone.[14] Two decades after that crash, however, the commercial paper market was to prove a weak point in the system and provide an early warning of the instability to come.

The deterioration in subprime ratings had a dramatic effect on the ABCP market, particularly issuances from SIVs. While most ABCP conduits held diversified portfolios of asset-backed securities (ABS), single-seller ABCP conduits were often used by banks to warehouse mortgages or mortgage-backed tranches prior to their securitization or issuance. Furthermore, SIVs, particularly SIV-lites (see Chapter 12), grew dramatically in 2006, as did the proportion of their assets invested in the AAA-rated tranches of RMBS and CDOs containing RMBS. By this time, the relatively low interest rates on AAA-rated tranches had dampened demand from investors; SIVs and ABCP conduits provided a way for securitizers to use unsold tranches as collateral for short-term funding.

Prime money market funds were the major purchasers of ABCP. As 2007 progressed, these buyers became increasingly aware of the deteriorating quality of the underlying collateral. Bear Stearns announced in June 2007 that it was halting redemptions from two highly visible hedge funds. The High-Grade Structured Credit Fund, begun in 2003, had enjoyed high returns through 2006, based on investments, leveraged 10-to-1, in supposedly low-risk assets including AAA-rated CDOs. In August 2006, the fund had been split to create a second fund, the Enhanced Leverage Fund, with even higher leverage. Into early 2007, the funds were reporting that they had about 6 percent of the assets in subprime mortgages, but that number did not include the subprime exposures of the CDOs they held, which constituted about 60 percent of assets.[15] Both funds were unable to meet margin calls from lenders and counterparties and were deemed valueless by mid July.

Prime money market fund investors, newly wary of the prime funds' mortgage exposures, fled them in favor of government money market funds that bought Treasury-backed assets.[16] Prime funds began to hoard cash in the expectation of further investor redemptions. ABCP issuance began a sharp fall-off in July 2007, while commercial paper backed by other types of assets remained stable (see Exhibit 14.2).

Then, in early August, French bank BNP Paribas announced that it was halting redemptions from two of its funds, saying:[17]

> Asset-backed securities, mortgage loans, especially subprime loans, don't have any business . . . it is no longer possible to value fairly the underlying US ABS assets in the . . . funds.

**EXHIBIT 14.2**

Commercial Paper Issuance

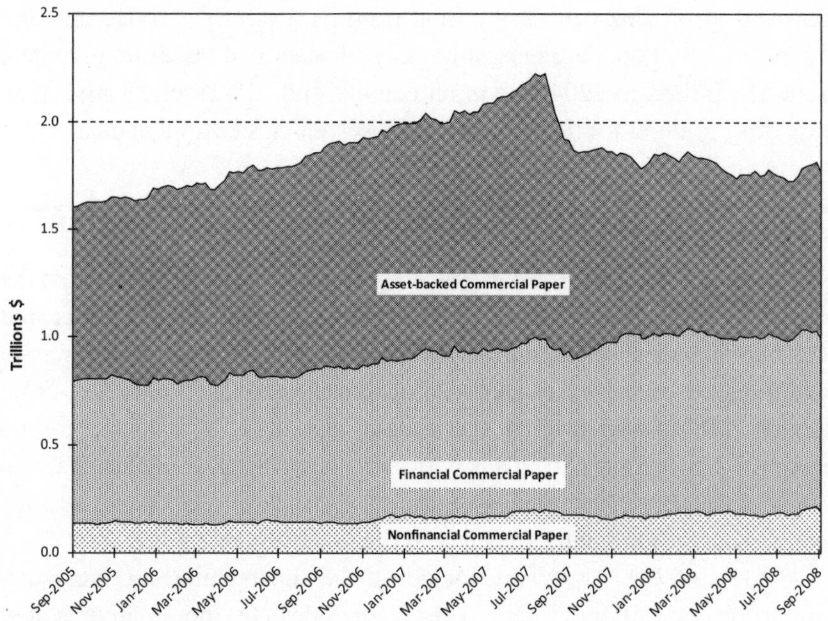


Source: Federal Reserve Board.

This announcement exacerbated the decline in the hardest-hit segments of the ABCP market. SIV's outstanding amount of ABCP fell about 80 percent from July to December 2007, while single-seller mortgage conduit ABCP fell from $23 billion to $2 billion.[18] No SIVs or SIV-lites survived the credit crisis.

In order to meet obligations on maturing paper in the absence of new investment, some ABCP conduits extended the maturities of their paper, which made potential buyers even more skittish. Bank balance sheets took a hit as the cash reserved to guarantee ABCP payments was drawn down. For some ABCP conduits and SIVs, declines in the value of collateral hit triggers that required sponsors to repurchase assets at face value or repay the paper at par, usually by liquidating assets.

SIV sponsors were particularly hard hit because, unlike ABCP conduits, most SIVs did not fully guarantee their paper, so sponsors did not recognize the full value of potential liabilities on their balance sheets. Most bank sponsors ended up paying off paper and note holders, leading to losses as unfunded SIV assets came back onto balance sheets or were liquidated at depressed values. In November 2007, HSBC had to take $35 billion in SIV assets back onto its balance sheet. Citigroup, the largest US player in SIVs, took back $49 billion from its seven SIVs in December.[19] By the end of 2008, commercial banks had sustained losses of anywhere from $68 billion to $204 billion on conduit and SIV assets. Rather than providing funding for their sponsors, these vehicles cost them dearly.

## COLLATERALIZED DEBT OBLIGATIONS FEEL THE HEAT

Fire sales of assets in SIVs and ABCP conduits put further pressure on the values of RMBS and CDOs,[20] as many subprime tranches that appeared on bank balance sheets had to be marked down to reflect new, lower asset values. Much of the wreckage was concentrated in CDO tranches. From August 2007 to March 2008, the market value of CDO tranches fell 60 percent.[21] Gross losses on CDOs with subprime collateral outpaced actual losses on mortgage loans because the CDOs' use of CDS to create synthetic exposures inflated exposures to the underlying debt.[22]

Holders of AAA tranches, including the super-senior cut, were disproportionately affected by write-downs, despite the relative safety of AAA tranches in comparison with mezzanine and equity tranches (see Exhibit 14.3). This reflected the sheer size of these tranches, which accounted for by far the largest bulk of the underlying collateral pool, and the predominance of AAA-rated tranches of mezzanine CDOs, which held BBB-rated tranches of RMBS and were thus able to offer higher rates than high-grade CDOs composed of AAA-rated tranches of RMBS. Banks were particularly affected, as they had retained a large number of super-senior tranches on their balance sheets.

Swiss bank UBS, for example, in a report to shareholders explaining its 2007 losses, said losses on its positions in US residential mortgages totaled about $18 billion. Half of these losses came from super-senior

**EXHIBIT 14.3**

Estimated Losses in Value of Various Collateralized Debt Obligation (CDO) Tranches

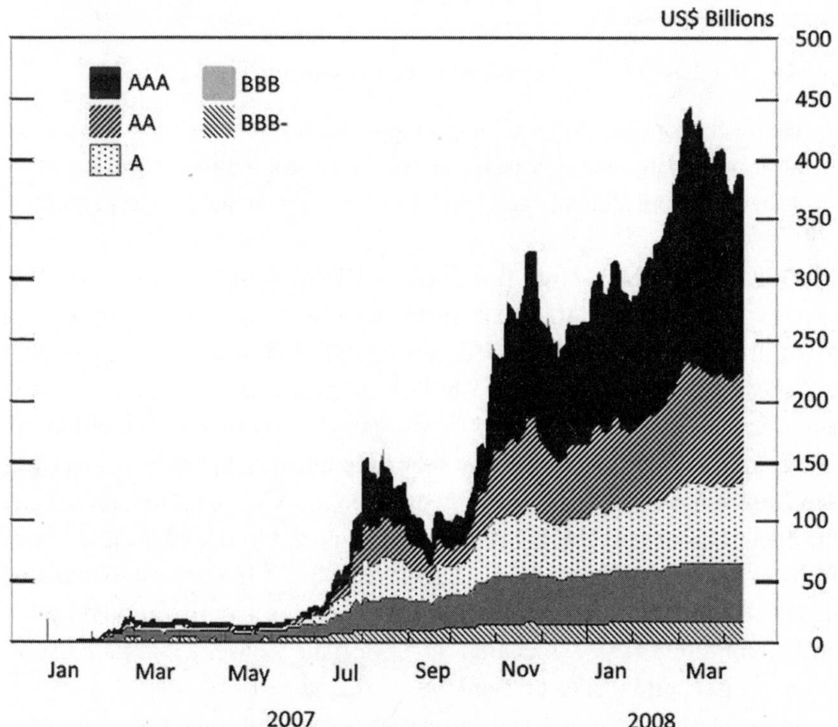


Source: Bank of England, *Financial Stability Report*, Issue 23, April 2008: 19.

CDO positions retained on the bank's balance sheet or purchased from third parties, with a significant portion representing unfunded, synthetic AAA-rated tranches. Two-thirds of super-senior tranche losses came from positions that were hedged for losses up to only 2 percent to 4 percent; a quarter came from losses on unhedged super-senior positions.

In some cases, UBS had not insured super-senior tranches deliberately because the tranches were considered to have very low risk exposure. In other cases, protection could not be obtained at less than prohibitive cost. UBS's statement notes the following.[23]

> Exit strategies contemplated by the CDO desk for the Super Senior positions included:
>
> - Sale of long positions;
> - Purchase of further first-loss protection for particular Super Seniors; and
> - Purchase of macro protection, such as shorting the ABX index.
>
> However, from July/August 2007, these strategies were not readily available, principally due to absence of counterparties willing to execute at prices that were mutually acceptable to both UBS and the counterparties.

Other banks with large positions in CDOs were similarly affected. Merrill Lynch, with large exposures to mezzanine CDOs, reported a $7.7 billion net loss for 2007. Citigroup, with $43 billion of super-senior tranches of CDOs out of its $55 billion subprime exposure, had to write down $5.7 billion in October 2007. Morgan Stanley took a $9.4 billion hit related to CDOs collateralized by subprime mortgage tranches. The average 2007 AAA-rated CDO was downgraded to CCC+ by 2008, increasing the capital a commercial bank would be required to hold for these bonds from $2 per $100 of bond value to $100 per $100.[24] In contrast, banks that had been reducing their commitments to mortgage securitization reported profits for 2007; these included J. P. Morgan Chase, Goldman Sachs, Credit Suisse, and Deutsche Bank.[25]

Investigations carried out after the crisis by the Securities and Exchange Commission (SEC) and the US Senate, as well as investor civil suits, revealed that a number of CDOs created in this period were materially motivated by parties such as hedge funds that wanted to bet against the mortgages in these CDOs. The Abacus series of CDOs initiated by Goldman Sachs in 2007 provides one example. Goldman Sachs disclosed to potential investors at the time that a monoline insurance firm had vetted the securities in the deal, but it did not mention that selection of those securities was influenced by a hedge fund manager, John Paulson & Co., which subsequently bet against them by shorting. Within a year of the first deal, virtually all the bonds in the CDO had been downgraded, costing investors more than $1 billion.[26] In July 2010, Goldman Sachs settled a civil suit brought by the SEC by paying a fine of $550 million. Other banks engaged in similar two-sided dealings.[27]

As house prices continued to decline and defaults increased, sponsors found it increasingly difficult to find buyers for their CDOs. One solution they found was to sell CDO tranches to other CDOs. Before 2006, about 5 percent of new CDOs constituted tranches from other CDOs. In 2007, 67 percent of CDO mezzanine tranches were apparently purchased by other CDOs, with sponsors shuffling tranches between their own deals or trading tranches with other CDO sponsors.[28]

Issuance of CDOs dropped from about $100 billion in each of the first two quarters of 2007 to $40 billion in the third quarter.[29] With securitizations declining, the resources available to buy subprime mortgages also shrank. Many subprime lenders found it difficult to sell mortgages remaining on their own books and impossible to raise funds for further lending. Their problems were exacerbated by the fact that many of the banks and other securitizers purchasing subprime loans had begun in 2006 to require sellers to buy back loans that had defaulted within three months of purchase.[30] A number of subprime lenders—including Fremont General Corporation, New Century Financial Corporation, American Home Mortgage Investment Corporation, and Ameriquest Mortgage—went under when they became unable to access further funding.

## Repo Retreats

Subprime RMBS and CDO tranches, particularly highly rated ones, were used as collateral for repo borrowing, a market estimated to be as large as $12 trillion at its peak.[31] With repo (repurchase) agreements, the lending party charges a fee that reflects the term of the loan and the riskiness of the borrower. It may also apply a "haircut" to the value of the assets posted as collateral, to reflect differences between its estimate of the price it may be able to sell the collateral for, if necessary, and the value placed upon the collateral by the borrowing party. Thus, a bank that borrows $100 million in a repo agreement may have to post collateral valued at more than $100 million.

Problems with the repo market had begun to show up after the troubles at the two Bear Stearns hedge funds emerged in June 2007. Merrill Lynch had encountered difficulties offloading the repo collateral Bear Stearns had placed with it; what it could sell went at significant discounts.[32] Much of the collateral consisted of the same kinds of mortgage-related instruments that had brought down the hedge funds.

Bear Stearns had been a pioneer and large player in the mortgage securitization business, and by 2006 it even originated 31 percent of the loans, largely subprime, it securitized.[33] As of November 2007, it had about $46 billion in mortgages, RMBS, CDOs, and CDS.[34] Following the demise of its two hedge funds in 2007, however, Bear Stearns faced increasing difficulty getting repo financing as lenders grew concerned about the value of the assets Bear Stearns could post as collateral. As Bear Stearns was calling on about $75 billion a day in repo financing,[35] access to the repo market was critical.

In March 2008, Bear Stearns ran out of willing lenders. Meanwhile, its prime brokerage clients, including many hedge funds, were pulling their assets out and reassigning their derivatives contracts to other counterparties. The SEC, which had been monitoring the firm, reported that Bear Stearns's cash balance was down to $2 billion by March 13. Bear Stearns could not satisfy the steadily increasing demands of its counterparties for cash and collateral, and it was forced to obtain emergency funding from the Federal Reserve on March 14.

On March 16, 2008, the Fed brokered the sale of Bear Stearns to J. P. Morgan Chase. Bear Stearns, which had a market value of $20 billion in January 2007, agreed to be purchased for $236 million.[36] That figure was later revised upward to about $1.5 billion. The Fed provided J. P. Morgan Chase with $30 billion in financing for Bear Stearns's less liquid assets, including subprime tranches, and opened its discount window to investment banks, for the first time allowing them to borrow at the same terms as commercial banks.

Bear Stearns was hardly the only firm affected by concerns over collateral for repo. The entire repo market became more and more infected as questions about collateral quality and counterparty risk heightened and spread from subprime collateral to most collateral other than government bonds. In early 2007, repo lenders had regarded subprime mortgage collateral as riskier than collateral based on corporate bonds or tranches of collateralized loan obligations and CDOs based on non-mortgage-related debt. By 2008, however, fees and "haircuts" on these types of collateral were rising substantially, and most subprime-related collateral had been priced out of the repo market.[37] Substantial liquidity was being drained from the credit market.

## CREDIT DEFAULT SWAP PROTECTION CRUMBLES

The CDS market had doubled in size between 2006 and 2007, from $34 trillion in notional value to $62 trillion, according to the International Swaps and Derivatives Association (ISDA). In 2001, the notional amount of CDS outstanding had totaled less than $1 trillion, at $919 billion. US banks' exposure to counterparty credit risk expanded with the expansion of the market for CDS.

The CDS market's growth reflected several developments. First, the ISDA's guidelines for CDS on ABS, introduced in 2005, facilitated CDS transactions, while the ABX indexes, created in early 2006, provided a liquid venue for taking positions on CDS and the underlying housing market. Second, sponsors' need for mezzanine RMBS tranches to create AAA-rated tranches of mezzanine CDOs and their demand for protection on retained super-senior tranches drove up demand for CDS. Third, deterioration of the underlying subprime housing market and an expanding series of downgrades of subprime tranches increased market participants' perception of risk and desire for protection.[38]

CDS usually require mark-to-market payments between counterparties as the riskiness of the reference assets changes. Large downgrades could require significant payments from protection sellers to protection buyers. Even if the underlying asset does not eventually default and the seller ultimately recovers this amount, such payments can strain the protection seller's resources in the meanwhile.

Exchanges of collateral are supposed to provide protection against counterparty default. In the case of CDS written on subprime tranches and collateralized by subprime tranches, however, difficulties in the underlying market may lead a protection seller to default, while at the same time eroding the value of the collateral (as counterparties to the Bear Stearns hedge funds found out in early 2007). Similarly, protection buyers assumed that, in the event of default by a seller, they could merely replace the protection on a still-viable asset by going to another seller. But if the default by the initial seller is related to conditions that also affect the asset, it may be impossible to replace protection at a reasonable cost.[39]

Perhaps most pertinent to the systemic risk potential of CDS is the ability of protection sellers to meet their commitments. If a protection seller defaults, there is significant risk of a chain reaction. The failure of the seller can lead to the failure of a protection buyer, whose failure can lead to more losses down the line. Interconnections between core banking institutions combined with the concentration of the market create a fragile system in which the failure of one or a few large protection sellers can bring down other key players.

## Markdowns on Monolines

In 2007, the ABX indexes on variously rated subprime RMBS tranches began to indicate substantial deterioration of underlying tranche value and increasing volatility (see Exhibit 14.4). The ABX indexes use CDS to represent values in the subprime RMBS market. The values of all the tranches fell beginning in late 2006, with the lowest-rated tranches falling the most, to nearly zero by late 2008. The tumult in the CDS market had dire consequences for the monolines that had insured so many senior subprime tranches.[40]

By 2007, banks and hedge funds were the primary sellers of CDS, each group accounting for about one-third of the market. Banks, however, bought more protection than they sold, whereas hedge funds were net sellers of protection. Monolines, municipal bond insurers that had branched out into securitized debt products, and other insurers had about an 18 percent share of the seller market, but only a 6 percent share of the buyer market.[41] Monolines had insured about $127 billion in CDO tranches, and their outstanding guarantees were leveraged by about 115 to 1.[42]

**EXHIBIT 14.4**

ABX Index Representing Various Subprime Residential Mortgage-Backed Security (RMBS) Tranches

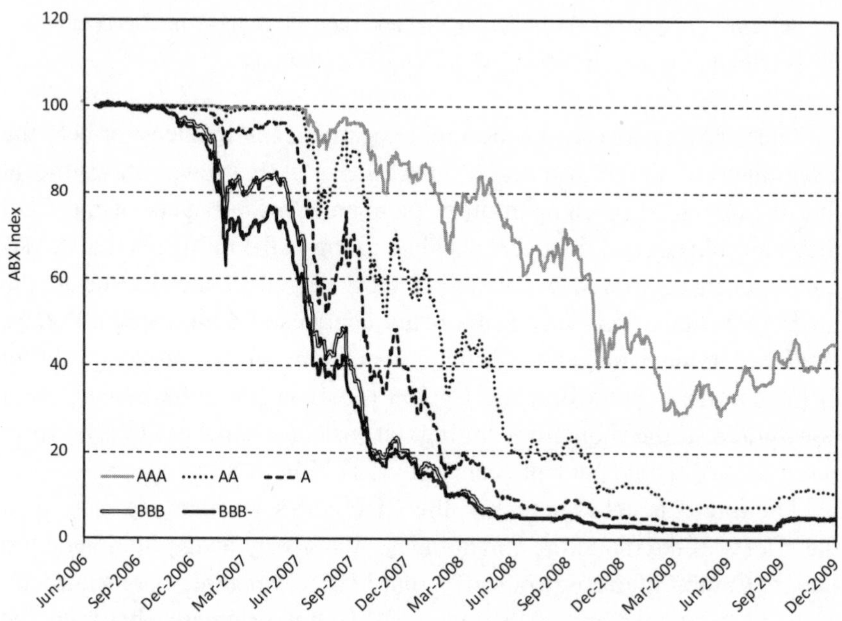


Source: Data on ABX 2006 2 Series from Markit Group.

In late 2007, monoline ACA Financial Guaranty Corp. (one-third owned by Bear Stearns), which had insured some $60 billion in CDS on mortgage and other debt, was downgraded from A to CCC by the Standard & Poor's rating agency. In January 2008, ACA could not meet its CDS obligations and was forced to unwind its insurance contracts. According to Standard & Poor's August 2008 report, Merrill Lynch had about $19 billion of CDS coverage on its mortgage-related assets. About one-quarter of this came from ACA. Assets Merrill Lynch thought were protected had to be written down.

In January 2008, Fitch Ratings downgraded Ambac Financial Group, Inc., which had sold about $60 billion of CDS on CDOs. In June, Moody's Investors Service and Standard & Poor's downgraded Ambac and another bond insurer, MBIA, Inc., which had a $125 billion commitment to CDS on CDOs. Moody's noted at the time:[43]

> MBIA's insured portfolio remained vulnerable to further economic deterioration, particularly given the leverage contained in the sizable portfolio of resecuritization [ABS CDO] transactions.

These downgrades had substantial negative consequences for both the monolines and their customers. A downgrade in their own ratings meant the monolines owed compensatory payments to the buyers of the CDS they had sold. But CDS buyers also had to lower the ratings on the AAA-rated tranches covered by monoline CDS to reflect the decline in the insurers' ratings. This led to significant declines in bank capital. Precise estimates of the damages are difficult to come by, given the private nature of the contracts, but a Barclays Capital report in late 2008 opined that a downgrade in the monolines' ratings of just one letter grade (say, from AAA to AA) would cut bank capital by $22 billion.[44]

The interconnected nature of the CDO and CDS markets magnified the effects of the monoline downgrades. A study by hedge fund Pershing Square Capital Management shows that MBIA was directly or indirectly exposed to 80 percent of the subprime CDOs originated between the beginning of 2005 and the end of 2007, while Ambac was exposed to 73 percent of them.[45] Furthermore, the opacity of the market made it difficult to know not only the size of losses and collateral transfers, but also the identities of the parties involved.

A general pullback from all markets perceived as risky accelerated. By the end of June 2008, the Dow Jones Industrial Average (DJIA) fell to a low for the year, down nearly 20 percent from its fall 2007 peak. International equity markets were down even more, with Germany, France, China, and India down the most. Prices of safe-harbor assets—gold and US Treasuries—continued to rise.

Calls for greater transparency in the market for CDS got louder. Timothy F. Geithner, then head of the Federal Reserve Bank of New York, pressured CDS traders to promise to establish a central clearinghouse to handle direct as well as dealer-intermediated CDS trading. Central clearing could provide greater price transparency, as well as lower counterparty risk, and provide better enforcement of margin requirements.[46]

## FALLOUT IN THE FALL

On September 7, 2008, the government put the Federal National Mortgage Association (Fannie Mae) and the Federal Home Loan Mortgage Corporation (Freddie Mac), guarantors of about three-quarters of new home mortgages, under conservatorship. The government-sponsored entities (GSEs) had accelerated their purchases and securitizations of nonconforming mortgages, mostly Alt-A and subprime, since 2005, in part as the result of political pressure from the White House and the US Congress. Fannie Mae had purchased or guaranteed some $270 billion of subprime and Alt-A loans since 2005. Government officials asserted that they were moved to action not by fears of an imminent collapse of the GSEs, but by increasing concerns about the GSEs' long-term viability and by pressure from foreign central banks heavily invested in them.[47]

Whatever the motives, the action effectively triggered clauses in the CDS contracts that required settlement of all CDS on the GSEs. It also heightened concerns over other CDS. In particular, the cost for CDS protection on Lehman Brothers debt rose sharply.

Lehman Brothers had expanded its investment in real estate-related assets since 2006, even as other investors were starting to pull back.[48] Lehman reported its overall leverage at about 30 times equity in late 2007. The firm was heavily dependent on ABCP conduits and the repo market for financing. Lehman was also a party or counterparty to over 900,000 derivatives contracts, including CDS, currency and interest rate swaps, options, and futures contracts, with a notional value of over $30 trillion.

Lehman made plans to sell off real estate positions in January 2008, but found buyers to be scarce.[49] Instead, as the subprime market continued to deteriorate, Lehman's stock price fell. The deterioration attracted unwelcome attention from credit rating agencies.[50] Lehman's derivatives and repo counterparties, already leery of the quality of Lehman Brothers' collateral and questioning its asset valuations, raised haircuts and demanded increased collateral.

On September 10, 2008, Lehman reported that it had liquid assets of $41 billion, but the real value was closer to $2 billion. Lehman was at the time engaging in an accounting maneuver known in the firm as "Repo 105." By treating repo transactions, which are essentially borrowings, as actual sales, the firm was able to reduce its reported debt levels substantially. Using this questionable, skirtingly legal tactic, Lehman was able to hide $50 billion in debt in mid 2008.[51]

On September 11, 2008, J. P. Morgan Chase demanded $5 billion in collateral from Lehman, and the rumor mill ground out the news that the rating agencies were threatening to downgrade the firm.[52] Over the weekend of September 12–14, the Federal Reserve Bank of New York, the US Treasury, and the SEC attempted to convince Wall Street firms to bail Lehman out, as they had Long-Term Capital Management (LTCM) in 1998, but no deal could be struck without any financial assistance from the government. On September 15, 2008, Lehman Brothers filed for bankruptcy.

Default triggered automatic termination of the derivatives contracts of Lehman. But no one knew the extent of the CDS contracts written on Lehman's debt, the identity of buyers or sellers, or the value of contracts Lehman itself may have issued or purchased.[53] Regulators convinced dealer-owned Depository Trust & Clearing Corporation (DTCC), a central registry of CDS trading by dealers, to release pertinent data. According to the DTCC, some $72 billion notional value of CDS had been written on Lehman debt. The DTCC was quick to note that most of these contracts were offsetting, and equally quick to announce, in October 2008, that eventual settlement resulted in net payments of only $5.2 billion.[54]

On the day following the Lehman Brothers bankruptcy, the Fed stepped in to rescue insurance giant American International Group (AIG) with an $85 billion bailout. AIG's London-based Financial Products unit had grown huge by securitizing and selling mostly mortgage-related securities and offering CDS protection on AAA-rated tranches of CDOs, mostly to European banks. Its revenues, $737 million in 1999, had reached $3.26 billion by 2005. Profits from CDS premiums reached $250 million-a-year.[55] By mid 2008, it had sold protection on about $400 billion notional value of super-senior tranches, including about $55 billion of CDO tranches with subprime exposure.[56]

As an insurance company, AIG was not subject to the leverage limitations imposed on commercial banks. In fact, its leverage amounted to about 11 times capital—modest by Lehman standards but gargantuan compared with other, non-monoline insurers, which were leveraged two to four times.[57] AIG had insured an enormous amount of mortgage securities, but it did not have the capital to cover substantial losses.

AIG had lost over $11 billion on its CDS in 2007, most of it due to subprime-related CDOs.[58] The values of the insured securities continued to decline in 2008, resulting in more write-downs and more collateral demands. In September, AIG's credit rating was lowered by the major rating agencies, primarily on the basis of the paucity of capital underlying the CDS contracts it had sold.[59] The company had to pay out $15 billion in collateral,[60] contributing to an $18 billion loss for the first three quarters of 2008.[61]

A default by AIG would have forced CDS protection buyers to put up to $300 billion in senior and super-senior tranches on their balance sheets as protection failed.[62] The rescue avoided this, but the near-wreck of AIG nevertheless sent shock waves through an already turbulent market. A shrinkage of lending in the interbank market was apparent immediately following the Lehman and AIG disasters, which, to make matters worse, were accompanied by the forced sale of Merrill Lynch to Bank of America. US, European, and Japanese central banks pumped billions into their financial systems, but Libor, the widely followed London interest rate benchmark, nevertheless doubled as banks' willingness to lend to each other shriveled.[63]

On September 21, 2008, the Sunday following the dramas at Lehman and AIG, the Federal Reserve announced that Goldman Sachs and Morgan Stanley, the last large surviving US investment banking firms, would become bank holding companies. The conversion would allow them to take deposits and bring them under the stricter regulatory regime of the Fed. According to Goldman Sachs Chairman Lloyd Blankfein, "such regulation provides its members with full prudential supervision and access to permanent liquidity funding."[64]

Banks were now hoarding cash. In the immediate wake of the shock, the daily excess cash reserve of US commercial banks grew 50-fold from its average levels.[65] Within a few weeks, bank lending to companies dropped 40 percent from the average beginning-of-year level.[66]

Global equity markets fell. Panicked investors withdrew upwards of $140 billion from money market funds.[67] The ABCP conduits market shrank further. CDS were priced practically out of reach. By June 2009, the ABX indexes on subprime tranches were implying extremely high mortgage default rates, some near 100 percent.[68] Subprime securitization disappeared. Ironically, but perhaps not surprisingly, among those hurt by the crisis were hedge funds run by former LTCM partners John W. Meriwether and Myron S. Scholes.

## THE ROLE OF SECURITIZATION

Securitization enabled financial institutions to free up capital for lending, to pass the risk of house price declines on to investors, to earn profits on the sales, and to retain low-risk products for their own portfolios. The imprimatur of agencies' credit ratings and the protection offered by monoline insurers and other CDS sellers enhanced the perception that subprime mortgage loans and structured finance products based on subprime mortgages were low risk.

The perceived low risk permitted commercial banks, investment banks, and other entities to increase lending for more mortgage loans and the purchase of more MBS. Securitization also allowed the expansion of funding for subprime mortgages to move beyond the leveraged financial sector to traditionally unleveraged investors such as insurance companies, pension funds, and mutual funds.

These incremental sources of credit increased the supply of funding for subprime loans and securitizations. At the same time, an expansion in the loan supply was perceived as an increase in funding liquidity, which reduced the perception of risk and the probability of default. This situation, in turn, resulted in further expansion of the credit supply, more lending, lower perceived risk, lower perceived probability of default, and so on.[69] The positive feedback initiated by the demand for subprime mortgages, and structured finance products based on them, was reinforced by the increase in available funding. As long as house prices kept rising, borrowers were encouraged to borrow more and lenders were encouraged to lend more, even if that meant lending to borrowers who might be likelier to default, all of which further increased the demand for, and prices of, houses.[70]

Of course, the entire leveraged system rested on a very shaky foundation: loans to high-risk subprime borrowers. Furthermore, subprime loans had themselves become increasingly leveraged, with loan-to-value ratios rising between 2001 and 2007.[71] When house price appreciation slowed and then reversed, delinquencies and defaults in the subprime sector increased beyond the expectations reflected in mortgage rates, RMBS yields, and CDS premiums. The real underlying risk of subprime mortgages, effectively hidden for so long by the instruments used to shift that risk, became apparent.

At the same time, the extent of the problem remained opaque. The complexity of CDOs and the web of obligations created by CDS, combined with the lack of publicly available information about them, made it difficult for market participants to discern which instruments and which entities were going to disintegrate next. The solvency of some critical institutions began to be questioned, counterparty risk came to the forefront of decision making, and liquidity dried up as banks hoarded their capital and declined to lend. This led to further declines in housing prices, more defaults and foreclosures, and more losses for mortgage holders and investors in mortgage-related products. The effects on both the US economy and the international economy were severe.

As with portfolio insurance in 1987, measures that purported to reduce risk for some—mortgage lenders and investors, in the case of structured finance products—ended up increasing risk for the financial system as a whole. What's more, the effects of the expansion and decline in the residential housing market in 2001–2008 were magnified by the massive amounts of leverage used to fund mortgages and mortgage-related instruments, just as leverage magnified the effects of the LTCM debacle.

# PART V

CHAPTER 15

# After the Storm, 2010–2018

*"Market participants and regulators . . . collectively underestimated how disruptions could spread horizontally across interconnected companies and markets and impair the functioning of the financial system, with severe consequences for the economy."*

—**Office of Financial Research**[1]

Portfolio insurance selling in October 1987 had repercussions primarily for the United States and, secondarily, for global equity markets. The effects of the unwinding of Long-Term Capital Management's (LTCM's) huge arbitrage positions were substantially confined to the US equity and bond markets. The disintegration of subprime-related instruments, however, reverberated globally and over a longer period of time. It caused major losses on equity holdings, fundamentally changed the geography of Wall Street, froze the credit market for borrowers large and small, and resulted in the longest recession the United States had experienced since the Great Depression.

The Bank of England estimates that the crisis globally destroyed one to three and one-half years of economic growth.[2] In the United States, $15 trillion in wealth disappeared, and some nine million individuals fell into poverty.[3] Corporate profits in the financial sector, which had reached a pre-crisis peak of $401.5 billion in the second quarter of 2006, turned into a $101.5 billion loss by the fourth quarter of 2008. Recovery from the downturn was much slower than for other post-World War II recessions.

US real gross domestic product (GDP) dropped at an annual rate of 8.2 percent in the fourth quarter of 2008, and real GDP growth did not turn positive until the third quarter of 2009. It rebounded to a fairly healthy annual rate of 2.5 percent in 2010. Over the next seven years, however, it never broke 3 percent and remained below 2 percent in three of those years. The unemployment rate more than doubled from 4.9 percent in February 2008 to 10 percent in October 2009. It remained at or above 9 percent through the third quarter of 2011, only declining below 5 percent in early 2016. It took over seven years for the unemployment rate to get back to its early 2008 level.

In part, the severity of the fallout from the credit crisis reflects the centrality of housing to the financial and private sectors. Mortgage lending and securitization constitute the largest portion of the US debt market, which is much bigger than the equity market. The US debt market in 2008 was about $30 trillion, versus equity market value of $15 trillion.[4] The collapse of house prices and the resulting losses for financial firms resulted in a substantial contraction of the entire financial sector and a consequent reduction in lending.[5]

The S&P/Case-Shiller US National Home Price Index, seasonally adjusted, reached its crisis-period peak in the first quarter of 2007. Housing prices in May 2011 declined to levels not seen since 2002, before the bubble started inflating,[6] but the S&P/Case-Shiller US National Home Price Index didn't bottom out until early 2012. Although prices in 10 of the 50 largest metropolitan areas were back to pre-crisis peaks by year-end 2013,[7] it wasn't until late 2016 that prices nationally attained and surpassed the peak reached in 2007.

Home values represent the largest portion of most individuals' actual and perceived wealth. By 2011, median household net wealth had declined by 35 percent from its 2005 peak.[8] Owners' equity in real estate had risen to about $13.4 trillion by the first quarter of 2006. By the first quarter of 2009, that figure had fallen by more than half, to about $6 trillion. It recovered only gradually, not reaching its 2006 peak until the first quarter of 2017.

Moreover, when house prices were increasing, a significant portion of homeowners refinanced with larger mortgages, taking out cash, which fueled spending.[9] Declining home prices brought an end to most borrowers' ability to refinance and extract equity. As these sources of cash withered, consumer spending, which had grown by 2.4 percent to 3.1 percent annually between 2004 and 2008, fell by 0.01 percent in 2009, depressing economic activity. In only one year since then, in 2011, did consumer spending grow by more than 2 percent, and from 2013 through 2016, growth remained below 1.5 percent annually.[10]

Delinquencies and defaults on single-family residential mortgages, which had picked up in mid 2006 and increased sharply starting in 2007, didn't peak until early 2010, as job woes pressured borrowers already struggling with declining house prices. Delinquencies and defaults remained close to crisis highs into 2013, with some 13 percent of mortgage holders still underwater in the third quarter of 2013. Foreclosures, which peaked in mid 2010, only returned to pre-crisis levels in early 2016, but were trending upward in late 2016 and early 2017. The good news has been that 70 percent of foreclosures were concentrated in loans originated during the housing boom and bust; those originated since 2009 are performing even better than the 1999–2003 vintages.[11]

The net profit for US banks and thrifts during the housing bubble had topped out at $40.2 billion in the fourth quarter of 2006, but that turned into a significant loss in the last quarter of 2008 and further losses in three of the next four quarters. Profitability returned in 2010, but did not top the pre-crisis peak until the first quarter of 2013. Growth was driven primarily by business loans,[12] but these too remained below their crisis-period peak until late 2016. Residential mortgage originations for first-lien purchases dropped fairly steadily from the bubble peak of about $1.5 trillion in 2007 to half that amount in 2011 before working their way back up to the $1 trillion mark in 2016.[13]

Non-agency issuance of residential mortgage-backed securities (RMBS), which had ballooned to a high of about $1.2 trillion in 2006, dropped by about one-third in the following year and fell off a cliff in 2008 to $52 billion, down more than 95 percent from the peak; it had not broken $100 billion through 2016. Subprime RMBS issuance virtually disappeared after 2007. The business of securitizing loans has fought its way back to life since 2010, with products based on junk bonds, credit card debt, and auto loans back on the market, but not mortgages.

The US equity market got off to a quick start on the path to recovery from the credit crisis and, notwithstanding a few significant stalls and setbacks, has performed strongly in the ensuing years (see Exhibit 15.1). From its post-crisis bottom of 6,547 on March 9, 2009, the Dow Jones Industrial Average (DJIA) rose by 59 percent during the rest of the year to 10,428 on December 31. This still left the index down substantially

**EXHIBIT 15.1**

The Dow Jones Industrial Average (DJIA) in 2009–2018

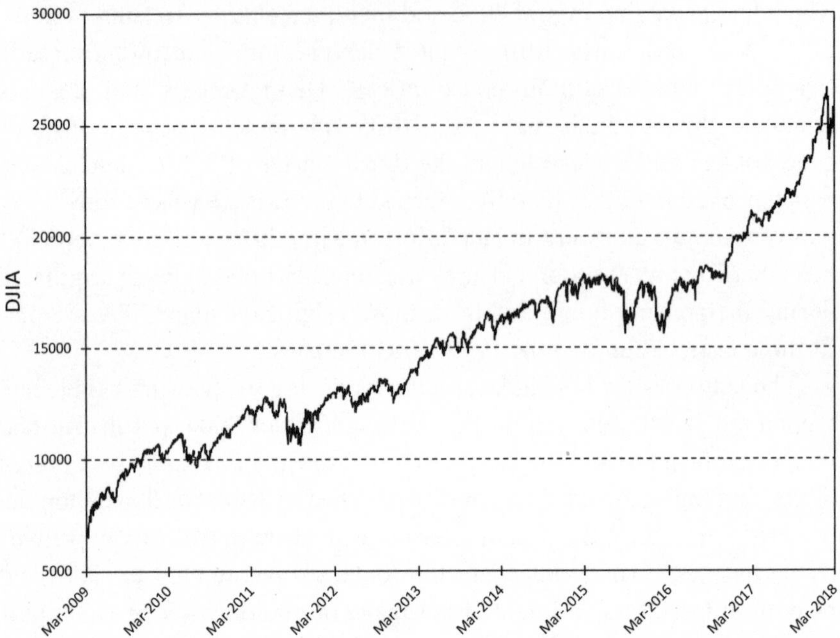


from its crisis-period high of 14,164 on October 9, 2007. The DJIA added another 11 percent in 2010, despite a flash crash in May that saw the DJIA down 600 points in one five-minute interval (see the sidebar, "High-Frequency Trading and Flash Crashes"). In 2011, however, the sovereign debt crisis in Europe, and the downgrading of the US credit rating, roiled both equity and bond markets worldwide and suppressed equity returns, despite increasingly strong company fundamentals.

## HIGH-FREQUENCY TRADING AND FLASH CRASHES

In the years following the 1987 crash, all exchanges stepped up replacement of time-consuming manual processes with automated systems that permit electronic routing and execution of orders. Improvements were also made to automated dissemination of trade information.

Nevertheless, by the close of the first decade of the twenty-first century, traditional exchanges such as the New York Stock Exchange (NYSE) and American Stock Exchange (AMEX) were being challenged by off-exchange trading venues.[14]

The ascendancy of electronic networks and private trading platforms (often called "dark pools" because of their lack of transparency), together with the speed with which trading can now occur on both these networks and more established exchanges, has given rise to a new set of problems, epitomized by the so-called flash crash. On the afternoon of May 6, 2010, with the DJIA already down more than 300 points (2.7%) from the open, the index fell almost 600 points in five minutes, only to recover most of this loss within one and a half minutes. In the interim, however, some stocks were selling at one cent per share, while the prices of other stocks, including Apple and Hewlett-Packard, topped $100,000.

An early report from the Securities and Exchange Commission (SEC) and Commodity Futures Trading Commission (CFTC) concluded that a US mutual fund manager using a computer trading program to sell Standard & Poor's 500 (S&P 500) futures set off a brief frenzy of trading by high-frequency traders.[15] These are institutional-size outfits that use computer algorithms and electronic networks to trade very rapidly, seeking to profit by turning over positions quickly rather than holding them. This, in turn, triggered a cascade of selling by arbitrageurs in the underlying stock market, which first scared away exchange market makers and then high-frequency traders. With the market bereft of buyers, prices dropped precipitously until a futures trading halt was triggered at the Chicago Mercantile Exchange.

A frequently used technique was cited in the 2010 Congressional testimony of SEC Chair Mary L. Schapiro.[16] She theorized that the automation of trading had contributed to the May 6 flash crash because high-frequency and other traders place market orders that do not discriminate between real bids and offers and so-called stub quotes. Stub quotes are quotes way outside current prices that are essentially place holders for market makers not inclined to trade. When market orders come from automated systems that seek immediacy, irrespective of price, these orders may be executed at irrational prices.

In the wake of the May 6, 2010 flash crash, exchanges instituted various trading-halt rules for individual securities. These did not stop flash crashes, however. On August 1, 2012, a newly installed automated trading system at brokerage firm Knight Capital Group began entering a series of irrational trades at the 9:30 a.m. opening. Millions of shares of almost 150 stocks were alternately bought and sold by the program, spiking the stocks' volumes and resulting in extreme price moves before the firm's managers could regain control of the trading program at 10:15 a.m. Although much of the trading took place on the NYSE, the exchange's trading halts did not kick in because they were not set to become effective until 30 minutes after the start of trading. Knight Capital Group took a loss of $400 million for the day and, by the end of the year, was acquired by Getco LLC, becoming KCG Holdings.

In 2015, the US Department of Justice charged a trader from England, Navinder Singh Sarao of Nav Sarao Futures, with causing the 2010 flash crash. The charges held that Sarao had used a computerized algorithm to engage in spoofing. "Spoofing" involves placing a large order that one never intends to execute in order to manipulate prices.[17] Sarao pled guilty in November 2016 to one count of wire fraud and one count of spoofing and was ordered to pay $38.4 million.[18] The emergence of automated, high-speed trading and the fragmentation of trading across numerous exchanges present problems for traditional circuit breakers and raise questions about the potential fragility of financial markets.

In 2012, with the crises in Europe easing and continued expansionary monetary policy, the DJIA was up again, although it remained below its previous high until 2013. It broke 15,000 for the first time ever in early May 2013, and then went on to surpass 16,000 in November 2013. The index broke 18,000 at the end of 2014, before turning in its first post-crisis annual loss in 2015. It recovered lost ground, and then some, in 2016, passing the 21,000 mark in March 2017 and exceeding 26,000 in early 2018.

## THE LEGAL FALLOUT

Another corner of the economy that has seen an upturn in business since the crisis is the legal profession. The US government, through the Department of Justice (DOJ), Securities and Exchange Commission (SEC), and

Federal Housing Finance Agency (FHFA), as well as various states' attorneys general, has collected billions of dollars from a flood of lawsuits against participants in the credit crisis. In 2010, Goldman Sachs paid a $550 million fine for its role in the Abacus collateralized debt obligation (CDO) (see Chapter 14, "Securitization and the Credit Crisis"). Citigroup in late 2011 paid $285 million to settle with the SEC over a similar CDO deal.[19] The FHFA has gone after 17 big financial institutions for hundreds of millions of dollars in recompense for poorly documented mortgages sold to the Federal National Mortgage Association (Fannie Mae) and the Federal Home Loan Mortgage Corporation (Freddie Mac).[20]

By early 2016, government actions against major banks (those with $100 billion-plus in assets) had netted over $118 billion in penalties for activities related to mortgage financing and securitization. Bank of America had paid out the largest share, some $56 billion, followed by J. P. Morgan Chase at $28 billion, Citigroup at $15 billion, Wells Fargo at $11 billion, Goldman Sachs at $9 billion, and Morgan Stanley at close to $5 billion.[21] In January 2017, Credit Suisse and Deutsche Bank reached settlements with the DOJ over their mortgage securitizations, agreeing to payments of $5.28 billion and $7.2 billion, respectively. The Royal Bank of Scotland settled with the FHFA for $5.5 billion in July 2016, with the State of New York for $500 million in March 2018, and with the DOJ for $4.9 billion in May 2018. The DOJ collected $2 billion in settlements from Barclays in March 2018 and another $2.09 billion from Wells Fargo in 2018. UBS paid $230 million to close out a case brought by New York State. Through later that year, financial settlements and penalties imposed by government agencies totaled about $150 billion.

Private parties filed mortgage-related lawsuits as well. A group of pension funds suing Wells Fargo over mortgage-backed securities (MBS) collected $125 million in 2011.[22] Bank of America, charged by shareholders with misleading them about its acquisition of Merrill Lynch, agreed to pay $2.438 billion.[23] Citigroup paid institutional investors $730 million in 2013 and $1.13 billion in 2014 to settle claims stemming from mortgage-related losses.[24] In March 2018, Lehman Brothers' bankruptcy estate paid out $2.4 billion to settle a lawsuit by investors in mortgage-related securities.

The internecine warfare has been intense. Morgan Stanley received $1.1 billion from MBIA, Inc. over guarantees on commercial and residential mortgage instruments.[25] Bank of America agreed to pay federal bailout beneficiary American International Group (AIG) $650 million to cover damages from MBS losses.[26]

There have been no successful criminal charges against a major player in the crisis.[27] A securities fraud trial of Ralph R. Cioffi and Matthew M. Tannin, managers of the Bear Stearns hedge funds that collapsed in 2007, resulted in acquittals, as did that of money market mutual fund creator Bruce R. Bent and his son and co-executive at the Reserve Primary Fund, which collapsed in September 2008 over its substantial holdings of Lehman Brothers' debt. Criminal investigations into Angelo R. Mozilo of Countrywide Financial and into executives at other mortgage brokers including Washington Mutual, IndyMac Bank, and New Century Financial Corporation have fallen by the wayside.[28]

## US CONGRESS AND REGULATORS STEP IN

Responses to the crisis included a spate of new and pending regulations, spawned by the passage in mid July 2010 of the Dodd-Frank Wall Street Reform and Consumer Protection Act (Dodd-Frank). The act set out a framework for reform, leaving many of the details to be filled in by the federal regulatory agencies. One of the immediate effects of Dodd-Frank, however, was to cap payments from the Troubled Asset Relief Program (TARP).

TARP, passed in 2008, had authority to pay out up to $700 billion to help relieve the credit crunch. Dodd-Frank capped that figure at $475 billion, and the authority to make further payments under TARP expired in October 2010. Program payouts were phased out in October 2010.[29] By then, all the largest banks except Citigroup had repaid their TARP loans, and General Motors and Chrysler had emerged from bankruptcy reorganization. Total TARP disbursements eventually amounted to about $439 billion.

As of September 30, 2017, the US Treasury had collected 103 percent of the TARP funds disbursed. Bank support yielded the largest profit, some $30 billion, while credit support, including funds for purchasing automaker stocks and asset-backed-security loans, netted $4.5 billion. Losses were incurred on the auto rescue program, primarily General Motors, and on the resale of AIG shares obtained by TARP. The latter loss was more than offset by gains on non-TARP shares held by the Treasury Department. Outside of TARP, Fannie Mae and Freddie Mac received about $187 billion from the government. Since they returned to profitability in 2012, virtually all their dividend payments have been swept to the Treasury (much to the consternation of shareholders, whose lawsuit challenging the government was turned away by the US Supreme Court in February 2018).[30]

One of the more publicized and controversial prescriptions of Dodd-Frank has been the so-called Volcker Rule, named after former Federal Reserve Board Chairman Paul Volcker. This rule aims to limit trading by banks for their own accounts, in part by curtailing banks' ownership of hedge funds and private equity funds, although allowing for hedging of a bank's own positions. The rule took effect in July 2015, although many banks had already begun to limit their proprietary trading by this time.[31] At the end of May 2018, the Fed released a proposal that would limit the rule's scope, exempting entirely smaller institutions that do not engage in a lot of trading.

Another problem uncovered by the credit crisis and targeted by Dodd-Frank is the role of credit rating agencies. The act sought to remove credit ratings from under the protection of the First Amendment; rating agencies had historically relied on First Amendment privilege to protect their ratings from legal liability. The legal implementation and consequences of this directive have so far been inconclusive. A judge in federal district court in Manhattan ruled in July 2012 that a rating agency's assertion that its ratings were merely opinions protected by the First Amendment could not protect the agency from liability for misleading ratings.[32] Nevertheless, by early 2013, some 41 legal actions against Standard & Poor's rating service were dropped based on a First Amendment defense.[33]

US federal and state governments have had more success pursuing the rating agencies under an earlier law passed after the savings and loan crisis of the 1980s—the Financial Institutions Reform, Recovery, and Enforcement Act of 1989. In a 2015 civil action brought by the DOJ and a number of states, Standard & Poor's agreed to a settlement of $1.375 billion for defrauding investors in RMBS and CDOs in the lead-up to the financial crisis; Standard & Poor's admitted it had falsely stated that its ratings were objective, independent, and not influenced by its business relationships with investment banks.[34] Moody's paid $864 million to settle a similar lawsuit in 2017; Moody's was found to have rated RMBS and CDOs using evaluation standards inferior to those it had publicized.[35]

Dodd-Frank directed that much of the trading of over-the-counter (OTC) derivatives, including credit default swaps (CDS) on indexes, be moved to clearinghouses. A clearinghouse, whose members are banks and other dealers, facilitates trade executions and stands ready to make good on any counterparty defaults. For these services, members deposit collateral, or margin. Margining and the ability to net exposures between different counterparties through central clearing have the potential to significantly reduce counterparty credit risk. Clearinghouses also increase transparency, insofar as they report transactional data to appropriate regulatory agencies, if not to the public generally. Under Dodd-Frank, information from trading in derivatives and swaps not required to trade on clearinghouses would have to be reported to repositories such as the Depository Trust & Clearing Corporation or to government agencies, with the aggregated data being disclosed to the public.

Various sections in the act address capital and leverage ratio requirements. In addressing the requirements of the act, and in response to annual stress tests conducted on US banks since 2012, the Federal Reserve Board, the Federal Deposit Insurance Corporation (FDIC), and the Office of the Comptroller of the Currency (OCC) have passed new capital and leverage ratio requirements, which become fully effective in 2019. These generally follow the guidelines set by the Bank for International Settlements in Basel III and impose more stringent requirements for larger banks and, particularly, for global, systemically important banks (see the sidebar, "Basel III Capital Requirements").

## BASEL III CAPITAL REQUIREMENTS

Basel III significantly strengthens capital requirements for banks and adds new measures to bolster capital reserves during crises. The new rules retain the 8 percent minimum total capital requirement from Basel II but require that banks hold Tier 1 capital equal to at least 6 percent of risk-adjusted assets, up from 4 percent. Furthermore, at least 75 percent of Tier 1 capital must consist of common equity from shareholders, up from 50 percent. Common equity is better able to absorb losses than other, more ephemeral forms of capital, such as subordinated debt, minority stakes in other financial firms, and deferred tax assets.

Banks will also be required to hold a "capital conservation buffer" consisting of common equity equal to 2.5 percent of risk-weighted assets. This buffer could be drawn on during periods of stress. Erosion of the buffer would trigger restrictions on bank dividends and payments of discretionary bonuses to bank executives. Including the buffer, banks will be required to hold total capital (Tier 1 and other capital) equal to 10.5 percent of risk-weighted assets.

Basel III also calls for a "countercyclical buffer," ranging from 0 to 2.5 percent of risk-weighted assets in the form of common equity or similar quality capital. National governments would have the option of adopting this buffer, which is designed to increase as credit and systemic risk grow in a national economy. This provision is intended to address concerns that the older Basel rules are too pro-cyclical, exacerbating business cycles by promoting excessive lending during good times and drastic cutbacks in downturns.

The Basel Committee on Banking Supervision also endorsed the use of a leverage ratio, a ratio of Tier 1 capital to non-risk-weighted assets, including derivatives, repo transactions, and off-balance-sheet exposures. This is designed to serve as a reality check for capital ratios based on risk-weighted assets, as it would presumably be more difficult for banks to avoid it by moving assets off balance sheet or into assets with lower risk weightings. The leverage ratio, which takes effect in 2018, requires banks to hold Tier 1 capital equal to at least 3 percent of non-risk-weighted assets.

Basel III introduces two new measures to enhance the liquidity of supervised financial institutions. The minimum liquidity coverage ratio would require banks to have enough liquid assets to withstand a 30-day stressed scenario set by supervisors. The net stable funding ratio requires funding that is reliably available for over a year and that equals or exceeds a level that varies depending on the liquidity and maturities of on- and off-balance-sheet assets and whether funding is short or long term, retail or wholesale. These requirements should reduce the incidence of runs on banks and other financial institutions and their need to offload assets at fire-sale prices.

Basel III requirements are scheduled to become effective in stages between 2013 and 2019. However, national governments can modify them and apply their own timetables.

US regulators have generally adopted the international standards, but have in some cases toughened them. For example, rules for defining Tier 1 capital and for calculating the liquidity coverage ratio are more stringent. In addition, Dodd-Frank establishes minimum capital requirements and leverage ratio requirements for systemically important non-bank financial companies. The act also imposes a capital floor, which says that capital requirements for bank holding companies can be no less stringent than those that apply to their deposit-taking subsidiaries. Dodd-Frank also removes any references to credit ratings supplied by credit rating agencies from regulatory guidance on determining capital requirements for banks and insurance companies and asset restrictions for money market mutual funds.

The US leverage ratio is also tougher on the largest banks than its international counterparts. All bank holding companies and deposit-taking institutions are required to hold Tier 1 capital equal to 4 percent of their on-balance-sheet assets. For larger banks with more than $250 billion in assets or $10 billion of foreign exposures, a 3 percent supplementary leverage ratio is imposed, and it applies to on- and off-balance-sheet exposures. The largest bank holding companies with more than $700 billion in assets or $10 trillion in custodial assets must meet a tougher supplementary leverage ratio standard—5 percent, rather than 3 percent—to avoid restrictions on distributions and discretionary bonus payments. The standard rises to 6 percent for the holding companies' federally insured banking subsidiaries.[36]

## A 'Whale' Surfaces in London

It is important to keep in mind that heightened restrictions may have negative as well as positive consequences. One risk consultant warned that proprietary trading (that is, the trading financial institutions do for their own accounts) would, as a result of the Volcker Rule, simply move to institutions' market-making areas, rendering banks (and markets) more reliant on clients to take the other sides of trades the institutions want to make.[37] Events at J. P. Morgan Chase in the spring and summer of 2012 gave some cause for concern.

By 2012, J. P. Morgan Chase had closed its proprietary desk and private equity business, but was nevertheless lobbying for dispensations that would allow banks to continue making large bets with their own money.[38] A trader in J. P. Morgan's investment office, who became known as "the London Whale," had made a series of sizable and complex trades in derivatives and CDS allegedly meant to hedge against a European recession and then to hedge against its own hedge.[39] These bets went suddenly sour in the spring, resulting in losses of as much as $7 billion. The size of the loss suggested that the supposed hedges were actually speculative bets.[40] The bank's investment office was essentially run by former hedge fund managers and operated like a proprietary trading desk.[41]

The Volcker Rule and possibly centralized clearing could have deleterious effects on market liquidity. Banks' proprietary trading has traditionally played a market-making role, whereby banks take the other side of trades that would not otherwise be filled. If that function is curtailed by the Volcker Rule, market making may be left to the less regulated "shadow-banking system," or to high-frequency traders, which may not be willing to put their capital at risk when markets are under stress.[42] Some argue that central clearing transforms counterparty risk into liquidity risk. In particular, central clearing requires actual and immediate margin payments, which can result in liquidity problems for firms even if they are solvent.[43]

## A NEW COUNCIL TO MONITOR RISK

Dodd-Frank established the Financial Stability Oversight Council (FSOC), headed by the Secretary of the Treasury and including heads of the OCC, the SEC, the CFTC, the FDIC, the FHFA, and the Fed among its 10 voting members. The mission of the council is to identify threats to the stability of the US financial system. It has the power to designate financial institutions, even non-banks, as systemically important and to apply appropriate supervision and standards.

The FSOC also has broad authority to request information needed to determine the source and extent of systemic risks. Information is obtained through the Office of Financial Research (OFR). This office represents the outcome of the efforts of the Committee to Establish the National Institute of Finance, a group of academics and practitioners formed in the wake of the crisis to shape a regulatory approach to disclosure requirements that would allow identification of systemic risks. According to its 2012 Annual Report, the OFR sees its mission as:

> developing metrics for measuring risks to financial stability; monitoring and investigating risks; conducting research on stability; and improving data standards. It may request that supervisory agencies require companies to disclose data, and unlike the individual supervisory agencies, the office takes a broad view of the entire financial sector. Such a macroprudential approach can help to fill in the unavoidable data gaps that result from a segmented regulatory system.

US regulators have been unanimous in identifying a need for international coordination of rule- and standard-setting. The sovereign debt crisis in Europe, which unfolded on the heels of the US credit crisis, underscores that developments external to any country's financial system can create a systemic risk that leads to economic instability across countries.

## SHORT-VOLATILITY STRATEGIES

On Friday, February 2, 2018, the US Department of Labor (DOL) reported unexpectedly strong wage gains during the previous month, a development that brought a sudden end to a prolonged period of stock market calm. Fears of resurgent inflation knocked US stock indexes down by 2 percent for the day. The following Monday, February 5, major US stock indexes fell more than 4 percent, wiping out the year's gains. By Thursday, February 8, three more days of volatile trading had dragged the Standard & Poor's 500 (S&P 500) and the Dow Jones Industrial Average (DJIA) into correction territory (losses of 10% or more from the indexes' peak values).

Even more concerning was the reappearance of sharp price reversals and chaotic trading conditions seen in earlier market meltdowns. In one 15-minute period an hour before the close on February 5, the DJIA plunged 900 points before finishing down nearly 1,600 points, the index's biggest single-day point decline since August 2011.[44] The sharp price movements had all the earmarks of a liquidity-driven sell-off by investors pressured to unload stocks into a market with few buyers. Trading in some hard-hit exchange-traded products (ETPs) tied to a stock-price-volatility index was halted on Monday and Tuesday.[45] Several major discount brokerages suffered system outages, locking clients out of their accounts for a brief period.[46]

What was behind the turmoil in the midst of an otherwise strong US economy? Fingers soon began pointing at a relatively new category of financial products focused on stock-price volatility, which is often seen as a proxy for risk. These products were inspired by the Chicago Board Options Exchange Volatility Index, known widely by its ticker symbol, VIX. Launched in 1993, the VIX tracks investor expectations of price volatility of the S&P 500 index.[47]

A rise in the VIX, known as Wall Street's "Fear Index," often portends trouble for stocks, because higher expected stock volatility is usually associated with declining stock prices. The VIX, thus, typically moves in the opposite direction of stock prices. VIX-related products—futures based on the index were introduced in 2004 and options in 2006—are often used to hedge stock portfolios.

In early 2018, VIX levels had been unusually low for a prolonged period, in part because of efforts by the Federal Reserve and other central banks to restrain interest rates and stabilize prices following the credit and sovereign debt crises. Over the previous three years, the VIX level had averaged close to 14, well below the index's 19.3 average since its inception.[48] In the 12 months leading up to February's turmoil, the average VIX level was a mild 11.3.[49] During this period it became popular, and profitable, to use volatility products to bet that the calm would continue—a strategy known as short volatility.

Short-volatility strategies involve selling insurance against market turbulence, and they bear a striking resemblance to portfolio insurance. Like portfolio insurance, short-volatility strategies became popular during a long period of rising markets and low volatility, during which the potential risks of these strategies seemed remote.

One of the simplest short-volatility strategies is to sell options. As discussed in Appendix B, an option seller earns a premium payment for agreeing, in the case of a put option, to buy shares of the underlying security at the exercise price if the shares fall below that price before the contract expires. In the case of call options, the call seller earns a premium for promising to sell the security to the call buyer at the exercise price if the share price rises above the exercise price before expiration. In both cases, if the security's price holds steady and does not cross the exercise price—a bet investors were increasingly willing to make during the prolonged period of market tranquility—the option expires worthless and the premium is the option seller's profit.[50]

As volatility expectations fall, however, premiums for selling puts and calls fall as well. In the low-volatility environment leading up to 2018, volatility sellers were forced to sell increasing numbers of option contracts to meet their income targets.

Volatility-related strategies take other forms as well. One, known as risk parity, constructs a portfolio targeted to have equal risk or volatility across asset classes, such as stocks, government bonds, corporate bonds, and commodities.[51] This is accomplished by using leverage to increase the position size of low-volatility assets in the portfolio. As the volatility of an asset increases, its position size in the portfolio is reduced, and vice versa. If stock volatility increases, the risk-parity portfolio will sell stocks and buy bonds to maintain risk parity. Therein lies the potential for a volatility-induced selloff, with increased stock volatility leading to stock sales, in turn causing more stock volatility and more stock sales.

The sensitivity of risk-parity portfolios to changes in volatility is amplified by their use of leverage. In February 2018, the average leverage target for risk-parity funds was estimated to be a record 2.8 times invested capital, and open interest in futures contracts used to boost stock exposure was at an all-time high.[52]

Financial institutions that sell variable annuities are also players in the short-volatility arena. Under pressure from regulators to protect annuity buyers from extreme market moves, annuity providers try to keep portfolio volatility in check by selling stock index futures as volatility increases (and stock prices fall) and purchasing stock futures as volatility falls (and stock prices rise). This strategy—in effect, replicating a put option—is similar to portfolio insurance: buying stocks as prices rise and selling as prices fall. Such trend-following trading programs can be destabilizing when pursued on a large enough scale (see Chapter 5, "Portfolio Insurance and the Crash").

Investors seeking to speculate directly on a rise or fall in market volatility can choose from at least 40 ETPs.[53] Most are designed to increase in value as the VIX rises, but "inverse" funds gain in value as the VIX declines and fall in value as the VIX rises. Two of the most popular inverse funds at the beginning of 2018 were sponsored by Credit Suisse and ProShares.

The two funds attracted a combined $3.6 billion in investment at their peak, including $1.7 billion during a record-setting month, January 2018.[54]

Investors had poured an estimated $2 trillion into volatility-linked strategies by February 2018.[55] This was enough to destabilize markets when conditions changed.

On Monday, February 5, as concerns triggered by Friday's DOL report spread, the level of the VIX, which had begun the day at 19.2, more than doubled to 38.8 before settling at 37.3, the highest close in two years. It was the index's largest one-day rise ever. On Tuesday, the VIX briefly surpassed 50 before closing at 30. Managers of leveraged funds that tracked the VIX index were forced to buy VIX futures, while managers of volatility-sensitive funds were forced to sell stocks or stock index futures to maintain their targeted volatility levels. Also in the market for futures were momentum traders and others hoping to profit from a rising VIX and/or falling stock indexes.

The surge in the VIX index was particularly problematic for inverse-VIX ETPs, designed to rise in value as the VIX index falls and fall in value as the VIX rises. This involves selling VIX futures, a strategy that produces a profit as long as volatility remains low. The funds had performed particularly well in 2017 and attracted substantial assets. By the close of trading on Friday, February 2, the two largest inverse-VIX funds were short about 200,000 contracts, equal to about three-quarters of the average daily volume of VIX futures expiring in March.[56]

The sharp rise in the VIX on February 5, however, meant sharp losses for inverse-VIX ETPs. To adhere to trading rules requiring them to rebalance their positions daily, they had to buy back the VIX futures they had sold, regardless of the current price. Furthermore, the immense size of their positions—the two largest funds held about 42 percent of the open contracts for March expiration[57]—was no secret, and sophisticated traders rushed to purchase VIX futures ahead of them, driving up their cost. In less than a minute, at 4:08 p.m. on February 5, close to 116,000 VIX futures contracts changed hands—about a quarter of all VIX futures contracts available at the time.[58]

The result was a scenario reminiscent of October 1987: a trend-following trading strategy that was orderly most of the time suddenly turned into a panic, overwhelming the market with buy orders for VIX futures and sell orders for stock index futures, with sophisticated investors trading in front of these orders. A positive feedback loop induced further trading. As purchases of VIX futures drove the VIX higher, leveraged and inverse funds based on the VIX index were forced to purchase more VIX futures. The turmoil spread to stocks as buyers of VIX futures hedged their exposures by selling S&P 500 futures, driving the index lower. A rising VIX also was a sell signal for other volatility-sensitive strategies, further pressuring stock prices.[59]

The combined value of the two largest inverse-VIX funds fell from more than $3 billion to just $150 million after the close of trading on February 5.[60] The Credit Suisse inverse-VIX fund, which lost 96 percent of its value that day, was liquidated shortly thereafter, along with a similar fund sponsored by Nomura.[61] The ProShares fund, which lost close to 90 percent of its value on February 5, remained in business but soon after changed its rules so that its share prices moved only half as much as before in response to changes in the VIX, an adjustment intended to dampen the fund's volatility.[62]

Even though losses from the blow-up in short-volatility strategies were largely confined to US stocks and VIX-related derivatives and the market disruptions were short-lived, the episode was a reminder that reduced-risk, high-return strategies still tend to lead toward destabilization. Thirty years after the stock market crash of 1987, those lessons must still be learned.

## CHAPTER 16

# The European Debt Crisis

*"We all lived through Lehman Brothers. I don't want another such threat to emanate from Europe."*

**—German Chancellor Angela Merkel**[1]

European banks have so far made only cameo appearances in our narrative. But it is not because they were bit players. Despite a perception that the global financial crisis was wholly a US phenomenon, European banks were deeply involved. They helped finance the creation of securities backed by subprime mortgages and were eager buyers of the finished products. Europe also experienced a credit bubble of its own, which gave rise to national housing booms—notably in Ireland and Spain—that were just as overheated as the one the United States experienced.

As the US boom in house prices ended, fault lines soon appeared in Europe. Falling US real estate values wreaked havoc on balance sheets of European banks, many of which had invested heavily in US mortgage-backed securities (MBS). The weakened banking sector would tie the hands of national governments as they tried to shore up their collapsing economies. Government officials would be further hampered by an ill-fitting currency union that left the region unprepared to deal with a debt crisis that emerged in Greece and quickly spread.

## ORIGINS OF EUROPE'S CREDIT BUBBLE

Earlier we discussed some of the factors behind the unprecedented increase in liquidity supplied by major central banks beginning in the 1990s (see Chapter 11, "Blowing Bubbles"). Among the factors were global economic competition after the fall of the Berlin Wall and attempts to cushion the coincident shocks of the September 11, 2001, attacks and the bursting of the tech stock bubble.

Another large part of this story was the excess savings that flowed to the United States from developing economies (the biggest of which were known collectively as "BRIC"—Brazil, Russia, India, China) as well as from Middle East oil producers and from other commodity exporters. But the widely accepted view—that these excess savings brought on low interest rates and shrinking risk premiums in the United States, Europe, and the rest of the developed world—tells only part of the story.

China and other emerging-market economies did indeed use their savings to accumulate large holdings of US public debt securities, helping to drive down interest rates. But at the same time, Europeans were building up equally impressive holdings of US securities, including privately issued MBS. European nations accounted for around half of total capital inflows to the United States in 2007.[2] Unlike the BRIC economies and oil exporters, however, Europeans financed their security purchases primarily with debt rather than with excess savings.

The 1999 creation within the European Union (EU) of a common currency, the euro, was also a major contributor to Europe's credit bubble.[3] The structure of the eurozone required the European Central Bank (ECB) to base its monetary policy on interest rates that were suitable for Germany, which had, by far, the largest economy. But rates that were suitable for Germany's well-oiled economy were far too low for less efficient economies on Europe's periphery. In theory, the market, by pricing in country-specific risks, would appropriately adjust individual countries' borrowing costs. But this did not happen until Europe became mired in crisis in 2010. For nearly a decade before that, every eurozone country was able to borrow at low interest rates similar to Germany's, thanks to the widespread belief that their individual economies would become more like Germany's (a process known as "convergence") or that they would be bailed out if they failed.

These illusions were reinforced by spending and debt limits that countries had to meet as a condition of membership in the currency bloc. These included stipulations that a member country's annual budget deficit not exceed 3 percent of its gross domestic product (GDP) and that the country's accumulated debt not exceed 60 percent of its GDP.[4] These conditions ostensibly ensured that governments would manage their fiscal affairs prudently. But there was plenty of wiggle room. Countries could exceed the deficit target on an "exceptional and temporary basis," and the debt target could be exceeded as well if the excess debt was diminishing "at a satisfactory pace." Thus, Italy and Belgium became founding members despite having more than twice the level of debt allowed.[5]

The assumption that all eurozone members were on the same fiscal footing allowed Greece, Italy, and others to issue sovereign debt—bonds backed by national governments—at yields that were only fractionally above those of Germany, despite large gaps in competitiveness and inflation rates. Greece's pre-euro 10-year bond yields, for example, were as high as 24.5 percent in 1993, but fell to 6.5 percent in 1999, the year the euro was launched.[6] From 1999 until mid July 2007, spreads of eurozone sovereign bond yields over German bond yields moved in a narrow range with only modest differences between countries.[7]

## A HOUSING BUBBLE INFLATES IN EUROPE

As in the United States, low interest rates fueled a credit binge in Europe. European household debt surged from 52 percent of GDP in 1999 to 70 percent in 2007 (though this was still below the US level of 95 percent).[8] Much of this borrowed money found its way into the housing market. Home prices rose from the late 1990s to 2007 in most European countries, and in many countries prices rose by more than they did in the United States. From 1996 until their peak a decade later, real house prices increased 182 percent in Ireland, 152 percent in the United Kingdom, 115 percent in Spain, 108 percent in France, and 51 percent in Italy.[9] The housing boom gave rise to construction booms in Spain and Ireland, where construction investment accounted for as much as 20 percent of GDP, far above the US level.[10]

Although cheap credit fed housing bubbles in both Europe and the United States, Europe's had its own distinct flavor. US-style securitization played a much smaller role in the European mortgage market than it did in the United States. There were various reasons for the difference.

The government itself was the dominant enabler of mortgage securitization in the United States. Government-sponsored entities (GSEs) such as the Federal National Mortgage Association (Fannie Mae) and the Federal Home Loan Mortgage Corporation (Freddie Mac) purchased qualifying mortgages, securitized them, and sold the MBS with guarantees of timely interest and principal payments.[11] Non-agency securitizers (banks, hedge funds, and others) also played a significant role in increasing the issuance of subprime and other mortgages not qualifying for US agency purchase. As we have noted, this type of securitization increased funding for more mortgages, freed up capital by reducing risky assets in bank portfolios, and reduced or eliminated the risks of nonpayment and prepayment for mortgage originators.

European governments had nothing comparable to Fannie Mae or Freddie Mac.[12] European mortgages were far more likely to be funded the traditional way—by bank deposits—rather than through securitization. The dominant role of securitization was unique to the United States, where 50 percent of mortgages were securitized in 2007. In Europe, just 13 percent of mortgages were securitized that year, although Spain and the United Kingdom had securitization rates as high as 24 percent and 28 percent, respectively.[13]

European banks also financed mortgages by issuing "covered bonds"—bonds backed by pools of performing mortgages that remained on lenders' balance sheets. Securitization that removed mortgages from the originator's balance sheet only emerged as a significant source of funding in Europe in 2002, and even then, only in the United Kingdom, Ireland, and the Netherlands.[14] In these countries, securitization served a key function of providing relief from capital requirements, as in the United States. But in Spain, which accounted for almost half of securitizations by euro area banks in 2007, and in Portugal, regulators required securitized mortgages to remain on the balance sheet. Securitization in these countries was used purely to raise capital to fund additional mortgage loans rather than to bypass regulatory capital requirements.[15]

The design of European mortgages and underwriting standards reflected the fact that securitization was seldom used as a vehicle for risk reduction. US-style long-term, fixed-rate loans were uncommon in Europe. Mortgages were far more likely to be adjustable-rate mortgages (ARMs) and ARM hybrids, which posed less interest-rate risk to lenders. Variable-rate mortgages and short-term (one- to three-year) fixed-rate loans were the most common forms of mortgage lending in Ireland, Spain, and the United Kingdom. In Germany and the Netherlands, rollover mortgages, which typically had a fixed rate for five years or 10 years and a 25- to 30-year amortization period, were popular. On all varieties of mortgages, severe penalties for early payment were common, and lenders typically had recourse to borrowers' non-housing wealth in case of default.[16]

Given the design of European mortgages, which shifted most interest-rate risk to the borrower, banks in Europe had less need for securitization as a risk-reduction measure than banks in the United States, where most borrowers could lock in interest rates for 30 years and prepay loans without penalty if interest rates fell. Cultural differences reduced the role of securitization as well. European banking has long been relationship based, and selling loans was sometimes considered a breach of the relationship.[17]

European mortgage underwriting was also generally stricter than in the United States. Loan-to-value ratios for mortgages that backed covered bonds typically topped out at 80 percent.[18] Subprime lending was rare outside the United Kingdom, where it peaked at 8 percent of the market in 2006, versus 25 percent in the United States.[19]

## EUROPE IMPORTS A SUBPRIME PROBLEM

European banks issued one-fifth as many residential mortgage-backed securities (RMBS), collateralized debt obligations (CDOs), and other forms of asset-backed securities (ABS) as US banks did in 2007.[20] Although CDOs constituted a higher proportion of the structured finance market in Europe than in the United States, banks in the United States still issued nearly three times more CDOs than European banks. European-issued structured finance products were primarily for local purchase; about 60 percent remained in European hands, while only one-third of those issued by US banks stayed in the hands of US investors.[21]

The lack of a sizable, homegrown subprime market in Europe did not turn out to be an impediment to participation in the subprime boom. US commercial and investment banks were more than happy to help their European counterparts indulge a growing appetite for subprime securities.

Not that European banks needed much convincing. Their balance sheets were expanding rapidly, growing by 53 percent between 2003 and 2007 in the eurozone.[22] By early 2008, European banks owned $30 trillion in foreign assets, 10 times the foreign holdings of US banks.[23] US private-label mortgage securities were a significant portion of those holdings, because they offered attractive yields compared with US Treasury and agency securities. They also came with AAA ratings that implied a high degree of safety.

These were not the only factors prompting banks to abandon their traditional bias toward assets in their home markets in favor of shopping internationally. The dollar was weakening against European currencies, which made dollar-denominated assets cheaper to buy. Furthermore, the shopping spree coincided with rapid growth in structured finance products, which was largely based in the United States.

Unlike many buyers from emerging markets, European buyers were willing to take on some credit risk. Europeans accounted for two-thirds of foreign purchases of US corporate debt from 2003 to 2007 and more than half of foreign purchases of ABS, such as RMBS and CDOs backed by subprime mortgages.[24] By mid 2007, European banks had accumulated more than $8 trillion in dollar-denominated assets over the previous decade.[25]

To finance their acquisition of US assets, European banks emulated their US counterparts by tapping more non-bank funding sources, particularly asset-backed commercial paper (ABCP) conduits. ABCP conduits were designed to allow banks to accumulate income-generating assets (primarily US MBS) with funds raised by the sale of commercial paper (CP) (see Chapter 12, "Weapons of Mass Destruction"). In July 2007, ABCP conduits held more than $1.2 trillion in assets worldwide. Though most paper issued by the conduits was denominated in dollars, US bank-sponsored conduits held only about $489 billion in assets. Conduits sponsored by European banks, especially those headquartered in Germany and the United Kingdom, held much of the rest.[26] Even though ABCP issuance fell sharply after 2007, holdings of the 15 largest US prime money market funds in mid 2008 show that about half their portfolios were invested in the CP and other short-term notes of non-US banks. Overall, US money market funds' investment in non-US banks reached an estimated $1 trillion in mid-2008.[27]

US banks preferred to keep conduit assets off their balance sheets to avoid a capital charge; their balance sheets did reflect bank capital set aside as liquidity guarantees, which were essentially promises to stand behind the conduit's obligations, or at least a portion of them. The Federal Reserve, the Federal Deposit Insurance Corporation (FDIC), and other US bank regulators essentially blessed this arrangement in 2004, reversing a policy requiring assets in ABCP conduits to be included in capital charge calculations. Bank regulators also ruled that only 10 percent of conduit assets covered by banks' liquidity guarantees needed to be reflected in the baseline 8 percent capital charge, an effective charge of less than 1 percent.[28]

In Europe, many banks were subject to accounting rules that required conduits to be consolidated on the balance sheet for financial reporting. But bank regulators in the United Kingdom, Germany, and some other countries did not require banks to hold any capital against assets in conduits. In 2006 and 2007, European banks began adopting Basel II rules, which required 20 percent of a bank's liquidity guarantee to be reflected on the balance sheet, an effective capital charge of 1.6 percent. But if the conduit was holding highly rated assets—and conduits held almost nothing but assets AAA-rated at issuance—the capital charge was even lower under Basel II's risk-weighting regime.[29]

## The Crisis Hits

When the US housing market began to slump in the summer of 2007, effects were felt almost immediately in Europe. In July, German lender IKB Deutsche Industriebank AG revealed crippling losses from US subprime mortgages and was immediately taken over by state-owned bank Kreditanstalt für Wiederaufbau (KfW). In August 2007, French bank BNP Paribas, complaining about the "complete evaporation of liquidity" for US mortgage securities, suspended redemptions from three of its funds that held them.[30] The following month, the failure of UK housing lender Northern Rock bank introduced a troubling new twist to the budding crisis: Northern Rock failed not because it held faulty US mortgage loans, but because it could not renew its own short- and medium-term loans that were being used to fund a solid portfolio of UK prime mortgages.[31]

Northern Rock's failure was an early signal of bank liquidity hoarding, something that would later mushroom.[32] It also highlighted the vulnerability of highly leveraged European banks. For every pound sterling of equity, Northern Rock held more than 86 pounds worth of assets.[33] While Northern Rock's 86-to-1 leverage ratio may have been an extreme case, the average European bank was leveraged 26-to-1 before the crisis hit, more than double the 12-to-1 average leverage ratio of US commercial banks.[34]

The prices of some eurozone sovereign bonds began falling after Northern Rock's failure, and many investors began retreating from structured assets. ABCP conduits encountered difficulties rolling over outstanding CP as key buyers, particularly US money market funds, shifted their investments toward safe government debt. The inability of conduits to renew their short-term funding was a key source of transmission of the crisis from the United States to Europe.

As the ABCP conduits collapsed, banks were forced to make good on their liquidity guarantees and step in with additional funding. This reduced the amount of money they had available to lend to others through the interbank market. That, combined with rising counterparty risk and mounting asset write-downs, led banks to begin to refuse to renew short-term loans.

In mid 2007, European banks also faced a severe dollar squeeze. They had $800 billion worth of short-term loans that needed to be repaid in dollars.[35] Other estimates put the dollar shortfall higher, between $1 trillion and $2.2 trillion.[36] This represented considerable exchange-rate risk, as European banks had to convert their home currency into dollars to meet these obligations.

With US money markets and the interbank market for dollars in turmoil, European banks' dollar demands soon overwhelmed currency swap markets. Spreads for overnight maturities ballooned to more than 7 basis points from just 0.1 basis points before the crisis.[37] The US Fed responded in late 2007 with the Term Auction Facility (TAF), which provided short-term loans to US banks and US branches of foreign banks. Of $500 billion in loans extended under the program by March 2009, almost 40 percent went to non-US banks.[38] The Fed, the ECB, and other central banks also put into place a system of currency swaps that provided unlimited supplies of dollars to foreign banks at prevailing exchange rates. Swap spreads decreased markedly after that and stabilized by the following January.[39] But banks remained dependent on dollar-based funding, and strains would reappear in 2011 when money market fund investors once again abandoned European banks in the wake of the sovereign debt crisis.

## European Banks Are Badly Damaged

Almost every European country committed substantial sums of taxpayer money to support its banks at the peak of the crisis in October

2008. Nevertheless, many European banks remained in a continuous state of fragility for years after the crisis erupted. Their recovery has been hindered by a number of structural and cultural factors. Generally, Europe's banks were far larger than their US counterparts. In 2009, for example, aggregate assets of the three largest banks in the Netherlands represented 406 percent of GDP and in the United Kingdom 336 percent of GDP, compared with 43 percent in the United States. Banks in Europe generally had a larger role in financial intermediation than in the United States, where a "shadow banking system" was a much larger factor.[40] European banks also were more thinly capitalized, as mentioned earlier.

Europe had no equivalent to the US's FDIC resolution process to wind down failing banks.[41] Regulators and central banks were more likely to bail them out or nationalize them than to dismantle them. Senior and junior bank creditors were made whole in almost every case.[42]

European bank bailout costs were staggering. From 2008 to 2011, EU governments committed nearly 4.5 trillion euros to support banks. About 1.7 trillion euros, or 13 percent of EU GDP, were actually paid out, mostly in the form of capital injections, asset purchases, and debt guarantees.[43] The Irish government, a notable example, committed to spend 64 billion euros to bail out its banks, a sum equal to roughly 14,000 euros for every resident,[44] and more than twice the nation's annual economic output.[45]

Costs were all the more difficult to bear as they occurred during a period when government budgets deteriorated sharply as the result of weakening economic activity and rising social welfare costs. In the second half of 2008, many European countries experienced a decline in real GDP for the first time in more than a decade. In many EU countries, residential building activity in 2008 fell almost to 1998 levels.[46]

## BANK DIFFICULTIES WEIGH ON GOVERNMENTS

European banks held large quantities of sovereign debt, issued primarily by their home countries, although their cross-border holdings were also significant. Sovereign bonds were attractive to banks because Basel Accord rules generally considered them risk-free and did not require any capital charge for holding them. In addition, the ECB accepted them, at face value, as collateral for loans to banks. Close ties between government and banking officials also encouraged banks to provide support to their governments through bond purchases. National governments were thus very dependent on the health of their banks, which served as a primary market for their sovereign debt.[47]

But bank bailouts sent troubling signals to investors about the governments' own health. Yields on 10-year Irish government bonds, for example, soared from a record low of 3.1 percent in 2005 to a record high of 14 percent in July 2011.[48] There was a clear rise in sovereign credit risk in the aftermath of bailout measures, evidenced by a large increase in the cost of credit default swaps (CDS) on sovereign debt.[49] The rise reflected the expectation of future taxation or inflation costs as well as a feedback mechanism by which bailouts caused government bonds to lose value, damaging the health of the banks that held the bonds and limiting the ability of governments to engage in further bailouts.

## The Greek Debt Crisis Breaks

In October 2009, George Papandreou led Greece's socialist party to a landslide election victory based on promises to boost government spending and increase wages. Greek 10-year bonds at the time yielded 4.58 percent. But upon taking office, the Papandreou government immediately revised the 2009 budget deficit estimate from an unhealthy 6.7 percent of GDP to 12.7 percent, and later above 15 percent. This prompted credit rating agencies to downgrade AAA-rated Greek government bonds, and their prices plummeted.

The budget revelations brought to light many problems in Greece that had long been ignored or downplayed, including pervasive yet inefficient state control of the economy and widespread tax evasion. Upon joining the euro bloc, Greece used its new access to credit mostly to invest in additional public-sector benefits rather than in enterprises that would help repay the debt. Government expenditures in 2009 accounted for half of Greece's GDP, and of that amount, three-quarters went toward public-sector wages and benefits. Deficits ballooned during the 2000s. Public debt reached 126 percent of GDP in 2009.[50]

The emerging Greek crisis also exposed serious flaws in the mechanisms that governed the eurozone. Although members shared a common currency and monetary policy, each country controlled its own domestic budget. In 1997, the Stability and Growth Pact imposed penalties for exceeding debt and fiscal deficit caps. They were weak to begin with and ultimately toothless in the face of the severe economic downturn that began in 2008, which decimated the fiscal budgets of well-off and struggling nations alike.

Greece could be criticized for failing to rein in public spending when credit was plentiful, but other countries that seemed to be on firmer fiscal footing were also swept up in the crisis. Buoyed by large inflows of private capital, Ireland's fiscal accounts were continually in surplus from 2001 to 2007. Private capital flows also helped Spain run budget surpluses between 2005 and 2007.[51] In fact, Ireland and Spain reduced their public debt as a percentage of GDP between 2001 and 2007.[52] But each found itself fending off insolvency as foreign private investment evaporated, tax revenues collapsed, and the urgent need to rescue their banking systems hampered their ability to service suddenly rising debt levels.

## Rescuing Greece

Opposition within the eurozone to rescuing Greece was weakened by the possibility of home-country banks having to absorb losses on their holdings of Greek debt, and by fear that the crisis would spread to other countries whose banks were large creditors. From 2000 to 2008, banks from wealthy eurozone members such as Germany and France, as well as from the United Kingdom, had invested close to 1.6 trillion euros in countries that were now struggling with debt that was high (Greece, Italy, Portugal) or rising precipitously (Spain, Ireland).[53]

Europe's wealthier countries dodged a bullet when the Irish government guaranteed virtually all its private banks' obligations, many of which were owed to other European lenders. But the rescue came at tremendous cost to Irish taxpayers, nearly quadrupling Ireland's national debt just as the collapse of its housing bubble threw its economy into reverse.[54] Meanwhile, Portugal's economy was suffering from many of the same ailments as Greece's, including low productivity, lack of competitiveness, high unemployment, and growth averaging just 1 percent annually in the previous 10 years.

Following an emergency summit in February 2010, the EU and the International Monetary Fund (IMF) had put together a loan package for Greece—110 billion euros over three years, at market rates. In return, Greece agreed to reform its economy and slash its budget deficit to less than 3 percent of GDP—a drastic reduction of 11 percentage points—by 2014. EU and eurozone countries also created temporary lending programs, totaling 500 billion euros, for eurozone members facing debt crises. In December 2010, Ireland accepted 67.5 billion euros in loans under the program, and in May 2011 Portugal received 78 billion euros in loans. Both countries agreed to slash public spending and submit to EU oversight of their fiscal budgets as conditions for the bailout. The ECB also began buying European bonds in the secondary market to prop up their prices, and aided banks by accepting lower-quality collateral in exchange for one-year loans.[55]

## Europe Retrenches

Across Europe, austerity measures were implemented in response to rising fiscal deficits. But the money-saving measures had the side effect of depressing economic growth, lowering tax revenues, and deepening the downturn. Adding to the burden was a mandate from the European Banking Authority requiring banks to create a temporary core Tier 1 capital buffer of 9 percent of risk-weighted assets (more stringent than the 7 percent Basel III baseline standard). The mandate forced banks to sell or write down assets or raise $142 billion in new capital,[56] much of it through asset sales. As a result, they were hardly in a position to provide new loans for economic expansion. This caused particular hardship for European businesses, which raised far more of their capital through bank loans than did US corporations.

European banks faced additional pressure from US prime money market mutual funds, which had to contend with large-scale redemptions from investors who wanted to reduce exposure to the eurozone. These funds had helped trigger the crisis by halting purchases of CP issued by ABCP conduits, many of which were sponsored by European banks. They began to return to Europe in a big way in 2011, lured by high yields. But on June 15, 2011, Moody's Investors Service placed three large French banks, BNP Paribas, Société Générale, and Crédit Agricole, on review for a possible credit downgrade because of their exposures to Greece. Fearing that other European banks were exposed to Greece and would suffer the same fate, investors redeemed $180 billion from US prime money market mutual funds. Assets under management for these funds fell 11 percent between June 8 and August 31, 2011. Investors withdrew as much as half the assets of some funds.[57] Central banks were forced to extend their dollar swap facilities and reduce the cost of dollar funds to help out the embattled euro banking system.

## Greece's Troubles Re-emerge

Bailout loans failed to pull Greece out of its downward spiral. In fact, austerity measures demanded by lenders as a condition of the bailout may have accelerated it. With the main engine of Greek economic growth—its government—sidelined, the economy continued to contract, reducing tax revenues, increasing the budget deficit and overall debt, and putting solvency further out of reach. Tourism and the country's relatively small export sector could not assist a recovery because Greece could not devalue its currency, as it might have done before the euro.

Over time, it became painfully clear to international creditors that Greece would need a new package of bailout loans, and that the old loans probably would not be paid back in full. In February 2012, the EU, ECB, and IMF agreed to provide 130 billion euros in new loans in return for a promise to implement even more stringent austerity measures than before. These included a 22 percent cut in the minimum wage and, over the following three years, layoffs of 150,000 government workers out of a total workforce of 800,000. As part of the deal, private bondholders would trade in their old bonds for a package of securities valued at around 23 cents on the euro, reducing Greece's sovereign debt by about 100 billion euros to 260 billion euros. Days after the deal was completed in March, Fitch Ratings and Moody's declared Greece in default, the first by a developed nation since 1946.[58]

The deal left the Greek economy, which in 2012 was suffering through its fifth year of recession, with barely a pulse. Its economic output had fallen by 25 percent since 2010. Some 68,000 businesses had closed, and another 53,000 of the 300,000 businesses still active were thought to be close to bankruptcy. More than $75 billion in bank deposits had left the country as wealthy Greeks moved their savings abroad.[59] Unemployment was at 25 percent.

The second bailout package was designed to reduce Greece's debt burden to 120 percent of GDP by 2020, the limit of what was considered sustainable. But Greece's deteriorating economy quickly threw that plan off track. In late 2012, the Greek government projected debt would rise to 189 percent of GDP in 2013, up from 159 percent of GDP in the third quarter of 2011.[60] After many rounds of negotiations, Greece was loaned an additional 11 billion euros to buy back, at a deep discount, about 32 billion euros of bonds issued only nine months earlier.[61]

## Spain in the Spotlight

It didn't take long after Greece's second bailout package was finalized for the spotlight to turn to Spain. Its private debt load, bloated by bad real estate loans, was 227 percent of GDP, one of the highest in Europe.[62] In addition, Spain's banks held nearly 325 billion euros of private property assets, about two-thirds of which were labeled problematic by Spain's central bank.[63] Yields on 10-year government bonds were 7 percent in mid-2012, a level that had led to earlier bailouts in Greece, Ireland, and Portugal.

Spain's troubles did not stem from reckless public spending. Public debt, though rising, remained a manageable 70 percent of GDP in 2012. However, newly vigilant European political leaders insisted that Spain bring its fiscal deficit, which rose as high as 11 percent of GDP in 2009,[64] below 3 percent by 2013. As in Greece, this would require tax increases and large cuts in public spending. It would place a burden on an economy that had already been in recession twice since 2007. A quarter of the workforce was idle.

A bailout of Spain, the eurozone's fourth-largest economy, would be a much more expensive proposition than rescuing Greece. Cost estimates ranged as high as 350 billion euros,[65] which would blow a large hole in Europe's 500-billion-euro temporary bailout fund (which was later replaced by a permanent bailout fund, also capped at 500 billion euros). If Spain fell, expectations were that Italy, with a long-stagnant economy and a debt-to-GDP ratio of 120 percent, would soon follow.

## United States and Others Feel Europe's Pain

By late 2012, economies accounting for 60 percent of Europe's output were stagnant or shrinking,[66] and the impact was being felt all over the world. Slowing growth in Asia was exacerbated by a slowdown in European business. China's economy was on track for its weakest annual expansion in more than 20 years, owing in part to weak exports to Europe, which until then was its largest export market. US manufacturers, particularly automakers and high-tech firms, were increasingly blaming disappointing results on Europe, the destination of about one-fifth of US exports. A pullback by Europe's giant banks was reducing global credit availability. In October 2012, the IMF declared that the risks of a global slowdown were "alarmingly high."

## THE EUROPEAN CENTRAL BANK STEPS IN

The eurozone was not without the means to solve its problems. The budget and current account deficits of the entire eurozone were smaller than those of the United States. But it had no mechanism for transferring funds from wealthier countries, primarily in the north, to the struggling economies in the south. The currency bloc's budget and debt limits were supposed to have prevented the need for collective financing of lagging nations in the first place. But having failed to accomplish that goal, Europe had no Plan B. Political leaders, and more importantly voters, in Germany, Finland, the Netherlands, and other relatively prosperous nations strongly opposed contributing to bailouts. They viewed their neighbors' struggles as the consequences of their own poor choices rather than as unavoidable fallout from a systemic financial crisis.

By design, the ECB was not a lender of last resort in the mold of the US Federal Reserve. Its role was officially limited to managing the bloc's monetary policy. The 1992 Maastricht Treaty, which framed the terms of the EU, barred eurozone members from taking on the liabilities of fellow members—a "no-bailouts clause." Germany, which wielded outsized influence within the currency bloc, interpreted this provision to preclude collective aid channeled through the ECB or the issuance of bonds jointly backed by eurozone governments.

But the ECB had other options. In December 2011, as investor confidence was waning and yields on Spanish and Italian debt reached worrisome levels, the ECB rolled out a program offering banks three-year loans (previously, a one-year limit) at low interest rates of about 1 percent against a broad range of collateral. Hundreds of banks took out close to 1 trillion euros in loans in late 2011 and early 2012. Much of the cash went to replace existing loans, but experts said as much as 520 billion euros of new money went into eurozone economies.[67] The three-year payback period appeared to provide a degree of stability.

In the weeks following the initial round of loans, banks also used the money to purchase sovereign debt. Yields on the debt of the eurozone's troubled economies began falling noticeably. A month after the first round, Italy's five-year bonds were trading at 5 percent, down from nearly 8 percent; Spain's 10-year rates fell to 5.5 percent from 7 percent.[68] The loans at least temporarily relieved governments of having to pump new money into their shaky banks and adding further to national debt loads. Rather, they created a virtuous circle. Against a backdrop of promised budget cuts by governments, banks were buying sovereign debt with the proceeds of the ECB loans.

The sense of relief brought about by the ECB loan program did not last long. By mid 2012, Spain's debt problems were growing worse, and Spanish and Italian bond yields were back at worrisome levels. Again the ECB stepped in, offering to stabilize Spain's banks with up to 100 billion euros in loans, of which Spain accepted 37 billion euros.[69] Several months later, the ECB announced a plan to purchase unlimited amounts of short-term debt directly from governments. Though no purchases were made, the open-ended nature of the program implied the ECB could focus considerable resources on keeping a participating country's debt costs in check. Yields on the long-term debt of Spain and Italy immediately began falling.

Still, the eurozone economy was hardly on solid ground, as Cyprus demonstrated the following spring. Its banks were decimated by losses on their holdings of Greek sovereign debt. The island nation was forced to accept a bailout deal in March 2013 with a harsh new twist. The EU, ECB, and IMF required bondholders and uninsured depositors of Cyprus's failed banks to contribute up to 13 billion euros of a 23 billion euro bailout package. This requirement virtually wiped out deposits above the insured level of 100,000 euros, decimating many small businesses.

## STUCK AT THE CROSSROADS

Amid growing confidence in the ECB's efforts to keep the currency union intact, Europe appeared to have regained its footing by 2015. Ireland, Portugal, and Cyprus all had exited their bailout programs (Ireland and Portugal in 2014, Cyprus in 2015) and were fiscally self-sufficient. Ten-year government bond yields in Spain and Italy neared all-time lows. But the eurozone economy was still smaller than it was before the crisis, and the pace of recovery was slower than it was after the Great Depression.

With deflation looming and Europe's leaders unable to stimulate economic growth, unemployment remained stubbornly high, particularly among the young. Widespread discontent, fueled by stagnant growth and immigration concerns, led to a troubling rise in support for nationalist and anti-EU political parties and the stunning success of a June 2016 ballot measure in the United Kingdom mandating an exit from the EU (Brexit). The previous year, a standoff between EU leaders and a newly elected left-wing government in Greece prompted billions of euros in capital to flee the country, crippling banks and once again crushing the Greek economy. Greek leaders had to accept 86 billion euros more in loans. Greece finally exited the bailout program in 2018.

Europe's ongoing economic problems can be traced back to many of the same origins as those that plagued the United States during its shorter-lived crisis. In both cases, an abundance of credit found its way into housing markets, inflating bubbles. While Europe's regulatory regime and banking culture limited its banks' issuance of subprime MBS, these factors did little to discourage banks' purchases of those securities for their own investment portfolios. European banks gorged on the securities, exhibiting the same misunderstanding of risk and herding tendencies as their US counterparts.

As US banks did, European banks financed highly leveraged purchases of mortgage securities with short-term borrowing arrangements that could not be renewed once the bubble burst. European banks then faced the added burden of having borrowed in a foreign currency—US dollars—to purchase dollar-denominated mortgage securities, forcing them to scramble not only to fund their liabilities but to do so in dollars that were becoming increasingly scarce in the global panic of late 2008 and again in 2011.

Through the early stages of the crisis, the consequences played out in Europe much as they did in the United States. As the twin engines of expansion—finance and housing—sputtered, economies on both sides of the Atlantic fell into deep recession. Governments were forced to step in with massive public expenditures to rescue banks and prop up faltering economies. But here is where the stories diverge.

As the US economy began to recover in 2009, the sudden emergence of a debt crisis in Greece exposed a case of misperceived risk that was perhaps even greater than the one centered on mortgage products. For more than a decade, investors had been lending to Greece and other risky economies on Europe's periphery at interest rates barely above those demanded by lower-risk, relatively efficient economies, such as that of Germany. These bargain interest rates were nothing more than a free lunch that would cause widespread indigestion when the bill was presented later. They were justified at the time by the expectation that the economies of every nation that adopted the common currency would converge, acquiring all the qualities that made Germany and others formidable while shedding those qualities that held back weaker players.

This was a classic case of excessive optimism and overconfidence.[70] While it lasted, it papered over the shortcomings of the currency bloc's political structure as well as chronic economic imbalances between the strong economies of the north and the weaker ones of the south. The promise of convergence seemed to minimize the risk of investing in Spain and Ireland even as their housing markets were overheating and the risk of acquiring sovereign debt issued by Greece, Portugal, and Italy as their economies were stagnating.

The admission in 2009 by Greece that its fiscal deficits had been grossly understated brought about an unusually sharp and swift change in sentiment. It also set in motion a feedback mechanism that allowed the problems of a small country accounting for less than 3 percent of the EU economy to quickly engulf the continent.

The collapsing value of Greek sovereign debt weakened Greek banks, and falling sovereign debt values in other struggling European nations had the same effect on the balance sheets of their own domestic banks. This increased the financial pressure on national governments as they were struggling to recapitalize their banking systems during a period of deep recession and diminished tax revenues. The unavailability of bank lending further dampened economic growth, which further reduced tax revenues and hampered the ability of governments to meet rapidly rising debt obligations. As public debt levels reached new highs, the cost of issuing new public debt soared, raising questions about governments' ability to meet their obligations. Those doubts depressed the value of previously issued sovereign bonds, further weakening the balance sheets of domestic banks that held them.

The currency union that tied European nations together served as an additional transmission channel of the crisis. In the absence of a single fiscal authority, the credibility of the euro rested upon the ability of members of the bloc to remain within agreed-upon debt and deficit boundaries. It quickly became clear that Greece could not. No longer able to borrow in international capital markets, Greece was forced to turn for help to other eurozone countries and the IMF. Many of the same factors that weighed upon the Greek economy forced Portugal, Ireland, and later Cyprus to request bailouts. Now the question was not only whether the eurozone could summon the political unity to mount an effective rescue program for its credit-starved members, but whether it could afford to do so if the contagion spread further to large countries like Spain and Italy.

Thanks in large part to timely interventions by the ECB, members of the eurozone have achieved enough unity (so far) to stave off economic catastrophe. But if Europe is ever to earn a clean bill of health, it must tackle not only the same issues of systemic risk in the banking system that the United States faces, but the much more difficult question of how to structure the economic union so that the problems of one member do not bring disaster to all.

CHAPTER 17

# Illusions of Safety and Market Meltdowns

*"Wall Street gets in its worst trouble not by taking risks but by following false prophets who promise to make finance risk-free."*

**—Martin Mayer**[1]

Part I of this book described the investment decision-making process as a tradeoff between the rewards and associated risks of various investment instruments and strategies. Much of quantitative finance is devoted to measuring and attempting to control this tradeoff. In theory, market prices are the result of a rational balancing act between risk and return.

Behavioral finance recognizes that this balancing act is often destabilized by the tendency of humans to act in less than perfectly rational ways. In the vernacular, markets are driven by emotions, by hope for future gains, and fear of future losses.[2] While hope and fear may be reined in by reason, one or the other is always ready to break out and upset the equilibrium, sometimes for extended periods.

The entire market can be swept along by hope or fear, leading to a repeating pattern of booms and busts. As noted earlier, economist Hyman P. Minsky has explained this pattern in terms of overly optimistic lending in good times leading to speculative bubbles, which are dependent on continuing price appreciation (see Chapter 2, "Black Monday 1987").[3] When prices fail to rise, or begin to fall, repayment of debt may require liquidation of assets, leading to fire sales and crashes.

Underlying this behavior may be "representativeness," one of the behavioral finance theories advanced by Daniel Kahneman and Amos

Tversky.[4] The theory suggests that in good times, investors may overestimate the likelihood that stock prices will continue to rise, ignore underlying fundamentals, and underestimate the probability of loss. Other cognitive biases may come into play.[5]

"Recency bias" may lead investors and others to focus on recent data and events, and neglect information from further in the past. "Regret aversion" may make investors reluctant to sell assets whose prices are rising because they believe they could profit more by waiting. Such biases may lead to asset bubbles, neglect of risk, excessive debt issuance, and eventual crisis.[6]

The crises we have discussed are occasions when investor emotion overcame investor rationality. Fear took over during the stock market crash of 1987, the market turmoil of late summer and fall 1998, and the credit crunch of 2007–2008. But before the fear, there was a feeling of hope. It was hope that had raised financial markets up to the pinnacles from which they fell. As we noted in the Introduction, these crises affected different markets: the first centered on the stock market; the second centered on international fixed-income and derivatives markets; and the third centered on international credit markets. In all these cases, however, certain investment strategies or instruments, products of highly sophisticated financial ingenuity, propelled market rises and contributed to market falls by channeling, first, investors' hopes and, later, investors' fears. Yet, all these products were designed to reduce risk and increase return.

## A FREE LUNCH

Portfolio insurance emerged in the 1980s out of the fertile ground of market efficiency and the Black-Scholes-Merton options pricing formula. It was marketed not only as a means of controlling risk by promising a predetermined floor for a portfolio's value, but as a means of increasing returns beyond a simple strategy of buying and holding a representative market index.

One 1982 ad by Leland O'Brien Rubinstein Associates (LOR) touted "a guaranteed equity investment"; it was accompanied by a diagram showing that "hypothetically over the 10 years ending 1981, one dollar invested in the S&P 500 would have returned . . . 6.5% per annum . . . one dollar invested in the S&P 500 and in T-bills in accordance with the principles of Dynamic Asset Allocation [portfolio insurance] would have returned . . . 10.0% per annum" (see Exhibit 17.1).[7] Another ad from LOR and Aetna promised "a guaranteed minimum rate of return" and showed a cumulative 10-year return for the strategy of 170%, versus 91% for the Standard & Poor's 500 (S&P 500) (see Exhibit 17.2).[8] A J. P. Morgan ad said, "We develop and implement strategies for our clients that

**EXHIBIT 17.1**

Assured Equity Investing: "A Guaranteed Equity Investment"

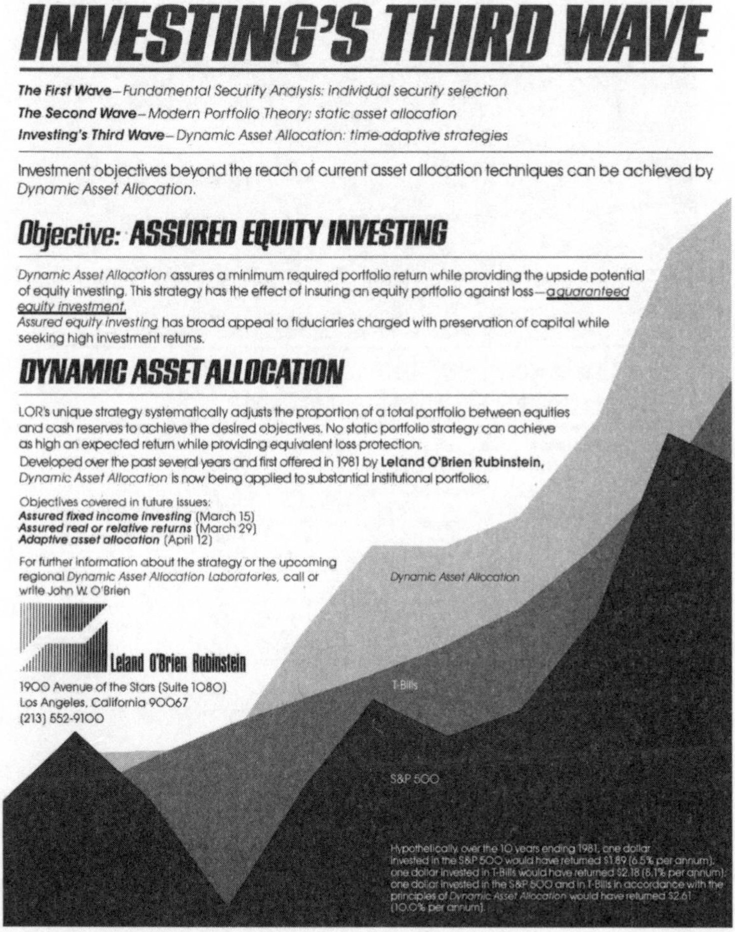

Source: *Pensions & Investment Age*, March 1, 1982.
Note: Underline added to a *guaranteed equity investment*.

**EXHIBIT 17.2**

Higher Cumulative Returns

**Read what happened when the pioneer of dynamic asset allocation met the manager of $25 billion in pension funds.**

*They came up with GEM, Ætna Life & Casualty's Guaranteed Equity Management strategy.*

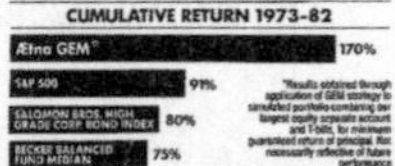


*What makes GEM unique is the combination it offers: Dynamic asset allocation, coupled with a guaranteed minimum rate of return which you select.*

*What's more, GEM offers the highest equity participation of any dynamic strategy available.*

*What else makes our GEM strategy so remarkable? The investment technology credentials of Leland O'Brien Rubinstein Associates (LOR) are impeccable. They provide dynamic asset allocation services and nothing but. Currently, they are serving twenty other portfolios totaling over $600 million.*

*Ætna's equity management credentials are equally impressive. Cumulatively, over a ten-year period, our largest pooled account performance has ranked in the top 9% of the P.I.P.E.R. universe.*

*And we provide pension and financial services to one out of four of America's largest corporations.*

*If you would like to learn more about GEM, get in touch with your Ætna Employee Benefits Representative, or call T. Jerald Moore, Vice President, at (203) 273-4734.*

***You'll be glad you met Ætna.***

Employee Benefits Division
Ætna Life Insurance Company
151 Farmington Avenue, Hartford, CT 06156

Source: *Pensions & Investment Age*, November 14, 1983.

systematically limit their exposure to market losses, yet allow them to participate in rising markets" (see Exhibit 17.3).

Risk was controlled by shifting portfolio assets between stock and cash, in accordance with the option pricing model, in order to replicate the behavior of a portfolio protected by a put option. As stock prices rose, portfolio insurance programs purchased more stock, and as stock prices

**EXHIBIT 17.3**

Limited Downside, Participation in Upside

**Portfolio Protection**

With nearly $6 billion in portfolio protection programs, J. P. Morgan Investment Management is a recognized leader in risk control. We develop and implement strategies for our clients that systematically limit their exposure to market losses, yet allow them to participate in rising markets.

Our emphasis on research has enabled us to develop proprietary management techniques including models and valuation procedures. Morgan specialists use these tools to design hedging strategies tailored to each client's precise needs.

J. P. Morgan Investment Management protects equity, fixed income, and balanced portfolios. We combine our risk control methods with our expertise in the related areas of immunization, equity management, and asset allocation to provide multi-dimensional protection programs. Call Douglas M. Fleming, Vice President, at (212) 837-1405.

**J. P. Morgan Investment Management**

**JPMorgan**

Source: *Pensions & Investment Age*, January 26, 1987: 19.

fell, programs sold stock. The amount bought or sold was dictated by the option pricing model and the parameters of the particular portfolio insurance strategy. In effect, the risk of stock market declines was to be shifted from "insured" investors to other stock market investors.

Long-Term Capital Management (LTCM), too, offered high returns at supposedly low risk. Myron S. Scholes and Robert C. Merton, creators of the option pricing model, were partners of the fund. Headed by John W. Meriwether, who had run one of Wall Street's most sophisticated quantitative bond trading desks at Salomon Brothers, LTCM's main line of business was bond arbitrage. Meriwether had brought with him to LTCM some of the most talented quantitative analysts (quants) from Salomon Brothers, and had recruited others from academia, as well as David W. Mullins Jr., a former vice chairman of the Federal Reserve Board (who had served on the Brady Commission charged with investigating the causes of the 1987 stock market crash).

LTCM's arbitrage strategies were designed to detect and exploit divergences from rational pricing. The strategies involved buying high-yielding (higher-risk) assets that were estimated to be "cheap" and selling short low-yielding (lower-risk) assets that were estimated to be "expensive." The aim was to profit from the spreads between high and low yields *and* from an increase in the prices of the assets bought and a decrease in the prices of the assets sold short.

To assess the risk of its strategies, LTCM conducted state-of-the-art risk analyses, including value-at-risk, as well as stress tests and scenario analyses. The overall portfolio was supposed to be neutral to broad changes in interest rates, stock market volatility, and currency rates. Exposures to these sources of systematic risk were controlled through offsetting long and short positions and the use of derivatives contracts such as futures, options, and swaps. LTCM's investors were informed in an October 1994 letter that there was only a 1-in-100 chance that the portfolio would sustain a loss of more than 20 percent.

In accordance with theory, these low-risk positions were expected to, and did, have low returns, a couple of cents on the dollar. High returns were achieved via leverage of 25-to-1, not taking into account the firm's derivatives positions. This leverage was justified on the basis of the supposedly extraordinarily low risk of the underlying positions.

Structured products like residential mortgage-backed securities (RMBS) and collateralized debt obligations (CDOs) based on subprime mortgages appeared also to be return-enhancing and risk-minimizing. The underlying subprime mortgages were inherently riskier than prime mortgages, hence commanded higher interest rates from borrowers. Much of the return was passed on to buyers of the structured products, including money market funds, which purchased commercial paper (CP) issued by structured investment vehicles (SIVs). At the same time, the risk was mitigated by the use of diversification and tranching.

Complex models of the co-movements of the underlying mortgages, including prepayment and default correlations, were supposed to ensure adequate diversification of the mortgage pools, thus insulating them from the specific risks of individual mortgage defaults. The magic of tranching transformed most of a pool into senior or super-senior debt cushioned by subordinated classes of debt that were to absorb virtually all losses. According to the models used by credit rating agencies, these senior tranches were near riskless, or near enough to qualify for the AAA rating accorded often to US government, and very few corporate, bonds.[9]

The financial intermediaries—banks, hedge funds, and insurance companies—that created and issued these products also used them to boost returns and lower risk. The products provided a means for mortgage lenders to reduce or eliminate the risk of mortgage defaults. This risk was transferred from the mortgage lenders to the RMBS or CDO buyers, the sellers of credit default swaps (CDS), and, to some extent, the buyers of CP. Financial intermediaries could profit by selling the products for more than their cost. They also collected hefty fees for structuring RMBS and CDOs.

Perhaps most importantly, transferring mortgage loans off their balance sheets via the sale of structured finance products allowed mortgage lenders to reduce the riskiness of their balance sheets. They could, therefore, lower the amount of capital they had to hold against assets. This boosted their reported return on equity. It also freed up funds they could use to make more mortgage and other loans.

## ILLUSIONS OF SAFETY

The strategies and instruments we have discussed all seem to offer a free lunch—increased return at reduced risk. These include portfolio insurance, the types of arbitrage strategies pursued by LTCM, and the mortgage products at the center of the 2007–2008 crisis. An offer of a free lunch is always hard to resist. Devout adherents of financial theory would argue that higher return can only be obtained by taking on higher risk. These products, however, were backed by the latest in investment theory and practice. They came with the imprimatur of finance professors, some of whom were Nobel Prize winners, leading Wall Street firms, and established credit rating agencies.

When free-lunch products attract a large number of followers, they can channel individual investors' hopes and fears in such a way that these sentiments become real market movers. This was the case with portfolio insurance, LTCM, and subprime mortgage products, which in essence turned investor hope and fear into systematic risk factors.

In the 1980s, portfolio insurance helped to lift the Dow Jones Industrial Average (DJIA) from 777 in August 1982 to 2,722 in August 1987. The amount of assets in portfolio insurance programs grew from nothing to as much as $100 billion in this period. Kidder Peabody, J. P. Morgan, Bankers Trust, Chase Manhattan, First Chicago, Aetna, Travelers, MassMutual, and BEA Associates, among others, joined LOR in offering portfolio insurance programs. Users included university endowments and the pension plans of numerous companies.

Since stock prices continued to rise, portfolio insurance programs called for more buying, which supported further stock price increases. Many investors, unaware of the extent to which purchases reflected the purely mechanistic and reactive responses of portfolio insurance programs, may have interpreted the demand from insurance programs as information-motivated buying, and been encouraged to buy along with insured investors. Portfolio insurance, thus, served to channel the hopes of both insured and uninsured investors in such a way as to move the market seemingly ever upward.

The illusion of safety provided by portfolio insurance encouraged its users to invest more in stocks than they otherwise would have. Furthermore, investors who were worried that continued stock price increases were unsustainable might have, in the normal course of events, sold stock in order to reduce portfolio risk, thereby lessening further price increases. Investors with portfolio insurance, however, "assured" of a given floor return, refrained from selling stock.

As the bulls charged through 1986 and into 1987, many investors began to worry about the possibility of being gored by a bull market about-face, and giving back the exceptional gains made over the past years. Rather than realizing those gains by selling stock, however, investors could turn to portfolio insurance, which promised to "put a lock on market gains," according to one LOR ad (see Exhibit 17.4).

**EXHIBIT 17.4**

Put a Lock on Market Gains

Source: *Institutional Investor*, January 1987: 88.

By discouraging stock sales, portfolio insurance contributed to the market's rise. As the market continued to rise, portfolio insurance programs continued to buy stock. This put more upward pressure on prices and encouraged other investors to buy. Ironically, portfolio insurance, a strategy that was designed to operate mechanistically in response to market movements—following the path made by the market—instead moved the markets.

Unlike portfolio insurance's trend-following activity, which can magnify market movements and cause prices to diverge from fundamentally rational values, the kind of arbitrage strategies pursued by LTCM should stabilize markets. LTCM sold short assets that it determined to be overpriced in relation to their fundamental values and purchased assets it determined to be underpriced. These actions should move prices toward levels justified by underlying fundamentals.

LTCM's competitors were awed by the reputations of its partners and, in its first few years, its sizable returns. Some of these competitors became counterparties to LTCM's trades in order to gain insights into the fund's strategies. Most attempted to copy LTCM's success by replicating its trades.

The effects of LTCM's trades on market prices were magnified by its mimicking competitors, just like investors trading in response to portfolio insurance purchases helped to magnify the effects of portfolio insurance programs. At first, such competition benefited the performance of LTCM's strategies. As more investors purchased underpriced assets and sold short overpriced assets, LTCM profited. Ultimately, however, increased competition diminished the potential opportunities for arbitrage. LTCM's returns started to decline.

As portfolio insurance helped to create the bull market of the 1980s, RMBS, CDOs, ABCP conduits, SIVs, and CDS extended the housing price bubble by fueling the market in subprime loans. Subprime lending more than doubled between 2003 and 2005, taking up the slack left by a slowdown in prime loans. Most of these subprime loans were made with the expectation that they would be packaged into RMBS and CDOs and sold, parked in ABCP conduits or SIVs, or insured by CDS. These products enabled mortgage lenders to insulate themselves from the risk of default, to reduce balance-sheet risk, and to garner large profits from sales and fees. Their appeal encouraged more subprime lending, which facilitated further demand for homes and further increases in housing prices.

As with LTCM, the whole system rested on a huge amount of leverage. Homebuyers put down only 10 percent to secure mortgage loans. The financial intermediaries sponsoring RMBS and CDOs funded their mortgage purchases with repo financing and short-term borrowing via sales of CP. Tradable indexes on subprime RMBS tranches and synthetic CDOs based on CDS allowed speculators to take on exposures to subprime structured finance products for very little, if any, initial outlay. Leverage amplified the demand for subprime products and, in turn, the funds available for lending, and their effects on the housing market.

## MARKET MELTDOWNS

The seemingly low risks and high returns of free-lunch products attract a substantial following. When the products are backed by seemingly rigorous mathematics, plausible theory, and early performance success, the interest in these products can translate into substantial dollars invested. The products can then have outsized effects on the very markets in which they trade.

When a market is behaving in line with the models and expectations underlying these products, the products' success in acquiring assets will tend to reinforce or even amplify that market behavior. Markets on the rise will rise more. Arbitrage trades will converge more, or more swiftly. This lends further credence to the products, attracting more followers and further magnifying their effects.

When investors are hopeful, these products will tend to focus and concentrate that hope. When hope turns to fear, however, seemingly low-risk approaches can amplify the fear. Low risk can quickly turn into high risk for investors in the products, and investors generally.

In the two weeks preceding the 1987 US stock market crash on Monday, October 19, stocks declined substantially, and portfolio insurance programs sold futures equivalent to about $4 billion in stock, exacerbating the downturn. Many investors, unaware of the extent of the mechanistic selling by portfolio insurers, sold along with the insurers, in the mistaken belief that the sales were based on bad news to which they were not privy.

Portfolio insurance sales combined with arbitrage between stock index futures and the stock market set off a downward cascade in both markets.

Investors not engaged in either insurance or stock index arbitrage were swept along. The US stock market sustained its greatest one-day percentage loss ever.

Among the victims of the 1987 stock market crash were portfolio insurance itself and the investors who thought they were insured. The strategy's assured floor—its promise of low risk—relied on being able to transfer risk to other market participants via the sale of stock. This, in turn, depended on the presence of counterparties ready and willing to buy stock when insured investors needed to sell. On October 19, at least, such buyers declined to step forward. They were overwhelmed by the sheer volume of portfolio insurers' selling demands and by the speed and extent of the market's decline, in no small measure the results of portfolio insurance trading.

The type of arbitrage trades undertaken by LTCM should, unlike portfolio insurance, be market-stabilizing. When they come undone, however, these strategies engage in trend-following trades much like the trades of portfolio insurers. For LTCM, a kind of chain reaction began when problems emerged in the mortgage-backed securities (MBS) market in early 1998. Not only did LTCM take losses on its significant MBS positions, it also suffered when hedge funds and other institutional investors liquidated their profitable emerging-market positions to make up for their own mortgage losses.

The real flight to quality began, however, with Russia's default on debt in August 1998. The spreads on LTCM's bread-and-butter arbitrage trades widened as demand for the less risky, lower-yield bonds it had sold short pushed their prices up and sales of the riskier, higher-yield bonds it had purchased sent their prices plummeting. Heightened volatility in European equity markets also meant that LTCM had to come up with cash to back its short option positions. As the value of LTCM's short positions increased and the value of its long positions fell, the fund's capital was depleted just as it had to deposit more collateral with lenders.

When LTCM was launched, in 1994, it was flush with cash and found plenty of opportunities in the volatile market environment of the time. It is not so easy, however, to raise capital in a highly volatile environment when you are losing money. The deliberate complexity and sheer number of LTCM's trades did not help matters, as it made it difficult for potential lenders and investors to discern either the profitability of the trades or their risk.

Current and potential investors declined to ante up. Lenders that had been so eager to feed LTCM's appetite for leverage pulled back. Counterparties, rather than relaxing the terms they offered to the fund, upped their demands for collateral. LTCM had to raise cash by liquidating positions, covering (buying) the lower-risk assets it had sold short, whose prices were already rising, and selling the higher-risk assets it held long, whose prices were already declining. Some of the fund's counterparties, along with other sophisticated investors, tried to anticipate LTCM's trades and execute before LTCM could get to market. Thus, much like portfolio insurance trading, the liquidation of LTCM's positions exacerbated existing market trends.

In the late summer and fall of 1998, US equity market volatility reached levels not seen since 1987. The yield on US Treasuries fell below 5 percent for the first time in 30 years, while the premiums on risky, high-yield bonds doubled between August and the middle of October. The market for emerging debt and US commercial mortgage-backed securities (CMBS) collapsed. As the market for securitized loans disappeared, lenders withdrew from providing credit, or demanded prohibitive rates. It took government action, in the form of an unexpected interest rate cut, to restore some calm to these markets.

Almost 10 years later, the government had to step in again to stanch the hemorrhaging of credit from the financial markets. As (highly leveraged) RMBS, CDOs, and CDS helped to enlarge the credit available to homeowners and thus inflate the housing bubble during the first half of the first decade of the twenty-first century, so too did they magnify the effects on the economy of the deterioration in the underlying subprime loans during the second half.

House-price appreciation slowed and then started to decline in 2006. Many subprime borrowers exercised the put options implicit in their mortgage contracts, passing the downside risk of house prices back to lenders and, via products like RMBS and CDOs, on to investors. Delinquencies and defaults in the subprime sector increased beyond the expectations embedded in mortgage rates, RMBS and CDO yields, and CDS premiums.

As losses on these structured finance products continued to increase, lenders became more and more reluctant to lend, and credit dried up. This led in turn to further declines in housing prices, more defaults, and more losses for mortgage holders and investors in mortgage-related products. The effects, magnified by the massive amounts of leverage used by banks and hedge funds, were soon felt in the economy. As with portfolio insurance in 1987, and the arbitrage strategies of LTCM in 1998, products that promised to reduce risk for some ended up increasing risk for the system as a whole.

## WHY?

Products that purport to reduce risk while promising increased return tend to encourage more risk-taking. This is true whether the presumed risk reduction comes from particular products and strategies or from a general perception of the market's risk. Thus, they can have an effect similar to that of the moral hazard captured by the "too big to fail" argument; that is, large banks, in the years preceding the 2007–2008 crisis, took on an inordinate amount of risk in the expectation that they could pocket any profits while the government would bail them out if they sustained losses too large to absorb.

With portfolio insurance, insured investors decided to buy more stock or maintain stock positions, rather than sell them, even when market prices reached levels that appeared to be unsustainable. With LTCM, the supposedly low risk of the fund's arbitrage positions seemed to justify high leverage ratios. AAA credit ratings encouraged banks, money market funds, and other investors to leverage their holdings of senior tranches of RMBS and CDOs.

The risks underlying these sophisticated products were essentially systematic in nature. Portfolio insurance was supposed to protect portfolios against equity market declines. LTCM's arbitrage strategies were designed to insulate the fund's profits from changes in interest rates, the equity market, and exchange rates. The AAA-rated tranches of RMBS and CDOs were supposed to be insulated from the risk of declines in underlying house prices.

Systematic risk cannot be diversified away. Control of systematic risk relies largely on being able to shift the risk from those who do not want it to those who will accept it in exchange for a compensatory return. This can be accomplished in many ways. With portfolio insurance, risk is shifted by selling stock from insured portfolios to other investors.

With arbitrage strategies, risk is offset by holding long and short positions in related assets, which requires other investors able to sell and buy the appropriate securities and derivatives. RMBS and CDOs shift risk from lenders to buyers of the products, and from buyers of AAA-rated tranches to buyers of subordinate tranches. CDS shift the risk of default from insurance buyers to insurance sellers.

The ability to shift risk is ultimately dependent on the willingness of counterparties to take on that risk. However, as the demand increases for products designed to reduce risk while increasing returns, the level of risk that must be shifted increases. The availability of counterparties to take on the risk becomes more and more questionable. Liquidity begins to dry up.

At this point, the markets affected by free-lunch products become fragile. Increases in underlying risk can have major destabilizing effects. In 1987, increasing volatility led to portfolio insurance sales that overwhelmed counterparties' willingness or ability to buy. In 1998, LTCM's liquidity demands went unmet by its investors, by lenders, and by buyers and sellers in the marketplace. In 2007–2008, banks' willingness to lend dried up as banks and other RMBS and CDO sponsors found themselves stuck with billions of dollars in deteriorating mortgage assets for which they could not find buyers. CDS sellers, flooded with demands for payouts on the assets they had supposedly provided insurance on, faced default, which would leave CDS buyers in the lurch.

As I foresaw in 2004, the government became the risk bearer of last resort in the 2007–2008 credit crisis. What I wrote then is just as pertinent now, and likely will be when the next crisis arises:

> Who then becomes the risk bearer of last resort? It may be the taxpayer, if the government decides that the firms that offered these products are 'too big to fail.' Often, it is investors in general, who must bear the risk in the form of the substantial declines in prices that are required to entice risk bearers back into the market. Ironically, products designed to reduce financial risk can end up creating even more risk.[10]

CHAPTER 18

# Taming the Tempest

*"What's past is prologue."*

**—William Shakespeare**[1]

Although option, arbitrage, and securitization strategies have the potential to destabilize underlying markets when they induce large numbers of investors to buy into rising markets and sell into falling markets, they can serve useful purposes—provided that their limitations are recognized. Options can enhance the ability of investors and others to hedge risk. Arbitrage strategies, despite the destabilizing effects they may have when they fail, serve to dampen unsustainable price increases and cushion price declines when they succeed. Securitization can increase credit availability and lower borrowing costs.

Furthermore, as the financial crises we have described illustrate, strategies and instruments can change over time. The markets in which they operate change. We cannot know today what the next destabilizing strategy will be, or in what market or markets it will emerge. We can, however, ask what characteristics shared by these strategies have proved problematic for market stability, and how these characteristics might better be understood and controlled.

## PROBLEM AREAS

The strategies at the heart of recent crises share certain characteristics that can foster market fragility. These include:

- opacity and complexity with regard to both the strategies and the relationships they forge between counterparties;

- leverage facilitated by the use of derivatives and borrowing; and
- option-like behavior leading to nonlinear returns.

These characteristics can interact in ways that produce an illusion of liquidity, a misperception of underlying risks, a flood of capital into the strategies, a magnification of the effects of the strategies on underlying markets and financial institutions, consequent feedback loops between the strategies and market behavior, and an increase in market fragility. Attempts to avoid or contain financial crises may be more successful by focusing on these general characteristics rather than on specific strategies or actors.

## Opacity

Opacity can arise from a lack of knowledge, from complexity in the strategies and/or instruments, and from the complexity of the network of actors involved in the strategy. Opacity to one degree or another was characteristic of all the crises we have covered; the subprime crisis provides a good example.

While mortgage securitization was not new in 2001, the degree of its extension to subprime housing was novel, and there was scant historical data available for rigorously estimating performance. Furthermore, securitizations became increasingly complex, with BBB-rated residential mortgage-backed securities (RMBS) being repackaged as AAA-rated collateralized debt obligations (CDOs), and BBB-rated CDOs being repackaged as AAA-rated $CDO^2$s. Equally complicated was the chain of production: independent, often largely unregulated, mortgage originators; banks originating or purchasing mortgages; special purpose vehicles (SPVs) creating RMBS and CDOs from mortgage pools; credit rating agencies evaluating the securities; institutional investors purchasing the securities; structured investment vehicles (SIVs) and asset-backed commercial paper (ABCP) conduits funding the purchase of securities through the issuance of commercial paper and notes; money-market funds funded by retail investors buying the paper and notes; and monolines and others selling credit default swaps (CDS) that insured RMBS and CDO tranches.

The lack of transparency hid the real risks of the underlying mortgages, facilitating the explosion in popularity of subprime RMBS as well as, importantly, their use by investment banks and others as collateral for borrowing. When the real risks became apparent, the values of RMBS and CDOs plummeted and a crisis ensued.[2] The complex network of relationships between the parties involved exacerbated the crisis. When the credit ratings of monoline insurers were downgraded, for example, the protection offered by the CDS they had sold was impaired. Bank assets covered by CDS became riskier, and banks had to increase the amount of regulatory capital held against them; this often required selling assets to raise capital. When mortgage securities pledged as collateral declined in value, borrowers often had to sell assets in order to meet margin calls.

Opacity abetted earlier crises as well. In the 1980s, most investors did not know about the large amount of assets subject to portfolio insurance, a novel strategy at the time. Many investors piled into a market inflated by portfolio insurance trading, exaggerating the run-up in stock prices and then exacerbating the abrupt decline on October 19, 1987. In the 1990s, the nature, size, and sheer complexity of Long-Term Capital Management's (LTCM's) arbitrage trades and the network of counterparties they created were also obscure. Hedge funds and proprietary trading desks attempted to reproduce LTCM's trades, initially reinforcing price movements that tended to stabilize markets. In "the flight to quality" in 1998, however, they tried to front run LTCM's anticipated unwinding, thereby magnifying market instability.

## Leverage

The perceived low risk of LTCM's arbitrage positions and of AAA-rated credit tranches encouraged the piling on of leverage. Although leverage was not the predominant factor in the 1980s, portfolio insurance programs did engage in margined futures trading, which accelerated the adoption of the strategy because the futures market was thought to be a separate haven of liquidity. Leverage can magnify a strategy's profits, but it can also magnify losses and the impact of the strategy on underlying markets.

This was certainly true of the unwinding of LTCM's highly leveraged arbitrage strategies in 1998. What's more, the effects of LTCM's deleveraging were amplified by the actions of other hedge funds and bank proprietary desks trading out of similar positions at the same time. Furthermore, LTCM's many derivatives positions constituted a kind of hidden leverage. They were established with little outlay of capital and added to the firm's profits when security prices were behaving as LTCM expected. When prices started to move adversely, however, these positions required the posting of maintenance margins, which further depleted LTCM's capital and heightened the pressure to sell.

The extent of leverage in the financial system may have been obscured by various practices in the years leading up to the credit crisis. An increase in leverage was facilitated by the growth of shadow banking, which included hedge funds, broker-dealers, and money-market funds. These parties operated largely outside regulatory banking controls, making it difficult to discern the level of leverage in the system and difficult for the government to respond with efforts to moderate credit growth.[3]

It became apparent after the collapse of the credit market that many, if not most, regulated banks obfuscated the true debt loads they labored under. They did so simply by adjusting their repo borrowing for reporting cycles. An investigation of 18 banks undertaken after the crisis found that the average reported debt level at the end of each quarter from the first quarter of 2009 to the first quarter of 2010 was 20 percent to 40 percent lower than the peak debt level during each quarter.[4]

As networks of borrowers and lenders develop and multiply, leverage intensifies the connectivity within the financial sector and between the financial sector and the broad economy. Increasingly complex interrelationships further reduce transparency. Potentially damaging feedback loops can develop. Leverage magnifies feedback and can lead to a downward spiral.

The index arbitrage-portfolio insurance cascade provides one example: Stock prices fall. Portfolio insurers sell stock futures to reduce their equity exposure. Arbitrageurs buy "cheap" futures and sell stock, further pressuring stock prices. Portfolio insurers sell more futures, and so on (see Chapter 4, "Portfolio Insurance and Futures Markets"). The unwinding of LTCM's heavily leveraged arbitrage positions in the fall of 1998 had similar effects on markets (see Chapter 8, "Long-Term Capital Management").

With the subprime crisis, declines in house prices led to defaults by subprime borrowers, which eventually led to downgrades of mortgage securities, which reduced their value as collateral, which hampered lenders' ability to borrow via repo, which led to a contraction in lending, which led to economic recession, which led to further declines in house prices, which led to more defaults by mortgage borrowers.

## Nonlinearity with Options and Leverage

In addition to reinforcing and exacerbating trends in underlying markets, the types of products implicated in the market crises of 1987, 1998, and 2007–2008 tend to create or increase nonlinearity in the markets in which they trade. When these products are in operation, prices have a greater tendency to jump up or gap down, rather than follow a more continuous, smoother path.

This effect reflects the option-like nature of many of these products. Option values can behave in very nonlinear ways. The value of an option varies as the price of the underlying asset changes. If the price of the asset is well below (or well above) the strike price of a call (or a put) option, the option is "deep out of the money," and its value changes little as the asset price changes. As the asset's price approaches the strike price of the option, the option's value becomes increasingly sensitive to changes in the asset's price. When the option is "deep in the money," its value moves closer to being linearly related to the price of the asset. Most dramatically, however, at expiration the option is worth either something if it is in the money, or nothing if it is out of the money.

Portfolio insurance is the most obvious illustration of this. Portfolio insurance was designed to replicate the behavior of a protective put option, that is, the behavior of an underlying asset protected by a put option (see Chapter 3, "Replicating Options"). The put option's strike price provides a floor below the value of the underlying asset. As the price of the underlying asset (the portfolio in the case of portfolio insurance) declines toward and below that floor, more and more risky assets must be sold. The portfolio becomes more and more invested in cash (or riskless bonds) and less and less affected by the movement of the risky asset. The dynamic hedging undertaken by option dealers attempting to offset the risk of their option positions works in a similar, nonlinear fashion (see Chapter 6, "After the Crash—Options").

This type of dynamic hedging passes on to other market participants the risk that is not wanted by the option replicators. The end result is that the trading needs of portfolio insurance impart to underlying markets the nonlinear behavior of options. Prices are prone to rise more, or rise more quickly, and to fall more, or fall more abruptly. Prices are more prone to gap down if there is a large volume of sales, as happened on October 19, 1987, as well as in the later "mini-breaks" of the 1980s and 1990s. Market participants end up bearing the risk of the "options" created by portfolio insurers and other option replicators.

The subprime mortgage products of the 2007–2008 crisis essentially constituted a giant put on the housing market. The puts implicit in the underlying mortgage loans were passed on by the original put sellers—that is, the lenders—to the investors in mortgage-backed securities (MBS) and to those providing insurance via guarantees or, more commonly, CDS on mortgage-backed products. Declines in house prices, however, made the puts increasingly valuable. More and more puts were exercised by homeowners, who defaulted on their mortgage loans. Losses mounted in a nonlinear fashion for investors in RMBS and CDOs holding RMBS. The highly leveraged monolines, which had sold CDS on "safe" RMBS and CDO tranches, faced increasing payouts to insurance buyers. As the monolines were downgraded by the rating agencies, or went bankrupt, the ultimate put protection—CDS—started to fail.

Leverage itself can also induce nonlinear effects.[5] This was a notable aspect of the LTCM crisis of 1998. The type of arbitrage strategies conducted by LTCM should be market-stabilizing. They should serve to contribute to the convergence of prices toward values that can be considered reasonable on the basis of the fundamentals of the underlying entity and economy.

As the case of LTCM illustrates, however, leverage gives lenders a trigger that can act like an option strike price and force borrowers to unwind arbitrage positions, often at losses. Losses consume capital, thereby further increasing a borrower's leverage, and can also undermine the value of collateral posted to secure loans. As losses mount, lenders will decline to extend more loans, will demand more collateral, or will call in loans and demand to be repaid. In the absence of additional funding, the borrower will have to unwind arbitrage positions. Forced unwinding of arbitrage strategies can destabilize markets because, similar to portfolio insurance, it requires selling long positions as they decline and covering (buying) short positions as they rise.

The option-like effects of leverage also were significant contributors to the 2007–2008 crisis. Bear Stearns and Lehman Brothers, both holding highly leveraged and deteriorating mortgage assets, provide notable examples of what happens when demand for collateral increases because of borrower losses. The effect is exacerbated by a decline in the value of the assets posted as collateral. Borrowers become subject to margin calls for increased collateral from repo counterparties and other lenders. These calls may force borrowers to sell assets at losses. As the credit crisis showed, forced sales can also create a "fire sale" dynamic, where sales lead to price declines, creating losses for other investors, who are forced to sell, enlarging losses.

## THE UNERRING SCIENCE OF QUANTITATIVE MODELING

Models may fail to recognize the likelihood of price discontinuity and instead assume that prices will move in small increments (continuous pricing) and that returns will be symmetrically distributed about the average return (normal distribution). This is true of the Black-Scholes-Merton options pricing model that underlies portfolio insurance. As a result, the costs of portfolio insurance were vastly underestimated early on. This, in turn, encouraged the adoption of the strategy and thus amplified the problems it created when the model's assumption of continuous pricing failed the test of reality.

In 1998, LTCM ignored the possibility that price gaps would leave the fund with collateral "bills" it would not be able to cover by selling assets at prices close to recent norms. The risk models used by credit rating agencies obviously discounted the possibility that defaults on mortgage loans would spike discontinuously and suddenly in the mid-2000s.

Furthermore, financial models may overlook certain risks that prove to be critical in the real world. The traditional mean-variance model, for example, the heart of modern portfolio theory, looks at risk in terms of variations in security returns but overlooks leverage as a source of risk. As the histories outlined in this book illustrate, the level of leverage assumed by investors is often based merely on the nature of the underlying strategy to be leveraged and the risk of the positions in that strategy. Thus LTCM undertook large amounts of borrowing to lever up the relatively small returns on its supposedly low-risk arbitrage positions.

I have proposed, with Ken Levy, a mean-variance-leverage model that considers leverage explicitly in the portfolio formation process.[6] We argue that leverage entails risks that are distinct from the risks inherent in asset volatility. For example, leverage entails the risk of margin calls, a consideration apparently ignored by American International Group; see Chapter

14, "Securitization and the Credit Crisis." Margin calls can become particularly problematic during periods of market disruption, because at these times it is difficult to either raise capital or liquidate assets at reasonable prices. Liquidation may be at extremely adverse prices, thereby worsening market conditions, and bankruptcy protection may be sought.

We believe such scenarios might be mitigated or avoided if investors consider explicitly their aversion to these unique risks of leverage when forming portfolios. Restraining leverage in and of itself may not prevent the creation of instruments and strategies that have the potential to destabilize financial markets or the tendency of investors to react emotionally. It may, however, dampen their effects.

A number of critics see quantitative modeling itself as a primary contributor to recent crises.[7] According to this view, mathematical models leave out real-world considerations that get in the way of a good equation. Practitioners are too willing and ready to rely on the infallibility of mathematical equations. Investors are led astray by a false sense of overconfidence.[8] Call it model "hubris."

Would we be better off if we ignored the models? As tempting as the idea may be, it is not the answer. Quantitative methods—which, as we have seen, do have the potential to contribute to market destabilization—also provide invaluable tools for imposing discipline, transparency, and accountability on the investment process. For the most part, their benefits outweigh their costs.

Investors are swayed by hope and fear, which can at times move market prices swiftly away from fundamental values. Behavioral economists who have studied investment decision-making in laboratory settings have catalogued a host of cognitive errors that can (like the more coarsely defined greed and fear) motivate investors to behave in ways contrary to their own long-term best interests. For example, investors tend to be loss averse and willing to take more risk than is warranted if the alternative is a sure loss. Investors tend to focus on short-term goals rather than long-term gains. Although they tend to be overconfident in their decision-making abilities, believing themselves to be above average, they also have a tendency to herd. The decisions of individual decision-makers thus tend to converge, reinforcing price movements.

Cognitive errors were evident in all the crises discussed in this book. Behavioral economist Hersh Shefrin points out how, in the latest crisis, excessive optimism and overconfidence, and the tendency to extrapolate current trends into the indefinite future, led astray large bank UBS, large credit rater Standard & Poor's, and large insurer AIG during the credit crisis.[9] Portfolio insurance buyers in the 1980s and LTCM in the 1990s benefited, but ultimately suffered, from the herd-like behavior of other investors trading in their footsteps.

Quantitative methods of security selection and portfolio construction impose discipline on the investment process. They allow for the construction of portfolios with preset performance goals and for the measurement of performance relative to those goals. Not only are such portfolios less likely to fall prey to cognitive errors, but they can be designed to take advantage of pricing discrepancies caused by such errors.

But it is also important to make a distinction between overconfidence based on ignorance and overconfidence based on willful disregard of the unrealistic assumptions underlying models. After the failure of portfolio insurance in 1987, much research went into pricing options when underlying asset prices are subject to sudden jumps. In fact, that crash propelled a plethora of research on identifying and modeling non-normal asset-price behavior, including discontinuous price changes and so-called fat tails (greater than expected occurrences of extreme return outcomes). Quantitative analysts at major financial institutions are very aware that the world is full of pitfalls that trip up models, which are often based on simplistic assumptions that do not represent reality. According to option-model creator Robert C. Merton:[10]

> I don't think anyone used Black-Scholes for actual trading or actual valuation. . . . Everyone knows we have stochastic volatility [volatility that varies over time]; in fact, we trade it—it's patently obvious that the formula doesn't hold.

In many cases, however, it seems that users and even creators of such quantitative tools as portfolio insurance and CDOs are aware of the potential pitfalls of their products and quantitative models, but they choose to downplay or ignore these problems for various reasons (monetary gain being the predominant but not necessarily sole reason). According to one financial journalist:[11]

> Bankers securitizing mortgages knew that their models were highly sensitive to house-price appreciation. If it ever turned negative on a national scale, a lot of bonds that had been rated triple-A, or risk-free, by computer-powered models would blow up. But no one was willing to stop the creation of CDOs, and the big investment banks happily kept on building more, drawing their correlation data from a period when real estate only went up.

Even more damningly, Matthew W. (Matt) Ridley, former chairman of the UK bank Northern Rock, stated in regard to the crisis: "very smart people in the financial sector thought it was fun and completely acceptable to use the fact that you were very smart to exploit people who were less smart."[12]

Too often, strategies and products such as portfolio insurance and CDOs are oversold—and overleveraged—on the basis of a strict and unrealistic view of the unerring "science" of investing. Too often, financial experts who know better use quantitative and statistical techniques and results to lend a false sense of certainty and precision in order to sell products and strategies to investment managers as well as investors. Too often, managers and investors fall prey to a level of certainty they know or should have known to be unattainable.

## CONFLICTS OF INTEREST

The financial sector is rife with conflicts of interest, and these conflicts played a large role in the financial crisis of 2007–2008. New regulations under the Dodd-Frank Wall Street Reform and Consumer Protection Act (Dodd-Frank) may ameliorate some of these conflicts. The Volcker Rule seeks to rein in banks' trading for their own accounts, which has at times been undertaken at the expense of clients. Banks and other entities that securitize loans will now have to retain a material (unhedged) portion of the credit risk on their own balance sheets. (It should be noted, however, that throughout the most recent crisis, banks had retained significant portions of the securitizations they sponsored.) Other measures have been recommended to deal with the conflicts of interest associated with asset-backed securities (ABS). These include expanded disclosure requirements to discourage sponsors from engaging in activities that may harm investors in their securitizations, such as taking short positions in the underlying assets or designing securitizations to benefit other parties that take short positions.

Dodd-Frank addresses some of the conflicts of interest inherent in agencies' rating of credit instruments. In particular, rating agencies must report the past performances of their various ratings categories over multiple horizons. They must also disclose information about their models and the assumptions underlying them. Rating agencies must review ratings made by analysts who subsequently leave an agency to work for clients that issue securitizations.

According to the *Wall Street Journal*, in the five years from the end of 2006 through 2011, over 100 credit rating analysts had left their agencies to join financial firms they had once rated.[13] A number of critics have pointed out that former Secretary of the Treasury Henry Paulson, instrumental in implementing the Troubled Asset Relief Program (TARP), had once headed Goldman Sachs, a beneficiary of the bailout. But the revolving door between government and industry has turned for hundreds of others.

The 2010 documentary *Inside Job* placed blame for the credit crisis on excessive debt, deregulation, and the growth of the financial sector and its influence on government. Along with lax oversight by all parties, from banks to credit raters to regulators, the film highlighted the often-close relationship between the financial service industry and those who regulate it, or advise the regulators. For instance, Martin Feldstein, chief economic advisor to President Ronald Reagan as well as his chairman of the Council of Economic Advisors (1982–1984), served on the board of American International Group (AIG) Financial Products during the credit bubble and crash. Laura Tyson, chair of President Bill Clinton's Council of Economic Advisors (1993–1995), subsequently joined the board of Morgan Stanley. Glenn Hubbard, chairman of President George W. Bush's Council of Economic Advisors (2001–2003), was on the board of Capmark Financial Group, a major commercial mortgage lender that went bankrupt in 2009.[14]

This is not to say that any illegalities occurred, or that regulation has been subverted by overt partisanship or financial remuneration. Indeed, outright lobbying efforts on behalf of the industry have undoubtedly had larger effects.[15] Furthermore, in the complex, highly quantitative world of modern finance, there is a relatively small pool of people with the requisite expertise, and they must be shared, both within and between private and public sectors. Nevertheless, the somewhat incestuous relationships that characterize this arcane world can have deleterious effects.

One solution is a "fiduciary duty standard" that extends beyond investment advisers to anyone who provides investment recommendations or advice.[16] Authorization for such a standard was included in Dodd-Frank, and a Labor Department fiduciary rule was supposed to apply to managers of retirement-account assets beginning in June 2017, but it was vacated by the Fifth Circuit Court of Appeals in 2018. In April 2018, however, the SEC proposed a "best interest" rule that would require brokers to disclose conflicts of interest to retail customers, to eliminate or mitigate some such conflicts, and to refrain from using the title of "financial adviser"; the proposal is currently in review.

A related approach is to require a wider and more forthcoming disclosure of relationships that have the potential to give rise to conflicts of interest. In late 2011, well after the crisis and following the release of *Inside Job*, the American Economic Association (AEA) established conflict-of-interest guidelines for authors of articles submitted to its journals. Interested-party conflicts can pose a significant barrier to the dissemination of critical research.

A decade earlier, as a result of my own experience, I successfully advocated for conflict-of-interest guidelines at the *Financial Analysts Journal*. What follows is a brief account of my quest for these guidelines, which began in June 1984, while I was at Prudential Asset Management Company. It describes my attempts to publish several papers that offered critical examinations of portfolio insurance, and the barriers erected by those with a vested interest in suppressing contrary views. This first-hand account has wider implications for everyone engaged in serious research and for everyone who applies such research to practice. In finance, or in any field of endeavor, progress is critically dependent on the free flow of ideas—even if those ideas may cast doubt on conventional wisdom or threaten incumbent business models.

In 1984, I submitted to the *Journal of Portfolio Management* a paper entitled "Is Portfolio Insurance Appropriate for the Long-Term Investor?" This was a formalization of my thoughts about the viability and appropriateness of the portfolio insurance strategy.[17] I had previously written some pieces that exposed the strategy's pitfalls and questioned whether it was appropriate for one of its major target clients—retirement plans—given these plans' long horizons.

I had debated the partners of the primary vendor and promoter of portfolio insurance, Leland O'Brien and Rubinstein Associates (LOR) (see "A Debate on Portfolio Insurance" in Chapter 5). The manuscript I submitted to the *Journal of Portfolio Management* was reviewed by Mark E. Rubinstein, a partner of LOR and member of the journal's editorial board. He was highly critical of the paper, and it was not accepted for publication. (Rubinstein gave the editor permission to reveal his identity and share his review.) The editor invited me to revise and resubmit the manuscript.

I had shared my ideas with Simon Benninga, a friend and colleague at my alma mater, the Wharton School of the University of Pennsylvania. He discussed my ideas with another professor, Marshall Blume. Together, they authored a paper that formalized some of my arguments, which was published in the *Journal of Finance* as "On the Optimality of Portfolio Insurance" in 1985.[18] When I subsequently saw Rubinstein at a conference, he said he could not believe that the *Journal of Finance* published the article, and remarked that these were my ideas, what happened? I replied that he was not supportive as the reviewer at the *Journal of Portfolio Management* and that I had shared my ideas at Wharton. It was then that he first called me his nemesis.

In September 1988, almost a year after the October 19, 1987 crash, I submitted a manuscript entitled "The Portfolio Insurance Debacle" to the *Financial Analysts Journal*. This was the official publication of the Financial Analysts Federation (FAF), an industry association for security analysts, which later became the Association for Investment Management and Research (AIMR), and, still later, the CFA Institute. Rubinstein was also on the editorial board of the *Financial Analysts Journal* and was one of the reviewers. He was highly critical of this paper, and it was not accepted for publication. (Again, Rubinstein allowed the editor to reveal his identity and share his review with me.) The editor invited me to revise and resubmit the manuscript. In a piece that appeared much later in *Pensions & Investments*, Rubinstein noted with regard to his reviews: "I did have a conflict of interest. The question is, did it affect my judgment? It didn't because I was the best qualified to evaluate it [the submission]. I look at myself as an academic first."[19]

In March 1990, I resubmitted a substantially revised and enlarged manuscript, "The Rise of Portfolio Insurance and the Crash of 1987," to the *Financial Analysts Journal*. Rubinstein was one of the reviewers. After a lengthy review process, the editor suggested that, given the manuscript's length, he could ask the Research Foundation of the FAF to publish it as a monograph. There was a condition, however; the discussion of LOR's promotion of the strategy had to be removed. That discussion was key to understanding the rapid adoption of portfolio insurance and its subsequent effect on the market, which were important lessons to be learned. So I declined the offer.

I enlarged the manuscript into a book, which was accepted by the academic publisher Blackwell. Nobel laureate Harry M. Markowitz, whom I had met at a conference of the Institute for Quantitative Research in Finance, offered to write the foreword. Robert R. Glauber, executive director of the Brady Commission and former Undersecretary of the Treasury, provided an endorsement for the book's jacket, as did Charles P. Kindleberger, author of *Manias, Panics, and Crashes: A History of Financial Crises*. My book, *Capital Ideas and Market Realities: Option Replication, Investor Behavior, and Stock Market Crashes*, was published in 1999.[20] At last, my ideas on portfolio insurance and the stock market crash of 1987 were shared publicly.

My primary aim in writing *Capital Ideas and Market Realities* was to alert investors to the way in which some investment theories, when put into practice, can interact with market realities to create unhealthy consequences for markets and investors. The book discusses not only portfolio insurance, but also similar strategies including over-the-counter (OTC) derivatives, hedging, and the type of highly leveraged arbitrage activity conducted by Long-Term Capital Management (LTCM).

One major thread linking all these strategies is the way in which they are marketed to potential clients. The way in which portfolio insurance was marketed by LOR and others was closely examined in *Capital Ideas and Market Realities* because this information is vital to understanding why markets were so affected. In brief, marketing that creates the false impression that such strategies offer high returns at low risk enables them to attract enormous investments, which can threaten market stability.

The allure of insuring portfolios may have been enhanced by its appeal to the self-interest (that is, job security) of investment officers responsible for pension plans.[21] In 1984, *Institutional Investor* ran an LOR-sponsored section containing an ad for Aetna's product GEM (see Exhibit 17.2). The ad stated: "If a sponsor chooses a 0 percent return, he's never going to have to go to his pension committee and explain losses."[22]

The July/August 2000 issue of the *Financial Analysts Journal* published a favorable review of *Capital Ideas and Market Realities*, in which the book review editor stated: "Jacobs' meticulously documented book presents compelling evidence . . . that portfolio insurance failed to deliver on its lofty promises."[23] In the January/February 2001 issue of *Financial Analysts Journal*, however, the same reviewer wrote a "Postscript" that retracted his earlier review, now implying that the statements LOR had used in order to sell portfolio insurance could be balanced (from a required disclosure viewpoint) by more cautious statements that LOR made in its published articles.[24]

Yet this argument is specious. Each advertisement of a registered investment adviser must meet the requirements of Section 206 of the Investment Advisers Act of 1940; disclosures in other venues cannot "make good" for a lack of required disclosure in the advertisements. Regulators have set high standards with respect to disclosure in the securities industry. LOR's advertisement touting portfolio insurance as a "guaranteed equity investment" would seem to breach those standards.[25] I believe that LOR's portrayal of portfolio insurance as a "guaranteed equity investment" was false and misleading. As the US Supreme Court pointed out in a 1963 ruling involving an investment advisor who offered an investment advisory service:[26]

> The Investment Advisers Act of 1940 was the last in a series designed to eliminate certain abuses in the securities industry, abuses which were found to have contributed to the stock market crash of 1929 and the depression of the 1930's . . . A fundamental purpose . . . was to substitute a philosophy of full disclosure for the philosophy of *caveat emptor* and thus to achieve a high standard of business ethics in the securities industry. . . . As we recently said in a related context, "It requires but little appreciation . . . of what happened in this country during the 1920's and 1930's to realize how essential it is that the highest ethical standard prevail" . . . in every facet of the securities industry.

In reply to my May/June 2001 response to his "Postscript," the book review editor stated that "the professionals whom I consulted [in writing the initial 'Postscript'] were neither purveyors of portfolio insurance nor investors who ultimately decided to buy the product."[27] But *Pensions & Investments* found out that the book review editor's "Postscript" was written at the behest of Rubinstein.[28] According to the article, Rubinstein had suggested that the book review editor "consider writing a 'correction' to his original review." The *Financial Analysts Journal*'s editor (also a vendor of portfolio insurance products) declined to investigate further, according to another article in *Pensions & Investments*.[29] The whole episode had the appearance of egregious conflicts of interest.

At the time, with the equity market suffering from the aftereffects of the bursting of the tech stock bubble, things were not going well for security analysts or, indeed, the industry. The SEC was investigating possible bubble-era abuses in the initial public offering (IPO) market, including promises by brokerage firms to supply select clients with scarce IPO allocations if the clients agreed either to buy more shares in the aftermarket or pay exorbitant commissions. The SEC ultimately levied a fine of $15 million on Jack B. Grubman, the managing director at Salomon Smith Barney responsible for investment banking in the telecom sector; he was also barred from the securities industry for issuing fraudulent and misleading research reports. The SEC also charged Henry Blodget, the managing director at Merrill Lynch and head of internet research, with issuing fraudulent research and misleading investors with forecasts inconsistent with privately expressed negative views; he paid $4 million in fines and was barred from the industry. The National Association of Securities Dealers finally laid down rules to address conflicts of interest in analysts' recommendations.

In July 2002, the AIMR proposed a series of Research Objectivity Standards designed to (among other things) prevent investment bankers and corporate issuers from influencing analyst recommendations and from taking retribution against analysts whose recommendations they disagreed with. I replied in August, noting that the proposed standards were welcome, but that the organization should look a little closer to home for conflicts of interest that have the potential to taint research and to inflict harm on investors (see Appendix E for my response). Just as the research conducted by analysts at brokerage firms and investment banks is susceptible to the influence of commercial interests that may conflict with the best interests of their clients, I noted, so too is the work done for and by the AIMR and its professional publications and conferences.[30] I advised that the Research Objectivity Standards be expanded to deal with these conflicts of interest—a recommendation picked up by the *Wall Street Journal* and supported by José M. Arau, principal investment officer at CalPERS, one of the world's largest pension funds.[31] In January 2003, the AIMR published conflict-of-interest policies for the *Financial Analysts Journal* that reflect many of the suggested standards proposed in my response.

Conflicts of interest in the rarified world of professional publications may seem like an arcane concern, unlikely to have much influence on the real world; and, of course, my story is just one small example of such conflict. But the implications can be profound, and they are the reason I was motivated to press the AIMR to establish guidelines. By permitting an editorial board member with a substantial financial interest in portfolio insurance products to quash criticism of the products, its journal effectively curtailed the free flow of ideas so necessary to an educated investment community and a healthy market.

A similar dynamic was on display during the 2007–2008 crisis, as the documentary *Inside Job* illustrates. Again, those with vested interests in the housing bubble and its money machine out-criticized and out-shouted the Cassandras who warned of an impending debacle.

The more closed a system of thinking becomes, the more defensive it is toward criticism, the tighter it holds onto its beliefs, and the less likely it is to be able to realize its own faults. A feedback loop is created, in which only affirmation of already held opinions is allowed. Conflict-of-interest standards can weaken the defenses that protect such a faulty system and thus encourage a freer flow of ideas and a healthier market.

It is time to declare that the efficient market hypothesis (EMH) and the rational investor are dead, inasmuch as they are meant to imply consistently correct market pricing. That sense of market efficiency should have died with the 1987 crash.[32] There is no excuse today for investors, investment professionals, or regulators to assume that market prices always represent "true" values for every asset, to assume that such prices will only move in a continuous fashion consistent with a normal distribution, or that investors, unlike any other group of people, will always act rationally.

Rather than scuttling modeling, however, we should harness its power to enlarge and fine-tune our representations of the complex realities of financial markets, including nonlinear price behavior, spikes, gaps, fat tails, and the effects of herding, feedback dynamics, and liquidity shortages. This may require the adoption of approaches that have so far been largely outside the boundaries of financial theory. Richard Bookstaber, a noted economist, states:[33]

> I am arguing against the equilibrium condition and for a process, one that has feedback that requires constant reorientation. It is agile modeling: the model is reoriented over the course of the process. The model changes with time and circumstances. There is no machine, there is no black box, there are no formal principles, no provably correct answers, no solution.

Alternatives may include network dynamics and agent-based models. For example, the Jacobs Levy Markowitz Market Simulator (JLMSim), an agent-based model, has demonstrated that a relatively low ratio of momentum investors to value investors is conducive to market stability, but as the ratio of momentum investors increases, so does market volatility. In other experiments, the simulator showed how flash crashes can occur when traders are not anchored to recent price levels.[34] Coupled with advances in behavioral finance, such models may offer keener insights into market dynamics and the limitations of solely mathematical solutions. As has been said, models are "decision aids, not decision makers."[35]

The recent crisis has made clear that investors, from the less sophisticated retail investor to the CEO of an investment bank offering and using the most complex, cutting-edge products, require better education about investment strategies and instruments, their risks, their returns, and their potential effects on markets. Researchers—quantitative, behavioral, or fundamental—must proactively commit to making their work more accessible to financial-product users who may not be as knowledgeable as they.

## REGULATORY REMEDIES

The ability of the regulatory process to prevent crises of the kind we have discussed in this book is often questioned (and not only by critics of government in general). Financial regulators, like generals, are always fighting the last war. After the stock market crash of 1987, circuit breakers were introduced in the hope of restraining volatility in the US stock market. These did not prevent market breaks in 1989, 1991, or 1997; nor did they prevent the market volatility following the takeover of LTCM in 1998, or the flash crashes of the new millennium.

In the wake of the LTCM debacle, international regulators, such as the Bank for International Settlements, and quasi-regulatory authorities, such as the Counterparty Risk Management Policy Group, proposed numerous guidelines to improve bank lending standards and rein in hedge fund leverage. These did not help banks, or investors, avoid the credit crisis of 2007–2008. In fact, according to at least one empirical study, banks that performed poorly during the 1998 crisis also performed poorly during the credit crisis; these poor performers were characterized, pre-crises, by high leverage and risky lending.[36]

As we have noted, the nature of financial crises changes over time. In the period we cover, crises occurred in global stock markets, as the result of investment practices of institutional investors; in the US stock and bond markets, as the result of hedge fund operations; and in global credit markets, largely as the result of the lending, securitization, and risk management practices of international banks. The next crisis is just as likely to arise outside the banking sector as inside it. Regulations addressing the last crisis are unlikely to prevent the next.

Regulations also tend to beget their own, often damaging, consequences. Regulatory changes affecting the levels and kinds of rates banks could charge borrowers motivated the creation of the subprime market (see Chapter 13, "Securitization and the Housing Bubble"). Also, regulatory capital requirements motivated banks to use securitization to remove assets from their balance sheets. A review of earlier crises shows that portfolio insurance was, in part, motivated by limits placed on the number of exchange-traded option positions that investment institutions could buy.

Some critics argue that regulations passed in the wake of the credit crisis will encourage the migration of many of the activities traditionally performed by banks to the non-bank entities in the shadow banking sector.[37] Indeed, a report from the International Monetary Fund (IMF) finds that, since the 2007–2008 crisis, credit intermediation has shifted from banks to the shadow banks (including exchange-traded funds, money market funds, hedge funds, and private equity funds).[38] The fear is that risk and fragility in the system overall may increase as a result, because these entities are subject to less oversight, less capital regulation, and fewer disclosure requirements.

Government works slowly, is often hostage to political ideologies and special interests, and is inclined to Byzantine parsing of power that facilitates regulatory arbitrage on the part of the would-be regulated. Furthermore, its solutions can have counterproductive effects and can promote a false sense of security. The implicit US government guarantees of securities issued by Freddie Mac and Fannie Mae, for example, conveyed a sense of safety that encouraged the proliferation of mortgage securitization by non-government issuers. Government sanction of credit ratings enabled money market funds to invest in what turned out to be highly risky mortgage securities. Critics of government regulation believe governments can only have adverse effects on economies and should allow free markets to exert their own discipline. Former Federal Reserve Chairman Alan Greenspan, a believer in free-market ideology, said on August 4, 2008, "the past has seen mounting global forces (the international version of Adam Smith's invisible hand) quietly displacing government control of economic affairs."[39]

Yet there are also limits to the ability of markets to regulate themselves. Competition among individual companies, each seeking to maximize its own profits, can have unintended consequences (so-called externalities) that are harmful to the economy as a whole and, in the end, to the companies themselves.[40] This was evident in the developments of the credit crisis. No one company can, or should, be held responsible for ensuring the integrity of the system as a whole; this leaves a role for government.

Effective regulatory reform needs to address the broad sources of potential financial instability, not just the proximate causes, and it needs to do so in a manner that, as far as possible, reduces the potential for boomerang effects that will end up magnifying, rather than limiting, financial instability.

Some of the mandates of the Dodd-Frank Wall Street Reform and Consumer Protection Act of 2010 (Dodd-Frank) have the potential to reduce the opacity that has fostered investor herding and excessive leverage in previous crises. Moving trading of over-the-counter derivatives, including CDS, to clearinghouses may increase the availability of information about the type and volume of trading and reduce counterparty credit risk. Increased disclosure could significantly reduce the kinds of problems encountered especially during the 1987 stock market crash and during the 2007–2008 credit crisis, when ignorance about the identity and motivations of sellers increased uncertainty and led to more selling, which further reduced asset prices.

The Financial Stability Oversight Council (FSOC) created by Dodd-Frank has focused on a macroprudential approach to the financial markets. Rather than focusing on risks to individual financial institutions, a macroprudential approach attempts to detect and control risks to the financial system as a whole. The FSOC's purview spans banks, nonbank financial companies, and other entities, including insurance companies and hedge funds, that it deems to have the potential to pose systemic risks to the US economy, as well as the various financial regulatory agencies of the government.

In determining whether an entity is systemically important to the financial system and the economy, the FSOC may look at a variety of factors. These include the entity's use of derivatives and borrowing, its purchase and sale of securitized products, its purchase and sale of financial guarantees, its activities in the repo market, the concentration of its positions, and the extent to which its asset prices are based on models rather than historical data or liquid market prices. The FSOC also has broad authority to ask the Office of Financial Research to obtain information needed to determine the source and extent of systemic risks.

## WARNING SIGNS

Since the financial crisis, the news media have pointed to numerous strategies and instruments that could pose the next systemic threat. One potential culprit—complex, leveraged exchange-traded products—did roil markets in early 2018 (see "Short-Volatility Strategies" in Chapter 15). Also concerning—but not yet disruptive—have been securitizations based on iffy home-improvement loans such as PACE (Property Assessed Clean Energy) notes, which offer tempting yields in a low-rate environment and are based on no-down-payment loans set up by local governments.[41]

The FSOC and regulators should focus on the features of investment products or strategies, such as option-like behavior and leverage, that can give rise to market problems. Products and strategies that trade mechanistically in the same direction as asset prices or asset volatility can exaggerate price movements, especially when other investors herd along with them, facilitating bubbles and crashes. Leverage, because of margin calls, can cause products and strategies to behave in nonlinear ways that are transferred to markets in the form of precipitous declines.

"Free lunch" products, whose appeal rests on their supposedly low risk or their offer of higher returns than seem warranted by the risks they do acknowledge, can attract substantial investments. But how is the risk reduction, or return enhancement, achieved? Reliance on the ability to shift risks to other investors is often based on an illusion of liquidity. Investors' willingness to take the other side of risk-shifters' trades vanishes quickly when investor hope turns into investor fear. At that point, the result can be asset liquidations at fire-sale prices. It then becomes apparent that the lower risk promised by free-lunch products and strategies was merely an illusion of safety.

Finally, regulators, and investors, should be wary of products and strategies that are opaque and overly complex. Regulators must understand not only the gist of the product or strategy itself, but also the ways in which it involves other market participants and how it may interact with the markets in which it trades. As previous crises have shown, products such as portfolio insurance and RMBS can create complex chains of interdependence and feedback loops that vastly complicate the task of anticipating the product's effects.

The bottom line is, if an investment product or strategy seems too good to be true, it probably is—particularly if it is opaque, highly leveraged, or appears guaranteed.

APPENDIX A

# Foreshadowing the Crises: The Crash of 1929

The US stock market crash of October 28 and 29, 1929, a wave of panic and jolting losses, saw trading volume records shattered and the Dow Jones Industrial Average (DJIA) fall 23 percent over two days. It brought an end to a decade of prosperity, during which stock prices had more than quadrupled.[1] Many telltale signs of a mania were evident during the run-up—easy credit, leverage, a hot new financial product, and widespread fascination with stocks fanned by news reports of easy riches. After the crash, stocks continued falling for more than two years, with the DJIA finally hitting bottom on July 8, 1932, at 41.2, off 89 percent from its peak of 381.17 on September 3, 1929.

Whether the Great Depression that followed was caused by the crash itself or by a series of policy errors by political leaders and central bank officials in the United States and Europe remains a matter of debate. But the experience left an indelible imprint on society. Many financial and social reforms that resulted from the decade-long downturn, the deepest and most severe in US history, remain with us today, including Social Security, bank deposit insurance, the Securities and Exchange Commission, and federal regulation of borrowing money to make stock purchases.

As traumatic as the crash and subsequent worldwide depression were, they did not put an end to the kinds of behavior that had caused them. Echoes of 1929 reverberated in the speculative bubbles that inflated and burst in the 1987 and 2007–2008 crises and in the financial turmoil that followed each time.

The events leading up to the 1929 crash began with a bull market driven by a 75 percent rise in corporate profits between 1922 and 1927. During the middle of the decade, signs of excess in the real estate market appeared. Housing construction jumped, commercial real estate boomed in Chicago, New York, and Detroit, and in Florida real estate experienced a spectacular bubble. But stock prices rose commensurately with profits, at least through mid 1927.[2]

Nevertheless, skeptics fretted that prices were being fueled by excessive lending to investors, who were buying stocks on margin, that is, with borrowed money. Margin loans rose from about $1 billion in the early 1920s to $3.5 billion in 1927.[3] When the Federal Reserve lowered its benchmark rate by 0.5 percentage points to 3.5 percent in July 1927, margin lending took off, and the DJIA gained 22 percent during the second half of 1927. Margin lending approached $6 billion by the end of the following year.[4]

Under fire, the Fed reversed course in February 1928 and raised the benchmark rate to 5 percent over the next three months. But by that point it was too late to apply the brakes. Brokers could demand as much as 12 percent for a margin loan, leaving ample profit even after the Fed move. Economist John Kenneth Galbraith later called margin lending "possibly the most profitable arbitrage operation of all time,"[5] so profitable, in fact, that by the first half of 1929, nonbank sources funded nearly three-quarters of margin loans.[6]

Contemporary accounts note that by 1928, small investors were avid participants in what had become a national obsession. Brokerage firm offices began popping up in small towns across the United States. Six hundred new offices opened in 1928 and 1929, increasing the total by half.[7] The enthusiasm was fueled by the fantastic success of glamour stocks like Radio Corporation of America, which soared from $11 a share in 1924 to $114 in 1929, as well as by rags-to-riches stories appearing in the press. One such article, "Everybody Ought to Be Rich," appeared in the August 1929 *Ladies Home Journal*.[8]

Half a century later, the stock market was convulsed by a series of similar episodes. The fad-like popularity of portfolio insurance drove up stock prices prior to the 1987 crash. As discussed in Chapter 5, "Portfolio Insurance and the Crash," the buyers in 1987 were institutional investors rather than individual investors.[9] In the 1990s, individual and institutional investors inflated internet stocks, which had been heavily promoted by Wall Street stock analysts (see sidebar, "Bursting of the Tech Stock Bubble," in Chapter 11). And in the run-up to 2007–2008, both individuals and institutions played a role in the housing boom and the overheated demand for toxic mortgage-backed securities.

The toxic financial products of the 1920s were known as investment trusts. These were vehicles created from a combustible combination of opacity, leverage, and cross-ownership. Although virtually nonexistent in the United States before the 1920s, roughly 750 trusts had been created by the end of 1929.[10] At their peak, these trusts controlled more than $8 billion in assets. Similar in basic structure to today's closed-end mutual funds, they sold debt and preferred stock to finance the purchase of common stocks in other companies. The trusts then ratcheted up the initial leverage by creating new investment trusts, which in turn took on debt to finance further stock purchases. The resulting pyramid structure was very profitable for the original sponsors, who received management fees and, by retaining a controlling interest in each layer, earned returns on their original investment, which grew geometrically as long as stock prices continued rising.

Despite their questionable investment architecture, trusts proved popular with the public, thanks to their steadily rising prices. Trust shares often traded for more than the value of their underlying assets; the premium was thought to reflect the benefit of the sponsors' expertise in assembling the security portfolios. During the darkest days of October 1929, however, the sponsors' expertise was worth far less. As falling stock prices shifted the effects of leverage into reverse, the trusts' common shares quickly lost value and could not be unloaded at any price in the weeks following the crash. This scenario foreshadowed the events of 1987, when mechanistic selling by portfolio insurers caused a rapid decline in market indexes, and of 2007–2008, when the evaporation of demand for mortgage-backed securities set off a panic that dragged down prices of all types of risky assets.

On August 8, 1929, the Fed raised its benchmark interest rate to 6 percent in an effort to cool off the market. This did not immediately succeed. Although the DJIA fell a record 14 points the next day, it rose 30 points in the following three weeks. But the Fed's tightening did have an impact on the broader economy, which fell into a recession by the end of August.

The first sign that the mania was ending came on Wednesday, October 23, 1929, when an unexplained rush of sell orders knocked the market down near the end of the day's trading. The next day, which came to be known as Black Thursday, panic set in. Indexes fell sharply during early trading before a group of Wall Street barons made a show of confidence by placing large buy orders for blue chips.[11] The DJIA rallied to close at 299, down just 6 points. Trading volume of 13 million shares was more than double the normal level.

Heavy selling resumed on October 28, later dubbed Black Monday, accelerated by margin calls, especially from the nonbank lenders who had been so eager to extend credit previously. By the close, the DJIA was down a record 38 points (12.8%), after 9 million shares traded. The next day, Black Tuesday, the DJIA lost another 31 points (11.7%) to close at 230 on volume of 16 million shares. The percentage of trading volume attributable to forced margin selling in October 1929 was similar in magnitude to the forced selling caused by mechanistic portfolio insurance trading in 1987,[12] and the two-day price decline of 23 percent in October 1929 was nearly identical to the 22.6 percent one-day drop on October 19, 1987.

The damage in 1929 could have been worse but for an effort spearheaded by the Federal Reserve Bank of New York to replace more than $1 billion in capital that had fled the margin loan market.[13] The Federal Reserve Board injected another $500 million into the banking system and cut interest rates beginning in November 1929. The DJIA bottomed that month at 199 and rallied in the spring of 1930 to 294, still 23 percent off its September 1929 peak. Fed easing ended that summer with the benchmark rate at 2.5 percent, and the economy and the stock market resumed a downward spiral.

The stock market crash in 1929 was a clear blow to the US economy. Business investment and consumer purchases fell sharply in the aftermath. During the Great Depression, industrial production fell by a remarkable 47 percent, and deflation knocked prices down by 30 percent.[14] Treasury Secretary Andrew Mellon insisted the economy was fundamentally sound and expressed hope that "enterprising people will pick up the wrecks from less competent people." But unemployment, which had stood at 1.5 million in the summer of 1929, doubled to 3.0 million by the spring of 1930.[15] It would reach a peak of 13 million, about a quarter of the work force, in 1933.[16]

A series of banking panics that began in the fall of 1930 wiped out one-fifth of US banks by 1933 and increased the severity of the downturn. Savers began hoarding cash rather than trusting banks; deposit insurance did not yet exist. This hoarding had the effect of severely contracting credit and the money supply.

The Fed's response to this problem was limited, in large part, by its allegiance to the international gold standard, a system by which central banks fixed the values of their currencies to the price of gold (and by extension to each others' currencies). While an expansion of the money supply might have eased economic conditions, it also might have raised concerns that the United States would devalue its currency. That, in turn, could prompt a run on the nation's gold reserves.

In fact, the gold standard required, in essence, that other nations match the contraction of the US economy in order to maintain their own gold reserves. This had the effect of turning the US depression into a worldwide phenomenon. Global economic output fell 15 percent from 1929 through 1932.[17] Similarly, the 1987 US crash unleashed a wave of volatility that quickly spread through international markets.[18] As discussed in Chapter 16, "The European Debt Crisis," the 2007–2008 crisis was felt immediately across Europe and triggered a sovereign debt crisis on the Continent that threatened to unravel the European Union.

The United States effectively abandoned the gold standard in 1933, initiating a four-year period during which economic output grew by 9 percent annually.[19] Although an ill-advised increase in interest rates in 1937 triggered another severe downturn, by mid-1938 the economy was once again showing strong growth. Economic output finally returned to its long-run trend line in 1942. The level of the DJIA, however, didn't surpass its pre-crash peak until 1954.

APPENDIX B

# Primer on Bonds, Stocks, and Derivatives

Any investment entails risk. It is anticipated that risk will be compensated with return. Higher risk should command higher return. Here we examine what those risks are for the most common investment securities.

## GOVERNMENT BONDS

Bonds are essentially IOUs issued in exchange for a loan. In the United States, where the national debt held by the public is $15 trillion, the federal government has issued an astonishing amount of Treasury bonds (30-year maturities), notes (maturities of two to 10 years), and bills (maturities of up to a year). But the United States has a sterling record of repaying its lenders. In fact, Treasury securities are considered virtually free of credit risk—the risk that the Treasury will be unable to make interest payments or return investors' principal—also known as default risk.

In addition, the market for US Treasuries is the most liquid of any bond market in the world. That means there is always a large pool of ready buyers for these securities. Although liquidity risk is not entirely absent, it is less of a concern for Treasuries than for other types of securities.

Treasuries are not completely risk free. They face certain risks that affect all types of bonds. Inflation, for example, is an ever-present concern. The higher the inflation rate, the lower the purchasing power of future interest and principal payments. There is also interest rate risk. An increase in interest rates will reduce the desirability, and therefore the resale value, of previously issued bonds that pay interest at a lower rate. Falling interest rates mean that future payments of interest and principal may have to be reinvested at a lower rate of return (reinvestment risk).

Risk differs across Treasuries of different maturities. Bonds with longer maturities stand a greater chance than shorter-term bonds of being affected by inflation and changes in interest rates. Duration is a measure of the sensitivity of the price of a bond to an interest rate change. The higher a bond's duration, the more sensitive it is to interest rate changes.

But even after taking all of these risks into account, Treasuries are close to a sure bet in investing. Treasury bills are considered virtually risk free because of their short-term maturities and lack of credit risk. Three-month Treasury bills are widely used as a proxy for cash.

## Agency and Entity Bonds

Many government agencies issue bonds to fund loans for housing, small businesses, and other undertakings. Like Treasuries, these bonds are backed by the full faith and credit of the federal government and are free of credit risk. The market for agency debt is generally liquid, although not as liquid as the market for Treasuries; therefore agency bonds must offer a higher interest rate.

Bonds issued by government-sponsored entities (GSEs) and certain government corporations, such as the Tennessee Valley Authority, are not explicitly backed by the federal government, so they carry credit risk. However, investors have long assumed that the federal government would not allow GSEs to default on their debts. This assumption allowed GSEs to issue bonds at interest rates only slightly above those of Treasuries. Indeed, in 2008 the federal government, in effect, nationalized two GSEs, the Federal National Mortgage Association and the Federal Home Loan Mortgage Corporation (Fannie Mae and Freddie Mac), to prevent default and preserve their central role in the mortgage market.

## Municipal Bonds

Municipal bonds, or munis, are issued by state and local governments and agencies. Because they are generally exempt from federal income taxes, and often exempt from state and local income taxes for local residents, they are more attractive to individual investors than to institutional investors, which are largely tax-exempt.

Although their historical default rate has been low, munis carry credit risk (although this is usually mitigated by guarantees from monoline insurance companies, which insure municipal debt). The degree of credit risk depends largely on which of two categories a municipal bond falls into. General obligation bonds are backed by the taxing authority of the issuer. Revenue bonds are repaid from tolls, rents, and other charges levied by the facilities financed by the bond issue. Owners of revenue bonds face relatively higher credit and default risk because of the possibility that revenues could fall short of expectations.

Munis offer nominal interest rates that can be lower than those of comparable Treasuries (due to their favorable tax treatment). But muni risk is generally higher, reflecting differences in credit, liquidity, and other factors.

## CORPORATE BONDS

Corporations issue a variety of bonds, and they are vulnerable to many of the same risks that affect government bonds, including maturity and duration risk, inflation and interest-rate risk, and reinvestment risk. For investors in corporate bonds, however, credit risk is a bigger issue than it is for government-bond investors. Corporations can, and sometimes do, default on their obligations, leaving bondholders vulnerable to loss of principal and future interest payments. Corporate bonds pay higher interest rates than Treasuries and other government debt instruments as compensation for the greater credit risk.

Determining which corporate bonds have a higher risk of default than others requires a great deal of research into the operations and financial conditions of thousands of companies. Many investors rely on research performed by credit rating agencies. The three largest rating agencies in the United States are Moody's Investors Service, Standard & Poor's, and Fitch Ratings. Each assigns letter-grade ratings signifying the relative risk of a particular issue. Moody's gives grades ranging from Aaa for the least-risky issues to a low of C for the most risky. Standard & Poor's and Fitch assign grades ranging from AAA to D. (See Exhibit 11.1 in Chapter 11, "Blowing Bubbles.")

Credit rating agencies rate many types of debt instruments, including those issued by governments. Bonds with lower ratings tend to pay higher interest rates to reflect a higher degree of risk. Interest rates for AAA-rated bonds may be only slightly higher than those of Treasuries, given their relative safety. Ratings are upgraded or downgraded in response to changing conditions. The possibility of a rating downgrade, which can lower a bond's resale value, is a component of credit risk.

Corporate bonds with noninvestment-grade ratings (Ba1 and below on the Moody's scale, BB+ and below on the Standard & Poor's and Fitch scales) are known as high-yield or junk bonds. As the name implies, these bonds pay higher interest rates to reflect their speculative nature and their relatively high risk of default. Some conservative endowments and pension funds cannot, by policy, hold them. Thus, a downgrade from an investment-grade to a noninvestment-grade rating can have a bigger impact on a bond's value than other downgrades because it could have the effect of reducing the pool of available buyers.

Many corporate bond issues are callable; that is, the issuer reserves the right to buy back, or call, its bonds at a stated price, usually after a period of years has passed since issuance. (The United States government has not issued callable Treasuries since the mid-1980s, but some government agency issues are callable; municipal bonds can also be callable.) Typically, bonds will be called if interest rates have fallen and the issuer can refinance the debt at lower rates. Call risk reflects the possibility that an investor will have to sell a relatively high-yielding bond sooner than expected and reinvest the proceeds in a lower-yielding environment. Even if an issue has not been called, the perception that it is likely to be called can adversely affect its resale value if it is trading above the price at which it will be called.

There are not as many ready buyers for corporate bonds as there are for Treasuries. Therefore, corporate bonds pose greater liquidity risk, the risk that buyers will not be willing to step forward when the investor wants to sell. Liquidity risk is even higher for bonds issued by small companies or issued in small quantities and for bonds that have low ratings or that have been recently downgraded. The seller of a thinly traded bond may have to offer a deeply discounted price to attract a buyer.

The market for bonds is less transparent than for stocks, adding another layer of risk. Most bonds do not trade on exchanges, so recent price quotes are not always available. Buyers and sellers must instead rely on dealer price quotes. It may be difficult to determine the fair value of a thinly traded bond because it may trade relatively infrequently and there may be few dealers willing to offer a price quote. Dealers also may impose additional mark-ups on purchases and sales of thinly traded bonds. This gap between market value and the dealer's price is known as the bid-ask spread.

The introduction in 2002 of a centralized reporting system for bond trades, known as TRACE (Transaction Reporting and Compliance Engine), has significantly reduced bid-ask spreads for corporate bonds. The system, mandated by the Securities and Exchange Commission (SEC), requires bond dealers to immediately report all corporate bond sales and transaction prices to a central database run by the Financial Industry Regulatory Authority, or FINRA.

## STOCKS

There is a fundamental difference between stock returns and risks and bond returns and risks. Virtually all of the returns on a (noncallable) bond held to maturity come from scheduled interest payments. A bondholder faces the risk that changes in interest rates may affect the bond's resale value, but if there is no default by the issuer, a bondholder will receive all of the promised interest payments plus a return of principal at maturity, regardless of economic or market conditions.

A stock represents partial ownership of, or equity in, a company, rather than a loan to a company. In return for this ownership, stockholders are entitled to a portion of a company's assets and profits, but the company is not obligated to return to the investor the original stock investment, as it is obligated to return a bond's principal at maturity. Furthermore, stockholders cannot claim their share of income until bondholders' claims are satisfied. Because an investment in stocks is generally riskier than an investment in bonds, stocks have historically provided a higher return than bonds, which compensates for the increased risk. This higher return is known as the equity risk premium.

### THE EQUITY RISK PREMIUM

From 1926 through 2017, large-company stock returns averaged 10.2 percent a year before adjusting for inflation. Long-term government bonds provided a 5.5 percent average annual return over the same period.[1] This difference in returns, 4.7 percentage points, is a simple and widely used measure of the historical US equity risk premium. It is an estimate of the extra reward investors require for taking on the added risk of owning stocks rather than relatively safe government bonds.

Whether it is an accurate measure is a matter of ongoing debate, however. Because it is based on historical averages, this particular measure of the equity risk premium is backward looking and does not necessarily reflect conditions ahead.

The long time span included in the averages may well obscure important differences between today's investing environment and that which existed decades ago. Today, accounting standards are more stringent, central banks are better able to keep inflation under control, worker productivity is higher, and global trade has increased economic efficiency. To the extent that these factors have produced a less risky investing environment for stocks, the equity premium may be lower today than it has been historically.

In addition, stock ownership is more common today than it was 50 or even 30 years ago, thanks to greater prosperity, substantially reduced trading commissions, and the rise of self-directed retirement accounts. This greater demand for stocks has increased their price. Stocks generally trade today at a higher price-to-earnings ratio than they did early in the twentieth century. The greater price relative to earnings implies that investors are willing to accept a lower return, and thus a reduced risk premium, for owning stocks.

Some researchers argue that the equity risk premium that appeared to prevail during the last century is simply too high to be justified by any actual difference in risk between stocks and bonds. They call this the "equity premium puzzle."[2] After all, US stocks have produced positive returns over every 20-year period since 1926.[3] Of course, many investors hold stocks for shorter periods of time, during which negative returns are a greater possibility. This is, perhaps, the key to solving the puzzle. Behavioral economists argue that investors' aversion to short-term losses is so strong that they require an extra premium to bear the risk of short-term losses.

Rather than rely on historical averages, some researchers prefer to calculate a forward-looking equity risk premium based on forecasts of future cashflows (dividends and stock repurchases) and earnings growth rates. Using this approach, Damodaran estimated a year-ahead US equity risk premium of 5.08 percent as of January 1, 2018.[4]

Whether the equity risk premium is 4.7 percent, 5.08 percent, or some other figure cannot be known with certainty. Still, understanding the relationship between risk and potential returns is the first step in determining how to manage risk.

## Dividends and Capital Appreciation

Returns on a stock come from periodic dividends the company may pay shareholders plus any increase in the value of the company's shares while they are held by the investor. Unlike fixed bond interest payments, stock dividend payments are at the discretion of each company. Companies can raise, lower, or suspend dividends without triggering a default; many companies do not pay any dividends. In any case, dividends represent only a portion of the historical return for stocks, just 4.0 percentage points of the average 10.2 percent annual return on stocks of large companies from 1926 through 2017.[5] Smaller companies tend to pay no or only a small amount of dividends. The majority of a stock's return (and risk) comes from changes in the price investors are willing to pay for the shares.

Both portions of a stock's return, dividend income and price change, are subject to several risks. The risk of bankruptcy is a key consideration. If a business fails and its assets are liquidated, owners of common stock are far back in the line for reimbursement, behind bondholders and owners of preferred stock (a class of stock that has some bond-like characteristics). It is not unusual for common stock investors to get nothing if a company is liquidated.

The sale of a stock, and any profit on that sale, may also be affected by the liquidity of the market for the company's shares. In a liquid market, with lots of buyers and sellers, sales and purchases are accomplished quickly and have little impact on the price of the shares. In an illiquid market, with buyers and sellers hard to come by, it may be difficult to sell or buy shares, and transactions may have fairly large effects on share prices.

Generally, this type of liquidity risk is greater for the shares of small companies than for the shares of large companies, because the former tend to have fewer investors. However, there may be periods, such as during market crises, when liquidity dries up, willing buyers disappear from the market, and it becomes very difficult to trade shares of large and small companies alike.

Because stocks are traded on exchanges, their prices are publicly available to all potential investors. Furthermore, stock markets are typically quite liquid, so prices generally reflect current, virtually real-time transaction prices. Some stocks, usually those of the smallest firms, trade more infrequently; their prices may represent transactions that took place hours or even days before. Compared with stocks, bonds are much more opaque, as most do not trade on exchanges and trade much more infrequently than stocks. Market crises may impair price transparency.

Stocks also face some interest-rate risk, though to a lesser extent than bonds. Rising interest rates, by increasing the costs companies must pay to borrow or by slowing economic growth, can impede profit growth, a key driver of stock returns. But inflation, at least moderate inflation, is generally not a risk for stocks as their prices tend to rise with inflation. In fact, stocks are often touted as a hedge against inflation. It is generally assumed that companies can pass inflationary cost increases on to consumers in the form of higher prices, preserving shareholder value.

## Specific and Systematic Risks

A stock's risk is generally measured as the variability of its return about the mean, or average, of the return over a given period. The statistical measure that is used is variance. A stock with a higher variance has returns that are more variable than those of a stock with a lower variance.

Financial theory developed in the 1960s posited that stocks should be compared not only in terms of their variances, but in terms of how their returns covary with changes in the overall market's return.[6] As a rising tide lifts all boats, a rising market tends to lift the prices of all stocks, even those of companies with low expectations of future profitability; in a falling market, the shares of even highly profitable companies tend to fall.

The comovement of the returns of a stock with the returns of the market is measured statistically by covariance. A stock's beta is its price sensitivity to changes in the overall market; beta can be calculated as the ratio of the stock's covariance with the market divided by the variance of the market. A stock with a beta of 1 is expected to move in tandem with the market; if the market rises 1 percent, the stock rises 1 percent, and if the market falls 1 percent, the stock falls 1 percent. A higher beta indicates greater sensitivity to market movements; a lower beta, less sensitivity. A stock with a negative beta moves counter to the market; its price is expected to rise as the market falls and to fall as the market rises.

Beta represents the *systematic* risk of a stock, the portion of its risk and return that derives from the system of which it is a part, the overall stock market. High-beta stocks and portfolios with a preponderance of high-beta stocks have greater systematic risk. They should, at least theoretically, offer higher expected returns to compensate investors for incurring more risk than would be found in lower-beta, lower-risk stocks and portfolios.[7]

A stock's beta does not account for all of its risk or return, however. A stock's return will usually include a residual portion of return that cannot be accounted for by overall market movements. This stock-specific, or idiosyncratic, risk represents the portion of the stock's return stemming from the particular attributes of the company. This portion of a stock's return is *specific* to the company and gives rise to the stock's alpha, the divergence of the stock's return from the return that would be expected from the stock's covariance with the market.

Finance theory holds that specific risk can be eliminated, or at least mitigated, through diversification—holding a portfolio that contains a variety of stocks whose specific risks are offsetting. For example, an increase in oil prices can be expected to result in increases in the prices of oil-company stocks but in price declines for the stocks of companies that are heavy users of oil, such as airlines. As another example, a portfolio that holds stocks of both importers and exporters can be expected to be somewhat protected against unexpected fluctuations in currency exchange rates.

Because specific risk is diversifiable, theory posits, it should not be rewarded. Only systematic risk, which cannot be diversified away, should be rewarded. Furthermore, as noted, higher systematic risk should be rewarded with a higher expected return. In an idealized world, investors could select from a continuum of portfolios offering different combinations of expected return and risk, from portfolios that offer low risk and low expected return to those that offer high risk and high expected return.

According to the efficient market hypothesis, stock prices reflect at all times all available information.[8] Trying to beat the market by selecting stocks based on predicting their price changes is thus presumed to be futile. According to this theory, the best a stock investor can do is to hold a portfolio representative of the overall market, such as a stock market index. The stock market index can be combined with a risk-free asset such as Treasury bills in order to achieve a lower level of overall risk at the cost of lower expected return (or leveraged by borrowing funds to invest in the index in order to increase overall expected return at the cost of added risk). However, new theories and technologies over the last several decades, including the field of behavioral finance, new statistical techniques, and ever increasing computer power, suggest that it may be possible for some investors to manage portfolios actively in order to achieve alpha, that is, a more favorable return than that implied by the portfolio's beta alone.

Achieving alpha requires either skill in stock selection (purchasing stocks that outperform the overall market or selling short stocks that underperform the overall market) or market timing (buying a stock market index before it rises and selling before it falls). In the absence of such skills, however, the best an investor can expect to achieve over time is a return commensurate with the investment's systematic risk, or beta.

## DERIVATIVES

A derivative is a contract that calls for one party to make payments to another based on the price movements of an underlying asset, such as a stock or stock index, bond or bond index, commodity, interest rate, or currency exchange rate. The value of a derivative is thus *derived* from the price of the underlying asset.

Derivatives may be used to enhance investment returns and to reduce risks. They also can provide investment exposures that may be otherwise prohibited by investment guidelines that apply to direct purchases.[9] Speculators use derivatives to bet on the future direction of the underlying asset's price movements. The initial payment to open a derivatives contract, known as margin, is generally a small fraction of what the underlying asset would cost. A derivatives position thus involves leverage and can potentially offer a greater return on investment than a direct investment in the underlying asset.

Derivatives are also used to manage risk. They may be used, for example, to turn a variable rate of return on an asset into a fixed rate of return on the same asset. Or they may be used in such a way that their cash flows or price changes partially or fully offset the cash flows or price changes on the underlying asset, so that the variability of the latter is reduced or eliminated. They may also be used to shape the returns on an asset to provide, for example, for returns within a certain range. Various types of derivatives are available on a variety of assets. Some of the most common are described below.

The most common form of derivative is the *swap*. A swap is an agreement between two parties to trade future cash flows. Usually, the counterparties exchange interest rates on a specified amount of an underlying asset, called the reference asset. One party pays a floating rate, which can rise or fall due to a variety of factors, and receives from the counterparty a fixed rate, which remains constant over the term of the contract.

Either side of such a swap may be risk-reducing. For example, a party that owns an asset that pays a fixed interest rate might engage in a fixed-for-floating swap to protect itself from an increase in interest rates. Conversely, a party that owns an asset that pays a floating interest rate might engage in a floating-for-fixed swap to protect itself from a decline in interest rates. Alternatively, either position may be taken as a speculative bet on the future direction of interest rates.

Swaps, as noted, are agreements between individual counterparties. They are not traded, like stocks, on an organized exchange; rather, they are traded among an informal network of dealers known as the over-the-counter (OTC) market. Entering into a swap thus can involve counterparty risk, the risk that a counterparty will not live up to the agreement.[10] Swaps also entail liquidity risk, as there is no secondary market in which to trade swap positions. A counterparty that wishes to get out of the obligations of its swap position may be able to find a third party that will take its position on, but doing so may be costly.

*Futures and forwards* are contracts to buy or sell an asset in the future at an agreed-upon price. Futures are standardized contracts and trade on organized exchanges. Forwards are customized contracts and trade over the counter, though, like swaps, these trades are increasingly overseen by a central counterparty clearinghouse (CCP).

Futures and forwards essentially lock in a price today for a transaction that will take place later. For example, a futures contract generally specifies the amount of the underlying asset covered, the future date at which it can be bought or sold (the contract maturity), and the price at which it can be bought or sold at that date. Futures are traded on many agricultural and energy commodities as well as on precious metals and financial products, such as individual stocks and stock indexes, bonds and bond indexes, and currency exchange rates. As with swaps, a buyer or seller can use futures and forwards to obtain exposure to a given amount of the underlying asset for much less than it would cost to actually purchase the underlying asset.

Futures and forwards, like swaps, may be used to speculate on the direction of the underlying asset's price or to hedge against movements in the underlying asset's price. The prices of futures and forward contracts move one for one, that is, in a linear fashion with the price of the underlying asset. If the price of the underlying asset increases (declines) by one dollar, the price of a futures or forward contract written on it will increase (decline) by a similar amount. At maturity, of course, the price of the futures and forward contracts and the underlying asset must converge. Thus, futures and forwards can act as surrogates for the underlying assets.

An *option*, like futures and forwards, may be traded on organized exchanges or over the counter. An option contract specifies a given amount of an underlying asset (again, this may be a commodity or a financial asset), a maturity date (the date at which the contract will expire), and an exercise price. The exercise price, or strike price, represents the price at which the option buyer may sell or buy the underlying asset. *May*, because an option, unlike a futures contract, does not confer an obligation to buy or sell, but a right to buy or sell.

The purchaser of a put option has the right to sell an underlying asset at the exercise price, and the purchaser of a call option has the right to buy an underlying asset at the exercise price. The put option seller (also called the option writer) takes the risk that the price of the underlying asset will fall below the exercise price. The call option seller takes on the risk that the price of the underlying asset will increase above the exercise price. The price of the option, called the premium, reflects this risk. So-called American options can be exercised at any time on or before the expiration date; so-called European options can be exercised only at expiration.

If the price of the asset covered by a put option drops below the exercise price, the put buyer can exercise the option, selling the asset to the put writer at the exercise price and avoiding a loss equal to the difference between the exercise price and the current (lower) price of the asset less the cost of the option premium. Alternatively, the buyer can sell the put option, unexercised, at a profit.

If the price of the asset covered by a call option rises above the exercise price, the call buyer can exercise the option, buying the asset from the call writer at the exercise price and making a profit equal to the difference between the current (higher) price of the asset and the exercise price, less the cost of the option premium. Alternatively, the buyer can sell the call option, unexercised, at a profit.

The major risk for the option buyer is that the underlying price will not move in the right direction or will not move enough to make exercise of the option worthwhile. In that case, the option buyer will not exercise the option. The option will expire worthless, and the premium paid by the option buyer will be a loss.

While the value of a futures or forward contract converges to the value of the underlying asset, an option at expiration may be worth either something or nothing. The relationship between the option and the underlying asset is more complicated than that between a futures or forward contract and the underlying asset.

Unlike the value of futures and forwards, the option's value does not move linearly with the price of the underlying asset. When the price of the underlying asset is far below the exercise price of the call option (the option is "deep out of the money"), the option's value hardly changes with changes in the price of the underlying asset. As the asset's price approaches the strike price of the option, however, the option's value becomes increasingly sensitive to changes in the asset's price. When the price of the underlying asset is well above the exercise price of a call option (the option is "deep in the money"), the option's value moves closer to being linearly related to the price of the underlying asset.

Derivatives in general pose the same risks as the underlying assets on which they are based, but there are other risks as well. Derivatives employ leverage. Buyers initially post cash (initial margin) equal to just a small fraction of the derivative instrument's price, representing just a small fraction of the underlying asset's price. This gives rise to leverage, which can magnify profits as well as losses. For example, a derivatives buyer who posts cash equal to 10 percent of a derivative contract's price can earn a 100 percent return on the posted cash if the underlying asset rises just 10 percent, but lose the entire amount posted if the underlying asset declines by 10 percent.

Futures and publicly traded options are listed on exchanges, but purchasers of nonstandardized OTC derivatives contracts, such as swaps, forwards, and some options, face counterparty risk; since the credit crisis, these transactions are increasingly steered through CCPs, which provide some mitigation of counterparty risk. Counterparty risk includes the risks that the counterparty will default on the payments owed or come up short or late in paying.

Liquidity risk can be high for derivatives that trade over the counter or have customized features that limit their appeal to other buyers. Price transparency may also be low for these instruments because they do not trade on an exchange, and the prices at which they transact are usually not publicly available.

The market for most exchange-traded derivatives is quite liquid, but some derivatives that trade on exchanges can have limited liquidity because they are based on an underlying asset with low liquidity or because they are deep out of the money, paying off at a price that is far from the current price of the underlying asset, hence trade infrequently.

Futures may also carry basis risk; their price movements may not fully offset the price movements of the assets they are intended to hedge. This can result from an unexpected divergence between the futures contract's price and the underlying asset's price, or because the expiration date of the futures contract differs from the end of the desired hedging period.

Model risk can be a factor, especially for complex derivatives, but it is also a factor in estimating the value of the underlying stocks or bonds. Estimating a company's expected future cash flows and calculating the present-day value of those cash flows, for example, require models, as does estimating the stock's expected returns and risks. Weaknesses in the assumptions behind the models, or errors in data inputs or in the model calculations, can impair investment results.

Derivatives are more complex than their underlying assets, and their prices and volumes are less transparent; hence they can pose greater risk than simple assets for their investors and for the markets in which they trade. Appendix D describes a number of derivatives-based disasters that plagued companies and local governments in the 1990s, when these types of instruments were relatively new and not well understood.

In general, the less familiar, the more complex, and the less transparent the instrument, the greater the misperception of risk. Portfolio insurance in the 1980s was a novel, relatively sophisticated strategy that offered little transparency in terms of the extent to which it was being used, the markets it could affect, and its anticipated costs. Long-Term Capital Management's arbitrage strategies were very complex, highly leveraged, and, by design, opaque to the fund's counterparties as well as to investors. The mortgage-backed products that became so popular in the 2000s were complex and lacking in transparency.

APPENDIX C

# The Debate on Portfolio Insurance

## Bruce Jacobs's "Memorandum to Prudential Insurance Company of America's Client Service and Sales Forces regarding Portfolio Insulation" – January 17, 1983

### Bruce Jacobs's Memorandum to Prudential Insurance Company of America's Client Service and Sales Forces regarding Portfolio Insulation

January 17, 1983

Memo to Bob Ferrari

Re: Portfolio Insulation

Recently, a few financial institutions and consulting organizations have started to market a "portfolio insulation" technique which claims to "protect" asset values. Leland, O'Brien and Rubinstein (LOR) were the first to package and market an insulation product and have since been emulated by Kidder Peabody and Wilshire. While these competitors employ the same basic methodology, their products have been alternately branded "Dynamic Asset Allocation," "Protective Portfolio Management," and "Portfolio Risk Control."

Portfolio insulation techniques utilize the concept of a "protective put." A "put" is on option to sell a stock at a specified price, the strike price, over a given period of time. A put purchased on a security in conjunction with a long position in that security affords downside protection. For the cost of the put, referred to as the "premium", the investor's capital can be protected, hence the term "protective put". If the security's price falls, the put can be "exercised," i.e., the security can be sold at the strike price. If the security appreciates, the gains accrue to the investor less the premium paid for the put.

Theoretically, an entire portfolio can be protected through the purchase of puts on each security in the portfolio. However, puts are not available for all securities. In addition, the cost associated with protecting the investment in each security would be far costlier than protecting the capital invested in the portfolio as a whole. This cost problem arises because the premium paid for a put is directly related to the volatility of the protected asset. The volatility of a portfolio of securities, however, is significantly less than the average volatility of the component securities. Thus the put premium for an entire portfolio would be substantially less than the sum of the put premiums across all underlying securities.

It has been recently recognized in the financial literature that a protective put can be synthetically created for any portfolio of securities. The methodology dichotomizes the total portfolio into two segments--an actively managed portfolio and a cash-equivalents portfolio. The actively managed portfolio can be an all equity, all debt, or a balanced portfolio.

The initial portfolio position would consist of both a cash-equivalent portion and an actively managed portion. The cash equivalent portion is in a sense a buffer to limit the extent of losses. If the actively managed portfolio falls in value, a portion would be liquidated and invested in cash equivalents. Asset value declines require a more conservative posturing to protect remaining capital. Conversely, cash equivalents would be traded for investments in the actively traded portfolio if it appreciates in value. Asset value appreciation permits a riskier posturing since the appreciation provides a larger buffer above the protected value. The premium is paid implicitly and is represented by the opportunity costs of the hedge position in cash equivalents.

-2-

Portfolio insulation is not intended as a market timing technique. There is no attempt to forecast returns, but rather trading is precipitated by past returns. The trades between the actively managed portion and the cash-equivalents portion of the portfolio are activated by recent performance.

The portfolio insulation technique protects asset values for any time period specified by the client, usually a calendar year. Since the chosen horizon bears no relationship to the duration of the liabilities, it is arbitrary. The client may be comforted by limiting losses year-by-year. However, the implicit premium on the synthetic put represented by the opportunity costs of the hedge, will hinder longer-term performance. While simulations of the portfolio insulation technique using the last decade as a sample period show favorable performance, this period was characterized by poor equity performance. Any methodology that would have had large cash positions would have performed favorably.

If the actively managed segment of the portfolio is a "balanced" portfolio, the portfolio insulation technique would trade a vertical slice of the balanced portfolio for cash when the balanced portfolio fell in value, and conversely, would trade cash for a vertical purchase of the balanced portfolio when the balanced portfolio rose in value. The asset mix of a balanced portfolio is appropriately determined by an efficient frontier analysis, which determines the mix of assets that maximizes expected return for any chosen level of risk. Trades between the balanced portfolio and the cash portfolio, required by the portfolio insulation technique, would alter the mix of assets and thereby be a violation of the long-run efficient frontier assumptions in order to reach a short-term goal of protecting asset values, alternatively stated as "assuring" returns, for an arbitrarily chosen time period. Short-run returns could be assured only by moving off the efficient frontier.

Compared to a traditionally managed portfolio, the trades required by the portfolio insulation technique would increase transaction costs, including both commissions and market impact costs. The insulation technique also requires that the actively managed portfolio consist of highly liquid securities. In fact, if the value of the actively traded portfolio falls significantly, the entire active segment will have to be liquidated. In this case, the portfolio would consist of cash equivalents until the beginning of the next performance period. Such asset categories as real estate, for example, may not be readily liquidated.

There are also potential slippages in the system so that the protected amount may not be fully protected. For example, since execution prices may differ from the price at the time of the sell signal, the entire portfolio value may fall below the protected amount. In addition, since the expected volatility of the actively managed portion determines the magnitude of the implicit premium on the synthetic put and thus the appropriate hedge, the technique may fail if the volatility of the actively managed portion is mis-specified.

-3-

On a more theoretical note, since the portfolio insulation technique trades cash for the actively traded portfolio when values appreciate, and conversely, trades the actively traded fund for cash when values fall, there is an implicit assumption that the investors utility for wealth displays decreasing risk aversion (increasing risk tolerance). An individual displaying decreasing risk aversion will commit an increasing (decreasing) proportion of his wealth to risky assets as his wealth rises (falls). The evidence in the financial literature is more supportive of the notion of constant proportional risk aversion, i.e., independent of wealth level, an individual will commit the same proportion of wealth to risky assets. That chosen proportion is of course unique to the individual.

Also, from a macro perspective, if a large number of investors utilized the portfolio insulation technique, price movements would tend to snowball. Price rises (falls) would be followed by purchases (sales) which would lead to further price appreciation (depreciation). Market prices would not be efficient and it would pay to not use portfolio insulation, since the resulting over- or under-valuation would represent opportunities for savvy investors.

A final criticism is that while it may be possible to assure nominal returns, after-inflation or real returns cannot be assured. While the plan sponsor may feel comfort in protecting nominal values for a chosen time period, purchasing power will remain unprotected. Since the plan sponsor's liabilities are real and not nominal in their nature, there is little comfort in assuring nominal returns, especially when the cost is a longer-run return sacrifice.

Bruce

Bruce I. Jacobs

BIJ:ls

Bruce Jacobs's "The Portfolio Insurance Puzzle" – August 22, 1983

Reprinted with permission from—

Pensions&Investments

The newspaper of corporate and institutional investing

August 22, 1983

# The portfolio insurance puzzle

## Techniques protect assets-and reduce long-term returns

By Bruce I. Jacobs

The financial community has recently shown a heightened interest in "portfolio insurance" techniques which have as their primary goal the "protection" of assets. My research indicates, however, that these techniques substantially reduce returns in the long run.

A number of financial institutions and consulting firms are marketing products under names such as "dynamic asset allocation/protective portfolio management," "portfolio insulation" and "portfolio risk control."

The portfolio insurance technique synthetically creates a "protective put" which attempts to limit downside risk. The initial portfolio position consists of both a cash equivalent portfolio and an actively managed portfolio.

If the actively managed investments fall in value, a portion of it would be liquidated and invested in cash equivalents to protect remaining capital.

Conversely, cash equivalents would be traded for additional investments in the actively managed portfolio if it appreciates in value. This is because asset value appreciation permits a riskier posture by providing a larger buffer to protect asset values.

Portfolio insurance is not a market timing technique. There is no attempt to forecast returns.

Trades between the actively managed portion and the cash-equivalents portion of the portfolio is triggered by past returns. Investors select a time interval, usually a calendar year, for asset value protection.

While investors may be comforted by limiting losses for short intervals, they should recognize that the opportunity costs of the hedged position in cash equivalents will seriously hinder longer-term performance of their portfolio.

For example, one dollar invested in January 1928 would have grown to $52.36 by the end of 1982 if invested in a Standard & Poor's 500 stock index portfolio that had been insured with an annual loss limitation of 5%. This, however, represents only one-half of the amount generated by an S&P 500 buy-and-hold strategy which would have returned $104.25.

After taking into account the relatively modest transaction costs estimated to be 1% for commissions and market impact, $1.00 invested in the S&P 500 portfolio using an insured strategy would have grown to only $36.97.

This is only one-third the level achieved by a buy-and-hold strategy.

Proponents of portfolio insurance often point to the last 10 years as a period when the technique would have produced favorable results. However, evidence from this period should be used with caution since this period was characterized by poor equity performance and unprecedented high short-term interest rates. Any strategy advocating large cash positions would have performed favorably.

For example, during the 10 years ending 1982, $1.00 invested in an insured S&P 500 portfolio having an annual loss limitation of 5% would have grown to $2.29 net of transaction costs.

A buy-and-hold strategy would have generated $1.90, but an investment in U.S. Treasury bills would have resulted in $2.27, a level greater than that achieved by investing in a buy-and-hold S&P 500 strategy, and only two cents less than the return achieved using the insured strategy.

The examples above use a calendar year as the time interval and an S&P 500 portfolio as the actively managed segment. Although this is not always the case, the fundamental conclusions remain the same whether the chosen horizon is one year or longer, or whether an actively managed equity portfolio is used rather than a passive equity index portfolio. In addition, the selected interval of protection usually bears no relationship to the duration of the liabilities and is therefore arbitrary.

*Mr. Jacobs is director of asset management at Prudential Insurance Co., Newark, N.J.*

A problem could arise if the value of the actively managed portfolio fell significantly, since the entire active portfolio would have to be liquidated.

The portfolio would then consist only of cash-equivalents until the beginning of the next performance period.

Accordingly, there would be no opportunity to participate in rising markets and the investor would be shut out of these gains, unless judgment was exercised to restart the technique.

This would have occurred for anyone using this strategy in 1933 when the entire active stock segment would have had to be liquidated early in the year. Subsequently the insured strategy would have produced a 5% loss for the calendar year vs. a 54% gain using a buy-and-hold S&P 500 strategy.

The pattern of the equity markets in 1982 came perilously close to producing a similar situation precluding investors from participating in the strong rally at yearend.

When using the insurance strategy, there are also potential slippages where the amount to be protected may not be fully protected. Since execution prices may differ from the price at the time of the sell signal, the entire protected value may fall below the protected amount.

In addition, since the expected volatility of the actively managed portion is a major factor in determining the size of the cash-equivalents position, the technique may fall if the volatility of the actively managed segment is misspecified. For example, the cash-equivalents position may be inadequate if the value of the actively managed segment happened to fall precipitously toward the end of the interval.

A portfolio allocated 61.75% to the S&P 500, and 38.25% to Treasury bills would have had the same volatility (as measured by the annual standard deviation) as the S&P 500 insured portfolio, but it would have also out-performed this portfolio. For the period 1928 to 1982, the return on an insured portfolio using this allocation would have exceeded that of one based on the S&P 500, by approximately 50 basis points. This is because transaction costs averaged 66 basis points for the insured portfolio.

Since the shifts between cash equivalents and the actively managed portions of the portfolio are not designed to profit from forecasted changes in relative returns, it is likely that an insured portfolio will underperform an allocated portfolio by the transaction costs incurred.

In addition, the vendors who insure the portfolios charge fees which I have not taken into account.

Because it has the same volatility, the allocated strategy would have provided the same average protection as that provided by the insured portfolio.

The pattern of annual losses would differ, however, based on the 5% maximum loss with portfolio insurance. So, the investor must address whether the 50 basis point sacrifice in annual return, plus the insurance vendor's fee, is a reasonable price to pay for the insured techniques's pattern of returns.

The insurance technique limited the magnitude of a loss in any one year to 5%, however, it generated losses in 24 out of the 55 years as compared to only 17 years of losses under the allocated strategy. And, in only four cases did these annual losses significantly exceed 5%. For two of these four years annual losses exceeded 10%, and for the other two exceeded 20%. The largest annual loss was 26.5%.

It should also be noted that in some years the loss limitation of the insurance technique would be comforting, while in others the opportunity cost of being shut out prior to a major market rally would be unsettling. In 1933, if an insured portfolio is compared to an allocated portfolio, the opportunity cost of being shut out was 38.4%.

In lieu of this, an appropriate approach to risk reduction would be to choose a balanced or multi-asset class portfolio. Such a portfolio should be broadly diversified across distinct asset classes to benefit from the lack of synchronization of asset class returns that lessens volatility. The mix of asset classes should be chosen in order to be efficient in maximizing expected return at any chosen level of volatility.

While with portfolio insurance the actively managed segment of the portfolio may be a multi-asset class portfolio, the trades between this balanced portfolio and the cash-equivalents portfolio would alter the mix of asset classes and thereby violate long-run efficiency.

Also keep in mind that equity real estate, an asset class highly recommended for balanced portfolios, may not be readily liquid at those times required by the insurance technique.

# Hayne Leland's "Portfolio Insurance Performance, 1928–1983" (1984)

## PORTFOLIO INSURANCE PERFORMANCE, 1928 — 1983

**Hayne Leland, Chairman**

Dynamic strategies or "portfolio insurance" can substantially raise expected portfolio returns, when contrasted with static investment strategies offering comparable protection against downside risk. Or so theoretical arguments indicate. With the availability of daily stock market data over the last 55 years (1/1/28 — 12/31/82), these contentions can now be examined empirically.

A recent article by Bruce Jacobs (*Pensions and Investments*, 8/22/83) questions whether portfolio insurance offers the advantages which have been heralded. We shall show that his conclusions are wrong. In fact, we shall show that 55 years of empirical experience fully supports the contention that portfolio insurance offers significant gains over static risk-equivalent alternatives.

How can two studies using the same data base reach such different conclusions? We shall show that Jacobs' conclusions result from two fundamental errors: (i) a failure to make appropriate risk comparisons, and (ii) a failure to use optimal portfolio insurance strategies.

The portfolio insurance program we initally focus on provides a minimum assured return each year of -5%, or "five percent deductible" protection. (Jacobs also examines this level of protection, although he uses a suboptimal implementation.)

LOR's Dynamic Asset Allocation strategy was applied to the 55 year period 1928 — 1983 for which a stock market index (the S&P 500 equivalent) was available. Results were as follows:

| Policy | Minimum Return | Compound Annual Return* | End Value of $1** |
|---|---|---|---|
| Insured "-5" | -5.0% | 7.0% | $41.32 |

It should be noted that the end period value using LOR's techniques exceeds Jacobs' ending value of $36.97 by more than 11%. This improvement is due to the superior LOR insurance technique.

What is the "risk equivalent" static strategy? Since we focus on downside risk, the question can be posed: What static mix of stock and Tbills would have produced no losses exceeding 5%? The answer to this question is a 14/86 mix. Any more than 14% in equities would result in at least one year with a loss exceeding 5%. Since the compound annual return of equities over the period 1/1/28 — 12/31/82 was 8.8%, and the return of Tbills 3.2%, the downside risk-equivalent static policy would have the following results:

| Policy | Minimum Return | Compound Annual Return | End Value of $1 |
|---|---|---|---|
| Static 14/86 | -5% | 4.0% | $8.65 |

Clearly, there are enormous gains to dynamic strategies when contrasted with static strategies providing exactly équivalent downside risk protection. The dynamic (insured) strategy offers 300 basis points more per year.

But perhaps asking for fully equivalent downside risk protection is too stringent. In many cases, investors wish "reasonable assurance" against losses exceeding some minimum, which is often interpreted as a 95% confidence level that such a result will not occur. What static strategy would provide such a confidence level?

A theoretical analysis indicates that a 35/65 static mix would provide 95% confidence that returns would equal or exceed -5%, given the risk and return of equities and Tbills. And, in fact, a 35/65 mix does provide returns exceeding -5% in 52 of 55 years, or 94.5% of the time. In the three years the mix fails, returns are -14.4, -12.1, and -7.1%. We may summarize the results for this static policy as follows:

| Policy | Minimum Return | Compound Annual Return | End Value of $1 |
|---|---|---|---|
| Static 35/65 | -14.4% | 5.2% | $16.25 |

1900 Avenue of the Stars
Suite 1080
Century City, California 90067
(213) 552-9100

707 Wilshire Boulevard
13th Floor
Los Angeles, California 90017
(213) 614-3173

122 East 42nd Street
17th Floor
New York, New York 10168
(212) 697-5535

Let's contrast the 35/65 static policy with the Insured "-5" policy. While providing *reasonable assurance* against losses exceeding 5%, the static policy still suffers a maximum loss of almost three times this level. And, more importantly, the static policy has an annual compound return which is lower by 180 basis points per year, after the transactions costs of the dynamic strategy are accounted for. At the end of the 55 year period, the investor following the dynamic strategy would have more than double the money of the investor following the static strategy, while never suffering a loss exceeding 5% in any year!

How, then, did Jacobs reach such differing conclusions? First, he contrasted the results of the insured program with an unprotected, 100% equity portfolio. The risks of the two are clearly totally different: unprotected equities suffered losses exceeding 5% in 15 of the 55 years, including losses of 43, 35, 27, and 25%!

Jacobs then contrasted the Insured "-5" policy with a 61.75/38.25 static mix, which he claimed was "risk equivalent." He based his claim on the assertion that this static allocation had the same average standard deviation as the insured portfolio. In fact, this is not correct when optimal insurance techniques are used: the LOR dynamic strategy creating the Insured "-5" had an average standard deviation of 9.1% per year, using daily data — as contrasted with the equity index's standard deviation of 19.8%. Easy calculations show the Insured program has the same standard deviation as a 46/64 portfolio (which would have had an annual compound return of 6.1%), rather than the 61.75/38.25 mix Jacobs claims.

More to the point, the appropriate comparison for investors concerned with downside risk is whether the 61.75/38.25 policy *did* provide equivalent downside risk protection. And here, the answer is again "no." Seven times the returns fell below -5%, including years with losses of 26, 21, 15, and 14%. Hardly "equivalent" loss protection! In fact, the 61.75/38.25 static policy provides 95% confidence of avoiding losses exceeding 14%. The appropriate comparison is with a dynamic strategy providing 100% confidence of avoiding losses exceeding 14%:

| Policy | Minimum Return | Compound Annual Return | End Value of $1 |
|---|---|---|---|
| 61.75/38.25 | -26% | 6.66% | $34.68 |
| Dynamic "-14" | -14% | 7.74% | $60.36 |

After transactions costs, the insured strategy returns more than 100 basis points more per year than the static strategy — and the investor following the insured strategy would have close to double the wealth of the investor following the static strategy by the end of 1982.

The reader may still have one lingering doubt: Is it possible to use portfolio insurance to *increase* expected return over that of the uninsured S&P 500, while still protecting against downside risk? Of course this cannot be done using the S&P 500 as such, since, for any given portfolio, a protected program (with less risk) will always have a lower expected return than an unprotected program.

But consider running a protected portfolio with beta 1.5 (with no residual risk: such a portfolio could be constructed, for example, by levering an index fund, or by using index futures).

We simulated the performance of such a levered portfolio over the 55 year period 1928 — 1982, protected at a maximum loss of (i) 5%, and (ii) 10% less than the Tbill rate. To the extent that Tbill rates provide an accurate tracking of inflation, simulation (ii) can be thought of as assuring a maximum *real* loss of 10%. Results of the simulations are as follows:

| Policy | Minimum Return | Compound Annual Return | End Value of $1 |
|---|---|---|---|
| -5% beta 1.5 | -5% | 9.0% | $114.40 |
| -10% real beta 1.5 | Tbill-10% | 9.8% | $171.10 |
| Uninsured beta 1.0 | -43% | 8.8% | $105.50 |

These figures, computed after payment of transactions costs estimated at 1.0%, show conclusively that portfolio protection programs can be used to increase return, while limiting downside risks. With the advent of index futures markets, beta 1.5 portfolios can easily be constructed, while keeping transactions costs to a minimum. Indeed, if transactions costs on futures were on the order of 0.25% (versus the assumed 1% on individual stocks), the insured programs would have had compound growth rates of 9.4% and 10.2%, respectively, yielding final values of $140 and $209. This contrasts with the $106 of the uninsured index, which (as the table indicates) has greater downside risk.

In sum, *the empirical evidence fully supports the contention that dynamic strategies can substantially increase portfolio performance while providing equivalent (or greater) protection against losses.* Average compound returns can be increased between 100 and 200 basis points per year, *after* the costs of trading are accounted for.

*These are compound annual returns *after* costs of trading are subtracted. Trading costs are estimated at 1 percent for round trip transactions. For the insured "-5" policy, turnover averages about 50% per year, although considerable variation occurs about this average. Note that if some active trading in a portfolio occurs when the mix of equities to Tbills is changed, *incremental* transactions costs may be less than assumed here. Also note that if index futures are used for hedging (rather than selling individual stocks), transactions costs are likely to be considerably lower — perhaps 1/4 to 1/10 the amount assumed here.

**This is the value that $1 invested in 1928 would become at the end of 1982, assuming interest and dividends are reinvested.

APPENDIX D

# Derivatives Disasters in the 1990s

Although agriculture and metals futures have been traded on exchanges for more than 100 years, the birth of modern financial derivatives markets can be traced to 1973. That year, the Black-Scholes options pricing model was published, and options on stocks began trading on the Chicago Board Options Exchange. Currency and interest rate futures also emerged in the 1970s, and the 1980s saw the creation of markets for eurodollar, energy, and stock index futures, index options, swaps, and other over-the-counter derivatives.

By the early 1990s, derivatives, much like portfolio insurance in the 1980s, had come to be seen as an all-purpose problem-solving tool, a way to hedge risk, to enhance returns, to lower costs, or simply to remove uncertainty from the planning horizon. Derivatives' early success in accomplishing those goals was due, in part, to benign economic conditions. As long as the markets performed as expected, so did derivatives.

That began to change in late 1993. Falling oil prices, and rising interest rates the following year, exposed some of the risks of derivatives that were not well understood. These included the leveraged nature of derivatives contracts, their opaque structure, and their complexity. Suddenly, derivatives were being blamed for some spectacular financial meltdowns. Here, we chronicle three of them.

## METALLGESELLSCHAFT

MG Corporation, the US arm of German conglomerate Metallgesellschaft AG, was a small player in the US oil market, but it had grand ambitions. By offering its customers long-term, fixed-price contracts for gasoline and other petroleum products, it hoped to rapidly expand its market share and transform its subsidiary, MG Refining and Marketing (MGRM), into a major US integrated oil company. Over the summer of 1993, MGRM signed contracts guaranteeing delivery of 160 million barrels of energy products, representing a potential nominal profit of $640 million.[1]

To counter the risk that rising oil prices would erode its profits, MGRM used a simple hedging strategy. For every barrel of oil it was obligated to deliver, MGRM purchased a barrel of oil in the futures or swaps markets. As a result, every $1 rise in the cost of its delivery obligation would be offset by a $1 rise in the value of its futures and swaps contracts, at least by MGRM's reckoning.

This barrel-for-barrel hedge was anything but perfect, however. Rather than matching the expiration of its futures and swap contracts with its contractually obligated delivery dates over a 10-year horizon, MGRM's entire hedge position consisted of a succession of short-dated contracts of three months or less. There was a pragmatic reason for this timing mismatch. Futures contracts with years-long maturities did not exist, and long-term forward or swap agreements that would have better aligned the hedges with delivery dates would have been prohibitively expensive.

There was a second motivation, however: MGRM thought it could cull additional profits. MGRM had to renew, or roll over, a major portion of its hedges each month, selling the maturing contracts and replacing them with new contracts that would expire a month or a few months later. If the old contracts could be sold for more than it cost to purchase the new contracts, MGRM would record a profit, known as roll yield.

Soon after MGRM began signing delivery contracts, however, energy markets took an unexpected turn. Crude prices began falling, from around $19 a barrel in June 1993 to less than $15 by December, following failed efforts by the Organization of Petroleum Exporting Countries to rein in excess production by some of its members. MGRM's long futures and swap positions declined in value as the spot price of the commodity fell. MGRM had to post additional collateral with the futures exchange, as well as with swap counterparties, to compensate for these unrealized losses.

Furthermore, as spot prices fell, near-term futures prices for crude dipped below the prices set for longer-term futures deliveries. Now, rather than receiving roll yield, MGRM had to put up extra cash to roll its hedges into new futures contracts that were more expensive than expiring contracts. MGRM's unrealized losses and collateral requirements exceeded

$900 million by late 1993, and its parent company replaced MGRM's management team and liquidated the hedge position. Losses exceeded $1 billion and ultimately wiped out half of the firm's capital.[2]

While MGRM's barrel-for-barrel hedging strategy had assumed that anything that changed the cost of its long-term delivery program would have an equal and offsetting impact on the cost of its short-term hedges, in fact the prices of its short-term futures contracts were far more sensitive to current supply and demand conditions than the cost of its long-term delivery obligations. When the value of its short-term hedge position fell drastically in the fall of 1993, the value of its long-term delivery contracts rose to a much smaller degree, creating a net loss.

MGRM's hedging strategy also overlooked the timing mismatch of the cash flows, just as banks did in the lead-up to the 2007–2009 crisis (see Chapter 14, "Securitization and the Credit Crisis").[3] Any decline in the value of MGRM's short-term hedges necessarily resulted in additional collateral demands, while any gains in the value of the long-term delivery contracts would not be realized until years later. Given the lower sensitivity of its long-term delivery obligations to market events, MGRM could have effectively hedged its obligations with a much smaller futures position, reducing its potential short-term funding risk.

## GIBSON GREETINGS

Gibson's derivatives problems began with a pair of relatively straightforward fixed-for-floating interest-rate swap agreements negotiated with BT Securities, a subsidiary of Bankers Trust, in November 1991. The goal of the swaps was ostensibly to hedge Gibson's payments on fixed-rate notes it had issued in May of that year. The first swap agreement called for Gibson to make fixed payments of 5.91 percent on a notional value of $30 million and receive floating-rate payments equal to the six-month London interbank offered rate (Libor). The swap would be in effect for 18 months, beginning June 1, 1992. In the second swap agreement, Gibson would make floating payments equal to six-month Libor, also on $30 million of notional value, and receive a fixed rate of 7.12 percent. This deal also began June 1, 1992, and was scheduled to remain in effect for four and a half years.[4]

For the first year and a half, during which the two swaps overlapped, the Libor payments would offset, and Gibson would wind up receiving a payment equal to the difference in the fixed interest rates, an annual rate of 1.21 percent on $30 million. During the latter three years, Gibson was, in effect, betting that the six-month Libor it was obligated to pay would not rise above the 7.12 percent fixed rate it would receive from BT.

The swap deal was in effect for only a little more than a month. Both parties agreed to terminate it on July 7, 1992, with BT paying Gibson $260,000 to reflect the increased value of Gibson's side of the deal in a declining interest rate environment.[5] Flush with success from this first deal, Gibson upped the ante the following October by entering into a leveraged transaction. Gibson agreed to receive fixed payments of 5.5 percent on a notional value of $30 million. But rather than pay BT a floating rate equal to Libor, as it would in a plain-vanilla swap, it agreed to make a payment equal to the square of six-month Libor divided by 6.[6]

The advantage of this more complicated structure over a straightforward plain-vanilla swap is not obvious. Squaring Libor had the effect of adding leverage, since small movements in Libor would now have a much bigger impact on payouts than they would have had otherwise. This leverage appeared to work more in BT's favor than Gibson's. The net payout to Gibson was effectively capped at 5.5 percent if Libor fell to zero, while the size of the payout to BT, which would increase with Libor, was potentially unlimited.

BT agreed to terminate the swap early in exchange for Gibson's entering into an even more complex swap. This pattern was repeated over the next several years. Gibson and BT would agree to terminate swap deals early in exchange for Gibson's agreement to enter into an even more exotic transaction. The Securities and Exchange Commission (SEC) later concluded that the serial deals—29 over a 29-month period, including amendments and terminations—came about in part because "Gibson consistently attempted to trade out of losses by agreeing to new or amended derivatives."[7]

Gibson reported a derivatives loss of $1 million to shareholders at the end of 1993,[8] but when interest rates began rising the next year, the losses exploded. In April 1994, it reported a $16.7 million loss, on top of a $3 million loss disclosed the previous month, and warned that the red ink could potentially reach $27.5 million. Following a lawsuit, Gibson and BT reached an out-of-court settlement reducing Gibson's combined $20.7 million obligation to $6.2 million.[9]

## ORANGE COUNTY, CALIFORNIA

In an era of shrinking property tax revenues and cutbacks in state aid, Robert Citron's ability to generate investment profits for municipal governments in Southern California was highly prized. Citron, who became treasurer of Orange County in 1972, delivered over the next 22 years an average annual return of 9.4 percent for the Orange County Investment Pool (OCIP), compared to an 8.4 percent return for the statewide investment pool.[10]

Citron was so successful that six cities and four agencies from outside the county had invested money in the pool, and several Orange County school districts floated bonds to raise additional cash to invest with Citron.[11] What these eager investors did not realize was that Citron's successful strategy was a one-way bet that interest rates would remain stable or decline, the trend for most of the previous two decades.

As long as Citron produced impressive returns, few people questioned how he accomplished it. Had they taken even a cursory look, they would have seen a portfolio that looked fairly typical for a municipal investment fund. The OCIP portfolio was filled primarily with short-maturity government and agency bonds that had little credit risk. But the portfolio was highly leveraged. In 1994, the pool had assets of $20.5 billion, almost three times the $7.6 billion in capital contributed by its members.[12] Citron had borrowed the difference in the repo market, a venue where large financial institutions can make or receive short-term loans.

With the pool's capital and billions in borrowed money, Citron had bought $12 billion in conventional fixed-rate notes with an average maturity of four years. The rest, about $8 billion, was invested in structured notes, customized bonds with interest payments linked to a variable rate.[13] A simple floating-rate note has interest payments that adjust periodically according to the level of a benchmark rate, such as Libor. Citron, however, preferred a variation known as an "inverse floater." As the name implies, these bonds have interest payments that move in the opposite direction of interest rates. For example, one of OCIP's inverse-floater holdings was a $100 million note that paid an interest rate equal to 10 percent minus Libor. As Libor rose, the payment received by OCIP declined, as did the resale value of the bond.[14]

Citron's bet on falling interest rates had worked well over the previous 20 years as rates trended downward. During this long period of relative calm, Citron became increasingly confident of his investing strategy and increasingly oblivious to the many risks it entailed. The most obvious was the high level of leverage, which had the effect of increasing the portfolio's duration, or interest-rate sensitivity. Even if the OCIP portfolio was filled with short-duration bonds, which would have been appropriate for a municipal investment portfolio, the nearly 3-to-1 leverage ratio would have almost tripled its duration.[15] Even without the leverage, the portfolio would have been highly vulnerable to interest-rate swings because of its reliance on inverse floaters, which are roughly twice as sensitive to interest rate changes as fixed-rate notes.[16]

As the value of the OCIP portfolio drifted downward during 1994 in response to rising interest rates, Citron seemed only vaguely aware of the approaching peril. He had always insisted that OCIP was not exposed to market risk and that day-to-day fluctuations in market value did not matter because he intended to hold all the bonds to maturity. But through his use of repo funding, he had engaged in a classic borrow-short, invest-long strategy, a potential trap that Bear Stearns and Lehman Brothers would fall into a decade later. The strategy would continue working only as long as his lenders were willing to renew their short-term loans, and they would do so only as long as they remained confident that they would be repaid. If lenders heard that losses were piling up, they would demand more collateral. That is indeed what occurred.

A county audit completed soon after the November election confirmed lenders' worst fears. The fund had suffered a loss in value of $1.5 billion or more, and the county was facing a cash crunch. Lenders demanded a return of their money. On December 4, Citron resigned as treasurer, and the next day, Orange County filed for bankruptcy.

After the pool was liquidated, its members' $7.6 billion in capital had shrunk to $5.7 billion, a loss of about 25 percent.[17] The loss forced Orange County to lay off about 10 percent of its workforce, reduce bus service, and squeeze funds from programs providing children's health care and nutrition to the homeless.[18] Other pool participants were forced to make similar cutbacks. It turned out to be an unexpected and painful lesson about the risks of leveraged derivatives.

APPENDIX E

# Bruce Jacobs's Research Objectivity Standards Proposal

## Bruce Jacobs's "Research Objectivity Standards Proposal" – August 12, 2002

### Bruce Jacobs's Research Objectivity Standards Proposal

August 12, 2002

Dear AIMR:

The proposed Research Objectivity Standards regarding analyst conflicts of interest are welcome, but AIMR should also look a little closer to home for conflicts of interest that have the potential to taint research and to inflict harm on investors. Just as the research conducted by analysts at brokerage firms and investment banks is susceptible to the influence of commercial interests that may conflict with the best interests of their clients, so too the work done for and by AIMR and its professional publications and conferences is susceptible to being influenced by interests that may conflict with the best interests of members and investors in general. I believe that the Research Objectivity Standards as proposed should be expanded to deal with these conflicts of interest.

For instance, AIMR's own *Financial Analysts Journal* (*FAJ*) plays a critical role in communicating the latest research and findings on investment instruments, techniques, and theories. Although the articles published generally do not make recommendations regarding individual securities, they do recommend particular strategies and instruments for investing, particular methods for evaluating stocks, and particular theories of how markets and/or investors "work." Many of these articles form the basis for investment research tools, quantitative analysis and portfolio decision-making. These articles can thus have very real effects in terms of shaping what investments are made and the way they are made and, consequently, on the results experienced by investors.

As a vital link between research and practice, the *FAJ* provides an invaluable service to the investing community. However, the procedures by which this service is rendered are too often rife with conflicts of interest. This is especially true today, as the boundary between the academic and practitioner research communities becomes ever more porous. Academics move back and forth between the university and Wall Street, take on paid consulting roles, and/or start their own businesses; investment firms, too, have taken a broader role in funding research undertaken by academics, either directly or indirectly via their support of bodies such as The Research Foundation of AIMR. In such an environment, it is all but inevitable that individuals' financial interests will influence (consciously or not) the types of research that are undertaken and that get published.

Transparency, in the form of disclosure of the business affiliations of authors of articles in the *FAJ* or of Research Foundation monographs, allows readers themselves to assess the possible effects of conflicts of interest on authors' research. However, readers are not privy to conflicts of interest affecting Editors, Editorial Board members, reviewers and others involved in the processes underlying publication, including peer reviews of manuscripts and grant proposals, which have the potential to bias decisions regarding what gets published (and what doesn't). Authors, readers, and the investment community in general could place greater trust in the objectivity of AIMR's publications if the organization had a clear, publicly stated policy explicitly governing conflicts of interest. In effect, AIMR is currently in the same position as the investment institutions and media it finds at fault for lacking such policies!

The medical profession has been grappling with the effects of conflicts of interest on their published research for about two decades.[1] A recent editorial in the *New England Journal of Medicine,* signed by the editors of the world's leading general medical journals, quotes extensively from the "Uniform Requirements for Manuscripts Submitted to Biomedical Journals," which begins with a statement on the importance of controlling conflicts of interest:[2]

> Public trust in the peer review process and the credibility of published articles depend in part on how well conflict of interest is handled during writing, peer review, and editorial decision making. Conflict of interest exists when an author (or the author's institution), reviewer, or editor has financial or personal relationships with other persons or organizations that inappropriately influence (bias) his or her actions. The potential for such relationships to create bias varies from negligible to extremely great; the existence of such relationships does not necessarily represent true conflict of interest . . . . The potential for conflict of interest can exist whether or not an individual believes that the relationship affects his or her scientific judgment. Financial relationships . . . are the most easily identifiable conflicts of interest and the most likely to undermine the credibility of the journal, the authors, and of science itself. Conflicts can occur for other reasons, however, such as personal and family relationships, academic competition, and intellectual passion.

In order to ameliorate the ill effects of conflicts of interest, the "Uniform Requirements" calls for "All participants in the peer review and publication process [to] . . . disclose all relationships that could be viewed as presenting a potential conflict of interest." Thus authors submitting a manuscript or letter are required to disclose all financial and personal relationships that may bias their work; it is up to the Editors to decide whether this information should be included if the manuscript is published.[3] Reviewers of manuscripts are required to state whether there exist conflicts of interest that could bias their opinion of the manuscript and to disclose such conflicts if they exist; they should disqualify themselves from reviewing particular manuscripts if appropriate. Editors can have no personal, professional, or financial involvement in any issues they might judge; other members of the editorial staff involved with editorial decisions must disclose to Editors their current financial interests and disqualify themselves from any decisions where they have a conflict of interest. Editors should avoid submitting research they have authored or co-authored to their own journals; if they do so, they should delegate editorial decisions on those manuscripts to others.[4] Editors should publish regular disclosure statements about potential conflicts of interest related to commitments of the journal's staff.

My own experience illustrates that conflicts of interest are not being controlled, or perhaps even considered, at the *FAJ*. For example, in the late 1980s, I submitted to the *FAJ* a manuscript on portfolio insurance and its contribution to the stock market crash of 1987. In the early 1980s, well prior to that crash, I had submitted a manuscript on the pitfalls of portfolio insurance to another journal. Those manuscripts were rejected for publication on the basis of reviews by the leading purveyor of portfolio insurance at the

3

time (who was also a member of the Editorial Boards of both journals). If conflict of interest standards had been in place and enforced, the Editor would not have assigned the work to this particular reviewer or, if the Editor had, the reviewer would have recused himself.

Of course, this was in the 1980s. One might hope that standards have improved since. My experience suggests otherwise. In 1999, I published a book, *Capital Ideas and Market Realities*, which discusses the dangers to market stability posed by certain derivatives-based strategies, using portfolio insurance and the crash of 1987 as an example.[5] Given my past experience with the *FAJ,* I was pleasantly surprised to see a favorable review of the book in the July/August 2000 issue. This review, written by the *FAJ*'s Book Review Editor, stated: "Jacobs' meticulously documented book presents compelling evidence . . . that portfolio insurance failed to deliver on its lofty promises." In the January/February 2001 issue of the *FAJ*, however, the same Book Review Editor published an unprecedented "Postscript," which charged that I had "marshaled selected quotations" to make my case and asserted, on the basis of various unnamed sources, that presentations made by the leading portfolio insurance purveyor were "candid in describing the likely impact of greater-than-expected volatility." (See my "Open Letter to AIMR and the *Financial Analysts Journal*," October 1, 2001, at http://www.CIMRbook.com/cimr/ethicalissues.html. [6])

*Pensions & Investments* subsequently uncovered the fact that the Book Review Editor wrote this "Postscript" at the suggestion of the same Editorial Board member and leading portfolio insurance purveyor who had rejected my original manuscripts.[7] It is interesting to note that, before the public was made aware of the influence this Editorial Board member had brought to bear on the book review process, the *FAJ*'s own Editor had declared that "If there was pressure from someone on the editorial board [in regard to the 'Postscript'], I would see that person would not be on the board."[8] After the facts were made public, the *FAJ*'s Editor (himself a vendor of portfolio insurance products) declined to investigate further. The whole episode has the appearance, at the very least, of egregious conflicts of interest.[9]

The problems I have encountered go beyond a mere matter of wounded pride. I believe, and my book argues, on the basis of copious evidence, that portfolio insurance and the way in which it was marketed in the 1980s had tremendous impact on the market (particularly in the 1987 crash) and has repercussions for the securities markets today. This view is open to debate. However, rather than allowing an open debate, the *FAJ*, by permitting an Editorial Board member with a substantial financial interest in portfolio insurance products (amounting to $54 billion in assets under management in 1987[10]) to quash criticism of it, effectively curtailed the free flow of ideas so necessary to an educated investment community and a healthy market. In the interests of fair and full disclosure to investors, AIMR now rightly seeks to institute standards that would prevent investment bankers and corporate issuers from influencing analyst recommendations and from taking retribution against analysts whose recommendations they disagree with. AIMR's own journal and its readership should benefit from similar standards.

How many manuscripts submitted to the *FAJ* have been subjected to review and dismissal by a reviewer with vested financial interests that would, under enforced conflict of interest standards, have disqualified him or her from vetting those manuscripts?[11] In most of these cases, we may assume that it was not the intent of the reviewer to reject the manuscript merely because it represented a threat to the reviewer's financial interests. Nevertheless, there is no way for the investment community to determine the *FAJ*'s independence and objectivity as long as it continues to operate under a cloak of secrecy, without publicly stated conflict of interest standards.[12] In the interest of fairness to authors and to the investment community in general, and in the interest of holding our professional journal to the highest ethical standards, even the appearance of conflict of interest should be avoided.[13]

AIMR states that one of the objectives of its proposed standards is to promote "a work environment for all investment professionals that supports, encourages, and rewards ethical behavior." I believe that the Research Objectivity Standards, which address "journalists and the media," do not go far enough to ensure this goal, especially as regards AIMR's own publications. For the *FAJ*, I believe that what is required are Research Objectivity Standards that directly reflect the AIMR Code of Ethics and Standards of Professional Conduct, something along the following lines:

I. Staff and volunteers associated with the *Financial Analysts Journal* (including the Editor and other members of the Editorial Board, whether or not members of AIMR or any of its constituent societies) shall be familiar with and abide by the AIMR Code of Ethics and Standards of Professional Conduct. This is in line with AIMR Standard I(A).

II. The person designated Editor or Editor-in-Chief shall be considered in a supervisory position vis-à-vis staff, other members of the Editorial Board, and others (including manuscript reviewers and authors) insofar as their activities contribute to the *FAJ*. Delegation of responsibilities connected with the *FAJ* does not absolve the designated Editor of supervisory responsibilities. The Editor is responsible for ensuring that those under his or her supervision abide by proposed *FAJ* Standard I above, including an annual acknowledgment of understanding and attestation of compliance. The Editor is responsible for ensuring that the independence and objectivity of the Editorial Board is maintained, that AIMR Code and Standards are followed as they relate to the *FAJ*, and that the Research Objectivity Standards for the *FAJ* are followed and enforced. This is in line with AIMR Standard III(E).

III. The person designated as the AIMR staff representative to the *FAJ* shall be considered in a supervisory position vis-à-vis the designated *FAJ* Editor and shall be responsible for the *FAJ*'s compliance with the Research Objectivity Standards (as outlined in *FAJ* Standard II above).

5

IV. Those persons falling under *FAJ* Standard I above have a duty to disclose to their supervisors at the *FAJ* or AIMR all matters that reasonably could be expected to interfere with the duties they undertake on behalf of the *FAJ* and/or their ability to make independent, objective and unbiased decisions. In this regard, the Editor should disclose to AIMR any interests, including personal business interests, that could interfere with his or her ability to carry out the duties of *FAJ* Editor in an independent, objective and unbiased manner. Other members of the Editorial Board should disclose same to the Editor. This is in line with AIMR Standard III(C).

V. The *FAJ* has a duty to disclose to readers material facts or conditions that could reasonably be expected to impair the independence and objectivity of the work published in the *FAJ*. Thus, the Editor as supervisor should solicit from prospective authors the existence of any such interests, and such interests should be disclosed with publication of authors' articles. This is in line with AIMR Standard IV(B).

VI. Persons falling under *FAJ* Standard I above shall use reasonable care and judgment to achieve and maintain independence and objectivity in undertaking their duties on behalf of the *FAJ*. Thus, for example, members of the Editorial Board or others who review manuscripts for possible publication in the *FAJ* should not be influenced by business or other interests that could interfere with their independence and objectivity in the review process. If a potential conflict of interest exists with regard to a particular manuscript, Editorial Board members should recuse themselves from the review process. This is in line with AIMR Standard IV(A).

VII. Persons who fall under *FAJ* Standard I above, when acting on behalf of the *FAJ*, have a duty to put the interests of the *FAJ* above their own interests. Thus, for example, members of the Editorial Board should not use their positions to further their own personal or business interests by influencing the editorial process or by other means. This is in line with AIMR Standard IV(B).

VIII. The standards under which the *FAJ* operates should be published annually in the *FAJ*, posted on the AIMR website, and made available to interested parties upon request.

IX. Transgressions regarding the standards should be subject to disciplinary proceedings by AIMR.

Although these proposed standards were written with particular reference to the *FAJ*, there is no reason that similar standards could not be adopted by other publications of AIMR, including the CFA Digest, Research Foundation monographs, conferences and proceedings, and webcasts and web-based seminars.[14] By adopting Research Objectivity Standards for its own publications and conferences, AIMR can demonstrate that it intends

6

to abide by the standards it is encouraging others to adopt. AIMR now has the opportunity to set the ethical bar for other publications and institutions of the financial community, for the betterment of all.

Sincerely,

Bruce I. Jacobs
AIMR Member and Principal, Jacobs Levy Equity Management

---

[1] See, for example, Relman, "Dealing with Conflicts of Interest," *New England Journal of Medicine* 310 (1984): 1182-1183, as well as the latest discussion in Drazen and Curfman, "Financial Associations of Authors," *New England Journal of Medicine* 346 (2002): 1901-1902.
[2] See Davidoff et al., "Sponsorship, Authorship, and Accountability," *New England Journal of Medicine* 345 (2001): 825-827.
[3] The *New England Journal of Medicine* goes beyond disclosure with regard to editorials and review articles; it does not allow publication of these if the authors have "any significant interest in a company (or its competitor) that makes a product discussed in the article." See Drazen and Curfman, "Financial Associations of Authors," op. cit.
[4] The *New England Journal of Medicine*, to "prevent the appearance of 'insider bias'," requires that all research articles by its editors or consultants be administered by an independent editor-at-large. See Curfman and Drazen, "Too Close to Call," *New England Journal of Medicine* 345 (2001): 832.
[5] Jacobs, *Capital Ideas and Market Realities: Option Replication, Investor Behavior, and Stock Market Crashes*, with a foreword by Harry M. Markowitz, Blackwell Publishers, Malden, MA, 1999.
[6] See also Jacobs, "FAJ, AIMR Ethical Issues," *Pensions & Investments*, October 1, 2001; Walters, "AIMR Strict on Ethics Code," *Pensions & Investments*, October 15, 2001; and Jacobs, "AIMR's Misinterpretation," *Pensions & Investments*, November 12, 2001.
[7] See Burr, "Praise for book turns to criticism," *Pensions & Investments*, June 25, 2001.
[8] Ibid.
[9] See Burr, "Rubinstein to stay on editorial board of FAJ despite talking with Fridson," *Pensions & Investments*, September 3, 2001. The *FAJ* Editor, Book Review Editor and Editorial Board member involved retain their positions as of this writing.
[10] According to the firm's 1987 ADV filing with the SEC.
[11] In the medical community, some have begun calling for a more open review process, including identification of reviewers, in part to ameliorate conflict of interest problems. See Godlee, "Making Reviewers Visible: Openness, Accountability, and Credit," *JAMA* 287 (2002): 2762-2763.
[12] When I pointed out the apparent conflicts of interest affecting conduct at the *FAJ*, the AIMR's Professional Conduct Officer's response was that proceedings regarding such complaints are undertaken in the utmost secrecy and cannot be discussed under any circumstances (see Walters, "AIMR Strict on Ethics Code," op. cit.). However, Rule 12 of AIMR's Rules of Procedure for Proceedings Related to Professional Conduct does permit public discussion of some complaints under certain conditions, which appear to hold in this instance (see Jacobs, "AIMR's Misinterpretation," op. cit.).
[13] According to AIMR Standard III(C), *Standards of Practice Handbook*, Eighth Edition, pp. 51-52: "The mere appearance of conflict of interest may create problems for a member . . . ."
[14] AIMR sponsors a series of "Industry Analysis" seminars and proceedings featuring leading sell side analysts. Under the Research Objectivity Standards, the analysts would presumably be required to disclose any potential conflicts of interest at the seminar and in any publication of the proceedings. But what conflict of interest standards govern the AIMR's behavior? How does AIMR deal with conflicts of interest that may arise in the decision of which analysts to invite as participants?

# ACRONYMS

**ABCP** – Asset-Backed Commercial Paper

**ABS** – Asset-Backed Security

**AIG** – American International Group

**ARM** – Adjustable-Rate Mortgage

**BIS** – Bank for International Settlements

**BRIC** – Brazil, Russia, India, China

**CBOE** – Chicago Board Options Exchange

**CCP** – Central Counterparty Clearinghouse

**CDO** – Collateralized Debt Obligation

**CDS** – Credit Default Swap

**CFTC** – Commodity Futures Trading Commission

**CLO** – Collateralized Loan Obligation

**CMBS** – Commercial Mortgage-Backed Security

**CME** – Chicago Mercantile Exchange

**CMO** – Collateralized Mortgage Obligation

**CP** – Commercial Paper

**CRA** – Credit Rating Agency

**DJIA** – Dow Jones Industrial Average

**DTCC** – Depository Trust & Clearing Corporation

**ECB** – European Central Bank

**EMH** – Efficient Market Hypothesis

**ETP** – Exchange-Traded Product

**EU** – European Union

**FCIC** – Financial Crisis Inquiry Commission

**FDIC** – Federal Deposit Insurance Corporation

**FHFA** – Federal Housing Finance Agency

**FICO** – Fair Isaac Corporation

**FINRA** – Financial Industry Regulatory Authority

**FSOC** – Financial Stability Oversight Council

**GAO** – Government Accountability Office

**GDP** – Gross Domestic Product

**GSE** – Government-Sponsored Enterprise

**IMF** – International Monetary Fund

**IPO** – Initial Public Offering

**ISDA** – International Swaps and Derivatives Association

**LEAPS** – Long-term Equity AnticiPation Security

**Libor** – London Interbank Offered Rate

**LTCM** – Long-Term Capital Management

**LTV** – Loan To Value

**MBS** – Mortgage-Backed Security

**MOC** – Market On Close

**Nasdaq** – National Association of Securities Dealers Automated Quotation

**NRSRO** – Nationally Recognized Statistical Rating Organization

**NYSE** – New York Stock Exchange

**OECD** – Organisation for Economic Co-operation and Development

**OFHEO** – Office of Federal Housing Enterprise Oversight

**OFR** – Office of Financial Research

**OTC** – Over The Counter

**RMBS** – Residential Mortgage-Backed Security

**SEC** – Securities and Exchange Commission

**SIFMA** – Securities Industry and Financial Markets Association

**SIV** – Structured Investment Vehicle

**SPV** – Special Purpose Vehicle

**SRB** – Single Resolution Board

**SSM** – Single Supervisory Mechanism

**TARP** – Troubled Asset Relief Program

**TRACE** – Trade Reporting and Compliance Engine

**VAR** – Value At Risk

# GLOSSARY

**ABX indexes** A series of indexes that track the value of subprime residential mortgage-backed securities based on the prices for credit default swaps on given subprime tranches. *See* Credit default swap, Index, Residential mortgage-backed security, Subprime loan, Tranche.

**Adjustable-rate mortgage loan** A loan with an initial interest rate that remains in effect for a limited period of time; thereafter, it adjusts periodically to changes in a benchmark interest rate, such as the London Interbank Offered Rate (Libor). Periodic rate increases are sometimes capped, and not all adjustable-rate mortgages have rates that adjust downward. *See* Benchmark, London Interbank Offered Rate (Libor).

**Alpha** The risk-adjusted return on an asset or portfolio that is not attributable to general market movements.

**Alt-A mortgage loan** A mortgage loan that occupies a middle ground between prime and subprime loans; extended to borrowers who are unable to qualify for a prime mortgage loan because of any of several reasons, including an uncertain or irregular income, an inability to fully document assets, a low down payment, high personal debt, or the intention of purchasing a vacation home or investment property rather than a primary residence. *See* Prime mortgage loan, Subprime loan.

**American option** An option that can be exercised at any time on or before its expiration. *See* European option, Option.

**Arbitrage** Trading that takes advantage of contemporaneous price discrepancies between the same asset in different markets or between asset surrogates in the same or different markets.

**Asset allocation** The deployment of investments across asset classes to take advantage of the risk and return characteristics of the classes and their correlations. *See* Asset class, Correlation, Diversification.

**Asset-backed commercial paper** Commercial paper collateralized by pools of loans, structured finance products, or other assets. *See* Collateral, Commercial paper, Conduit, Structured finance products.

**Asset-backed commercial paper conduit** A financing entity created by banks, often employing a special purpose vehicle. Issues commercial paper to finance medium- and long-term assets, such as mortgage loans and mortgage-backed securities. Assets do not appear on the sponsoring bank's balance sheet but are typically guaranteed by the sponsoring bank. *See*

Asset-backed commercial paper, Commercial paper, Securitization, Special purpose vehicle.

**Asset-backed security** A security collateralized by a specific asset, such as a pool of mortgages, loans, or credit card debt. *See* Collateral, Mortgage-backed security, Residential mortgage-backed security.

**Asset class** A group of securities with similar characteristics, e.g., stocks or bonds. *See* Asset allocation, Diversification.

**At the money** The state of an option when the underlying asset's price equals (or approximates) the option's strike price. *See* In the money, Option, Out of the money, Strike price, Underlying.

**Bank for International Settlements** An organization of national central banks, based in Basel, Switzerland, that provides banking services and research to its membership and serves as host for the Basel Committee on Banking Supervision. *See* Basel Capital Accord.

**Basel Capital Accord** An international agreement calling for the establishment of minimum standards for bank capitalization. The original accord, adopted in 1988 by the Basel Committee for Banking Supervision, is known as Basel I; the revised version, adopted in 2004, is known as Basel II. A further revision, Basel III, was adopted in 2010. *See* Bank for International Settlements, Capital charge.

**Basis point** One one-hundredth of 1 percent.

**Basis risk** Risk introduced by divergences in the prices of an asset or strategy and the asset or strategy it is designed to hedge or replicate. *See* Hedge.

**Bear market** A period during which market prices decline significantly. *See* Bull market.

**Behavioral finance** A branch of finance that seeks to understand how psychology affects financial decision-making and markets.

**Benchmark** A security or group of securities, such as an index, whose returns are used as a gauge of performance. *See* Index.

**Beta** A measure of an asset's or a portfolio's risk relative to a given market index. It reflects the sensitivity of an asset's or portfolio's returns to the returns of the market index. Beta is calculated as the covariance between the returns on the asset or portfolio and the market index's returns, divided by the variance of the market index returns. A portfolio with a beta of 1.5 relative to the S&P 500 index, for example, tends to go up or down by 1.5 percent in value if the market value of the S&P 500 goes up or down by 1 percent. *See* Covariance, Index, S&P 500, Variance.

**Bid-ask spread** The difference at a given time between the price at which buyers are willing to buy a security and the price at which sellers are willing to sell. *See* Spread.

**Black Monday** October 19, 1987, when the Dow Jones Industrial Average fell 22.6 percent; portfolio insurance is seen as a major cause. *See* Dow Jones Industrial Average, Portfolio insurance.

**Black-Scholes-Merton options pricing model** A formula for pricing options, developed by Fisher Black, Myron S. Scholes, and, separately, Robert C. Merton. *See* Call option, Option, Options pricing formula, Put option.

**Bond arbitrage** A form of arbitrage that calls for taking offsetting long and short positions in fixed-income instruments that appear to be mispriced. *See* Arbitrage, Fixed-income instruments, Long position, Short position.

**Brady Commission** A commission appointed by US President Ronald Reagan to investigate the market crash of October 1987; chaired by Nicholas F. Brady, then-chairman of investment bank Dillon, Read & Company and later Secretary of the Treasury under President George H.W. Bush. *See* Crash.

**Broker-dealer** A firm that trades securities for customers (as a broker) as well as for its own accounts (as a principal or dealer). *See* Dealer.

**Bubble** A price increase to an extreme level that cannot be justified by the fundamental characteristics of an asset or market; typically followed by an abrupt price collapse. *See* Crash.

**Bull market** A period during which market prices increase significantly. *See* Bear market.

**Call option** An option that grants the owner the right to buy a certain security at a specified price within a specified period of time. *See* Option, Put option.

**Cap** A maximum value for a security or for its return, specified in a contract or offered by a derivatives position. *See* Derivative, Floor.

**Capital charge** The amount of capital a bank is required to hold under the Basel Capital Accord to cover unexpected losses. *See* Basel Capital Accord.

**Carry trade** A strategy that involves borrowing at a low interest rate and investing the funds at a higher interest rate.

**CDO-cubed** A collateralized debt obligation backed by tranches of other CDO-squared securities; sometimes written as $CDO^3$. *See* Collateralized debt obligation, Tranche.

**CDO-squared** A collateralized debt obligation backed by tranches (usually mezzanine tranches) of other collateralized debt obligations; sometimes written as $CDO^2$. *See* Collateralized debt obligation, Mezzanine tranche, Tranche.

**Central counterparty clearinghouse (CCP)** A corporation, backed by financial institutions, that steps in to become the counterparty to both sides of certain derivatives transactions and guarantees performance of the contract. The guarantee is backed by the clearinghouse's own capital as well as by capital contributions from participating financial institutions and the mandatory posting of margin by the trading parties. *See* Counterparty, Derivative, Margin.

**Chicago Board Options Exchange (CBOE)** The largest US exchange for trading stock options, including index options on the S&P 100 and S&P 500. *See* Options, S&P 100, S&P 500.

**Chicago Mercantile Exchange (CME)** A US exchange for trading futures, and options on futures, on financial instruments such as the S&P 500, and on agricultural products. *See* Derivative, Futures contract, Options, S&P 500.

**Circuit breakers** A system of trading restrictions and halts on stock and futures exchanges, usually triggered by substantial price movements.

**Clearing** The process of reconciling orders and transferring funds between transacting parties on an exchange. *See* Central counterparty clearinghouse.

**Collateral** An asset used to secure the obligation of a borrower to repay a loan. In short selling, a deposit of cash or high-grade liquid securities provided to a securities lender to secure delivery of securities borrowed to sell short. *See* Short position, Short sale.

**Collateralized debt obligation (CDO)** A security backed by pools of loans or other securities that has been divided into tranches with differing risk attributes and payoff schedules. *See* Synthetic CDO, Tranche.

**Collateralized loan obligation (CLO)** A security, backed by pools of corporate loans, that has been divided into tranches with differing risk attributes and payoff schedules; a type of collateralized debt obligation. *See* Collateralized debt obligation, Tranche.

**Collateralized mortgage obligation (CMO)** A mortgage-backed security that has been divided into tranches with differing risk attributes and payoff schedules. *See* Mortgage-backed security, Tranche.

**Commercial bank** An institution that serves as a financial intermediary by accepting deposits and making loans. *See* Investment bank.

**Commercial mortgage-backed security (CMBS)** A security backed by principal and interest payments from a pool of commercial property mortgages; a form of asset-backed security. *See* Asset-backed security, Mortgage-backed security.

**Commercial paper** Short- or medium-term unsecured (no collateral) debt instruments issued by a bank or corporation; prior to the 2007–2008 credit crisis, used by banks to finance investments in mortgage-backed securities. *See* Asset-backed commercial paper, Collateral, Mortgage-backed security.

**Commodity Futures Trading Commission (CFTC)** A US federal regulatory agency that oversees US futures and options markets. *See* Futures contract, Options.

**Conduit** An off-balance-sheet financing vehicle formed by a sponsor, typically a bank, to borrow money through the issuance of asset-backed commercial paper and invest the proceeds in longer-term, investment-grade securities; similar to a structured investment vehicle except that its obligations are backed by explicit guarantees from the sponsor. *See* Asset-backed commercial paper, Structured investment vehicle.

**Conforming mortgage loan** A home mortgage loan that meets certain underwriting requirements and dollar-amount limits and is eligible to be purchased in the secondary market by Fannie Mae and Freddie Mac. *See*

Government-sponsored enterprise, Fannie Mae, Freddie Mac, Jumbo mortgage loan.

**Constant-mix portfolio strategy** A strategy that calls for holding a static mix of assets (such as 60 percent stocks/40 percent bonds) and rebalancing periodically. *See* Rebalancing.

**Contagion** The "infectious" transmittal of price movements from one financial market to another.

**Convergence trade** A trade that takes offsetting positions in two or more related assets with the expectation of profiting from the eventual convergence of the assets' prices.

**Correlation** A scaled version of covariance; measures the strength of the relationship between two variables; values range from –1 (variables move inversely) to +1 (variables move together). A value of 0 implies no relationship. *See* Covariance.

**Counterparty** The party on the other side of a trade or transaction. When two parties enter a contract, each is a counterparty to the other. *See* Central counterparty clearinghouse.

**Covariance** A measure of the degree to which changes in two variables are related; similar to correlation, which is a scaled version of covariance. A positive (negative) covariance implies that the two variables move together (inversely). *See* Correlation, Diagonal model.

**Crash** A sudden and widespread outbreak of panic selling, resulting in a rapid and steep decline in asset prices; often occurs following a speculative bubble. *See* Bubble.

**Credit default swap** An agreement that gives the buyer the right to sell a bond or a tranche of a securitized debt product for its face value in the event of a default by a borrower. *See* Securitization, Tranche.

**Credit rating** A credit rating agency's formal estimate, usually expressed as a letter grade, of the likelihood that a government, enterprise, or debt instrument will default. A rating of BBB– or better from S&P Global Ratings or Baa3 or better from Moody's Investor Service signifies that an issue is investment grade, indicating it is relatively low risk and considered safe for investors. *See* Credit rating agency.

**Credit rating agency** A company that assigns credit ratings to issuers of debt and to debt instruments. *See* Credit rating.

**Credit risk** The risk of loss stemming from a default or deterioration in the financial condition of a borrower.

**Dealer** A financial intermediary, especially in over-the-counter markets, that primarily trades with other entities as a principal (buying or selling from its own account). *See* Broker-dealer, Over the counter.

**Deductible** The amount of loss an insured party agrees to be exposed to before insurance coverage begins to provide protection. In general, the larger the deductible, the lower the cost of insurance.

**Delta hedging** *See* Dynamic hedging, Option replication.

**Depository Trust & Clearing Corporation (DTCC)** A financial services company that provides clearing and settlement for, as well as data on, securities, derivatives, and money market instruments. *See* Clearing, Derivative, Settlement.

**Derivative** A financial instrument whose value is contingent on the value of an underlying security; for example, a futures contract or an option. *See* Futures contract, Option, Underlying.

**Diagonal model** A model for simplifying the portfolio selection process developed by William F. Sharpe, who was later awarded the Nobel Prize in Economics; the model assumes security returns are related through a common relationship with the overall market return. *See* Covariance.

**Discontinuity** A significant difference or gap in the price of a security or a market index from one trade to the next. *See* Index.

**Diversification** Distribution of investments across a variety of assets, asset classes, investment themes, and/or geographically so as to reduce portfolio risk.

**Dow Jones Industrial Average (DJIA)** A price-weighted average of the share prices of 30 large US publicly traded companies.

**Duration** A measure of a bond's price sensitivity to changes in interest rates. The calculation takes into account the weighted average length of time until each interest and principal payment on a bond is due.

**Dynamic asset allocation** *See* Dynamic hedging.

**Dynamic hedging** The process of creating an option-like payoff pattern by taking and trading positions in an underlying asset or derivatives on an underlying asset. *See* Derivative, Option, Option replication, Underlying.

**Efficient frontier** The set of portfolios each of which has the highest expected return for any given level of volatility risk, or alternatively, the lowest volatility risk for any given level of expected return; or the set of portfolios each of which has the highest expected return for any given level of investor volatility tolerance (or inversely, volatility aversion or risk aversion). *See* Modern portfolio theory, Risk aversion, Volatility, Volatility aversion, Volatility tolerance.

**Efficient market hypothesis** The theory that market prices fully and instantaneously reflect all available information.

**Equilibrium** A condition of stability in which the demand for and supply of an asset are in balance.

**Equity-linked note** A type of structured note consisting of a debt instrument, such as a bond, that offers additional returns linked to the performance of a stock, basket of stocks, or stock index. *See* Structured note.

**Equity premium** The expected return on equities in excess of the return on the risk-free asset. *See* Risk-free (riskless) asset, Risk premium.

**Equity swap** An over-the-counter derivatives contract in which two parties agree to exchange payments, at least one of which is based on the performance of an underlying stock or stock index; generally, one party pays a fixed stream of cashflows and the other party makes payments that vary according to the performance of the stock or stock index. *See* Derivative, Index, Over the counter, Underlying.

**Equity tranche** The lowest-rated and highest-yielding tranche of a mortgage-backed security or collateralized debt obligation, designed to be the last to receive scheduled payments from the underlying instruments. *See* Collateralized debt obligation, Credit rating, Mortgage-backed security, Tranche, Underlying.

**European option** An option that can be exercised only on its expiration date. *See* American option, Option.

**Exchange-traded fund (ETF)** An investment fund traded on a public stock exchange; a type of exchange-traded product (ETP).

**Exchange-traded note (ETN)** A type of exchange-traded product (ETP) backed by an unsecured senior debt note of the issuer.

**Exchange-traded product (ETP)** A security traded on a public stock exchange that is based on the value of an underlying fund, bond, or other security.

**Exercise price** *See* Strike price.

**Expected return** The return that a security or portfolio is anticipated to provide over a given holding period. *See* Mean.

**Expiration date** The date beyond which an option may no longer be exercised. *See* Option.

**Fad** A behavioral phenomenon in which a practice is pursued with an exaggerated interest that tends to wane over time.

**Fair price** The price at which a security should be traded in an efficient market. *See* Efficient market hypothesis.

**Fannie Mae (Federal National Mortgage Association)** A government-sponsored enterprise and public company, created by Congress in 1938 to reduce the cost of home ownership by purchasing and securitizing home mortgages and guaranteeing payments on the resulting securities. *See* Government-sponsored enterprise, Freddie Mac, Securitization.

**Fat-tailed distribution** A probability distribution characterized by a larger-than-normal occurrence of values that diverge widely from the average value. *See* Normal distribution, Probability distribution.

**Federal Deposit Insurance Corporation (FDIC)** A US government agency created in 1933 to maintain stability and public confidence in the banking system by insuring deposits (up to $250,000 per account as of October 3, 2008, versus $100,000 previously), supervising financial institutions, and resolving insolvent lenders.

**Federal Housing Finance Agency (FHFA)** A US regulatory agency that replaced the Office of Federal Housing Enterprise Oversight (OFHEO) in 2008; oversees government-sponsored enterprises, including Fannie Mae and Freddie Mac, and serves as conservator since 2008 of Fannie Mae and

Freddie Mac. *See* Government-sponsored enterprise, Fannie Mae, Freddie Mac.

**Feedback** Occurs when an outcome of a system becomes an input affecting the system so as to create a cause-and-effect loop. Positive feedback is reinforcing, while negative feedback is stabilizing.

**Feedback traders** Traders who act on the basis of price changes rather than fundamentals. *See* Feedback, Negative feedback, Positive feedback.

**FICO score** A consumer credit score on a scale of 350 to 800 awarded by a private firm, Fair Isaac Corporation, on the basis of a consumer's debt load, record of on-time loan payments, and length of credit history; used by mortgage lenders to determine eligibility for prime mortgage loans. *See* Prime mortgage loan.

**Financial Crisis Inquiry Commission (FCIC)** Created by the Fraud Enforcement and Recovery Act of 2009, the 10-member body was appointed by US Congressional leaders and charged with investigating the causes of the 2007–2008 credit crisis. The commission reported its findings to Congress in 2011.

**Financial Stability Oversight Council (FSOC)** Created in 2010 by the Dodd-Frank Wall Street Reform and Consumer Protection Act, the 10-member body is charged with identifying, monitoring, and responding to threats to the stability of the US financial system. *See* Office of Financial Research.

**Fixed income instruments** Debt instruments paying a known interest rate.

**Flash crash** A May 6, 2010, incident in which the prices of many US-listed stocks suddenly plunged—some to as low as a penny per share—and recovered within minutes.

**Floor** A minimum value for a security, or for its return, specified in a contract or offered by a derivatives position. *See* Cap, Derivative.

**Freddie Mac (Federal Home Loan Mortgage Corporation)** A government-sponsored enterprise and public company, created by Congress in 1970 to reduce the cost of home ownership by purchasing and securitizing home mortgages and guaranteeing payments on the resulting securities. *See* Government-sponsored enterprise, Fannie Mae, Securitization.

**Front running** Trading with knowledge of other investors' anticipated trades in an attempt to profit by buying or selling ahead of their trades.

**Fundamentals** Economic-, industry-, or company-related information that may affect a firm's profitability.

**Futures contract** A standardized, exchange-traded contract to buy or sell, for a specified price, an asset to be delivered and paid for at a specified future date. Can be settled by delivery of the asset (typically for commodities) or by cash payment. Contract value is typically marked to market daily. *See* Marking to market.

**Government Accountability Office (GAO)** A US government agency that reports to Congress and investigates how taxpayer funds are spent. Formerly known as the General Accounting Office.

**Government-sponsored enterprise (GSE)** Corporations, such as Fannie Mae or Freddie Mac, created by Congress to facilitate funding of certain sectors of the economy, particularly housing, often by purchasing and securitizing mortgage loans and guaranteeing payments on the resulting securities. *See* Fannie Mae, Freddie Mac, Securitization.

**Gross domestic product (GDP)** The value of all finished goods and services produced by a country over a given period; a measure of a country's economic output and a benchmark for other economic statistics, which are often expressed as a ratio to gross domestic product. *See* Benchmark.

**Guaranteed equity** A type of investment in which the issuer offers to guarantee the return of most or all of an investor's initial capital plus a portion of any gains from a specified stock index. *See* Index.

**Haircut** A discount applied to the value of an asset offered for collateral. *See* Collateral.

**Hedge** An asset position used to offset the risk of another asset position.

**Hedge fund** An investment pool, structured as a private partnership, that typically pursues a wider variety of investment strategies and faces fewer regulatory requirements than funds such as mutual funds; may employ short selling, derivatives, and non-traditional assets. *See* Derivatives, Mutual fund, Short sale.

**Hedge ratio** The ratio of the size of a position in hedging instruments to the size of the position being hedged. *See* Hedge.

**Herding** The tendency of individuals to conform their behavior to that of others; the tendency of a stock analyst, for example, to adjust earnings estimates to be in line with the estimates of other analysts.

**Idiosyncratic risk** The portion of an asset's total risk not attributable to sources of variability common to all assets in the same market. *See* Diversification, Systematic risk.

**Implied volatility** The volatility of an underlying stock or stock index inferred from the prices of options on the stock or stock index and an options pricing formula. *See* Black-Scholes-Merton options pricing model, Index, Option, Underlying.

**Index** A statistical average of the prices of securities selected to represent a particular market (e.g., stocks or bonds) or subgroup of a market (e.g., growth, value, small-capitalization).

**Index arbitrage** An arbitrage strategy designed to profit from deviations from the normal relationship between stock index futures and their underlying stocks. *See* Arbitrage, Futures contract, Index, Underlying.

**Informational cascade** A situation that occurs when investors base their decisions on information, such as price changes, passed on by others, while ignoring information, such as fundamentals, gathered on their own; a price collapse that occurs when investors who have been basing their bullish investment decisions on the prior actions of other investors begin to act on their own bearish private information. *See* Fundamentals.

**Informationless trade** A trade undertaken for reasons other than changes in fundamentals due to liquidity needs, portfolio rebalancing, or dynamic hedging. *See* Dynamic hedging, Fundamentals, Rebalancing.

**Interest rate swap** An over-the-counter derivatives contract between two parties to exchange payments based on underlying interest rates; generally, one party makes a fixed stream of payments and the other party makes payments that vary with changes in an interest rate such as Libor. *See* Derivative, Index, London interbank offered rate, Over the counter, Underlying.

**In the money** The state of a call option when the price of the underlying asset is higher than the strike price; the state of a put option when the price of the underlying asset is lower than the strike price. *See* At the money, Call option, Option, Out of the money, Put option, Strike price, Underlying.

**Investment bank** Traditionally, an institution focused primarily on the business of underwriting securities and advising businesses seeking access to public securities markets. More recently, investment banks have moved into other lines of business, including asset management, brokerage, derivatives, and securities trading. *See* Commercial bank, Derivative, Underwriting.

**Investment grade** A rating from a credit rating agency (BBB– or better from S&P Global Ratings, Baa3 or better from Moody's Investor Service) that indicates a bond is of relatively low risk and safe for conservative investors. *See* Credit rating, Credit rating agency.

**Investment safety** The goal of investment products and strategies designed to reduce the risk of losses. *See* Hedge, Portfolio insurance, Protective put.

**Jacobs Levy Markowitz Market Simulator** A dynamic simulation model of an equity market that assumes a system changes at discrete, uneven time intervals as it moves from one event to the next; allows users to model the evolution of market prices and volumes or find the values of parameters such as equilibrium-implied expected security returns.

**Jumbo mortgage loan** A mortgage loan that exceeds the size limit established by Congress (typically $453,100, although it can range up to $679,650 in some markets) for loans that are eligible to be purchased in the secondary market by Fannie Mae and Freddie Mac. *See* Conforming mortgage loan, Fannie Mae, Freddie Mac, Government-sponsored enterprise.

**Leverage** The use of borrowed funds, short positions, or derivatives to increase exposure to an asset's price changes beyond the limits of an investor's capital. *See* Derivative, Leverage ratio, Short position, Unique risks of leverage.

**Leverage aversion** A measure of an investor's level of aversion to (or, inversely, tolerance for) leverage risk. *See* Leverage, Leverage tolerance, Mean-variance-leverage efficient frontier, Unique risks of leverage.

**Leverage ratio** Generally, the degree to which an entity relies on borrowed money. Under Basel III, the ratio of a bank's Tier 1 capital to non-risk-weighted assets, both on- and off-balance-sheet; designed as a reality check for Basel-mandated capital charges based on risk-weighted assets. *See* Basel Capital Accord, Capital charge, Leverage, Risk-weighted assets, Tier 1 capital.

**Leverage tolerance** A measure expressing an investor's level of tolerance for (or, inversely, aversion to) leverage risk. *See* Leverage, Leverage aversion, Mean-variance-leverage efficient frontier, Unique risks of leverage.

**Liar loan** A mortgage loan based on a borrower's unverified loan application. *See* Low-/no-doc loan, NINJA loan.

**Liquidity** A market's ability to absorb a sizable trade without substantial impact on the security's price; also the ease with which a particular security can be converted into cash (market liquidity); also the ease with which funds can be obtained for trading or supporting investment positions (funding liquidity).

**Loan-to-value (LTV) ratio** A measure of lending risk calculated by dividing the amount of the loan by the market value or estimated value of the collateral. The higher the loan-to-value ratio, the riskier the loan. *See* Collateral.

**London Interbank Offered Rate (Libor)** The average of the interest rates that leading London banks anticipate paying to borrow from other banks; formerly a widely used benchmark, but because of alleged manipulation by large banks, being phased out in favor of new measures, including the Overnight Bank Funding Rate in the United States. *See* Benchmark, Overnight Bank Funding Rate.

**Long position** The ownership position established by purchasing a financial asset or instrument. *See* Short position.

**Long-short portfolio** A portfolio that contains short and long positions in expectation of profiting from both undervalued securities (held long) and overvalued securities (sold short) and of benefiting from the ability of the short positions to cushion the portfolio from broad market declines. *See* Long position, Short position, Short sale.

**Long-term equity anticipation securities (LEAPS)** Publicly traded options contracts with terms of greater than one year. *See* Option.

**Loss aversion** The tendency of investors to act myopically by focusing on losses over the short term rather than returns over the long term.

**Low-/no-doc loan** A mortgage loan requiring little or no documentation of a borrower's loan application claims; essentially, a liar loan. *See* Liar loan, NINJA loan.

**Margin** A portion of an investment position's market value that an investor must deposit and maintain with a broker or exchange to serve as collateral. *See* Collateral, Margin call.

**Margin call** A demand by a broker that a margined customer deposit more collateral to cover losses from adverse moves in the customer's position in order to maintain margin requirements. *See* Broker-dealer, Collateral, Margin, Unique risks of leverage.

**Market capitalization** The market value of a publicly traded company's common stock, determined by multiplying share price by the number of shares outstanding.

**Market impact** The portion of the cost of a market transaction that reflects movement in the price of a traded asset in response to the trade itself. *See* Transaction costs.

**Market maker** A dealer in financial assets that maintains an inventory of securities and stands ready to buy or sell on demand. *See* Dealer.

**Market-neutral long-short portfolio** A long-short portfolio that holds long and short positions of roughly equal dollar amounts and roughly equal market sensitivities so as to eliminate the portfolio's sensitivity to broad market moves. *See* Long position, Long-short portfolio, Short position.

**Market-on-close order** A market order to be executed at the end of the trading session.

**Marking to market** The process of revaluing assets or liabilities as their market prices change; may necessitate collateral payments between short sellers and security lenders or between counterparties in derivatives transactions. *See* Collateral, Counterparty, Derivative, Short sale.

**Mean** The arithmetic average of several values, or for a weighted mean, a weighted average of several values. If all weights are equal, the weighted mean equals the arithmetic mean. Weighted means are commonly used to calculate portfolio expected return. *See* Expected return.

**Mean-variance efficient frontier** The set of portfolios each of which has the highest expected return for any given level of volatility risk, or alternatively, the lowest volatility risk for any given level of expected return; or the set of portfolios each of which has the highest expected return for any given level of investor volatility tolerance (or inversely, volatility aversion or risk aversion). *See* Mean-variance-leverage efficient frontier, Modern portfolio theory, Risk aversion, Volatility, Volatility aversion, Volatility tolerance.

**Mean-variance-leverage efficient frontier** For a given level of investor leverage tolerance (or, inversely, leverage aversion), the set of portfolios each of which has the highest expected return for any given level of volatility risk, or alternatively, the lowest volatility risk for any given level of expected return. The set of all such efficient portfolios comprises the mean-variance efficient frontier for a given level of investor leverage tolerance. *See* Leverage, Leverage aversion, Leverage tolerance, Mean-variance efficient frontier, Modern portfolio theory, Volatility, Volatility aversion, Volatility tolerance.

**Mezzanine tranche** A mid-level tranche in the capital structure of a mortgage-backed security or collateralized debt obligation, riskier and higher yielding than the senior tranche but less risky and lower yielding than the equity tranche. *See* Collateralized debt obligation, CDO-cubed, CDO-squared, Equity tranche, Mortgage-backed security, Senior tranche, Tranche.

**Modern portfolio theory** A theory and approach for constructing an optimal portfolio; it suggests selecting an optimal portfolio using a mean-variance efficient frontier. A key insight is that an asset should be considered in the context of how it contributes to the portfolio's overall risk and return. The theory quantifies the benefits of asset diversification. *See* Mean-variance efficient frontier, Mean-variance-leverage efficient frontier.

**Momentum investing** An investing strategy that assumes prices follow trends and that buys as prices rise and sells as prices fall. *See* Trend-following trading.

**Monoline insurer** Originally, a firm that guaranteed the timely repayment of bonds issued by municipal governments; later expanded to guarantee payments made by issuers of securitized debt products, such as collateralized debt obligations. *See* Collateralized debt obligation, Securitization.

**Moral hazard** A situation created when an event, such as the purchase of insurance, anticipated government intervention, or looming bankruptcy, creates an incentive to take unwarranted risks.

**Mortgage-backed security (MBS)** A security backed by principal and interest payments from a pool of residential or commercial mortgages; a form of asset-backed security. *See* Asset-backed security, Residential mortgage-backed security.

**Mutual fund** An investment fund regulated under the Investment Company Act of 1940 that pools money from many investors.

**Nasdaq** National Association of Securities Dealers Automated Quotations System, an electronic marketplace for over-the-counter stocks. *See* Over the counter.

**Nationally Recognized Statistical Rating Organization (NRSRO)** A credit rating agency that is registered with the Securities and Exchange Commission, and whose ratings can thus be used by financial institutions for certain regulatory purposes. *See* Credit rating agency, Securities and Exchange Commission.

**Negative-amortization loan** A loan that allows for periodic payments that are less than the amount of interest incurred during the period, resulting in a loan balance that increases rather than decreases.

**Negative feedback** The result of trading in the opposite direction of current market price changes (for example, buying as market prices fall); inherently stabilizing. *See* Positive feedback.

**Neoclassical economics** A school of economic thought that holds that people act rationally to make economic decisions that maximize their personal satisfaction, and that these actions, in aggregate, lead to an efficient allocation of resources in an economy.

**NINJA loan** A mortgage loan extended to a borrower with no verification of income, job, or assets, hence its name "no income, no job, and no assets." *See* Liar loan, Low-/no-doc loan.

**Noise** Security price movements induced by trading not related to fundamentals.

**Nonlinearity** A characteristic of a system or relationship when a change in an input causes a disproportionate response. For example, a small percentage change in the price of a stock can cause a large percentage change in the value of an option on the stock. *See* Option.

**Normal distribution** A probability distribution of the possible values of a random variable in which most of the possible values cluster symmetrically around the average value and diminish in number as the distance from the average value increases; the result is a bell-shaped curve. Also called Gaussian distribution. *See* Fat-tailed distribution, Probability distribution.

**Notional value** The nominal face amount used to calculate swap payments. In an interest rate swap, for example, rates are multiplied by notional amounts to determine counterparty obligations. *See* Counterparty, Swap.

**Off-balance-sheet** An asset or liability not reflected on a firm's financial statements.

**Office of Financial Research (OFR)** Established in 2010 by the Dodd-Frank Wall Street Reform and Consumer Protection Act to analyze potential risks to the financial system and to provide its research and data to the Financial Stability Oversight Council. *See* Financial Stability Oversight Council.

**Open interest** The number of listed option or futures contracts outstanding at any point in time. *See* Futures contract, Option.

**Option** A financial instrument that conveys the right, but not the obligation, to buy (call option) or sell (put option) an underlying asset at a specified price (the strike price) on or before a specified future date (the expiration date). *See* Call option, Put option, Strike price.

**Option premium** The amount of money an option buyer pays for an option. *See* Option.

**Option replication** A technique for duplicating or hedging an option's payoff pattern by taking and trading positions in the underlying asset or in derivatives of the underlying asset; also known as delta hedging or dynamic hedging. *See* Derivative, Dynamic hedging, Option, Options pricing formula, Portfolio insurance, Underlying.

**Options pricing formula** A mathematical model for estimating the value of an option, based on the equivalence of the option price and the price of a replicating portfolio containing the asset underlying the option and a risk-free asset. *See* Black-Scholes-Merton options pricing model, Option, Option replication, Risk-free (riskless) asset, Underlying.

**Options pricing model** *See* Options pricing formula.

**Out of the money** The state of a call option when the price of the underlying asset is lower than the strike price; the state of a put option when the price of the underlying asset is higher than the strike price. *See* At the money, Call option, In the money, Option, Put option, Strike price, Underlying.

**Over the counter (OTC)** An informal market for securities and instruments not traded on an organized exchange. *See* Dealer.

**Overcollateralization** Posted collateral worth more than the value of the loan being secured; used to reduce the lender's exposure to default risk. For an asset-backed security, the amount by which the security's assets exceed its liabilities. *See* Asset-backed security, Collateral.

**Overnight Bank Funding Rate** The average interest rate at US-based banks at which the most creditworthy banks borrow from or lend to other creditworthy banks in the overnight market. *See* London Interbank Offered Rate (Libor).

**Overreaction** The tendency of investors to respond to news by buying or selling more than is warranted by the fundamental information contained in the news. *See* Fundamentals.

**Portfolio insurance** An option replication strategy designed to protect a portfolio against losses exceeding a predetermined limit. *See* Option replication, Put option, Protective put.

**Positive feedback** The result of trading in the direction of current market price changes (for example, selling as market prices fall); inherently destabilizing. *See* Negative feedback.

**Price/earnings ratio** The ratio of a company's share price to the company's earnings per share, often used as a measure of a stock's valuation.

**Prime broker** A broker who executes and settles trades for a margin account and arranges to borrow shares for a customer to sell short. *See* Broker-dealer, Margin, Short sale.

**Prime money market fund** A mutual fund that invests primarily in highly liquid, short-term corporate debt securities with low credit risk. *See* Credit risk, Liquidity, Mutual fund.

**Prime mortgage loan** A mortgage loan extended to the most creditworthy borrowers who have a strong history of on-time loan repayments and who can document their financial capacity to repay the loan. *See* Alt-A mortgage loan, FICO score, Subprime loan.

**Private-label security** A mortgage-backed security that is neither issued nor guaranteed by a government-sponsored enterprise. *See* Government-sponsored enterprise, Mortgage-backed security.

**Probability distribution** A statistical description of all possible values of a random variable and their likelihoods. *See* Fat-tailed distribution, Normal distribution.

**Program trading** The use of computers to deliver simultaneous orders for a large number of securities; used to facilitate strategies such as index arbitrage. *See* Arbitrage, Index.

**Proprietary trading** Trading by a financial institution for its own benefit.

**Protective put** A long asset position combined with a put option on that asset. *See* Long position, Option, Put option.

**Public futures volume** The volume of futures trading exclusive of trading by dealers for their own accounts. *See* Dealer, Futures contract.

**Put option** An option that grants the owner the right to sell a certain security at a specified price within a specified period of time. *See* Option.

**Rational expectations** A theory explaining how security prices are determined; it holds that investors use all pertinent information and always make consistent, rational choices.

**Rebalancing** The act of realigning the weightings of assets in a portfolio in order to maintain desired investment objectives. *See* Informationless trade.

**Regulation T (Reg T)** US Federal Reserve Board regulation governing extension of credit by financial intermediaries for transactions involving margin accounts. *See* Margin.

**Regulatory arbitrage** Attempting to benefit from a more lenient regulatory regime by restructuring transactions or by moving business activity to a different jurisdiction.

**Relative-value trade** A trade that takes offsetting long and short positions in two or more related assets with the expectation of profiting from their relative price movements. *See* Long position, Long-short portfolio, Short position.

**Repo (repurchase agreement)** A short-term, collateralized loan in the form of an agreement to sell a security to a buyer and to repurchase it at a specified time and price; the repurchase price includes a premium corresponding to the appropriate short-term interest rate. *See* Collateral, Reverse repo.

**Residential mortgage-backed security (RMBS)** A security backed by principal and interest payments from a pool of residential mortgages; a form of asset-backed security. *See* Asset-backed security, Mortgage-backed security.

**Reverse repo** A repurchase agreement from the perspective of the security buyer (lender). *See* Repo (repurchase agreement).

**Risk aversion/tolerance** A measure of the willingness of an investor to accept additional risk as a trade-off for additional expected return. The more risk-averse (risk-tolerant) the investor the larger (smaller) the incremental return demanded for a given increase in the level of risk assumed.

**Risk-free (riskless) asset** An asset that offers a certain return, bearing no credit risk, generally proxied by US Treasury bills.

**Risk-free (riskless) return** The return on a risk-free asset. *See* Risk-free (riskless) asset.

**Risk premium** The expected return on an asset in excess of the return on a risk-free asset; the premium provides compensation for bearing risk. *See* Risk-free (riskless) asset.

**Risk sharing** Distributing risk among similarly situated parties, such as holders of fire insurance policies issued by the same insurer.

**Risk shifting** Transferring risk to counterparties who agree to assume it in exchange for a benefit or potential benefit, or, alternatively, to unwitting parties.

**Risk-weighted assets** A measure used to determine the capital charge; higher-risk assets, as determined by regulators, carry more weight than lower-risk assets in calculations used to determine the capital charge. *See* Basel Capital Accord, Capital charge.

**S&P 100** A capitalization-weighted index of 100 large-capitalization US publicly traded companies selected by Standard & Poor's. *See* Index.

**S&P 500** A capitalization-weighted index of 500 large-capitalization US publicly traded companies selected by Standard & Poor's. *See* Index.

**Safety** *See* Investment safety.

**Securities and Exchange Commission (SEC)** US federal agency charged with regulating the US securities industry.

**Securitization** The creation of securities from a pool of assets. *See* Asset-backed security, Mortgage-backed security, Residential mortgage-backed security, Special purpose vehicle.

**Sell short** *See* Short sale.

**Senior tranche** The top-level tranche in the capital structure of an asset-backed security with first rights to cashflows (absent a super-senior tranche) of the underlying securities; usually carrying a top, AAA or similar, rating from a credit rating agency. *See* Asset-backed security, Collateralized debt obligation, Credit rating, Credit rating agency, Super-senior tranche, Tranche, Underlying.

**Settlement** The completion of a transaction between the parties to a trade.

**Shadow banking system** An informal network of financial intermediaries involved in creating credit across the global financial system and largely beyond the control of government regulators. May include activities undertaken by banks and other regulated institutions that are not subject to regulatory regimes.

**Short covering** Closing out or partially closing out a short position by buying the shares shorted and returning them to the lender. *See* Short sale.

**Short position** The position established by a short sale. *See* Long position, Short sale.

**Short sale** A transaction in which a party borrows securities from another party (the lender), then sells those securities to a third party, with the agreement to deliver to the lender at a future date securities identical to those borrowed. Often done in anticipation of a decline in the securities' prices that will allow the borrower to profit from repaying the lender with securities that are reduced in value. *See* Short position.

**Short-volatility strategy** An investment strategy designed to profit from stable or falling levels of market volatility. *See* Volatility.

**Shut out** The condition occurring when a portfolio insurance program is stopped out and cannot benefit from a subsequent increase in the value of the insured asset. *See* Portfolio insurance, Stop out.

**Simulation** A technique that uses historical or probabilistic data and quantitative models to determine the likely outcomes of an investment program over a given historical or hypothetical environment.

**Sovereign debt** Bonds issued and guaranteed by a national government.

**Special purpose vehicle (SPV)** A legally separate, off-balance-sheet entity created for a specific purpose; used by banks or other sponsors to securitize mortgages or other loans. *See* Mortgage-backed security, Off-balance-sheet, Securitization.

**Specialist** A dealer of exchange-listed stocks who stands ready to buy or sell a given stock on demand and is obligated to maintain orderly markets. *See* Dealer.

**Specific risk** *See* Idiosyncratic risk.

**Speculator** A person who takes large risks on a short-term basis in anticipation of large gains.

**Spot market** The market in which transactions in securities or commodities are settled currently, rather than at some future date; the market underlying a derivatives contract. *See* Derivative, Underlying.

**Spot price** The price in spot markets. *See* Spot market.

**Spread** The difference between two prices or between two interest rates. *See* Bid–ask spread.

**Standard deviation** A statistical measure of the dispersion of a set of observations about their mean (average); often used as a measure of stock volatility. Equals the square root of variance. *See* Mean, Variance, Volatility.

**Stochastic** Random and varying over time; a stochastic variable may be analyzed statistically but cannot be predicted precisely.

**Stock index** *See* Index.

**Stock index futures** A futures contract on an underlying stock index. *See* Futures contract, Stock index.

**Stock index option** An option on a stock index. *See* Index, Option

**Stop-loss order** An order to sell a security if its price drops to or below a specified level.

**Stop out** The state of a transaction following the execution of a stop-loss order; the state of an insured portfolio when its value falls below the insured floor. *See* Floor, Portfolio insurance, Shut out, Stop-loss order.

**Strike price** The price specified in an option contract at which the option holder can buy or sell the underlying asset; also known as the exercise price. *See* Option, Underlying.

**Structured finance products** Investment products designed to offer particular risk-return profiles; often created via securitization of assets, special purpose vehicles, or structured investment vehicles. *See* Securitization, Special purpose vehicle, Structured investment vehicle.

**Structured investment vehicle** An off-balance-sheet financing vehicle formed by a sponsor, typically a bank, to borrow money through the issuance of short-term instruments, such as commercial paper, and invest the proceeds in longer-term, higher-yielding securities, such as mortgage-backed securities; similar to a conduit, but with fewer financial guarantees from the sponsor. *See* Commercial paper, Conduit, Mortgage-backed security, Off-balance-sheet.

**Structured note** A derivative that is structured to offer payouts that reflect a combination of returns on a security plus a derivative; a structured note that offers a return with some downside protection plus appreciation tied to a stock or bond index might be created by combining a bond with a call option on an index. *See* Call option, Derivative, Equity-linked note, Index.

**Subprime loan** A loan extended to a borrower who poses a high risk of default because of low credit scores, undocumented or uncertain income sources, or a history of late loan payments, defaults, or bankruptcy. *See* Alt-A mortgage loan, FICO score, Prime mortgage loan.

**Super-senior tranche** A tranche carved from the top-level senior tranche in the capital structure of an asset-backed security; ostensibly safer than, but carrying the same credit rating as, the senior tranche. *See* Asset-backed security, Collateralized debt obligation, Credit rating, Senior tranche, Tranche.

**Swap** A contract between two parties who agree to exchange future streams of payments based on the price behavior of specified underlying assets. *See* Underlying.

**Synthetic CDO** A collateralized debt obligation that holds credit default swaps. *See* Collateralized debt obligation, Credit default swap.

**Synthetic option** An option-like payoff pattern created by taking and trading positions in the underlying asset or derivatives of the underlying asset. *See* Derivative, Dynamic hedging, Option, Option replication, Portfolio insurance, Underlying.

**Systematic risk** The portion of an asset's total risk attributable to sources of variability common to all assets in the same market. *See* Beta, Idiosyncratic risk.

**Systemic risk** The risk that the failure of one or a few components of a system or market will cause failure of the entire system or market.

**Tier 1 capital** A measure of the adequacy of a bank's capital, composed primarily of common stock. Also known as core capital. *See* Basel Capital Accord.

**Trading collar** A New York Stock Exchange restriction that allows stocks to be traded only within a specific range of their closing prices from the previous trading session.

**Trading halt** A pause in trading due to price-limit restrictions, order imbalances, news dissemination, or other events.

**Tranche** A group of securities created from a single underlying pool of assets or asset-backed securities that shares characteristics such as risk attributes, credit ratings, or payoff sources. *See* Asset-backed security, Collateralized debt obligation, Credit rating, Equity tranche, Mezzanine tranche, Senior tranche, Super-senior tranche, Underlying.

**Transaction costs** The costs of executing a trade, including brokerage commissions, market impact cost, and opportunity cost of not being able to execute in a timely fashion. *See* Market impact.

**Transparency** The availability of accurate and timely information on asset positions, their prices, and trading volume.

**Treasury bill** A US government debt issue with a maturity of one year or less.

**Trend-following trading** Buying securities after their prices rise and selling securities after their prices fall. *See* Momentum investing.

**Troubled Asset Relief Program (TARP)** US federal program enacted in 2008 to provide funds to financial institutions in order to relieve the stress on lenders and stabilize markets and the economy in the midst of the credit crisis.

**Underlying** A security upon which a derivative security is based; changes in the market value, cashflows, or other characteristics of the underlying trigger changes in the value and characteristics of related derivatives. *See* Derivative.

**Underwater mortgage** A mortgage on a property whose value has fallen below the amount of the principal owed on the loan.

**Underwriting** The process of raising capital for a securities offering or of credit or risk analysis for a loan or insurance policy.

**Unique risks of leverage** These include the risks and costs of margin calls, which can force borrowers to liquidate securities at adverse prices due to illiquidity; losses exceeding the capital invested; and the possibility of bankruptcy. *See* Leverage, Leverage aversion, Liquidity, Margin call, Mean-variance-leverage efficient frontier.

**Value at risk (VAR)** An estimate of the loss that could be incurred with a given probability over a given period of time.

**Value investing** An investment strategy that favors assets that are undervalued by some measure, such as, in the case of stocks, low price/earnings ratio or high dividend yield. *See* Price/earnings ratio, Yield.

**Variance** A statistical measure of the dispersion of a set of observations about their average value (mean). Equals the square of the standard deviation. *See* Mean, Standard deviation.

**Volatility** The degree to which the price of a security or the value of a portfolio fluctuates over time, usually measured statistically by standard deviation or variance. *See* Standard deviation, Variance.

**Volatility aversion** A measure expressing an investor's level of aversion to (or, inversely, tolerance for) volatility risk. *See* Leverage aversion, Mean-variance efficient frontier, Mean-variance-leverage efficient frontier, Volatility, Volatility tolerance.

**Volatility tolerance** A measure expressing an investor's level of tolerance for (or, inversely, aversion to) volatility risk. *See* Leverage aversion, Mean-variance efficient frontier, Mean-variance-leverage efficient frontier, Volatility, Volatility aversion.

**Volcker Rule** A provision of the 2010 Dodd-Frank Wall Street Reform and Consumer Protection Act that imposes restrictions on the buying and selling of securities by deposit-taking US banks when trading for their own accounts;

also prohibits bank ownership of hedge funds and private equity funds. *See* Hedge fund.

**Whipsaw** A sharp price movement in one direction followed quickly by a sharp price reversal.

**Write** The act of selling, or taking a short position in, an option. *See* Option, Short position.

**Yield** The income generated by an asset over a given period (typically a year) as a percentage of the asset's price. For stocks, the annual dividends per share divided by the price per share.

# ENDNOTES

## INTRODUCTION

1. From *Prometheus Bound*, translation by David Grene. In D. Grene and R. Lattimore, eds., *Greek Tragedies Volume I* (Chicago: University of Chicago Press, 1960).
2. Eugene F. Fama, "Perspectives on October 1987, or what did we learn from the crash?" in R.J. Barro et al., eds., *Black Monday and the Future of Financial Markets* (Homewood, IL: Mid-America Institute for Public Policy Research and Dow Jones-Irwin, 1989): 81.
3. Mark Rubinstein, "Portfolio Insurance and the Market Crash," *Financial Analysts Journal* 44, no. 1 (1988): 38–47.
4. Hayne E. Leland and Mark Rubinstein, "Comments on the Market Crash: Six Months After," *Journal of Economic Perspectives* 2, no. 3 (1988): 45–50.
5. Michael Lewis, "How the Eggheads Cracked," *New York Times Magazine*, January 24, 1999.
6. Myron S. Scholes, "The Near Crash of 1998: Crisis and Risk Management," *American Economic Review Papers and Proceedings* 90, no. 2 (2000): 17–21.
7. William D. Cohan, *House of Cards: A Tale of Hubris and Wretched Excess on Wall Street* (New York: Doubleday, 2009): 146.
8. Richard S. Fuld, Jr., Speech to Marcum MicroCap Conference, New York, May 28, 2015; quoted in D. Gelles, "Ex-Lehman Boss Breaks Silence," *New York Times*, May 29, 2015: B1.
9. Bruce I. Jacobs, "Momentum Trading: The New Alchemy," *Journal of Investing* 9, no. 3 (2000): 6–7.
10. Gregory Zuckerman, *The Greatest Trade Ever: The Behind-the-Scenes Story of How John Paulson Defied Wall Street and Made Financial History* (New York: Broadway Books, 2009); Michael Lewis, *The Big Short: Inside the Doomsday Machine* (New York: W. W. Norton & Co., 2010).
11. Bruce I. Jacobs, "Memorandum to Prudential Insurance Company of America's Client Service and Sales Forces regarding Portfolio Insulation," January 17, 1983; reprinted in Appendix C.
12. Bruce I. Jacobs, "The Portfolio Insurance Puzzle," *Pensions & Investment Age*, August 22, 1983; Bruce I. Jacobs, "A Public Debate On Dynamic Hedging," in *Innovative Portfolio Insurance Techniques: The Latest Developments in "Dynamic Hedging"* (videotape) (New York: Institute for International

Research, 1986); Trudy Ring, "Portfolio Insurance's Merits Spur Debate," *Pensions & Investment Age*, July 7, 1986.

13. Michael Clowes, "More to Say About Crash," *Pensions & Investments*, July 12, 1999.
14. Roger Lowenstein, "Why Stock Options Are Really Dynamite," *Wall Street Journal*, November 6, 1997.
15. Mark Rubinstein, Correspondence to Michael Brennan, February 14, 2000. This was shared with the editor of *Derivatives Strategy* at its 2000 Hall of Fame Roundtable, "Portfolio Insurance Revisited," New York, April 14, 2000. The roundtable discussion was published in the August 2000 issue of *Derivatives Strategy*.
16. Bruce I. Jacobs, "Viewpoint on Portfolio Insurance: It's Prone to Failure," *Pensions & Investment Age*, November 16, 1987; Bruce I. Jacobs, "The Darker Side of Option Pricing Theory," *Pensions & Investments*, November 24, 1997; Bruce I. Jacobs, "Option Pricing Theory and Its Unintended Consequences," *Journal of Investing* 7, no. 1 (1998): 12–14; Bruce I. Jacobs, "Option Replication and the Market's Fragility," *Pensions & Investments*, June 15, 1998.
17. Bruce I. Jacobs, *Capital Ideas and Market Realities: Option Replication, Investor Behavior, and Stock Market Crashes* (Malden, MA: Blackwell, 1999).
18. In the foreword, Markowitz compares modern portfolio theory with portfolio insurance. He shows with a simple example that a portfolio insurance strategy produces inefficient portfolios in terms of expected return and volatility of return. He goes on to say that portfolio insurance is destabilizing: "Jacobs will show us that portfolio insurance did not in fact work, partly because it destabilized the market and then had liquidity problems as a consequence . . . the reason that portfolio insurance destabilized the market was because it bought when the market went up and sold when the market went down. The rebalancing strategies that portfolio theory implies . . . sell when the market rises and buy when the market falls, tend to stabilize the market. Thus . . . portfolio *theory* is . . . more environmentally friendly than portfolio *insurance*." See Harry M. Markowitz, "Foreword," in B.I. Jacobs, *Capital Ideas and Market Realities*.
19. Bruce I. Jacobs, "Long-Term Capital's Short-Term Memory," *Pensions & Investments*, October 5, 1998; Bruce I. Jacobs, "When Seemingly Infallible Arbitrage Strategies Fail," *Journal of Investing* 8, no. 1 (1999): 9–10; Bruce I. Jacobs, "A Tale of Two Hedge Funds," in B.I. Jacobs and K.N. Levy, eds., *Market Neutral Strategies* (New York: Wiley, 2005): 147–171.
20. Bruce I. Jacobs, "Risk Avoidance and Market Fragility," *Financial Analysts Journal* 60, no. 1 (2004): 26–30; citing my article, *Forbes* noted that risk-reducing products "could really backfire." William P. Barrett, "Weapons of Mass Panic," *Forbes*, March 15, 2004.

21. Jacobs, "Risk Avoidance and Market Fragility": 28.
22. Bruce I. Jacobs, "Tumbling Tower of Babel: Subprime Securitization and the Credit Crisis," *Financial Analysts Journal* 65, no. 2 (2009): 17–30.

## CHAPTER 1

1. Quoted in Michael Siconolfi, Anita Raghavan, and Mitchell Pacelle, "How Salesmanship and Brainpower Failed to Save Long-Term Capital," *Wall Street Journal*, November 16, 1998. Sharpe received the Nobel Prize in economics in 1990 for his work on the development of the capital asset pricing model. See William F. Sharpe, "Capital Asset Prices: A Theory of Market Equilibrium Under Conditions of Risk," *Journal of Finance* 19, no. 3 (1964): 425–442.
2. This was the insight of Harry M. Markowitz, who developed modern portfolio theory, for which he received the Nobel Prize in economics in 1990. Harry M. Markowitz, "Portfolio Selection," *Journal of Finance* 7, no. 1 (1952): 77–91 and *Portfolio Selection: Efficient Diversification of Investments* (New Haven: Yale University Press, 1959).
3. Bruce I. Jacobs and Kenneth N. Levy, "Leverage Aversion and Portfolio Optimality," *Financial Analysts Journal* 68, no. 5 (2012): 89–94; Bruce I. Jacobs and Kenneth N. Levy, "Leverage Aversion, Efficient Frontiers, and the Efficient Region," *Journal of Portfolio Management* 39, no. 3 (2013): 54–64; Bruce I. Jacobs and Kenneth N. Levy, "Traditional Optimization is Not Optimal for Leverage-Averse Investors," *Journal of Portfolio Management* 40, no. 2 (2014): 1–11; Bruce I. Jacobs and Kenneth N. Levy, "The Unique Risks of Portfolio Leverage: Why Modern Portfolio Theory Fails and How to Fix It," *Journal of Financial Perspectives* 2, no. 3 (2014): 113–126.
4. Short sales may also be subject to disclosure requirements, as they are in the European Union, and may be banned in stressed markets, as they were in the United States, Canada, Australia, and many European countries during the 2007–2010 crises. In the United States, short sales of individual stocks are also restricted if the stock experiences a significant price decline.

## CHAPTER 2

1. From *Pudd'nhead Wilson* (New York: Simon & Schuster, 2010), Ch. XIII.
2. *New York Times*, October 25, 1987: F6
3. *New York Times*, October 28, 1977: D14
4. *New York Times*, October 21, 1987: D14
5. *Boston Globe*, October 19, 1997: F1.
6. *New York Times*, October 19, 1997: C4
7. Frederic S. Mishkin and Eugene N. White, "U.S. Stock Market Crashes and Their Aftermath: Implications for Monetary Policy," National Bureau of Economic Research Working Paper 8992, June 2002.
8. Carmen M. Reinhart and Kenneth S. Rogoff, *This Time is Different: Eight Centuries of Financial Folly* (Princeton, NJ: Princeton University Press, 2009).

9. Eugene F. Fama, "Perspectives on October 1987, or What Did We Learn from the Crash?" in R.J. Barro et al., eds., *Black Monday and the Future of Financial Markets* (Homewood, IL: Mid-America Institute for Public Policy Research and Dow Jones-Irwin, 1989): 81. Fama received the Nobel Prize in economics in 2013 for his work on asset pricing.
10. Joseph A. Schumpeter, *Capitalism, Socialism and Democracy* (New York: Harper and Brothers, 1942).
11. Friedrich A. Hayek, "The Use of Knowledge in Society," *American Economic Review* 35, no. 4 (1945): 519–530; Milton Friedman and Anna J. Schwartz, *A Monetary History of the United States, 1867–1960* (Washington, DC: National Bureau of Economic Research, 1963). Hayek received the Nobel Prize in economics in 1974 and Friedman in 1976.
12. Justin Fox, *The Myth of the Rational Market: A History of Risk, Reward, and Delusion on Wall Street* (New York: Harper Business, 2009): 92.
13. John Cassidy, *How Markets Fail: The Logic of Economic Calamities* (New York: Farrar, Straus and Giroux, 2009): 76–77.
14. Irving Fisher, *The Money Illusion* (New York: Adelphi, 1928).
15. John M. Keynes, *The General Theory of Employment, Interest, and Money* (London: Macmillan, 1936). Reprint, New York: Harcourt Brace, 1964.
16. Amos Tversky and Daniel Kahneman, "Judgment Under Uncertainty: Heuristics and Biases," *Science* 185, no. 4157 (Sep. 27, 1974): 1124–1131. Kahneman received the Nobel Prize in economics in 2002 for his work with Tversky on behavioral economics; Tversky had died in 1996, hence was ineligible for the award.
17. Ivo Welch, "Herding Among Security Analysts," *Journal of Financial Economics* 58, no. 3 (2000): 369–396.
18. Robert J. Shiller, *Irrational Exuberance* (Princeton, NJ: Princeton University Press, 2000). Shiller received the Nobel Prize in economics in 2013 for his work on asset pricing.
19. Hyman P. Minsky, "The Financial Instability Hypothesis," Jerome Levy Economics Institute of Bard College Working Paper 74, May 1992.

## CHAPTER 3

1. Quoted in Donald MacKenzie, *An Engine, Not a Camera* (Cambridge, MA: MIT Press, 2006): 136.
2. Gary L. Gastineau, *The Options Manual*, 3rd ed. (New York: McGraw-Hill, 1988).
3. For a more complete description of options contracts, their properties, and how they are valued, see Appendix B, "Option Basics," in Bruce I. Jacobs, *Capital Ideas and Market Realities: Option Replication, Investor Behavior, and Stock Market Crashes* (Malden, MA: Blackwell, 1999): 309–319.
4. Fischer Black and Myron S. Scholes, "The Pricing of Options and Corporate Liabilities," *Journal of Political Economy* 81, no. 3 (1973): 637–654; Robert

C. Merton, "Theory of Rational Option Pricing," *Bell Journal of Economics and Management Science* 4, no. 1 (1973): 141–183.

5. Quoted in MacKenzie, *An Engine*: 158.
6. For a more complete description of how an option on a stock can be replicated by a portfolio consisting of the stock and a risk-free asset, as well as the dynamic trading in the underlying stock required in response to its price changes, see Appendix C, "Option Replication," in Jacobs, *Capital Ideas and Market Realities*: 321–333.
7. I had noted this potential problem early on, when portfolio insurance began to be adopted by financial firms. See Bruce I. Jacobs, Memorandum to Prudential Insurance Company of America's Client Service and Sales Forces regarding Portfolio Insulation, January 17, 1983; reprinted in Appendix C.

**CHAPTER 4**

1. Brady Commission, *Report of the Presidential Task Force on Market Mechanisms* (Washington, DC: Government Printing Office, 1988).
2. The investor in a stock index futures contract puts up a fraction of the contract price, which is referred to as the initial margin. The stock index futures contract, whether a long or a short position, is subject to daily marks-to-market, giving rise to a daily profit or loss. Ample money needs to be available to cover potential losses; this is referred to as maintenance margin. Stock index futures contracts are settled at expiration in cash, because of the difficulty of delivering the stocks in the index and in their weighted proportions.
3. Fischer Black, "Noise," *Journal of Finance* 41, no. 3 (1986): 529–543
4. Bruce I. Jacobs and Kenneth N. Levy, "Long-Short Equity Investing," *Journal of Portfolio Management* 20, no. 1 (1993): 52–63; Bruce I. Jacobs and Kenneth N. Levy, "20 Myths About Long-Short," *Financial Analysts Journal* 52, no. 5 (1996): 81–85.
5. Franklin R. Edwards, "Does Futures Trading Increase Stock Market Volatility?" *Financial Analysts Journal* 44, no. 1 (1988): 63–69.
6. Securities and Exchange Commission, "The Role of Index-Related Trading in the Market Decline on September 11 and 12, 1986" (Washington, DC: Division of Market Regulation, SEC, 1987): 21.
7. Ibid.: 22–23.
8. Joanne M. Hill and Frank J. Jones, "Equity Trading, Program Trading, Portfolio Insurance, Computer Trading and All That," *Financial Analysts Journal* 44, no. 4 (1988): 29–38.
9. Brady Commission, *Report*: 29.
10. Jack L. Treynor, "Portfolio Insurance and Market Volatility," *Financial Analysts Journal* 44, no. 6 (1988): 71–73.
11. Ibid.

## CHAPTER 5

1. Mark Rubinstein and Hayne E. Leland, "Replicating Options with Positions in Stock and Cash," *Financial Analysts Journal* 37, no. 4 (1981): 69. This statement is qualified only in a footnote to the article, which says "the analogy to insurance breaks down under a sudden catastrophic loss that does not leave sufficient time to adjust the replicating portfolio."
2. For a description and critical analysis of portfolio insurance, see Bruce I. Jacobs, *Capital Ideas and Market Realities: Option Replication, Investor Behavior, and Stock Market Crashes* (Malden, MA: Blackwell Publishers, 1999).
3. One ad that ran in a Leland O'Brien Rubinstein Associates-sponsored section of *Institutional Investor* in 1984 (p. 7) stated that, with a portfolio insurance plan in effect, "more of the fund's assets can be placed in higher expected return albeit riskier asset classes. The net effect can be to increase the total fund's expected return by 1 to 2 percent per annum."
4. The conference, sponsored by the University of California, Berkeley, took place in Monterey, CA, from September 16 to September 19, 1984.
5. Hayne E. Leland, "Portfolio Insurance Performance, 1928–1983," Leland O'Brien Rubinstein Associates, 1984; Bruce I. Jacobs, "The Portfolio Insurance Puzzle," *Pensions & Investment Age*, August 22, 1983. Appendix C includes both pieces. See also John W. O'Brien, "Research Questioned" (letter), *Pensions & Investment Age*, September 19, 1983, and Bruce I. Jacobs, "Mr. Jacobs Responds" (letter), *Pensions & Investment Age*, November 14, 1983.
6. Transaction costs are based on round-trip trades for individual stocks.
7. Leland, "Portfolio Insurance Performance."
8. Lake Wobegon is immortalized in "A Prairie Home Companion," Minnesota Public Radio.
9. At some seminars, LOR offered a prize of $1,000 if anyone could adjust the numbers in LOR's computer program to make the theories underlying portfolio insurance fail. See William Falloon, "The Invisible Hedge," *Intermarket*, October 1984.
10. Bruce I. Jacobs, "Memorandum to Prudential Insurance Company of America's Client Service and Sales Forces regarding Portfolio Insulation," January 17, 1983; reprinted in Appendix C. I wrote the memo at the request of higher-ups at Prudential, J. Robert (Bob) Ferrari and Edward (Ed) D. Zinbarg, who headed, respectively, the Pension Asset Management Group and the Common Stock Department, both parts of Prudential Asset Management Company, the institutional investment arm of Prudential Insurance Company of America. The memo was distributed to the client service and sales forces to inform them of Prudential's viewpoint.
11. LOR's simulation results, presented in a March 1, 1982, advertisement in *Pensions & Investment Age* (reprinted as Exhibit 17.1 in Chapter 17,

"Illusions of Safety and Market Meltdowns"), showed that $1 invested in its portfolio insurance strategy would have returned $2.61, for a 10 percent annual compound growth rate over the 10-year period ending in 1981, whereas $1 invested in the S&P 500 would have returned just $1.89, for a 6.5 percent annual rate.

12. Jacobs, "The Portfolio Insurance Puzzle."
13. Annual renewals of portfolio insurance lead an investor to rebalance back to the same constant-mix strategy at the start of each calendar year, if the same level of insurance protection is desired and market conditions remain the same. So the behavior of that investor across calendar years (following a constant-mix strategy) would appear inconsistent with the investor's behavior during each calendar year (following a dynamic portfolio insurance strategy).

    An interesting result is obtained for a portfolio insurance investor having a moving horizon of constant length, such as three years, that is updated daily. In this case, each day represents the start of a new interval of protection having the same length (three years). This investor would re-establish the same hedge ratio between stocks and cash equivalents every day. For such an investor, the "insurance strategy" is actually a constant-mix strategy. Bruce I. Jacobs, "Is Portfolio Insurance Appropriate for the Long-Term Investor?" Prudential Asset Management Company, 1984.
14. Aetna's GEM provided an insurance company guarantee on a minimum rate of return, but did not reimburse for shortfalls on the upside. GEM was discontinued after the crash. Ralph Tate, "The Insurance Company Guarantee," in D. Luskin, ed., *Portfolio Insurance: A Guide to Dynamic Hedging* (New York: John Wiley, 1988): 182–185.
15. Leland, "Portfolio Insurance Performance."
16. Jacobs, "The Portfolio Insurance Puzzle"; Jacobs, "Mr Jacobs Responds."
17. Robert Ferguson, "How to Beat the S&P 500 (without losing sleep)," *Financial Analysts Journal* 42, no. 5 (1986); Robert Ferguson, "An Open Letter" (letter), *Financial Analysts Journal* 42, no. 5 (1986).
18. Mark Rubinstein, "Portfolio Insurance and the Market Crash," *Financial Analysts Journal*, 44, no. 1 (1988): 40.
19. "A Public Debate on Dynamic Hedging," in *Innovative Portfolio Insurance Techniques: The Latest Developments in "Dynamic Hedging"* (videotape) (New York: Institute for International Research, 1986).
20. See Exhibit 17.4 in Chapter 17.
21. Robert J. Shiller, "Investor Behavior in the October 1987 Stock Market Crash: Survey Evidence," in R.J. Shiller, *Market Volatility* (Cambridge, MA: MIT Press, 1989).
22. Robert J. Shiller, "Portfolio Insurance and Other Investor Fashions as Factors in the 1987 Stock Market Crash," in S. Fischer, ed., *NBER Macroeconomics Annual 1988* (Cambridge, MA: MIT Press, 1988): 291.

23. Brady Commission, *Report of the Presidential Task Force on Market Mechanisms* (Washington, DC: Government Printing Office, 1988): 9.
24. Securities and Exchange Commission, "The October 1987 Market Break" (Washington, DC: Division of Market Regulation, SEC, 1988): 3.15.
25. Nicholas Katzenbach, "An Overview of Program Trading and its Impact on Current Market Practices" (New York: New York Stock Exchange, 1987): 28.
26. General Accounting Office, "Preliminary Observations on the October 1987 Crash (Financial Markets GAO/GGD 38–88)" (Washington, DC: GAO, 1988): 38.
27. As Rubinstein and co-author John C. Cox note in their 1985 textbook, "index option prices provide important, otherwise unobtainable, information [including information about future price volatility] to the economy." John C. Cox and Mark Rubinstein, *Options Markets* (Englewood Cliffs, NJ: Prentice-Hall, 1985).

    Jacobs (*Capital Ideas and Market Realities*, p. 139) points out that portfolio insurance does not provide any such information to the public or indeed to users of portfolio insurance, as it does not use exchange-traded options, where the price is explicit. Rather, the price of an option replication strategy such as portfolio insurance is dependent on the volatility of the underlying portfolio over the life of the strategy and is known only at termination of the strategy. Because the price of the strategy is obscured, it is difficult for investors to know the expected cost of the strategy. If the cost of the strategy is underestimated, investor demand will be greater than otherwise. An increased demand for portfolio insurance trading can increase market volatility, and thereby increase the cost of the strategy. Further, the cost may skyrocket if the positive feedback trading of the insurance strategy induces a vicious cycle and destabilizes the market.
28. Mark L. Mitchell and Jeffry M. Netter, "Triggering the 1987 Stock Market Crash: Anti-Takeover Provisions in the Proposed House Ways and Means Tax Bill?" *Journal of Financial Economics* 24, no. 1 (1989): 37–68.
29. *Wall Street Journal*, October 16, 1987: 28
30. *New York Times*, October 16, 1987: 1
31. *Wall Street Journal*, October 16, 1987: 3
32. Brady Commission, *Report*: 29.
33. Ibid.
34. Ibid.
35. As program trading came to account for an increasing share of market volume in the 1980s, some in the financial industry and in the press expressed concerns that it would increase volatility and perhaps destabilize markets. A detailed look at the events of October 19, 1987, however, indicates that the problem was not program trading per se, but the cause behind it—portfolio insurance. Program trading was merely the messenger.
36. Brady Commission, *Report:* 36.

37. Securities and Exchange Commission, "The October 1987 Market Break": 2.15–2.16.
38. Commodity Futures Trading Commission, "Final Report on Stock Index Futures and Cash Market Activity During October 1987" (Washington, DC: Divisions of Economic Analysis and Trading and Markets, CFTC, 1988): 137.
39. Brady Commission, *Report*: III.21–22.
40. Securities and Exchange Commission, "The October 1987 Market Break": xiii. In a 2011 piece that reiterates many of the arguments in Jacobs, *Capital Ideas and Market Realities*, Leland relates that a trader at LOR opined at one point during the 19th: "If I place all the sell orders that I should, the [S&P 500 futures] market will go to zero"; he was advised to restrain his trading. Hayne E. Leland, "Leverage, Forced Asset Sales, and Market Stability: Lessons from Past Market Crises and the Flash Crash," The Future of Computer Trading in Financial Markets—Foresight Driver Review—DR9 (London: Government Office for Science, 2011).
41. Brady Commission, *Report*: 36.
42. Securities and Exchange Commission, "The October 1987 Market Break": 2.15–2.16.
43. Brady Commission, *Report*: III.21–III.22.
44. Ibid.: 36.
45. Albert S. Kyle and Anna A. Obizhaeva, "Large Bets and Stock Market Crashes," University of Maryland Working Paper, January 26, 2016.
46. Securities and Exchange Commission, "The October 1987 Market Break": 2.21.
47. Ibid.
48. Brady Commission, *Report*: 40.
49. Ibid.: 57.
50. Securities and Exchange Commission, "The October 1987 Market Break": 2.21.
51. LOR offered several reasons why portfolio insurance was not responsible. These were reviewed and dismissed in Bruce I. Jacobs, *Capital Ideas and Market Realities*, chapters 11 and 12.
52. As described in the opening quotation.
53. S. Grannis, "Viewpoint on Portfolio Insurance: It Proved its Worth," *Pensions & Investment Age*, November 16, 1987: 3.
54. Securities and Exchange Commission, "The October 1987 Market Break": 2.15.
55. See Exhibit 17.4 in Chapter 17, "Illusions of Safety and Market Meltdowns."
56. Brady Commission, *Report*: V.17.
57. Trudy Ring, "66 percent drop in portfolio insurance," *Pensions & Investment Age*, January 25, 1988.
58. Asset figures are from LOR's Form ADVs filed with the SEC.

59. Richard Roll, "The International Crash of October 1987," *Financial Analysts Journal* 44, no. 5 (1988): 22.
60. *New York Times*, October 21, 1987: D16
61. *Wall Street Journal*, October 20, 1987: 50
62. *New York Times*, October 20, 1987: D1
63. Securities and Exchange Commission, "The October 1987 Market Break": 11.8.
64. The International Stock Exchange, "Report of the International Stock Exchange of Great Britain," in R.J. Barro et al., eds., *Black Monday and the Future of Financial Markets* (Homewood, IL: Mid-America Institute for Public Policy Research and Dow Jones-Irwin, 1989): 281.

## CHAPTER 6

1. Peter L. Bernstein, *Against the Gods: The Remarkable Story of Risk* (New York: Wiley, 1996): 305.
2. Securities and Exchange Commission, "Trading Analysis of October 13 and 16, 1989" (Washington, DC: Division of Market Regulation, SEC, 1990): 34.
3. Goldman Sachs, "Global Derivatives: 1997 Review–1998 Issues," Goldman Sachs Equity Derivatives Research, January 1998.
4. Securities and Exchange Commission, "Trading Analysis": 19–20.
5. Betsey A. Kuhn, Gregory J. Kuserk, and Peter Locke, "Do Circuit Breakers Moderate Volatility? Evidence from October 1989," *Review of Futures Markets* 10, no. 1 (1991): 139.
6. Commodity Futures Trading Commission, "Report on Stock Index Futures and Cash Market Activity During October 1989" (Washington, DC: Division of Economic Analysis, CFTC, 1990).
7. Securities and Exchange Commission, "Trading Analysis": 19–20
8. Ibid.: 23.
9. Securities and Exchange Commission, "Market Analysis of October 13 and 16, 1989" (Washington, DC: Division of Market Regulation, SEC, 1990): 72.
10. Ibid.: 21–23.
11. Securities and Exchange Commission, "Trading Analysis": 1.
12. Ibid.: 53.
13. Securities and Exchange Commission, "Market Analysis": 23–25.
14. Securities and Exchange Commission, "Trading Analysis": 54.
15. Ibid: 1.
16. Securities and Exchange Commission, "Market Analysis": 35.
17. Commodity Futures Trading Commission, "Stock Index Futures": 18, 20, 60–61.
18. Securities and Exchange Commission, "Trading Analysis": 37.
19. Ibid.: 44.
20. Ibid.: 44–45.
21. Ibid.: 68–69.

22. Securities and Exchange Commission, "Trading Analysis of November 15, 1991," Staff Report, Division of Market Regulation, SEC, 1992.
23. Securities and Exchange Commission, "Market Decline on November 15, 1991," Memorandum from William H. Hayman, Director, Division of Market Regulation, to SEC Chairman Breeden (Washington DC: Division of Market Regulation, SEC, December 24, 1991): 7.
24. International Monetary Fund, "World Economic Outlook: Crisis in Asia, Regional and Global Implications" (Washington, DC: IMF, 1997).
25. Ibid.: 18.
26. Goldman Sachs, "Global Derivatives."

## CHAPTER 7

1. John M. Keynes, *The General Theory of Employment, Interest, and Money* (London: Macmillan, 1936). Reprinted New York: Harcourt Brace, 1964.
2. *New York Times*, August 5, 1998: A1.
3. *Wall Street Journal*, August 5, 1998: C1.
4. *Wall Street Journal*, October 7, 1998: A18.
5. *New York Times*, September 9, 1998: C6.
6. *Wall Street Journal*, August 31, 1998.
7. *Wall Street Journal*, September 5, 1998.
8. *Wall Street Journal*, August 5, 1998: C28.
9. *Wall Street Journal*, August 12, 1998: C13.
10. *Wall Street Journal*, August 25, 1998: C16.
11. *Wall Street Journal*, August 28, 1998: C13.
12. *New York Times,* September 2, 1998: C1.
13. *New York Times*, September 1, 1998: C7.
14. *Wall Street Journal*, September 1, 1998: C1.
15. *Wall Street Journal*, September 14, 1998: C4.
16. *Wall Street Journal*, September 16, 1998: B18B.
17. *New York Times*, September 9, 1998: C1.
18. *Wall Street Journal*, September 11, 1998: C1.
19. *Wall Street Journal*, September 16, 1998: B18B.

## CHAPTER 8

1. Quoted in Roger Lowenstein, *When Genius Failed: The Rise and Fall of Long-Term Capital Management* (New York: Random House, 2000): 65.
2. *New York Times*, October 1, 1998: C1.
3. *New York Times*, October 13, 1998: C9.
4. *Wall Street Journal*, August 28, 1998: A1.
5. For descriptions of some of LTCM's strategies see the following: David M. Modest, "Long-Term Capital Management: An Internal Perspective," Presentation to the Institute for Quantitative Research in Finance, Palm Springs, CA, October 18, 1999; Nicholas Dunbar, *Inventing Money: The Story of Long-Term*

*Capital Management and the Legends Behind It* (New York: John Wiley & Sons, 2000); Philippe Jorion, "Risk Management Lessons from Long-Term Capital Management," *European Financial Management* 6, no. 3 (2000): 277–300; Lowenstein, *When Genius Failed*; Philippe Jorion, "Medium-Term Risk Management: Lessons from Long-Term Capital Management," in P. Field, ed., *Modern Risk Management: A History* (London: Risk Books, 2003).

6. Modest, "An Internal Perspective."
7. André F. Perold, "Long-Term Capital Management L.P.," Harvard Business School Case 9-200-007, 1999.
8. In early 2007, as risk in the mortgage market increased, the haircut on mortgage-related assets posted as collateral could be as much as 10 percent, and it would go up from there as risk proceeded to build. Mark D. Griffiths, Vladimir Kotomin, and Drew B. Winters, "A Crisis of Confidence: Understanding Money Markets During the Financial Crisis," *Journal of Applied Finance* 22, no. 2 (2012): 39–59.
9. Gary B. Gorton, "Questions and Answers about the Financial Crisis," Presentation prepared for the Financial Crisis Inquiry Commission, Washington, DC, February 2010.
10. Peter Hördahl and Michael R. King, "Developments in Repo Markets During the Financial Turmoil," *BIS Quarterly Review*, December 2008: 37–53.
11. *New York Times*, October 15, 1998: C6.
12. President's Working Group on Financial Markets, "Hedge Funds, Leverage, and the Lessons of Long-Term Capital Management," Washington, DC, April 1999.
13. Ibid.
14. Jorion, "Medium-Term Risk Management."
15. Bank for International Settlements, "Recent Developments in Bond Markets. A Report to the Ministers and Governors by the Chairman of the Group of Deputies," Basel, Switzerland: BIS, April 1994: 2.
16. Harrison J. Goldin, "Final Report of Harrison J. Golden, Trustee to The Honorable Stuart M. Bernstein, Judge, United States Bankruptcy Court, Southern District of New York," In re Granite Partners, L.P., Granite Corporation and Quartz Hedge Fund, New York, April 18, 1996: 25.
17. Ibid.
18. Ibid.
19. Lowenstein, *When Genius Failed*: 110.
20. Ludwig B. Chincarini, *The Crisis of Crowding: Quant Copycats, Ugly Models, and the New Crash Normal* (Hoboken, NJ: Bloomberg Press, 2012).
21. Satyajit Das, "Liquidity Risk Part 3: Long-Term Capital Management," *Futures and Options World*, February 2002.
22. Jorion, "Risk Management Lessons."
23. David Shirreff, *Dealing With Financial Risk* (New York: Bloomberg Press, 2004).
24. President's Working Group, "Hedge Funds."

25. Chincarini, *The Crisis of Crowding.*
26. Dan Tudball, "Whodunit?" (interview with Robert C. Merton), *Wilmott Magazine*, May 2009.
27. William J. McDonough, "Statement before the U.S. House of Representatives Committee on Banking and Finance Services," Washington, DC, October 1, 1998.
28. *New York Times*, October 23, 1998: C22.
29. *Wall Street Journal*, September 25, 1998: C1.
30. *Wall Street Journal*, September 29, 1998: C1.
31. *New York Times*, September 30, 1998: C1.
32. *New York Times*, October 23, 1998: C22
33. *New York Times*, October 10, 1998: C2
34. *Wall Street Journal,* October 28, 1998: C1

## CHAPTER 9

1. Quoted in Donald MacKenzie, *An Engine, Not a Camera* (Cambridge, MA: MIT Press, 2006): 228.
2. Quoted in Michael Lewis, "How the Eggheads Cracked," *New York Times Magazine*, January 24, 1999.
3. Bruce I. Jacobs, *Capital Ideas and Market Realities: Option Replication, Investor Behavior, and Stock Market Crashes* (Malden, MA: Blackwell, 1999); Bruce I. Jacobs, "When Seemingly Infallible Arbitrage Strategies Fail," *Journal of Investing* 8, no. 1 (1999): 9–10.
4. Quoted in William Poundstone, *Fortune's Formula: The Untold Story of the Scientific Betting System that Beat the Casinos and Wall Street* (New York: Hill and Wang, 2005).
5. Myron S. Scholes, "The Near Crash of 1998: Crisis and Risk Management," *American Economic Review Papers and Proceedings* 90, no. 2 (2000): 17–21; David M. Modest, "Long-Term Capital Management: An Internal Perspective," Presentation to the Institute for Quantitative Research in Finance, Palm Springs, CA, October 18, 1999.
6. Quoted in Lewis, "How the Eggheads Cracked."
7. President's Working Group on Financial Markets, "Hedge Funds, Leverage, and the Lessons of Long-Term Capital Management," Washington, DC, April 1999.
8. Nicholas Dunbar, *Inventing Money: The Story of Long-Term Capital Management and the Legends Behind It* (New York: Wiley, 2000).
9. Andrei Shleifer and Robert W. Vishny, "The Limits of Arbitrage," *Journal of Finance* 52, no. 1 (1997): 35–55.
10. Markus K. Brunnermeier and Lasse H. Pedersen, "Market Liquidity and Funding Liquidity," *Review of Financial Studies* 22, no. 6 (2009): 2201–2238.
11. Quoted in Gregory Zuckerman, "Long-Term Capital Chief Acknowledges Flawed Tactics," *Wall Street Journal*, August 21, 2000.

12. *Wall Street Journal*, October 5, 1998: C1.
13. Franklin R. Edwards and Frederic S. Mishkin, "The Decline of Traditional Banking: Implications for Financial Stability and Regulatory Policy," *Federal Reserve Bank of New York Economic Policy Review* 1, no. 2 (1995): 27–45.
14. Henry Kaufman, "Structural Changes in the Financial Markets: Economic and Policy Significance," *Federal Reserve Bank of Kansas City Economic Review* 79, no. 2 (1994): 11.

## CHAPTER 10

1. Quoted in Tunku Varadarajan, "Wall Street's Fortune Teller," *Daily Beast*, May 13, 2010. Available at: www.thedailybeast.com/wall-streets-fortune-teller.
2. International Monetary Fund, "Global Financial Stability Report: Market Developments and Issues" (Washington, DC: IMF, 2006): 51.
3. Financial Crisis Inquiry Commission, *The Financial Crisis Inquiry Report: Final Report of the National Commission on the Causes of the Financial and Economic Crisis in the United States (Financial Crisis Inquiry Commission)* (New York: PublicAffairs, 2011): 15.
4. Gary B. Gorton, Andrew Metrick, and Lei Xie, "An Econometric Chronology of the Financial Crisis of 2007–2008," Working Paper, Yale School of Management, New Haven, CT, April 28, 2015.
5. Adair Turner, *Between Debt and the Devil: Money, Credit, and Fixing Global Finance* (Princeton, NJ: Princeton University Press, 2016).
6. Timothy F. Geithner, *Stress Test: Reflections on Financial Crises* (New York: Crown, 2014).
7. David Adler, *The New Economics of Liquidity and Financial Frictions* (Charlottesville, VA: CFA Institute Research Foundation, 2014); Arvind Krishnamurthy, Stefan Nagel, and Dmitry Orlov, "Sizing Up Repo," *Journal of Finance* 69, no. 6 (2014): 2381–2417.
8. Amir E. Khandani and Andrew W. Lo, "What Happened to the Quants in August 2007: Evidence from Factors and Transactions Data," *Journal of Financial Markets* 14, no. 1 (2011): 1–46.
9. Financial Crisis Inquiry Commission, *Report*: 288.
10. Rosalind Z. Wiggins, Thomas Piontek, and Andrew Metrick, "The Lehman Brothers Bankruptcy A: Overview," Yale Program on Financial Stability Case Study 2014-3A-V1, Yale School of Management, New Haven, CT, October 1, 2014.
11. Geithner, *Stress Test*.
12. *Wall Street Journal*, December 12–13, 2009.
13. Ben S. Bernanke, *The Federal Reserve and the Financial Crisis* (Princeton, NJ: Princeton University Press, 2013): 85.
14. The Group of Twenty includes Argentina, Australia, Brazil, Canada, China, the European Union, France, Germany, India, Indonesia, Italy, Japan,

Mexico, Russia, Saudi Arabia, South Africa, South Korea, Turkey, the United Kingdom, and the United States.

## CHAPTER 11

1. From a presentation to the Economic Club of New York, May 19, 2005.
2. Robert J. Shiller, *Irrational Exuberance*, 2nd ed. (Princeton, NJ: Princeton University Press, 2005).
3. Eli Ofek and Matthew Richardson, "DotCom Mania: The Rise and Fall of Internet Stock Prices," *Journal of Finance* 58, no. 3 (2003): 1113–1137.
4. Alan Greenspan, Presentation to the Annual Dinner and Francis Boyer Lecture of the American Enterprise Institute for Public Policy Research, Washington, DC, December 5, 1996. Available at: http://www.federalreserve.gov/boarddocs/speeches/1996/19961205.htm.
5. James K. Glassman and Kevin A. Hassett, "Dow 36,000," *The Atlantic,* September 1999.
6. In essence, momentum traders are trying to obtain the benefits of a call option without paying an option premium. See Bruce I. Jacobs, "Another 'Costless' Strategy Roils Market," *Pensions & Investments*, May 29, 2000; Bruce I. Jacobs, "Momentum Trading: The New Alchemy," *Journal of Investing* 9, no. 3 (2000): 6–7.
7. Jeremy J. Siegel, *Stocks For the Long Run* (Burr Ridge, IL: Irwin Professional Publishing, 1994).
8. Michael J. Brennan, "How Did It Happen?" *Economic Notes* 33, no. 1 (2004): 3–22.
9. Roger Lowenstein, *Origins of the Crash: The Great Bubble and Its Undoing* (New York: The Penguin Press, 2004): 125.
10. Ibid.: 211.
11. Robert F. Bruner, "The Dynamics of a Financial Dislocation: The Panic of 1907 and the Subprime Crisis," in L.B. Siegel, ed., *Insights into the Global Financial Crisis* (Charlottesville, VA: Research Foundation of the CFA Institute, 2009).
12. *Wall Street Journal*, December 12, 2007.
13. Carmen M. Reinhart and Kenneth S. Rogoff, *This Time is Different: Eight Centuries of Financial Folly* (Princeton, NJ: Princeton University Press, 2009).
14. *Financial Times*, July 2007.
15. John M. Keynes, *The General Theory of Employment, Interest, and Money* (London: Macmillan, 1936). Reprint, New York: Harcourt Brace, 1964.
16. Robert J. Shiller, "Investor Behavior in the October 1987 Stock Market Crash: Survey Evidence," in R.J. Shiller, *Market Volatility* (Cambridge, MA: MIT Press, 1989).
17. Bruner, "The Dynamics of a Financial Dislocation."
18. Viral V. Acharya, Matthew Richardson, Stijn Van Nieuwerburgh, and Lawrence J. White, *Guaranteed to Fail: Fannie Mae, Freddie Mac and the*

*Debacle of Mortgage Finance* (Princeton, NJ: Princeton University Press, 2011).

19. Reinhart and Rogoff, *This Time is Different.*
20. Adam B. Ashcraft and Til Schuermann, "Understanding the Securitization of Subprime Mortgage Credit," *Federal Reserve Bank of New York Foundations and Trends in Finance* 2, no. 3 (2008): 191–309.
21. Christopher Mayer, Karen Pence, and Shane M. Sherlund, "The Rise in Mortgage Defaults," *Journal of Economic Perspectives* 23, no. 1 (2009): 27–50.
22. Elsewhere, such as in Europe, lenders may have recourse to a defaulting borrower's non-housing assets. See Chapter 16, "The European Debt Crisis."
23. Gary B. Gorton, "The Panic of 2007," in *Maintaining Stability in a Changing Financial System, Proceedings of the 2008 Jackson Hole Conference* (Kansas City, MO: Federal Reserve Bank of Kansas City, 2008).
24. Acharya et al., *Guaranteed to Fail.*
25. Financial Crisis Inquiry Commission, *The Financial Crisis Inquiry Report: Final Report of the National Commission on the Causes of the Financial and Economic Crisis in the United States (Financial Crisis Inquiry Commission)* (New York: PublicAffairs, 2011).
26. Alan Greenspan, Testimony before the Financial Crisis Inquiry Commission Hearing on Subprime Lending and Securitization and Government-Sponsored Enterprises (GSEs), April 7, 2010.
27. Financial Crisis Inquiry Commission, *Report*: 123.
28. Acharya et al., *Guaranteed to Fail.*
29. Financial Crisis Inquiry Commission, *Report*: 312
30. Ibid.
31. Acharya et al., *Guaranteed to Fail.*
32. Financial Crisis Inquiry Commission, *Report*: 123.
33. Acharya et al., *Guaranteed to Fail.*
34. Financial Crisis Inquiry Commission, *Report*: 119.
35. In contrast, Adelino finds evidence that investors did not rely exclusively on credit ratings but considered the fundamentals underlying the individual mortgages in a pool. Manuel Adelino, "How Much Do Investors Rely on Credit Ratings? The Case of Mortgage Backed Securities," Working Paper, Sloan School of Management, Massachusetts Institute of Technology, 2009.
36. John Cassidy, *How Markets Fail: The Logic of Economic Calamities* (New York: Farrar, Straus and Giroux, 2009).
37. Bank for International Settlements, "The Role of Ratings in Structured Finance: Issues and Implications," Committee on the Global Financial System Working Group Report, Basel, Switzerland, BIS, January 14, 2005.
38. Randall S. Kroszner and Robert J. Shiller, *Reforming U.S. Financial Markets: Reflections Before and Beyond Dodd-Frank* (Cambridge, MA: MIT Press, 2011).

39. Securities and Exchange Commission, "Summary Report of Issues Identified in the Commission Staff's Examinations of Select Credit Rating Agencies," Office of Compliance Inspections and Examinations, Division of Trading and Markets and Office of Economic Analysis, SEC, July 2008.
40. Joshua D. Coval, Jakob W. Jurek, and Erik Stafford, "Re-Examining the Role of Rating Agencies: Lessons from Structured Finance," Working Paper, 2008.
41. Eric S. Rosengren, "Asset Bubbles and Systemic Risk," Presentation to the Global Interdependence Center Conference on Financial Interdependence in the World's Post-Crisis Capital Markets, Philadelphia, March 3, 2010.
42. Financial Crisis Inquiry Commission, *Report*: 121.
43. Bank for International Settlements, "Ratings in Structured Finance: What Went Wrong and What Can be Done to Address Shortcomings?" Committee on the Global Financial System Working Paper 32, July 2008.
44. Efraim Benmelech and Jennifer Duglosz, "The Credit Rating Crisis," *NBER Macroeconomics Annual* 24, no. 1 (2010): 161–208.
45. Bank for International Settlements, "Ratings in Structured Finance."
46. Financial Crisis Inquiry Commission, *Report*: 121.
47. Benmelech and Duglosz, "Credit Rating Crisis," for example, found that issues with one rating, as opposed to ratings from two or three of the CRAs, were problematic in terms of both the number and size of subsequent downgrades. This suggests that issuers may have engaged in "ratings shopping," selecting a ratings agency with laxer standards.
48. Efraim Benmelech and Jennifer Duglosz, "The Alchemy of CDO Credit Ratings," *Journal of Monetary Economics* 56, no. 6 (2009): 617–634.
49. Ashcraft and Schuermann, "Understanding the Securitization of Subprime Mortgage Credit."
50. Giovanni Dell'Ariccia, Deniz Igan, and Luc Laeven, "Credit Booms and Lending Standards: Evidence from the Subprime Mortgage Market," *Journal of Money, Credit and Banking* 44, no. 2–3 (2012).
51. Ashcraft and Schuermann, "Understanding the Securitization of Subprime Mortgage Credit."
52. Financial Crisis Inquiry Commission, *Report*: 96–97.
53. Ibid.: 94.
54. Ibid.: 95.
55. David Faber, *And Then the Roof Caved In: How Wall Street's Greed and Stupidity Brought Capitalism to Its Knees* (Hoboken, NJ: Wiley, 2009).
56. Yuliya Demyanyk, "Ten Myths about Subprime Mortgages," *Federal Reserve Bank of Cleveland Economic Commentary*, 2009.
57. Ashish Das and Roger M. Stein, "Underwriting Versus Economy: A New Approach to Decomposing Mortgage Losses," *Journal of Credit Risk* 5, no. 2 (2009): 19–41.

58. Reported in Diane Pendley, Glenn Costello, and Mark Kelsch, "The Impact of Poor Underwriting Practices and Fraud in Subprime RMBS Performance," Fitch Ratings Structured Finance US Mortgage Special Report, 2007.
59. Yuliya Demyanyk and Otto Van Hemert, "Understanding the Subprime Mortgage Crisis," *Review of Financial Studies* 24, no. 6 (2011): 1848–1880; Geetesh Bhardwaj and Rajdeep Sengupta, "Subprime Loan Quality," Working Paper 2008-036E, Research Division, Federal Reserve Bank of St. Louis, September 2011.
60. Adam B. Ashcraft, Paul Goldsmith-Pinkham, and James Vickery, "MBS Ratings and the Mortgage Credit Boom," Federal Reserve Bank of New York Staff Report 449, May 2010.
61. William D. Cohan, "How Wall Street Hid Its Mortgage Mess," Opinionator blog, *New York Times*, October 14, 2010. Available at: http://opinionator.blogs.nytimes.com/2010/10/14/how-wall-street-hid-its-mortgage-mess/.

## CHAPTER 12

1. Warren Buffett, chairman of the board of Berkshire Hathaway, is credited with popularizing the phrase "financial weapons of mass destruction," which he used in his February 21, 2003 letter to shareholders to describe derivatives. See *Berkshire Hathaway 2002 Annual Report*, available at: http://www.berkshirehathaway.com/2002ar/2002ar.pdf.
2. Janet M. Tavakoli, "Beware of Geeks Bearing Grifts," *Risk Professional*, December 2009.
3. The Government National Mortgage Association (Ginnie Mae) is another government corporation that facilitates mortgage lending. It neither issues nor buys mortgages or mortgage securitizations, but provides explicit US government guarantee of timely payments on the securitizations of select private lenders. Buyers of Ginnie Mae securities essentially take on no credit risk. If the underlying mortgages suffer defaults, the US government will cover any losses to the security holders. Buyers may, however, be exposed to interest rate risk and prepayment risk, depending upon the nature of the securities they have purchased.
4. Frank J. Fabozzi and Vinod Kothari, "Securitization: The Tool of Financial Transformation," Yale ICF Working Paper 07-07, Yale University, New Haven, CT, 2007.
5. This results in a relatively shorter duration for the senior tranche, another source of risk reduction. An unexpected increase in prepayments of mortgages in the pool will further shorten the durations of senior tranches.
6. Gary B. Gorton, "The Subprime Panic," *European Financial Management* 15, no. 10 (2009): 10–46.
7. Henry Tabe, *The Unravelling of Structured Investment Vehicles: How Liquidity Leaked Through SIVs. Lessons in Risk Management and Regulatory Oversight* (Chatham, Kent, UK: Thoth Capital, 2010).

8. Ibid.
9. Richard Stanton and Nancy Wallace, "The Bear's Lair: Indexed Credit Default Swaps and the Subprime Mortgage Crisis," *Review of Financial Studies* 24 (2011): 3250–3280.
10. Janet M. Tavakoli, *Structured Finance & Collateralized Debt Obligations*, 2nd ed. (Hoboken, NJ: Wiley, 2008).
11. *Wall Street Journal*, May 3, 2010.

## CHAPTER 13

1. From *Alice's Adventures in Wonderland*, Chapter VII, "A Mad Tea Party," in Lewis Carroll and Martin Gardner, *The Annotated Alice* (New York: Bramhall House, 1960): 102.
2. Adam B. Ashcraft and Til Schuermann, "Understanding the Securitization of Subprime Mortgage Credit," *Foundations and Trends in Finance* 2, no. 3 (2008): 191–309.
3. David Greenlaw, Jan Hatzius, Anil K. Kashyap, and Hyun Song Shin, "Leveraged Losses: Lessons from the Mortgage Market Meltdown," *Proceedings of the U.S. Monetary Policy Forum 2008*, 2008.
4. Ashcraft and Schuermann, "Understanding the Securitization of Subprime Mortgage Credit."
5. Souphala Chomsisengphet and Anthony Pennington-Cross, "The Evolution of the Subprime Mortgage Market," *Federal Reserve Bank of St. Louis Review*, January/February 2006.
6. Ibid.
7. Ibid.
8. Ibid.
9. Adam B. Ashcraft, Paul Goldsmith-Pinkham, and James Vickery, "MBS Ratings and the Mortgage Credit Boom," Federal Reserve Bank of New York Staff Report 449, May 2010; Chomsisengphet and Pennington-Cross, "The Evolution of the Subprime Mortgage Market."
10. William N. Goetzmann, Liang Peng, and Jacqueline Yen, "The Subprime Crisis and House Price Appreciation," *Journal of Real Estate and Economics* 44, no. 1–2 (2012).
11. Gorton argues that, in fact, lenders designed subprime loans in such a way as to give themselves a call option on the underlying equity. The mortgage contracts were designed to reset after two or three years to higher spreads over Libor (London Interbank Offered Rate, a widely used interest rate benchmark), and included prepayment penalties (relatively rare in prime mortgage contracts). In essence, these features tended to transfer the call option usually held by home buyers (the ability to refinance and extract equity from houses that have appreciated in value) to the mortgage lender. Gary B. Gorton, "The Subprime Panic," *European Financial Management* 15, no. 10 (2009): 10–46.

12. Federal Reserve Bank of San Francisco, "The Subprime Mortgage Market: National and Twelfth District Developments," *2007 Annual Report*, San Francisco, CA: FRBSF, 2008; Michel G. Crouhy, Robert A. Jarrow, and Stuart M. Turnbull, "The Subprime Credit Crisis of 07," *Journal of Derivatives* 16, no. 1 (2008).
13. Sheri Markose, Simone Giansante, and Ali Rais Saghaghi, "'Too Interconnected to Fail' Financial Network of US CDS Market: Topological Fragility and Systemic Risk," *Journal of Economic Behavior and Organizations* 83 (2012): 627–646.
14. Walter W. Eubanks, "The Basel Accords: The Implementation of II and the Modification of I," Library of Congress Congressional Research Service, Washington, DC, June 16, 2006.
15. International Monetary Fund, "Global Financial Stability Report: Containing Systemic Risks and Restoring Financial Soundness" (Washington, DC: IMF, 2008). Available at http://www.imf.org/external/pubs/ft/gfsr/2008/01/index.htm.
16. Bank for International Settlements, "The Role of Valuation and Leverage in Procyclicality," Committee on the Global Financial System Working Paper 34, April 2009.
17. Gary B. Gorton, *Slapped by the Invisible Hand: The Panic of 2007* (New York: Oxford University Press, 2010).
18. Eric Dash and Julie Creswell, "Citigroup Pays for a Rush to Risk," *New York Times*, November 23, 2008.
19. Gregory Zuckerman, *The Greatest Trade Ever: The Behind-the-Scenes Story of How John Paulson Defied Wall Street and Made Financial History* (New York: Broadway Books, 2009).
20. David Murphy, *Unravelling the Credit Crunch* (Boca Raton, FL: CRC Press, 2009).
21. UBS, "Shareholder Report on UBS's Write-Downs," 2008. Available at: www.ubs.com/1/ShowMedia/investors/shareholderreport?contentId=140333&name=080418ShareholderReport.pdf.
22. Federal Reserve Bank of San Francisco, "Subprime Mortgage Market."
23. Ibid.
24. Crouhy et al., "The Subprime Credit Crisis of 07."
25. Ashcraft and Schuermann, "Understanding the Securitization of Subprime Mortgage Credit."
26. Yuliya Demyanyk and Otto Van Hemert, "Understanding the Subprime Mortgage Crisis," *Review of Financial Studies* 24, no. 6 (2011): 1848–1880; Atif Mian and Amir Sufi, "The Consequences of Mortgage Credit Expansion: Evidence from the U.S. Mortgage Default Crisis," *Quarterly Journal of Economics* 124, no. 4 (2009): 1446–1496.
27. Demyanyk and Van Hemert, "Understanding the Subprime Mortgage Crisis."

28. Financial Crisis Inquiry Commission, *The Financial Crisis Inquiry Report: Final Report of the National Commission on the Causes of the Financial and Economic Crisis in the United States (Financial Crisis Inquiry Commission)* (New York: PublicAffairs, 2011): 88.
29. John Cassidy, *How Markets Fail: The Logic of Economic Calamities* (New York: Farrar, Strauss and Giroux, 2009).
30. Securities Industry and Financial Markets Association, Global CDO Issuance—Quarterly Data From 2000 to 2010. Available at: http://www.sifma.org/research/statistics.aspx.
31. Joseph R. Mason and Joshua Rosner, "Where Did the Risk Go? How Misapplied Bond Ratings Cause Mortgage Backed Securities and Collateralized Debt Obligation Market Disruption," Working Paper, May 14, 2007.
32. Bank for International Settlements, "Credit Risk Transfer: Developments from 2005 to 2007," Consultative Document, Basel, Switzerland, April 2008.
33. Ibid.
34. Janet M. Tavakoli, *Structured Finance & Collateralized Debt Obligations*, 2nd ed. (Hoboken, NJ: Wiley, 2008).
35. Charles W. Calomiris, "The Subprime Turmoil: What's Old, What's New, and What's Next," *Journal of Structured Finance* 15, no. 1 (2009); Gillian Tett, *Fool's Gold: How the Bold Dream of a Small Tribe at J. P. Morgan Was Corrupted* (New York: Simon & Schuster, 2009).
36. Crouhy et al., "The Subprime Credit Crisis of 07."
37. International Monetary Fund, "Global Financial Stability Report: Containing Systemic Risks and Restoring Financial Soundness."
38. Ashcraft and Schuermann, "Understanding the Securitization of Subprime Mortgage Credit."
39. CDOs with subprime RMBS were often perceived as more diversified than the underlying RMBS because the CDO tranches were backed by more geographically diverse mortgage pools. See Sarai Criado and Adrian Van Rixtel, "Structured Finance and the Financial Turmoil of 2007–2008: An Introductory Overview," Banco de España Occasional Paper 0808, September 2, 2008.
40. Kristopher Gerardi, Andreas Lehnert, Shane M. Sherlund, and Paul Willen, "Making Sense of the Subprime Crisis," *Brookings Papers on Economic Activity*, Fall 2008.
41. Keys et al. modeled securitization of mortgage loans and found that investors were not well protected in this regard: Mortgages likely to be chosen for securitization defaulted at a rate as much as 20 percent higher than that of mortgages with similar characteristics but with a lower probability of being securitized. Benjamin J. Keys, Tanmoy Mukherjee, Amit Seru, and Vikrant Vig, "Did Securitization Lead to Lax Screening? Evidence from Subprime Loans," *Quarterly Journal of Economics* 125, no. 1 (2010): 307–362.

42. Bruce I. Jacobs, "Momentum Trading: The New Alchemy," *Journal of Investing* 9, no. 3 (2000): 6–7.

## CHAPTER 14

1. The flaw Greenspan says he found was in his own belief that "free, competitive markets are by far the unrivaled way to organize economies. We have tried regulation; none meaningfully worked." See Alan Greenspan, Testimony before the Committee on Oversight and Government Reform, US House of Representatives, October 23, 2008.
2. The S&P/Case-Shiller US National Home Price Index shows stronger price rises and declines than the national home price index compiled by the Office of Federal Housing Enterprise Oversight (OFHEO), now the Federal Housing Finance Agency. OFHEO prices, for example, show a decline of only 7.9 percent between their April 2007 peak and the end of the third quarter of 2008. Office of Federal Housing Enterprise Oversight, "Mortgage Markets and the Enterprises in 2007," July 2008. Available at: www.fhfa.gov/PolicyProgramsResearch/Research/PaperDocuments/20080721_RP_Mortgage%20MarketsEnterprises_2007_N508.pdf. One of the notable differences between the two series is the S&P/Case-Shiller Home Price index's inclusion of more homes purchased with subprime lending.
3. Juerg M. Syz and Pauolo Vanini, "Property Derivatives and the Subprime Crisis," *Wilmott Journal* 1, no. 3 (2009): 163–166.
4. Dan Tudball, "Whodunit?" (interview with Robert C. Merton), *Wilmott Magazine*, May 2009.
5. Toby Daglish, "What Motivates a Subprime Borrower to Default?" *Journal of Banking & Finance* 33 (2009): 681–693.
6. According to one study, only 7.4 percent of homeowners surveyed would default strategically (that is, even if they could afford the mortgage payments) if the shortfall equaled 10 percent of the home's value; by contrast, 12.4 percent would default strategically if the shortfall were 40 percent to 50 percent. Luigi Guiso, Paola Sapienza, and Luigi Zingales, "The Determinants of Attitudes toward Strategic Default on Mortgages," *Journal of Finance* 68, no. 4 (2013): 1473–1515.
7. One study of 1999 foreclosures in Chicago suggests that each home within one-eighth of a mile from a foreclosed home declines in value by almost 1 percent. Dan Immergluck and Geoff Smith, "The External Costs of Foreclosure: The Impact of Single-Family Mortgage Foreclosures on Property Values," *Housing Policy Debate* 17, no. 1 (2006).
8. An analysis of foreclosures and house prices in the 2007–2009 period suggests that foreclosures in the United States led to a 33 percent fall in house prices. Atif Mian, Amir Sufi, and Francesco Trebbi, "Foreclosure, House Prices, and the Real Economy," *Journal of Finance* 70, no. 6 (2015): 2587–2633.

9. Guiso et al., "The Determinants of Attitudes toward Strategic Default on Mortgages."
10. Christopher Mayer, Karen Pence, and Shane M. Sherlund, "The Rise in Mortgage Defaults," *Journal of Economic Perspectives* 23, no. 1 (2009): 27–50.
11. Atif Mian and Amir Sufi, "Household Leverage and the Recession of 2007–09," *IMF Economic Review* 58, no. 1 (2010): 74–117.
12. See Adam B. Ashcraft and Til Schuermann, "Understanding the Securitization of Subprime Mortgage Credit," *Foundations and Trends in Finance* 2, no. 3 (2008): 191–309.
13. Michel G. Crouhy, Robert A. Jarrow, and Stuart M. Turnbull, "The Subprime Credit Crisis of 07," *Journal of Derivatives* 16, no. 1 (2008). Fitch downgraded an unprecedented number of subprime tranches in the third quarter of 2006; Charles W. Calomiris, "The Subprime Turmoil: What's Old, What's New, and What's Next," *Journal of Structured Finance* 15, no.1 (2009). In early July 2007, Moody's downgraded 399 subprime tranches; Ashcraft and Schuermann, "Understanding the Securitization of Subprime Mortgage Credit."
14. Richard R. Lindsey and Anthony P. Pecora, "10 Years After: Regulatory Developments in the Securities Markets Since the 1987 Market Break," *Journal of Financial Services Research* 13, no. 3 (1998): 283–314.
15. William D. Cohan, *House of Cards: A Tale of Hubris and Wretched Excess on Wall Street* (New York: Doubleday, 2009).
16. Bank for International Settlements, "Ratings in Structured Finance: What Went Wrong and What Can Be Done to Address Shortcomings," Committee on the Global Financial System, Working Paper 32, July 2008.
17. *Bloomberg News*, August 9, 2007.
18. Daniel Covitz, Nellie Liang, and Gustavo A. Suarez, "The Evolution of a Financial Crisis: Collapse of the Asset-Backed Commercial Paper Market," *Journal of Finance* 68, no. 3 (2013): 815–848.
19. Viral V. Acharya, Philipp Schnabl, and Gustavo Suarez, "Securitization Without Risk Transfer," *Journal of Financial Economics* 107, no. 3 (2013): 515–536; Steven Goldstein, "Update: HSBC to Provide $35 Billion in Funds to Structured Vehicles," *MarketWatch*, November 26, 2007. Available at: http://www.marketwatch.com/story/hsbc-to-provide-35-billion-in-funds-to-structured-vehicles-2007-11-26; Liz Moyer, "Citigroup Goes It Alone to Rescue SIVs," *Forbes*, December 13, 2007.
20. Bank for International Settlements, "Ratings in Structured Finance."
21. International Monetary Fund, "Financial Stress and Deleveraging: Macro-Financial Implications and Policy" (Washington, DC: IMF, October 2008). Available at: http://www.imf.org/external/pubs/ft/gfsr/2008/02/index.htm.
22. Bank for International Settlements, "Ratings in Structured Finance."

23. UBS, "Shareholder Report on UBS's Write-Downs," 2008. Available at www.ubs.com/1/ShowMedia/investors/shareholderreport?contentID=140333&name=080418ShSHareholderReport.pdf.
24. *Wall Street Journal*, December 27, 2007; Jeffrey Friedman and Wladimir Kraus, *Engineering the Financial Crisis: Systemic Risk and the Failure of Regulation* (Philadelphia: University of Pennsylvania Press, 2011).
25. Goldman had started pulling back in 2006 and sold $6 billion worth of subprime mortgage-related securities in 2007. Credit Suisse had downsized its securitization business by 22 percent in 2006; *New York Times*, December 6, 2007.
26. In its defense, Goldman said that it had lost as much as $100 million, net of the $15 million it made in fees from Paulson; *Wall Street Journal*, April 20, 2010. But these losses appear to have resulted from the firm's failure to find buyers for all portions of the deal; *New York Times*, April 21, 2010.
27. UBS allegedly worked with New York money manager Tricadia Capital to create CDOs that included assets that Tricadia-affiliated funds were betting against. In 2005–2006, according to a civil suit, Merrill Lynch, with hedge fund Magnetar Capital, set up a CDO that Magnetar Capital subsequently bet against. *Wall Street Journal*, April 19, 2010. The US unit of Deutsche Bank also created CDOs that its hedge fund clients bet against. The SEC subsequently subpoenaed Citigroup, Deutsche Bank, J. P. Morgan Chase, Morgan Stanley, and UBS while looking into CDOs created with the support of hedge funds and other investors betting against the securities in the deals.
28. Jake Bernstein and Jesse Eisinger, "Banks' Self-Dealing Super-Charged Financial Crisis," *ProPublica*, August 26, 2010.
29. Securities Industry and Financial Markets Association, Global CDO Issuance—Quarterly Data From 2000 to 2010. Available at: http://www.sifma.org/research/statistics.aspx. Issuance of RMBS and CDOs would lag mortgage originations, as it might take two to six months to package the securities.
30. Allan N. Krinsman, "Subprime Mortgage Meltdown: How Did It Happen and How Will It End?" *Journal of Structured Finance* 13, no. 2 (2007): 13–29.
31. Gary B. Gorton, *Slapped by the Invisible Hand: The Panic of 2007* (New York: Oxford University Press, 2010).
32. Financial Crisis Inquiry Commission, *The Financial Crisis Inquiry Report: Final Report of the National Commission on the Causes of the Financial and Economic Crisis in the United States (Financial Crisis Inquiry Commission)* (New York: Public Affairs, 2011): 240.
33. Lewis S. Ranieri is widely credited with creating mortgage-backed securities in the 1970s while at investment bank Salomon Brothers. In a 2017 interview, he said he and other MBS creators never imagined that credit rating agencies and regulators would allow MBS to evolve into a "Frankenstein." See

"I Blew Up the World: War Stories" (video), *Institutional Investor*, November 9, 2017. Available at: https://www.institutionalinvestor.com/article/b160qlmj90f9g7/i-blew-up-the-world-war-stories?utm_medium=email&utm_campaign=The%20Essential%20II%20Daily%2012132017&utm_content=The%20Essential%20II%20Daily%2012132017%20CID_582a28f5e8089b5ad239195686ddb504&utm_source=CampaignMonitorEmail&utm_term=I%20Blew%20Up%20the%20World%20War%20Stories.

34. *New York Times*, March 16, 2008.
35. Cohan, *House of Cards*.
36. *Wall Street Journal*, March 17, 2008.
37. Gary B. Gorton and Andrew Metrick, "Securitized Banking and the Run on Repo," *Journal of Financial Economics* 104, no. 3 (2012): 425–451.
38. Some supporters of CDS suggest that the contribution of CDS to the credit crisis has been exaggerated; Peter J. Wallison, "Everything You Wanted to Know About Credit Default Swaps: But Were Never Told," *Journal of Structured Finance* 15, no. 2 (2009). One argument is that CDS commitments are offsetting. As each short position is matched by a long position, there is no net exposure for the system. Thus the notional amount of CDS contracts, which counts the full value of the debt referenced by both long and short positions, grossly overstates the risk exposure of these derivatives. But this does not account for the distribution of positions, which is not perfectly balanced. A dealer selling protection to one bank will generally execute a contract to buy a like amount of protection from another bank or hedge fund. But individual banks, hedge funds, insurers, and asset managers are likely to have net long or short positions. As the credit crisis unfolded, the largest banks were, as a whole, net buyers of protection, but some parties only bought and some, monolines for example, were net sellers of protection. Sheri Markose, Simone Giansante, Mateusz Gatkowski, and Ali Rais Shaghaghi, "Too Interconnected to Fail: Financial Contagion and Systematic Risk in Network Model of CDS and Other Credit Enhancement Obligations of US Banks," University of Essex Discussion Paper Series 683, February 2010.
39. René M. Stulz, "Credit Default Swaps and the Credit Crisis," *Journal of Economic Perspectives* 24, no. 1 (2010): 73–92.
40. A study by Chen et al. suggests that monoline and multiline sellers of credit insurance (CDS) have relatively high systematic risk because their performance is closely linked to that of the assets they insure; the study finds that, indeed, the correlation between these insurers and the banking sector increased by about half during the crisis. Fang Chen, Xuanjuan Chen, Zhenzhen Sun, Tong Yu, and Ming Zhong, "Systemic Risk, Financial Crisis, and Credit Risk Insurance," *Financial Review* 48 (2013): 417–442.
41. Markose et al., "Too Interconnected to Fail."
42. Crouhy et al., "The Subprime Credit Crisis of 07."

43. *Bloomberg News*, June 20, 2008.
44. Christine S. Richard, *Confidence Game: How Hedge Fund Manager Bill Ackman Called Wall Street's Bluff* (Hoboken, NJ: Wiley, 2010).
45. Ibid.
46. *Wall Street Journal*, August 1, 2008.
47. *Wall Street Journal*, September 8, 2008.
48. In 2007, Lehman Brothers' commercial and residential real estate assets, including MBS and CDOs, more than doubled in value to over $110 billion, or some four times the firm's equity; Rosalind Z. Wiggins and Andrew Metrick, "The Lehman Brothers Bankruptcy G: The Special Case of Derivatives," Yale Program on Financial Stability Case Study 2014-3G-V1, Yale School of Management, New Haven, CT, April 7, 2015.
49. Rosaline Z. Wiggins, Thomas Piontek, and Andrew Metrick, "The Lehman Brothers Bankruptcy A: Overview," Yale Program on Financial Stability Case Study 2014-3A-V1, Yale School of Management, New Haven, CT, October 1, 2014.
50. *Bloomberg News*, September 24, 2008.
51. Anton R. Valukas, "Report of Examiner Anton R. Valukas in re Lehman Brothers Holdings Inc., et al.," United States Bankruptcy Court Southern District of New York, Chapter 11 Case 08-13555 (JPM), 2010.
52. *Wall Street Journal*, October 6, 2008.
53. See, for example, Satyajit Das, "In the Matter of Lehman Brothers," *Wilmott Magazine*, May 20–28, 2012.
54. *Bloomberg News*, November 4, 2008. The DTCC data likely underestimated the full impact of Lehman Brothers' demise, however, because not all contracts were settled through the DTCC. There are estimates that CDS contracts on Lehman really totaled $200 billion to over $400 billion, including structured products sold by unrelated banks and brokers. See Wiggins and Metrick, "The Lehman Brothers Bankruptcy G," who estimate that losses on derivatives amounted to some $33 billion. See also Das, "In the Matter of Lehman Brothers."
55. *New York Times*, September 27, 2008.
56. Stulz, "Credit Default Swaps and the Credit Crisis."
57. Andrew Sullivan, "AIG's Failure Is So Much Bigger Than Enron," *The Motley Fool*, September 17, 2008.
58. Robert McDonald and Anna Paulson, "AIG in Hindsight," *Journal of Economic Perspectives* 29, no. 2 (2015): 81–106.
59. *Bloomberg News*, September 24, 2008.
60. *New York Times*, September 27, 2008.
61. *Wall Street Journal*, September 17, 2008.
62. Jeffrey Rosenberg, "Toward a Clear Understanding of the Systemic Risks of Large Institutions," *Journal of Credit Risk* 5, no. 2 (2009): 77–85.
63. *Wall Street Journal*, September 17, 2008.

64. Michael J. de la Merced, Vikas Bajaj, and Andrew Ross Sorkin, "As Goldman and Morgan Shift, a Wall Street Era Ends," DealBook blog, *New York Times*, September 21, 2008.
65. *Wall Street Journal*, September 20–21, 2008.
66. *Wall Street Journal*, October 10, 2008.
67. *Wall Street Journal*, September 20–21, 2008.
68. Richard Stanton and Nancy Wallace, "The Bear's Lair: Indexed Credit Default Swaps and the Subprime Mortgage Crisis," *Review of Financial Studies* 24 (2011): 3250–3280.
69. Hyun Song Shin, "Securitisation and Financial Stability," *Economic Journal* 119, no. 536 (2009): 309–332.
70. Anand M. Goel, Fengshua Song, and Anjan V. Thakor, "Correlated Leverage and Its Ramifications," *Journal of Financial Intermediation* 23 (2014): 471–503.
71. Yuliya Demyanyk and Otto Van Hemert, "Understanding the Subprime Mortgage Crisis," *Review of Financial Studies* 24, no. 6 (2011): 1848–1880.

## CHAPTER 15

1. From the Office of Financial Research, *2012 Annual Report* (Washington, DC: US Department of the Treasury, 2012).
2. *New York Times*, May 23, 2012.
3. Timothy F. Geithner, *Stress Test: Reflections on Financial Crises* (New York: Crown, 2014).
4. Omar Masood, "Balance Sheet Exposures Leading Toward the Credit Crunch in Global Investment Banks," *Journal of Credit Risk* 5, no. 2 (2009): 57–75.
5. There is a large body of literature on the transmission of financial shocks to the real economy. See Ben S. Bernanke, Mark Gertler, and Simon Gilchrist, "The Financial Accelerator in a Quantitative Business Cycle Framework," in J.B. Taylor and M. Woodford, eds., *Handbook of Macroeconomics, Volume I* (Amsterdam: Elsevier, 1999); Markus K. Brunnermeier and Yuliy Sannikov, "A Macroeconomic Model with a Financial Sector," *American Economic Review* 104, no. 2 (2014): 379–421. Some studies of the credit crisis indicate that disruptions in the financial sector led to illiquidity that hampered research and development at the company level (Pablo Guerron-Quintana and Ryo Jinnai, "Liquidity, Trends, and The Great Recession," Federal Reserve Bank of Philadelphia Working Paper 14-24, August 21, 2014); declines in industrial production (Stefan Mittnik and Willi Semmler, "Overleveraging, Financial Fragility and the Banking-Macro Link: Theory and Empirical Evidence," Center for European Economic Research Discussion Paper 14-110, November 20, 2014); and increases in unemployment in manufacturing (Samuel Haltenhof, Seung Jung Lee, and Viktors Stebunovs, "Bank Lending Channels During the Great Recession," Federal Reserve Board, October 15,

2013), particularly for small firms (Burcu Duygan-Bump, Alexey Levkov, and Judit Montoriol-Garriga, "Financing Constraints and Unemployment: Evidence from the Great Recession," Finance and Economics Discussion Series, Divisions of Research and Statistics and Monetary Affairs, Federal Reserve Board, Washington, DC, 2014).

6. *Wall Street Journal*, June 1, 2011.
7. *Wall Street Journal*, December 29, 2013.
8. Alfred Gottschalck, Marina Vornovitsky, and Adam Smith, "Household Wealth in the U.S.: 2000–2011," US Census Bureau, December 16, 2016.
9. Between 2001 and 2004, as home prices rose, 45 percent of US homeowners with mortgages refinanced them; one-third of these extracted equity from their homes; Gerald F. Davis, *Managed By the Markets: How Finance Re-Shaped America* (New York: Oxford University Press, 2009).
10. Demyanyk et al. find that housing wealth was an important determinant of consumer spending both in the housing bubble and the following recession; Yuliya Demyanyk, Dmytro Hryshko, Maria José Luengo-Prado, and Bent E. Sørensen, "The Rise and Fall of Consumption in the '00s," Federal Reserve Bank of Boston, October 16, 2015. Fair, too, traces the slow recovery to the fall in household wealth and spending; Ray C. Fair, "The Financial Crisis and Macroeconomic Activity: 2008–2013," Cowles Foundation Discussion Paper 1944, Yale University, New Haven, CT, February 2015.
11. Frank Nothaft, "Single-Family Mortgage Default Rate Falls to pre-Recession Level," CoreLogic Insights blog, June 2, 2016. Available at: http://www.corelogic.com/blog/authors/frank-nothaft/2016/06/single-family-mortgage-default-rate-falls-to-pre-recession-level.aspx#.WjrCwlWnGM8.
12. *Wall Street Journal*, August 11, 2014.
13. Bill McBride, "Black Knight: Mortgage 'Origination Volumes in 2016 Highest Level Seen in Nine Years'," Calculated Risk, March 9, 2017. Available at: www.calculatedriskblog.com/2017/03/black-knight-mortgage-origination.html.
14. The American Stock Exchange, now known as NYSE American, was acquired in 2008 by NYSE Euronext, which was formed by the 2007 merger of the New York Stock Exchange and Euronext. In 2013, NYSE Euronext was acquired by Intercontinental Exchange.
15. Commodity Futures Trading Commission and Securities and Exchange Commission, "Findings Regarding the Market Events of May 6, 2010: Report of the Staffs of the CFTC and SEC to the Joint Advisory Committee on Emerging Regulatory Issues" (Washington, DC: CFTC and SEC, September 30, 2010).
16. Mary L. Schapiro, "Testimony Concerning the Severe Market Disruption on May 6, 2010," Testimony Before the Subcommittee on Capital Markets, Insurance and Government-Sponsored Enterprises of the United States House of Representatives Committee on Financial Services, May 11, 2010.

17. *Wall Street Journal*, April 22, 2015, April 23, 2015, and May 7, 2015.
18. Sarao's firm and US authorities have had difficulties locating the funds, however, which seem to be distributed among several questionable ventures and difficult-to-access offshore accounts. See Liam Vaughan, "How the Flash Crash Trader's $50 Million Fortune Vanished," *Bloomberg Markets*, February 9, 2017; available at: www.bloomberg.com/news/features/2017-02-10/how-the-flash-crash-trader-s-50-million-fortune-vanished.
19. *New York Times*, October 20, 2011.
20. *Wall Street Journal*, September 3–4, 2011; *New York Times*, June 11, 2012.
21. Philip Mattera, *The $160 Billion Bank Fee: What Violation Tracker 2.0 Shows About Penalties Imposed on Major Financial Offenders* (Washington, DC: GoodJobsFirst.Org, 2016).
22. *Wall Street Journal*, December 7, 2011.
23. *Wall Street Journal*, September 29–30, 2012.
24. *Wall Street Journal*, March 18, 2013; Associated Press, April 7, 2014.
25. *Wall Street Journal*, December 14, 2011.
26. *Wall Street Journal*, July 16, 2014.
27. Government prosecutors and regulators brought charges related to the 2007–2008 crisis against 47 employees of Wall Street's 10 largest banks. Most of those charged pleaded guilty or settled civil cases. Of 11 cases that went to trial, the government won convictions in only five, and at least one conviction was overturned on appeal. See *Wall Street Journal*, May 27, 2016. Executives at smaller banks with assets of $10 billion or less did not fare as well. At least 59 were convicted of crisis-era crimes, including fraud cases related to the Troubled Asset Relief Program (TARP). Thirty-five were sentenced to prison. See CNNMoney, April 28, 2016.
28. *Wall Street Journal*, August 6–7, 2011.
29. *New York Times*, September 30, 2010.
30. Bloomberg.com, February 21, 2017; Reuters, February 20, 2018.
31. *Wall Street Journal*, July 22, 2015.
32. *New York Times*, July 3, 2012.
33. "Free Speech or Knowing Misrepresentation?" *Economist*, February 5, 2013.
34. Department of Justice, "Justice Department and State Partners Secure $1.375 Billion Settlement with S&P for Defrauding Investors in Lead Up to the Financial Crisis," Department of Justice Office of Public Affairs, February 3, 2015.
35. Department of Justice, "Justice Department and State Partners Secure Nearly $864 Million Settlement with Moody's Arising from Conduct in the Lead Up to the Financial Crisis," Department of Justice Office of Public Affairs, January 13, 2017.
36. Office of the Comptroller of the Currency, Federal Reserve System, and Federal Deposit Insurance Corporation, "Regulatory Capital Rules: Regulatory Capital, Enhanced Supplementary Leverage Ratio Standards for Certain

Bank Holding Companies and Their Subsidiary Insured Depository Institutions Final Rule," *Federal Register* 79, no. 84 (2014).

37. Satyajit Das, noted in Jesse Eisinger, "In Trading Scandal, a Reason to Enforce the Volcker Rule," *New York Times*, September 28, 2011.
38. *New York Times*, May 12, 2012.
39. *Wall Street Journal*, May 16, 2012.
40. Andrew Ross Sorkin, "At JP Morgan, 'Perfect Hedge' Still Elusive," *New York Times*, May 15, 2012.
41. *New York Times*, April 19, 2012.
42. Jack Bao, Maureen O'Hara, and Alex Zhou, "The Volcker Rule and Market-Making in Times of Stress," Federal Reserve Board, December 2016; Satyajit Das, "Crash Course or the Cascade of Financial Woes," *Wilmott Magazine*, November 2016.
43. Rama Cont, "Central Clearing and Risk Transformation," *Financial Stability Review (Banque de France)* 21, April (2017).
44. "Machines Had Their Fingerprints All Over a Dow Rout for the Ages," *Bloomberg News*, February 5, 2018; "Stock Plunge Deepens in Asia After a U.S. Sell-Off: Markets Wrap," *Bloomberg News*, February 6, 2018.
45. "How Two Tiny Volatility Products Helped Fuel Sudden Stock Slump," *Bloomberg News*, February 7, 2018; "VIX at 38 Is Waterloo for Short Vol Trade That Everyone Adored," *Bloomberg News*, February 6, 2018.
46. "System Outages Leave Retail Investors Fuming," *Financial Times*, February 5, 2018.
47. Originally based on the S&P 100 index, the VIX has been based on the S&P 500 index since 2003. Volatility expectations are for a 30-day period and are derived by inputting prices paid for options on the S&P 500 index into the Black-Scholes-Merton options pricing model. See Chapter 3, "Replicating Options."
48. "VIX at 38 Is Waterloo for Short Vol Trade That Everyone Adored."
49. "VIX May Form 'Mother of All Inverted Vs' as Positioning Calms," *Bloomberg News*, February 7, 2018.
50. Bhansali and Harris noted that endowments and pension funds sell options to improve investment yields, and managers of large institutional investment portfolios sell options to augment returns and thereby attract more assets. When it works, option-selling strategies offer positive expected returns and high Sharpe ratios. From the clients' vantage point, the income provided by these strategies is indistinguishable from returns earned by the managers' stated investment objective. Vineer Bhansali and Lawrence Harris, "Everybody's Doing It: Short Volatility Strategies and Shadow Financial Insurers," *Financial Analysts Journal,* 74, 2 (2018): 12–23.
51. Correlations are often incorporated to equalize risk contributions so that all asset classes have the same marginal contribution to the total risk of the portfolio.
52. Bhansali and Harris, "Everybody's Doing It."

53. "The Unstoppable Rise of Trading Market Volatility," *Financial Times*, February 9, 2018.
54. "How Two Tiny Volatility Products Helped Fuel Sudden Stock Slump."
55. Ibid. This figure likely includes purchases by large institutional investors of assets with embedded option-like characteristics, such as mortgage-backed securities. A low-volatility environment dampens these securities' substantial prepayment and default risks. See Bhansali and Harris, "Everybody's Doing It."
56. "Wall Street's Volatility Products in the Spotlight," *Financial Times*, March 5, 2018.
57. "VIX-Related Fund Did Go 'Poof'," *Wall Street Journal*, March 5, 2018.
58. "BIS Says Volatility Funds 'Amplified' Equity Turmoil in February," *Financial Times*, March 12, 2018.
59. M. Kolanovic and B. Kaplan, "Flash Crash, Flows, and Investment Opportunities—ALERT," JP Morgan market commentary, February 5, 2018.
60. "Quant-Blame Game, 'Crack Analysis' Behind the Flash Crash," *Bloomberg News*, February 6, 2018.
61. "Credit Suisse and Nomura Liquidate ETN Products Amid Market Volatility," *Financial Times*, February 6, 2018.
62. "VIX-Related Fund Did Go 'Poof'."

## CHAPTER 16

1. Quoted in *Bloomberg News*, June 19, 2011.
2. Claudio Borio and Piti Disyatat, "Global Imbalances and the Financial Crisis: Link or No Link?" Bank for International Settlements Working Paper 346, May 2011.
3. The European Union has 28 members, 19 of which have adopted the euro. The currency bloc began with 11 members: Belgium, Germany, Spain, France, Ireland, Italy, Luxembourg, the Netherlands, Austria, Portugal, and Finland. They were joined by Greece in 2001, Slovenia in 2007, Cyprus and Malta in 2008, Slovakia in 2009, Estonia in 2011, Latvia in 2014, and Lithuania in 2015. Nine EU members maintain their own currencies: Bulgaria, Croatia, Czech Republic, Denmark, Hungary, Poland, Romania, Sweden, and the United Kingdom (UK). In 2016, UK voters approved a ballot measure calling for an exit from the European Union—Brexit—although the United Kingdom remains an EU member while details of its departure are negotiated.
4. A 1997 agreement, the Stability and Growth Pact, bound all members of the currency bloc to those same spending and debt limits on an ongoing basis and called for significant financial penalties against violators. But it was not vigorously enforced.
5. Jacob F. Kirkegaard, "The Euro Area Crisis: Origin, Current Status, and European and U.S. Responses," Testimony before the US House Committee on Foreign Affairs Subcommittee on Europe and Eurasia, October 27, 2011.

6. Rebecca M. Nelson, Paul Belkin, and Derek E. Mix, "Greece's Debt Crisis: Overview, Policy Responses, and Implications," Congressional Research Service Report 7-5700, Washington, DC, August 18, 2011.
7. Ashoka Mody and Damiano Sandri, "The Eurozone Crisis: How Banks and Sovereigns Came to be Joined at the Hip," *Economic Policy* 27, no. 70 (2012): 199–230.
8. Paul De Grauwe, "Fighting the Wrong Enemy," *Vox,* May 19, 2010. Available at: http://www.voxeu.org/index.php?q=node/5062; Hans-Joachim Dübel and Marc Rothemund, "A New Mortgage Credit Regime for Europe: Setting the Right Priorities," Centre for European Policy Studies Special Report, June 2011.
9. Frank Nothaft, "The Boom, the Bubble, and the Bust Abroad," Freddie Mac Executive Perspectives Blog, February 14, 2011. Available at: http://www.freddiemac.com/news/blog/frank_nothaft/20110214_boom_bubble_and_bust_abroad.html.
10. Daniel Gros, "Is Europe's Housing Market Next?" *Project Syndicate*, February 8, 2008.
11. Although, as noted in Chapter 12, the US government did not explicitly guarantee securities issued by Fannie Mae and Freddie Mac.
12. Direct government support for housing in Europe had been shrinking since the 1990s (Dübel and Rothemund, "New Mortgage Credit Regime"). Despite the pullback, Spain, Ireland, and the United Kingdom had home ownership rates that exceeded that of the United States. Other western European countries had lower ownership rates than the United States, in part because of strong government support for middle-class rental housing. Michael Lea, "Alternative Forms of Mortgage Finance: What Can We Learn From Other Countries?" Paper prepared for Harvard Joint Center for Housing Studies National Symposium, April 2010.
13. Ibid.
14. European Central Bank, "Housing Finance in the Euro Area," ECB Occasional Paper Series 101, March 2009; Dübel and Rothemund, "New Mortgage Credit Regime."
15. European Central Bank, "Housing Finance in the Euro Area."
16. Lea, "Alternative Forms of Mortgage Finance."
17. European Central Bank, "Housing Finance in the Euro Area."
18. Lea, "Alternative Forms of Mortgage Finance."
19. Ibid.
20. European Central Bank, "The Incentive Structure of the 'Originate and Distribute' Model" (Frankfurt am Main, Germany: ECB, December 2008).
21. Ibid.
22. European Central Bank, "EU Banks' Funding Structures and Policies" (Frankfurt am Main, Germany: ECB, May 2009).

23. Naohiko Baba, Robert N. McCauley, and Srichander Ramaswamy, "US Dollar Money Market Funds and Non-US Banks," *BIS Quarterly Review*, March 2009: 65–81.
24. Ibid.
25. Bank for International Settlements, "79th Annual Report" (Basel, Switzerland: BIS, June 2009).
26. Viral V. Acharya and Philipp Schnabl, "Do Global Banks Spread Global Imbalances? Asset-Backed Commercial Paper During the Financial Crisis of 2007–09," *IMF Economic Review* 58, no. 1 (2010): 37–73.
27. Baba et al., "US Dollar Money Market Funds."
28. Ibid.
29. Ibid.
30. *New York Times*, August 9, 2007.
31. Hyun Song Shin, "Reflections on Northern Rock: The Bank Run that Heralded the Global Financial Crisis," *Journal of Economic Perspectives* 23, no. 1 (2009): 101–119.
32. The British government took over the failing lender in February 2008.
33. Shin, "Reflections on Northern Rock."
34. Kirkegaard, "Euro Area Crisis." However, the difference in the average leverage ratio between European and US banks in part reflected US banks' off-balance-sheet treatment of many assets and US accounting rules that allowed banks to report the net amount of long and short positions in derivatives contracts.
35. European Central Bank, "EU Banks' Funding Structures."
36. Patrick McGuire and Goetz von Peter, "The Dollar Shortage in Global Banking and the International Policy Response," *International Finance* 15, no. 2 (2012): 155–178.
37. European Central Bank, "EU Banks' Funding Structures."
38. Tanju Yorulmazer, "Case Studies on Disruptions During the Crisis," *FBRNY Economic Policy Review* 20, no. 1 (2014): 17–28.
39. Bank for International Settlements, "Annual Report."
40. Nicolas Véron, "The European Debt and Financial Crisis: Origins, Options, and Implications for the U.S. and Global Economy," Testimony before the US Senate Committee on Banking, Housing, and Urban Affairs Subcommittee on Security and International Trade and Finance, September 22, 2011.
41. Eurozone countries have since established within the ECB a joint regulatory agency, the Single Supervisory Mechanism (SSM), which assumed supervisory duties over large banks from national authorities in November 2014. The Frankfurt-based SSM is governed by a Brussels-based decision-making body, the Single Resolution Board, which would handle the resolution of failing banks and have the authority to force bank bondholders to absorb losses. The creation of these structures appeared to signal an intent to move away

from direct government bailouts of failing banks. Nicolas Véron, "Europe's Radical Banking Union," Bruegel Essay and Lecture Series, May 2015. Still, the Italian government committed 17 billion euros to bail out two regional banks in 2017 rather than force bondholders to absorb the losses under the resolution mechanism (*Wall Street Journal*, June 26, 2017).

42. Véron, "European Debt and Financial Crisis."
43. International Monetary Fund, "European Union: Publication of Financial Sector Assessment Program; Documentation—Technical Note on Progress with Bank Restructuring and Resolution in Europe," IMF Country Report 13/67, March 2013.
44. Barry Eichengreen, *Hall of Mirrors: The Great Depression, the Great Recession, and the Uses—and Misuses—of History* (New York: Oxford University Press, 2015).
45. Viral V. Acharya and Sascha Steffen, "Analyzing Systemic Risk of the European Banking Sector," in J.-P. Foque and J.A. Langsam, eds., *Handbook on Systemic Risk* (New York: Cambridge University Press, 2013).
46. European Mortgage Federation, "Hypostat 2008: A Review of Europe's Mortgage and Housing Markets" (Brussels: EMF, November 2009).
47. Véron, "European Debt and Financial Crisis."
48. Arthur L. Centonze, "The Irish Banking Crisis," *Review of Business and Finance Studies* 5, no. 2 (2014).
49. Viral V. Acharya, Itamar Drechsler, and Philipp Schnabl, "A Pyrrhic Victory? Bank Bailouts and Sovereign Credit Risk," *Journal of Finance* 69, no. 6 (2014).
50. Nelson et al., "Greece's Debt Crisis."
51. Esteban Pérez-Caldentey and Matias Vernengo, "The Euro Imbalances and Financial Deregulation: A Post-Keynesian Interpretation of the European Debt Crisis," Levy Economics Institute of Bard College Working Paper 702, January 2012.
52. Gunther Tichy, "The Sovereign Debt Crisis: Causes and Consequences," *Austrian Economic Quarterly* 17, no. 2 (2012): 95–107.
53. International Monetary Fund, "European Union: Publication of Financial Sector Assessment Program; Documentation—Technical Note on Financial Integration and Fragmentation in the European Union," IMF Country Report 13/71, March 2013.
54. Fernando M. Martin and Christopher J. Waller, "Sovereign Debt: A Modern Greek Tragedy," *Federal Reserve Bank of St. Louis Annual Report 2011* (2012): 4–17.
55. Nelson et al., "Greece's Debt Crisis." Hungary, Latvia, and Romania also received loans under a longstanding EU aid program for non-eurozone countries; Javier Villar Burke, "The Financial Crisis and the EU Response B: Supporting the Financial System and Sovereigns Under Financial Stress," European Commission, August 2014.

56. *New York Times*, December 8, 2011.
57. Sergey Chernenko and Adi Sunderam, "Frictions in Shadow Banking: Evidence from the Lending Behavior of Money Market Mutual Funds," *Review of Financial Studies* 26, no. 6 (2014).
58. Martin and Waller, "Sovereign Debt."
59. *New York Times*, January 16, 2012.
60. *New York Times*, February 7, 2012.
61. Jeromin Zettelmeyer, Christoph Trebesch, and Mitu Gulati, "The Greek Debt Restructuring: An Autopsy," *Economic Policy* 28, no. 75 (2013): 513–563.
62. *New York Times*, March 24, 2012.
63. *New York Times*, April 19, 2012.
64. *Wall Street Journal*, December 9, 2011.
65. *New York Times*, June 4, 2012.
66. *Wall Street Journal*, August 15, 2012.
67. *New York Times*, March 1, 2012.
68. *New York Times*, January 21, 2012.
69. *Wall Street Journal*, November 29, 2012.
70. Or it could be argued, perhaps cynically, that banks and other non-government investors acted quite rationally, assuming (correctly) they would be bailed out if catastrophe struck, a moral hazard.

## CHAPTER 17

1. Opening quotation from a presentation to the American Institute for Economic Research, June 25, 2009.
2. Hersh Shefrin, *Beyond Greed and Fear: Understanding Behavioral Finance and the Psychology of Investing* (Boston: Harvard Business School Press, 2000). For a brief discussion of behavioral finance and its relationship to neoclassical finance, see "Economic Theories of Crashes" in Chapter 2.
3. Hyman P. Minsky, "The Financial Instability Hypothesis," Jerome Levy Economics Institute of Bard College Working Paper 74, May 1992.
4. Daniel Kahneman and Amos Tversky, "Subjective Probability: A Judgment of Representativeness," *Cognitive Psychology* 3 (1972): 430–454.
5. Economist and Nobel laureate (2017) Richard Thaler argued that people can be irrational in predictable ways and that their behavior can be modeled. See Roger Lowenstein, "Exuberance Is Rational," *New York Times Magazine*, February 11, 2001.
6. Nicola Gennaioli, Andrei Shleifer, and Robert W. Vishny, "Neglected Risks: The Psychology of Financial Crises," *American Economic Review: Papers and Proceedings* 105, no. 5 (2015): 310–314.
7. For a discussion of LOR's 10-year simulation ending in 1981, and its problematic promise of what portfolio insurance can provide, see "A Debate on Portfolio Insurance" in Chapter 5. For a discussion of Leland's 1928–1983 portfolio insurance simulation, see Chapter 5, "Portfolio Insurance and the Crash."

8. Aetna did provide a guarantee of its portfolio insurance strategy GEM, but Aetna's guarantee did not reimburse for shortfalls on the upside. See Ralph Tate, "The Insurance Company Guarantee," in D. Luskin, ed., *Portfolio Insurance: A Guide to Dynamic Hedging* (New York: John Wiley, 1988): 182–185. LOR and other portfolio insurance vendors did not provide a guarantee, although LOR advertising described the strategy as a "guaranteed equity investment" (see "Conflicts of Interest" in Chapter 18).
9. Moody's and Fitch accord the US government an AAA rating or equivalent; Australia, Canada, Denmark, Germany, Luxembourg, the Netherlands, Norway, Singapore, Sweden, and Switzerland receive AAA-equivalent ratings from Moody's, Fitch, and Standard & Poor's.
10. Bruce I. Jacobs, "Risk Avoidance and Market Fragility," *Financial Analysts Journal* 60, no. 1 (2004): 28. This quote was the basis for William P. Barrett's piece, "Weapons of Mass Panic," in *Forbes*, March 15, 2004.

## CHAPTER 18

1. From *The Tempest*, Act II, Scene 1. Samuel Wells and Gary Taylor, eds., *William Shakespeare: The Complete Works* (Oxford, UK: University Press).
2. Gennaioli et al. posit a model in which financial intermediaries neglect unlikely risks in creating securities that will fulfill investor demand when safe assets are in short supply; such markets are inherently fragile and can lead to crises even in the absence of excessive leverage or fire sales. Nicola Gennaioli, Andrei Shleifer, and Robert W. Vishny, "Neglected Risks, Financial Innovation, and Financial Fragility," *Journal of Financial Economics* 104 (2012): 452–468.
3. Within the banking system, specific tactics, such as Lehman Brothers' Repo 105 (see Chapter 14), as well as the propensity of banks to deleverage when they knew the government was monitoring leverage, disguised the true risk of individual entities, encouraging more lending than would otherwise have occurred.
4. *Wall Street Journal*, April 21, 2010.
5. Thurner et al. present a model of the dynamics of leverage and nonlinearity. Stefan Thurner, J. Doyne Farmer, and John Geanakoplos, "Leverage Causes Fat Tails and Clustered Volatility," *Quantitative Finance* 12, no. 5 (2012): 695–707.
6. Bruce I. Jacobs and Kenneth N. Levy, "Leverage Aversion and Portfolio Optimality," *Financial Analysts Journal* 68, no. 5 (2012); Bruce I. Jacobs and Kenneth N. Levy, "Leverage Aversion, Efficient Frontiers, and the Efficient Region," *Journal of Portfolio Management* 39, no. 3 (2013); Bruce I. Jacobs and Kenneth N. Levy, "A Comparison of the Mean-Variance-Leverage Optimization Model and the Markowitz General Mean-Variance Portfolio Selection Model," *Journal of Portfolio Management* 40, no. 1 (2013); Bruce I. Jacobs and Kenneth N. Levy, "The Unique Risks of Portfolio Leverage:

Why Modern Portfolio Theory Fails and How to Fix It," *Journal of Financial Perspectives* 2, no. 3 (2014): 113–126; Bruce I. Jacobs and Kenneth N. Levy, "Traditional Optimization is Not Optimal for Leverage-Averse Investors," *Journal of Portfolio Management* 40, no. 2 (2014).

7. See, e.g., Nassim N. Taleb, *The Black Swan: The Impact of the Highly Improbable* (New York: Random House, 2007).
8. One LOR marketing document stated: "It doesn't matter that formal insurance policies are not available. The mathematics of finance provide the answer. . . . The bottom line is that financial catastrophes can be avoided at a relatively insignificant cost." Robert Ferguson and Larry D. Edwards, "General Characteristics of 'Portfolio Insurance' as Provided by Fiduciary Hedge Programs," Leland O'Brien Rubinstein Associates, Los Angeles, August 1985.
9. Hersh Shefrin, "How Psychological Pitfalls Generated the Global Financial Crisis," in L.B. Siegel, ed., *Insights Into the Global Financial Crisis* (Charlottesville, VA: Research Foundation of the CFA Institute, 2009).
10. Dan Tudball, "Whodunit?" (interview with Robert C. Merton), *Wilmott Magazine*, May 2009.
11. Felix Salmon, "Recipe for Disaster: The Formula That Killed Wall Street," *Wired*, February 23, 2009. Available at: https://www.wired.com/2009/02/wp-quant/.
12. Quoted in Patrick Jenkins, "A Decade on from the Financial Crisis, What Have We Learned?" *Financial Times*, August 31, 2017.
13. *Wall Street Journal*, December 2, 2011.
14. *Inside Job,* Charles Ferguson, director; Sony Pictures Classics, Representation Pictures, and Screen Pass Pictures, producers, 2010.
15. One study found that Washington lobbying by lenders was associated with greater risk-taking and lower subsequent stock performance. Deniz Igan, Prachi Mishra, and Thierry Tressel, "A Fistful of Dollars: Lobbying and the Financial Crisis," NBER Working Paper 17076, May 2011.
16. A fiduciary standard requires that a client's best interests be placed ahead of the fiduciary's own interests. Registered investment advisors regulated by the Securities and Exchange Commission already must meet a fiduciary standard. Certain financial planners are currently held to a lower standard of "suitability," which allows them to recommend suitable products, even if they may cost the client more than other products that are just as suitable. A fiduciary standard, if extended, would, for example, discourage such a financial planner from recommending a product that pays the planner a higher commission than another product that meets the client's needs.
17. See "A Debate on Portfolio Insurance" in Chapter 5, particularly endnote 13.
18. Simon Benninga and Marshall Blume, "On the Optimality of Portfolio Insurance," *Journal of Finance* 40, no. 5 (1985): 1341–1352.
19. Quoted in Barry B. Burr, "Praise for Book Turns to Criticism," *Pensions & Investments*, June 25, 2001.

20. Bruce I. Jacobs, *Capital Ideas and Market Realities: Option Replication, Investor Behavior, and Stock Market Crashes* (Malden, MA: Blackwell, 1999).
21. Jacobs, *Capital Ideas and Market Realities*: 45.
22. LOR-sponsored section, *Institutional Investor*, 1984.
23. Martin S. Fridson, "*Capital Ideas and Market Realities*" (book review), *Financial Analysts Journal* 56, no. 4 (2000).
24. Martin S. Fridson, "Postscript" (book review), *Financial Analysts Journal* 57, no. 1 (2001).
25. See LOR's advertisement illustrated in Exhibit 17.1, "Assured Equity Investing," which states, "This strategy has the effect of insuring an equity portfolio against loss—a *guaranteed equity investment*" [emphasis in the original]. Another LOR advertising display entitled "What LOR's Sophistication Means" (discussed in the *Wall Street Journal*, January 4, 1988, page B4) states: ". . . all the implications and expectations of the selected strategy are known in advance. No unhappy surprises."
26. Securities and Exchange Commission v. Capital Gains Research Bureau, Inc., et al., Supreme Court of the United States 375 U.S. 180 (1963).
27. Bruce I. Jacobs, "Postscript: Author's Comment," *Financial Analysts Journal* 57, no. 3 (2001); this is a substantially abridged version of a longer response that is available as "The Complete Text of Bruce I. Jacobs's Abbreviated 'Postscript: Author's Comment'" at jlem.com/documents/FG/jlem/p2954381/580747_www.jlem.com_articles_cimr_FajResp3a.pdf. Martin S. Fridson, "Postscript: Reviewer's Response," *Financial Analysts Journal* 57, no. 3 (2001).
28. Burr, "Praise Turns to Criticism."
29. Barry B. Burr, "Rubinstein to Stay on Editorial Board of *FAJ* Despite Talking with Fridson," *Pensions & Investments*, September 3, 2001.
30. Bruce I. Jacobs, "AIMR and 'Best Practices' on Ethics," *Pensions & Investments*, December 9, 2002.
31. "Bids & Offers: Analyst, Heal Thyself," *Wall Street Journal*, September 13, 2002; "AIMR's Objectivity Lesson," *Global Investor*, November 2002.
32. Bruce I. Jacobs, *Capital Ideas and Market Realities.*
33. Richard Bookstaber, *The End of Theory: Financial Crises, the Failure of Economics, and the Sweep of Human Interaction* (Princeton, NJ: Princeton University Press, 2017): 179.
34. Bruce I. Jacobs, Kenneth N. Levy, and Harry M. Markowitz, "Financial Market Simulation," *Journal of Portfolio Management* 30, no. 5 (2004); Bruce I. Jacobs, Kenneth N. Levy, and Harry M. Markowitz, "Simulating Security Markets in Dynamic and Equilibrium Modes," *Financial Analysts Journal* 66, no. 5 (2010): 42–53.
35. Jeffrey A. Brown, Brad McGourty, Til Schuermann, and Oliver Wyman, "Model Risk and the Great Financial Crisis: The Rise of Modern Model Risk

Management," in D.D. Evanoff, A.G. Haldane, and G.G. Kaufman, eds., *The New International Financial System: Analyzing the Cumulative Impact of Regulatory Reform* (Hackensack, NJ: World Scientific, 2015).

36. Rüdiger Fahlenbrach, Robert Prilmeier, and René M. Stulz, "This Time is the Same: Using Bank Performance in 1998 to Explain Bank Performance During the Recent Financial Crisis," NBER Working Paper 17038, May 2011.
37. Robert Jarrow, "Capital Adequacy Rules, Catastrophic Firm Failure, and Systemic Risk," *Review of Derivatives Research* 16 (2013): 219–231.
38. International Monetary Fund, "Global Financial Stability Report April 2015: Navigating Monetary Policy Challenges and Managing Risk" (Washington, D.C.: IMF, 2015).
39. Alan Greenspan, "Repel the Calls to Contain Competitive Markets," *Financial Times* August 4, 2008. Greenspan also opposed regulating off-exchange derivatives markets. In testimony before the US Congress in October 2008, Greenspan said: "I took a very strong position on the issue of derivatives and the efficacy of what they were doing for the economy as a whole, which, in effect, is essentially to transfer risk from those who... have great difficulty in absorbing it, to those who have the capital to absorb losses if and when they occur. These derivatives are working well." He also said, "Credit default swaps, I think, have serious problems associated with them. But, the bulk of derivatives, and, indeed, the only derivatives that existed when the major discussion started in 1999, were those of interest rate risk and foreign exchange risk." See Alan Greenspan, Testimony before the Committee on Oversight and Government Reform, US House of Representatives, October 23, 2008.
40. Dimitrios Bisias, Mark Flood, Andrew W. Lo, and Stavros Valavanis, "A Survey of Systemic Risk Analytics," *Annual Review of Financial Economics* 4 (2012): 255–296.
41. Plumbers and contractors broker the loans with little supervision, and lenders appear to care little about borrowers' creditworthiness, bringing to mind the freewheeling sales environment of subprime mortgage loans before the 2007–2008 credit crisis. See "America's Fastest-Growing Loan Category Has Eerie Echoes of Subprime Crisis," *Wall Street Journal*, January 10, 2017; "More Borrowers Are Defaulting on Their 'Green' PACE Loans," *Wall Street Journal*, August 15, 2017; "FBI, SEC Look Into Business Practices of Country's Largest 'Green' Lender," *Wall Street Journal*, September 26, 2017.

## APPENDIX A

1. C. D. Romer, "Great Depression," in *Encyclopaedia Britannica* (Chicago: Encyclopaedia Britannica, 2003).

2. Liaquat Ahamed, *Lords of Finance: The Bankers Who Broke the World* (New York: The Penguin Press, 2009): 308.
3. John Kenneth Galbraith, *The Great Crash 1929* (1997 ed.) (New York: Mariner Books, 1954): 21.
4. Ibid.: 21.
5. Ibid.: 31.
6. Barry Eichengreen, *Hall of Mirrors: The Great Depression, the Great Recession, and the Uses—and Misuses—of History* (New York: Oxford University Press, 2015).
7. Ibid.
8. Ahamed, *Lords of Finance*: 311.
9. Bruce I. Jacobs, *Capital Ideas and Market Realities: Option Replication, Investor Behavior, and Stock Market Crashes* (Malden, MA: Blackwell, 1999).
10. Galbraith, *The Great Crash 1929*: 48–50.
11. Ahamed, *Lords of Finance*: 354.
12. After the 1987 crash, some defenders of portfolio insurance pointed out that the strategy was an unlikely cause of the crash because the market had also crashed in 1929, long before the advent of portfolio insurance. Hayne E. Leland, for example, argued that "any plausible theory of market crashes must be able to explain more than just the crash of October 1987. . . . This would seem to preclude blaming the 1987 crash solely on instruments and techniques that were not available in 1929"; Hayne E. Leland, "On the Stock Market Crash and Portfolio Insurance," University of California, Berkeley, 1987. Jacobs (*Capital Ideas and Market Realities*), however, provides a detailed comparison of forced margin sales in 1929 and forced portfolio insurance selling in 1987 (pp. 174–176) and concludes that the two had very similar effects. Margin sales constituted about 25 percent of sales volume on October 28 and 29, 1929, and portfolio insurance sales constituted about 25 percent of sales volume on October 19, 1987. Furthermore, margin purchases and portfolio insurance purchases helped to increase stock prices in the years preceding the crashes. Leland seems to come around to this viewpoint in a later paper; Hayne E. Leland, "Leverage, Forced Asset Sales, and Market Stability: Lessons from Past Market Crises and the Flash Crash," The Future of Computer Trading in Financial Markets—Foresight Driver Review—DR9 (London: Government Office for Science, 2011).
13. Ahamed, *Lords of Finance*: 360.
14. Romer, "Great Depression."
15. Ahamed, *Lords of Finance*: 361.
16. Galbraith, *The Great Crash 1929*: 168.
17. Eichengreen, *Hall of Mirrors*.
18. Jacobs, *Capital Ideas and Market Realities*: 180–181.
19. Romer, "Great Depression."

## APPENDIX B

1. Roger Ibbotson, ed., *2018 SBBI Yearbook* (Hoboken, NJ: Wiley, 2018).
2. Rajnish Mehra and Edward C. Prescott, "The Equity Premium: A Puzzle," *Journal of Monetary Economics* 15, no. 2 (1985): 145–161.
3. Ibbotson, *2018 SBBI Yearbook.*
4. Aswath Damodaran, "Equity Risk Premiums (ERP): Determinants, Estimation and Implications—The 2018 Edition," New York University Stern School of Business Working Paper, March 2018.
5. Ibbotson, *2018 SBBI Yearbook.*
6. William F. Sharpe developed the diagonal model, which assumes that the returns of the securities are related through a common relationship with the overall market return. See William F. Sharpe, "A Simplified Model for Portfolio Analysis," *Management Science* 9, no. 2 (1963): 277–293.
7. According to Sharpe's capital asset pricing model (CAPM), a stock's systematic risk, or beta, is the determinant of a stock's expected return. See William F. Sharpe, "Capital Asset Prices: A Theory of Market Equilibrium Under Conditions of Risk," *Journal of Finance* 19, no. 3 (1964): 425–442. Sharpe was awarded the Nobel Prize in economics in 1990 for this insight. Some empirical findings suggest, however, that low-beta or low-volatility stocks outperform on a risk-adjusted basis. Baker et al. argue that this low-volatility anomaly stems from behavioral biases and impediments to arbitrage, such as barriers to leverage and shorting. See Malcolm Baker, Brendan Bradley, and Jeffrey Wurgler, "Benchmarks as Limits to Arbitrage: Understanding the Low-Volatility Anomaly," *Financial Analysts Journal* 67, no. 1 (2011): 40–54.
8. Eugene F. Fama, one of the foremost proponents of the efficient market hypothesis, was awarded the Nobel Prize in economics in 2013.
9. For example, some institutional investors may operate under guidelines that prohibit direct investment in physical commodities but allow commodities exposure through futures and other types of derivatives.
10. In Europe, and increasingly in the United States since the passage of the Dodd-Frank Act, swaps are "cleared" by a central counterparty clearinghouse, which steps in to become the counterparty to both sides of the swap transaction and guarantees performance of the contract. The guarantee is backed by the clearinghouse's own capital as well as by capital contributions from participating financial institutions and the mandatory posting of margin by the trading parties.

## APPENDIX D

1. Franklin R. Edwards and Michael S. Canter, "The Collapse of Metallgesellschaft: Unhedgeable Risks, Poor Hedging Strategy, or Just Bad Luck?" *Journal of Futures Markets* 15, no. 3 (1995): 211–264.
2. Ibid.

3. For banks, the timing mismatch involved issuing short-term debt in the form of commercial paper to purchase long-term mortgage assets held in asset-backed commercial paper conduits and structured investment vehicles.
4. James Overdahl and Barry Schachter, "Derivatives Regulation and Financial Management: Lessons from Gibson Greetings," *Financial Management* 24, no. 1 (1995): 68–78.
5. Ibid.
6. Ibid.
7. Securities and Exchange Commission, "In the Matter of Gibson Greetings, Inc., Ward A. Cavanaugh, and James H. Johnsen," Accounting and Auditing Enforcement Release No. 730, October 11, 1995: 4.
8. Frank Partnoy, *F.I.A.S.C.O. The Inside Story of a Wall Street Trader* (New York: Penguin Books, 1999).
9. Overdahl and Schachter, "Derivatives Regulation and Financial Management."
10. Philippe Jorion, *Big Bets Gone Bad: Derivatives and Bankruptcy in Orange County, the Largest Municipal Failure in U.S. History* (San Diego, CA: Academic Press, 1995).
11. Phelim Boyle and Feidhlim Boyle, *Derivatives: The Tools That Changed Finance* (London: Risk Waters Group, 2001).
12. Ibid.
13. Jorion, *Big Bets Gone Bad.*
14. Frank Partnoy, *Infectious Greed: How Deceit and Risk Corrupted the Financial Markets* (New York: Times Books, 2003).
15. Jorion, *Big Bets Gone Bad.*
16. Ibid.
17. Ibid.
18. Ibid.

# BIBLIOGRAPHY

"2000 Hall of Fame Roundtable: Portfolio Insurance Revisited" (2000). *Derivatives Strategy*, August.

"A Prairie Home Companion," Minnesota Public Radio.

Acharya, V.V. and P. Schnabl (2010). "Do Global Banks Spread Global Imbalances? Asset-Backed Commercial Paper During the Financial Crisis of 2007–09." *IMF Economic Review* 58 (1): 37–73.

Acharya, V.V. and S. Steffen (2013). "Analyzing Systemic Risk of the European Banking Sector." In J.-P. Foque and J.A. Langsam (eds.), *Handbook on Systemic Risk*. New York: Cambridge University Press.

Acharya, V.V., I. Drechsler, and P. Schnabl (2014). "A Pyrrhic Victory? Bank Bailouts and Sovereign Credit Risk." *Journal of Finance* 69 (6).

Acharya, V.V., P. Schnabl, and G. Suarez (2013). "Securitization without Risk Transfer." *Journal of Financial Economics* 107 (3): 515–536.

Acharya, V.V., M. Richardson, S. Van Nieuwerburgh, and L.J. White (2011). *Guaranteed to Fail: Fannie Mae, Freddie Mac, and the Debacle of Mortgage Finance*. Princeton, NJ: Princeton University Press.

Adelino, M. (2009). "How Much Do Investors Rely on Credit Ratings? The Case of Mortgage-Backed Securities." Working Paper, Sloan School of Management, Massachusetts Institute of Technology, Cambridge, MA.

Adler, D. (2014). *The New Economics of Liquidity and Financial Frictions*. Charlottesville, VA: CFA Institute Research Foundation.

Aeschylus (1960). *Prometheus Bound*, translation by David Grene. In D. Grene and R. Lattimore (eds.), *Greek Tragedies Volume I*. Chicago: University of Chicago Press.

Ahamed, L. (2009). *Lords of Finance: The Bankers Who Broke the World*. New York: The Penguin Press.

"AIMR's Objectivity Lesson" (2002). *Global Investor*, November.

Ashcraft, A.B. and T. Schuermann (2008). "Understanding the Securitization of Subprime Mortgage Credit." *Foundations and Trends in Finance* 2 (3): 191–309.

Ashcraft, A.B., P. Goldsmith-Pinkham, and J. Vickery (2010). "MBS Ratings and the Mortgage Credit Boom." Federal Reserve Bank of New York Staff Report 449, May.

Baba, N., R.N. McCauley, and S. Ramaswamy (2009). "US Dollar Money Market Funds and Non-US Banks." *BIS Quarterly Review*, March: 65–81.

Baker, M., B. Bradley, and J. Wurgler (2011). "Benchmarks as Limits to Arbitrage: Understanding the Low-Volatility Anomaly," *Financial Analysts Journal* 67 (1): 40–54.

Bank for International Settlements (1994). "Recent Developments in Bond Markets. A Report to the Ministers and Governors by the Chairman of the Group of Deputies." Basel, Switzerland: BIS, April.

——— (2005). "The Role of Ratings in Structured Finance: Issues and Implications." Committee on the Global Financial System Working Group Report. Basel, Switzerland: BIS, January 14.

——— (2008). "Credit Risk Transfer: Developments from 2005 to 2007." Consultative Document. Basel, Switzerland: BIS, April.

——— (2008). "Ratings in Structured Finance: What Went Wrong and What Can be Done to Address Shortcomings?" Committee on the Global Financial System Working Paper 32, July.

——— (2009). "79th Annual Report." Basel, Switzerland: BIS, June.

——— (2009). "The Role of Valuation and Leverage in Procyclicality." Committee on the Global Financial System Working Paper 34, April.

Bank of England (2008). *Financial Stability Report*, Issue 23, April.

Bao, J., M. O'Hara, and A. Zhou (2016). "The Volcker Rule and Market-Making in Times of Stress." Federal Reserve Board, December.

Barrett, W.P. (2004). "Weapons of Mass Panic." *Forbes*, March 15.

Benmelech, E. and J. Duglosz (2009). "The Alchemy of CDO Credit Ratings." *Journal of Monetary Economics* 56 (6): 617–634.

——— (2010). "The Credit Rating Crisis." *NBER Macroeconomics Annual* 24 (1): 161–208.

Benninga, S. and M. Blume (1985). "On the Optimality of Portfolio Insurance." *Journal of Finance* 40 (5): 1341–1352.

Bernanke, B.S. (2013). *The Federal Reserve and the Financial Crisis*. Princeton, NJ: Princeton University Press.

Bernanke, B.S., M. Gertler, and S. Gilchrist (1999). "The Financial Accelerator in a Quantitative Business Cycle Framework." In J.B. Taylor and M. Woodford (eds.), *Handbook of Macroeconomics,* Volume I. Amsterdam: Elsevier.

Bernstein, J. and J. Eisinger (2010). "Banks' Self-Dealing Super-Charged Financial Crisis." *ProPublica*, August 26.

Bernstein, P.L. (1996). *Against the Gods: The Remarkable Story of Risk*. New York: Wiley.

Bhansali, V. and L. Harris (2018). "Everybody's Doing it: Short Volatility Strategies and Shadow Financial Insurers." *Financial Analysts Journal* 74 (2): 12–23.

Bhardwaj, G. and R. Sengupta (2011). "Subprime Loan Quality." Working Paper 2008-036E, Research Division, Federal Reserve Bank of St. Louis, September.

"Bids & Offers: Analyst, Heal Thyself" (2002). *Wall Street Journal*, September 13.

Bisias, D., M. Flood, A.W. Lo, and S. Valavanis (2012). "A Survey of Systemic Risk Analytics." *Annual Review of Financial Economics* 4: 255–296.

Black, F. (1986). "Noise." *Journal of Finance* 41 (3): 529–543.

Black, F. and M.S. Scholes (1973). "The Pricing of Options and Corporate Liabilities." *Journal of Political Economy* 81 (3): 637–654.

Bookstaber, R. (2017). *The End of Theory: Financial Crises, the Failure of Economics, and the Sweep of Human Interaction.* Princeton, NJ: Princeton University Press.

Borio, C. and P. Disyatat (2011). "Global Imbalances and the Financial Crisis: Link or No Link?" Bank for International Settlements Working Paper 346, May.

Boyle, P. and F. Boyle (2001). *Derivatives: The Tools That Changed Finance.* London: Risk Waters Group.

Brady Commission (1988). *Report of the Presidential Task Force on Market Mechanisms.* Washington, DC: Government Printing Office.

Brennan, M.J. (2004). "How Did it Happen?" *Economic Notes* 33 (1): 3–22.

Brown, J.A., B. McGourty, T. Schuermann, and O. Wyman (2015). "Model Risk and the Great Financial Crisis: The Rise of Modern Model Risk Management." In D.D. Evanoff, A.G. Haldane, and G.G. Kaufman (eds.), *The New International Financial System: Analyzing the Cumulative Impact of Regulatory Reform.* Hackensack, NJ: World Scientific.

Bruner, R.F. (2009). "The Dynamics of a Financial Dislocation: The Panic of 1907 and the Subprime Crisis." In L.B. Siegel (ed.), *Insights into the Global Financial Crisis.* Charlottesville, VA: Research Foundation of the CFA Institute.

Brunnermeier, M.K. and L.H. Pedersen (2009). "Market Liquidity and Funding Liquidity." *Review of Financial Studies* 22 (6): 2201–2238.

Brunnermeier, M.K. and Y. Sannikov (2014). "A Macroeconomic Model with a Financial Sector." *American Economic Review* 104 (2): 379–421.

Buffett, W. (2003). "Chairman's Letter." *Berkshire Hathaway 2002 Annual Report.* Available at: http://www.berkshirehathaway.com/2002ar/2002ar.pdf.

Bullard, J., C.J. Neely, and D.C. Wheelock (2009). "Systemic Risk and the Financial Crisis: A Primer." *Federal Reserve Bank of St. Louis Review* 95 (1).

Burke, J.V. (2014). "The Financial Crisis and the EU Response B: Supporting the Financial System and Sovereigns Under Financial Stress." European Commission, August.

Burr, B.B. (2001). "Praise for Book Turns to Criticism." *Pensions & Investments*, June 25.

——— (2001). "Rubinstein to Stay on Editorial Board of *FAJ* Despite Talking with Fridson." *Pensions & Investments*, September 3.

Calomiris, C.W. (2009). "The Subprime Turmoil: What's Old, What's New, and What's Next." *Journal of Structured Finance* 15 (1).

Carroll, L. and M. Gardner (1960). *The Annotated Alice.* New York: Bramhall House.

Cassidy, J. (2009). *How Markets Fail: The Logic of Economic Calamities.* New York: Farrar, Straus and Giroux.

Centonze, A.L. (2014). "The Irish Banking Crisis." *Review of Business and Finance Studies* 5 (2).

Chen, F., X. Chen, Z. Sun, T. Yu, and M. Zhong (2013). "Systemic Risk, Financial Crisis, and Credit Risk Insurance." *Financial Review* 48: 417–442.

Chernenko, S. and A. Sunderam (2014). "Frictions in Shadow Banking: Evidence from the Lending Behavior of Money Market Mutual Funds." *Review of Financial Studies* 26 (6).

Chincarini, L.B. (2012). *The Crisis of Crowding: Quant Copycats, Ugly Models, and the New Crash Normal.* Hoboken, NJ: Bloomberg Press.

Chomsisengphet, S. and A. Pennington-Cross (2006). "The Evolution of the Subprime Mortgage Market." *Federal Reserve Bank of St. Louis Review,* January/February.

Clowes, M. (1999). "More to Say About Crash." *Pensions & Investments,* July 12.

Cohan, W.D. (2009). *House of Cards: A Tale of Hubris and Wretched Excess on Wall Street.* New York: Doubleday.

——— (2010). "How Wall Street Hid Its Mortgage Mess." Opinionator blog, *New York Times,* October 14. Available at: http://opinionator.blogs.nytimes.com/2010/10/14/how-wall-street-hid-its-mortgage-mess/.

Commodity Futures Trading Commission (1988). "Final Report on Stock Index Futures and Cash Market Activity During October 1987." Washington, DC: Divisions of Economic Analysis and Trading and Markets, CFTC.

——— (1990). "Report on Stock Index Futures and Cash Market Activity During October 1989." Washington, DC: Division of Economic Analysis, CFTC.

Commodity Futures Trading Commission and Securities and Exchange Commission (2010). "Findings Regarding the Market Events of May 6, 2010: Report of the Staffs of the CFTC and SEC to the Joint Advisory Committee on Emerging Regulatory Issues." Washington, DC: CFTC and SEC, September 30.

Cont, R. (2017). "Central Clearing and Risk Transformation." *Financial Stability Review (Banque de France)* 21, April.

Coval, J.D., J.W. Jurek, and E. Stafford (2008). "Re-examining the Role of Rating Agencies: Lessons from Structured Finance." Working Paper.

Covitz, D., N. Liang, and G.A. Suarez (2013). "The Evolution of a Financial Crisis: Collapse of the Asset-Backed Commercial Paper Market." *Journal of Finance* 68 (3): 815–848.

Cox, J.C. and M. Rubinstein (1985). *Options Markets.* Englewood Cliffs, NJ: Prentice-Hall.

Criado, S. and A. Van Rixtel (2008). "Structured Finance and the Financial Turmoil of 2007–2008: An Introductory Overview." Banco De España Occasional Paper Series 0808, September 2.

Crouhy, M.G., R.A. Jarrow, and S.M. Turnbull (2008). "The Subprime Credit Crisis of 07." *Journal of Derivatives* 16 (1).

Daglish, T. (2009). "What Motivates a Subprime Borrower to Default?" *Journal of Banking & Finance* 33: 681–693.

Damodaran, A. (2018). "Equity Risk Premiums (ERP): Determinants, Estimation and Implications—The 2018 Edition." New York University Stern School of Business Working Paper, March.

Das, A. and R.M. Stein (2009). "Underwriting Versus Economy: A New Approach to Decomposing Mortgage Losses." *Journal of Credit Risk* 5 (2): 19–41.

Das, S. (2002). "Liquidity Risk Part 3: Long-Term Capital Management." *Futures and Options World*, February.

——— (2012). "In the Matter of Lehman Brothers." *Wilmott Magazine*, May: 20–28.

——— (2016). "Crash Course or the Cascade of Financial Woes." *Wilmott Magazine*, November.

Dash, E. and J. Creswell (2008). "Citigroup Pays for a Rush to Risk." *New York Times*, November 23.

Davis, G.F. (2009). *Managed by the Markets: How Finance Reshaped America.* New York: Oxford University Press.

De Grauwe, P. (2010). "Fighting the Wrong Enemy." *Vox,* May 19. Available at: http://www.voxeu.org/index.php?q=node/5062.

de la Merced, M.J., V. Bajaj, and A.R. Sorkin (2008). "As Goldman and Morgan Shift, a Wall Street Era Ends." DealBook blog, *New York Times*, September 21.

Dell'Ariccia, G., D. Igan, and L. Laeven (2012). "Credit Booms and Lending Standards: Evidence from the Subprime Mortgage Market." *Journal of Money, Credit and Banking* 44 (2–3).

Demyanyk, Y. (2009). "Ten Myths about Subprime Mortgages." *Federal Reserve Bank of Cleveland Economic Commentary.*

Demyanyk, Y. and O. Van Hemert (2011). "Understanding the Subprime Mortgage Crisis." *Review of Financial Studies* 24 (6): 1848–1880.

Demyanyk, Y., D. Hryshko, M.J. Luengo-Prado, and B.E. Sørensen (2015). "The Rise and Fall of Consumption in the '00s." Federal Reserve Bank of Boston, October 16.

Department of Justice (2015). "Justice Department and State Partners Secure $1.375 Billion Settlement with S&P for Defrauding Investors in Lead Up to the Financial Crisis." Department of Justice Office of Public Affairs, February 3.

——— (2017). "Justice Department and State Partners Secure Nearly $864 Million Settlement with Moody's Arising from Conduct in the Lead Up to the Financial Crisis." Department of Justice Office of Public Affairs, January 13.

Dübel, H.-J. and M. Rothemund (2011). "A New Mortgage Credit Regime for Europe: Setting the Right Priorities." Centre for European Policy Studies Special Report, June.

Dunbar, N. (2000). *Inventing Money: The Story of Long-Term Capital Management and the Legends Behind It.* New York: Wiley.

Duygan-Bump, B., A. Levkov, and J. Montoriol-Garriga (2014). "Financing Constraints and Unemployment: Evidence from the Great Recession." Finance and Economics Discussion Series, Divisions of Research and Statistics and Monetary Affairs, Federal Reserve Board, Washington, DC.

Edwards, F.R. (1988). "Does Futures Trading Increase Stock Market Volatility?" *Financial Analysts Journal* 44 (1): 63–69.

Edwards, F.R. and M.S. Canter (1995). "The Collapse of Metallgesellschaft: Unhedgeable Risks, Poor Hedging Strategy, or Just Bad Luck?" *Journal of Futures Markets* 15 (3): 211–264.

Edwards, F.R. and F.S. Mishkin (1995). "The Decline of Traditional Banking: Implications for Financial Stability and Regulatory Policy." *Federal Reserve Bank of New York Economic Policy Review* 1 (2): 27–45.

Eichengreen, B. (2015). *Hall of Mirrors: The Great Depression, the Great Recession, and the Uses—and Misuses—of History.* New York: Oxford University Press.

Eisinger, J. (2011). "In Trading Scandal, a Reason to Enforce the Volcker Rule." *New York Times*, September 28.

Eubanks, W.W. (2006). "The Basel Accords: The Implementation of II and the Modification of I." Library of Congress Congressional Research Service, Washington, DC, June 16.

European Central Bank (2008). "The Incentive Structure of the 'Originate and Distribute' Model." Frankfurt am Main, Germany: ECB, December.

——— (2009). "Housing Finance in the Euro Area." ECB Occasional Paper Series 101, March.

——— (2009). "EU Banks' Funding Structures and Policies." Frankfurt am Main, Germany: ECB, May.

European Mortgage Federation (2009). "Hypostat 2008: A Review of Europe's Mortgage and Housing Markets." Brussels, Belgium: EMF, November.

Faber, D. (2009). *And Then the Roof Caved In: How Wall Street's Greed and Stupidity Brought Capitalism to Its Knees.* Hoboken, NJ: Wiley.

Fabozzi, F.J. and V. Kothari (2007). "Securitization: The Tool of Financial Transformation." Yale ICF Working Paper 07-07, Yale University, New Haven, CT.

Fahlenbrach, R., R. Prilmeier, and R.M. Stulz (2011). "This Time Is the Same: Using Bank Performance in 1998 to Explain Bank Performance During the Recent Financial Crisis." NBER Working Paper 17038, May.

Fair, R.C. (2015). "The Financial Crisis and Macroeconomic Activity: 2008–2013." Cowles Foundation Discussion Paper 1944, Yale University, New Haven, CT, February.

Falloon, W. (1984). "The Invisible Hedge." *Intermarket*, October.

Fama, E.F. (1989). "Perspectives on October 1987, or What Did We Learn from the Crash?" In R.J. Barro et al. (eds.), *Black Monday and the Future of Financial Markets*, 71–82. Homewood, IL: Mid-America Institute for Public Policy Research and Dow Jones-Irwin.

Federal Reserve Bank of San Francisco (2008). "The Subprime Mortgage Market: National and Twelfth District Developments." *2007 Annual Report*. San Francisco, CA: FRBSF.

Ferguson, R. (1986). "An Open Letter" (letter). *Financial Analysts Journal* 42 (5).

——— (1986). "How to Beat the S&P 500 (without losing sleep)." *Financial Analysts Journal* 42 (5).

Ferguson, R. and L.D. Edwards (1985). "General Characteristics of 'Portfolio Insurance' as Provided by Fiduciary Hedge Programs." Leland O'Brien Rubinstein Associates, Los Angeles, August.

Financial Crisis Inquiry Commission (2011). *The Financial Crisis Inquiry Report: Final Report of the National Commission on the Causes of the Financial and Economic Crisis in the United States (Financial Crisis Inquiry Commission).* New York: PublicAffairs.

Fisher, I. (1928) *The Money Illusion*. New York: Adelphi.

Fox, J. (2009). *The Myth of the Rational Market: A History of Risk, Reward, and Delusion on Wall Street*. New York: Harper Business.

"Free Speech or Knowing Misrepresentation?" (2013). *Economist*, February 5.

Fridson, M.S. (2000). "Capital Ideas and Market Realities" (book review). *Financial Analysts Journal* 56 (4).

——— (2001). "Postscript" (book review). *Financial Analysts Journal* 57 (1).

——— (2001). "Postscript: Reviewer's Response." *Financial Analysts Journal* 57 (3).

Friedman, J. and W. Kraus (2011). *Engineering the Financial Crisis: Systemic Risk and the Failure of Regulation*. Philadelphia: University of Pennsylvania Press.

Friedman, M. and A.J. Schwartz (1963). *A Monetary History of the United States, 1867–1960*. Washington, DC: National Bureau of Economic Research.

Fuld, R.S. Jr. (2015). Speech to Marcum MicroCap Conference, New York, May 28; quoted in D. Gelles, "Ex-Lehman Boss Breaks Silence." *New York Times*, May 29: B1.

Galbraith, J.K. (1954). *The Great Crash 1929* (1997 ed.). New York: Mariner Books.

Gastineau, G.L. (1988). *The Options Manual* (3rd ed.). New York: McGraw-Hill.

Geithner, T.F. (2014). *Stress Test: Reflections on Financial Crises*. New York: Crown.

General Accounting Office (1988). "Preliminary Observations on the October 1987 Crash. Financial Markets GAO/GGD 88-38." Washington, DC: GAO.

Gennaioli, N., A. Shleifer, and R.W. Vishny (2012). "Neglected Risks, Financial Innovation, and Financial Fragility." *Journal of Financial Economics* 104: 452–468.

——— (2015). "Neglected Risks: The Psychology of Financial Crises." *American Economic Review: Papers and Proceedings* 105 (5): 310–314.

Gerardi, K., A. Lehnert, S.M. Sherlund, and P. Willen (2008). "Making Sense of the Subprime Crisis." *Brookings Papers on Economic Activity*, Fall.

Glassman, J.K. and K.A. Hassett (1999). "Dow 36,000." *The Atlantic*, September.

Goel, A.M., F. Song, and A.V. Thakor (2014). "Correlated Leverage and Its Ramifications." *Journal of Financial Intermediation* 23: 471–503.

Goetzmann, W.N., L. Peng, and J. Yen (2012). "The Subprime Crisis and House Price Appreciation." *Journal of Real Estate and Economics* 44 (1–2).

Goldin, H.J. (1996). "Final Report of Harrison J. Golden, Trustee to The Honorable Stuart M. Bernstein, Judge, United States Bankruptcy Court, Southern District of New York, "In re Granite Partners, L.P., Granite Corporation and Quartz Hedge Fund," New York, April 18.

Goldman Sachs (1998). "Global Derivatives: 1997 Review–1998 Issues." Goldman Sachs Equity Derivatives Research, January.

Goldstein, S. (2007). "Update: HSBC to Provide $35 Billion in Funds to Structured Vehicles." *MarketWatch*, November 26. Available at: http://www.marketwatch.com/story/hsbc-to-provide-35-billion-in-funds-to-structured-vehicles-2007-11-26.

Gorton, G.B. (2008). "The Panic of 2007." In *Maintaining Stability in a Changing Financial System, Proceedings of the 2008 Jackson Hole Conference.* Kansas City, MO: Federal Reserve Bank of Kansas City.

——— (2009). "The Subprime Panic." *European Financial Management* 15 (10): 10–46.

——— (2010). "Questions and Answers about the Financial Crisis." Presentation prepared for the Financial Crisis Inquiry Commission, Washington, DC, February.

——— (2010). *Slapped by the Invisible Hand: The Panic of 2007.* New York: Oxford University Press.

Gorton, G.B. and A. Metrick (2012). "Securitized Banking and the Run on Repo." *Journal of Financial Economics* 104 (3): 425–451.

Gorton, G.B., A. Metrick, and L. Xie (2015). "An Econometric Chronology of the Financial Crisis of 2007–2008." Working Paper, Yale School of Management, New Haven, CT, April 28.

Gottschalck, A., M. Vornovitsky, and A. Smith (2016). "Household Wealth in the U.S.: 2000–2011." US Census Bureau, December 16.

Grannis, S. (1987). "Viewpoint on Portfolio Insurance: It Proved Its Worth." *Pensions & Investment Age*, November 16.

Greenlaw, D., J. Hatzius, A.K. Kashyap, and H.S. Shin (2008). "Leveraged Losses: Lessons from the Mortgage Market Meltdown." *Proceedings of the U.S. Monetary Policy Forum 2008.*

Greenspan, A. (1996). Presentation to the Annual Dinner and Francis Boyer Lecture of the American Enterprise Institute for Public Policy Research,

Washington, DC, December 5. Available at: http://www.federalreserve.gov/boarddocs/speeches/1996/19961205.htm.

——— (2005). Presentation to the Economic Club of New York, May 19.

——— (2008). "Repel the Calls to Contain Competitive Markets." *Financial Times*, August 4.

——— (2008). Testimony before the Committee on Oversight and Government Reform, US House of Representatives, October 23.

——— (2010). Testimony before the Financial Crisis Inquiry Commission Hearing on Subprime Lending and Securitization and Government-Sponsored Enterprises (GSEs), April 7.

Griffiths, M.D., V. Kotomin, and D.B. Winters (2012). "A Crisis of Confidence: Understanding Money Markets During the Financial Crisis." *Journal of Applied Finance* 22 (2): 39–59.

Gros, D. (2008). "Is Europe's Housing Market Next?" *Project Syndicate*, February 8.

Guerron-Quintana, P. and R. Jinnai (2014). "Liquidity, Trends, and The Great Recession." Federal Reserve Bank of Philadelphia Working Paper 14–24, August 21.

Guiso, L., P. Sapienza, and L. Zingales (2013). "The Determinants of Attitudes toward Strategic Default on Mortgages." *Journal of Finance* 68 (4): 1473–1515.

Haltenhof, S., S.J. Lee, and V. Stebunovs (2013). "Bank Lending Channels during the Great Recession." Federal Reserve Board, October 15.

Hayek, F.A. (1945). "The Use of Knowledge in Society." *American Economic Review* 35 (4): 519–530.

Hill, J.M. and F.J. Jones (1988). "Equity Trading, Program Trading, Portfolio Insurance, Computer Trading and All That." *Financial Analysts Journal*, 44 (4): 29–38.

Hördahl, P. and M.R. King (2008). "Developments in Repo Markets During the Financial Turmoil." *BIS Quarterly Review*, December: 37–53.

Ibbotson, R.G. (ed.) (2018). *2018 SBBI Yearbook*. Hoboken, NJ: Wiley.

Igan, D., P. Mishra, and T. Tressel (2011). "A Fistful of Dollars: Lobbying and the Financial Crisis." NBER Working Paper 17076, May.

Immergluck, D. and G. Smith (2006). "The External Costs of Foreclosure: The Impact of Single-Family Mortgage Foreclosures on Property Values." *Housing Policy Debate* 17 (1).

*Inside Job* (2010). Charles Ferguson, director; Sony Pictures Classics, Representation Pictures, and Screen Pass Pictures, producers.

International Monetary Fund (1997). "World Economic Outlook: Crisis in Asia, Regional and Global Implications." Washington, DC: IMF.

——— (2006). "Global Financial Stability Report: Market Developments and Issues." Washington, DC: IMF.

——— (2008). "Financial Stress and Deleveraging: Macro-Financial Implications and Policy." Washington, DC: IMF, October. Available at: http://www.imf.org/external/pubs/ft/gfsr/2008/02/index.htm.

——— (2008). "Global Financial Stability Report: Containing Systemic Risks and Restoring Financial Soundness." Washington, DC: IMF. Available at http://www.imf.org/external/pubs/ft/gfsr/2008/01/index.htm.

——— (2013). "European Union: Publication of Financial Sector Assessment Program; Documentation—Technical Note on Progress with Bank Restructuring and Resolution in Europe." IMF Country Report 13/67, March.

——— (2013). "European Union: Publication of Financial Sector Assessment Program; Documentation—Technical Note on Financial Integration and Fragmentation in the European Union." IMF Country Report 13/71, March.

——— (2015). "Global Financial Stability Report April 2015: Navigating Monetary Policy Challenges and Managing Risk." Washington, DC: IMF.

International Stock Exchange (1989). "Report of the International Stock Exchange of Great Britain." In: R.J. Barro et al. (eds.), *Black Monday and the Future of Financial Markets*. Homewood, IL: Mid-America Institute for Public Policy Research and Dow Jones-Irwin: 269–340.

Jacobs, B.I. (1983). "Memorandum to Prudential Insurance Company of America's Client Service and Sales Forces regarding Portfolio Insulation," January 17.

——— (1983). "The Portfolio Insurance Puzzle." *Pensions & Investment Age*, August 22.

——— (1983). "Mr. Jacobs Responds" (letter). *Pensions & Investment Age*, November 14.

——— (1984) "Is Portfolio Insurance Appropriate for the Long-Term Investor?" Prudential Asset Management Company.

——— (1986). "A Public Debate on Dynamic Hedging." In *Innovative Portfolio Insurance Techniques: The Latest Developments in "Dynamic Hedging"* (videotape). New York: Institute for International Research.

——— (1987). "Viewpoint on Portfolio Insurance: It's Prone to Failure." *Pensions & Investment Age*, November 16.

——— (1997). "The Darker Side of Option Pricing Theory." *Pensions & Investments*, November 24.

——— (1998). "Option Pricing Theory and Its Unintended Consequences." *Journal of Investing* 7 (1): 12–14.

——— (1998). "Option Replication and the Market's Fragility." *Pensions & Investments*, June 15.

——— (1998). "Long-Term Capital's Short-Term Memory." *Pensions & Investments*, October 5.

——— (1999). *Capital Ideas and Market Realities: Option Replication, Investor Behavior, and Stock Market Crashes*. Malden, MA: Blackwell.

——— (1999). "When Seemingly Infallible Arbitrage Strategies Fail." *Journal of Investing* 8 (1): 9–10.

——— (2000). "Another 'Costless' Strategy Roils Market." *Pensions & Investments*, May 29.

——— (2000). "Momentum Trading: The New Alchemy." *Journal of Investing* 9 (3): 6–7.

——— (2001). Complete Text of Bruce I. Jacobs's Abbreviated "Postscript: Author's Comment." Available at jlem.com/documents/FG/jlem/p2954381/580747_www.jlem.com_articles_cimr_FajResp3a.pdf.

——— (2001). "Postscript: Author's Comment." *Financial Analysts Journal* 57 (3).

——— (2002). "AIMR and 'Best Practices' on Ethics." *Pensions & Investments*, December 9.

——— (2004). "Risk Avoidance and Market Fragility." *Financial Analysts Journal* 60 (1): 26–30.

——— (2005). "A Tale of Two Hedge Funds," 147-171. In B.I. Jacobs and K.N. Levy (eds.). *Market Neutral Strategies.* New York: Wiley.

——— (2009). "Tumbling Tower of Babel: Subprime Securitization and the Credit Crisis." *Financial Analysts Journal* 65 (2): 17–30.

Jacobs, B.I. and K.N. Levy. (1993). "Long-Short Equity Investing." *Journal of Portfolio Management* 20 (1): 52–63.

——— (1996). "20 Myths About Long-Short." *Financial Analysts Journal* 52 (5): 81–85.

——— (2012). "Leverage Aversion and Portfolio Optimality." *Financial Analysts Journal* 68 (5): 89–94.

——— (2013). "A Comparison of the Mean-Variance-Leverage Optimization Model and the Markowitz General Mean-Variance Portfolio Selection Model." *Journal of Portfolio Management* 40 (1).

——— (2013). "Leverage Aversion, Efficient Frontiers, and the Efficient Region." *Journal of Portfolio Management* 39 (3): 54–64.

——— (2014). "Traditional Optimization Is Not Optimal for Leverage-Averse Investors." *Journal of Portfolio Management* 40 (2): 1–11.

——— (2014). "The Unique Risks of Portfolio Leverage: Why Modern Portfolio Theory Fails and How to Fix It." *Journal of Financial Perspectives* 2 (3): 113–126.

Jacobs, B.I., K.N. Levy, and H.M. Markowitz (2004). "Financial Market Simulation." *Journal of Portfolio Management* 30 (5).

——— (2010). "Simulating Security Markets in Dynamic and Equilibrium Modes." *Financial Analysts Journal* 66 (5): 42–53.

Jarrow, R. (2013). "Capital Adequacy Rules, Catastrophic Firm Failure, and Systemic Risk." *Review of Derivatives Research* 16: 219–231.

Jenkins, P. (2017). "A Decade on from the Financial Crisis, What Have We Learned?" *Financial Times*, August 31.

Jobst, A. (2008). "What Is Securitization?" *Finance and Development: A Quarterly Magazine of the IMF* 45 (3).

Jorion, P. (1995). *Big Bets Gone Bad: Derivatives and Bankruptcy in Orange County, the Largest Municipal Failure in U.S. History.* San Diego, CA: Academic Press.

——— (2000). "Risk Management Lessons from Long-Term Capital Management." *European Financial Management* 6 (3): 277–300.

——— (2003). "Medium-Term Risk Management: Lessons from Long-Term Capital Management." In P. Field (ed.), *Modern Risk Management: A History*, 475–484. London: Risk Books.

Kahneman, D. and A. Tversky (1972). "Subjective Probability: A Judgment of Representativeness." *Cognitive Psychology* 3: 430–454.

Katzenbach, N. (1987). "An Overview of Program Trading and Its Impact on Current Market Practices." New York: New York Stock Exchange.

Kaufman, H. (1994). "Structural Changes in the Financial Markets: Economic and Policy Significance." *Federal Reserve Bank of Kansas City Economic Review* 79 (2): 5–15.

Keynes, J.M. (1936). *The General Theory of Employment, Interest, and Money*. London: Macmillan. Reprinted New York: Harcourt Brace, 1964.

Keys, B.J., T. Mukherjee, A. Seru, and V. Vig (2010). "Did Securitization Lead to Lax Screening? Evidence from Subprime Loans." *Quarterly Journal of Economics* 125 (1): 307–362.

Khandani, A.E. and A.W. Lo (2011). "What Happened to the Quants in August 2007: Evidence from Factors and Transactions Data." *Journal of Financial Markets* 14 (1): 1–46.

Kirkegaard, J.F. (2011). "The Euro Area Crisis: Origin, Current Status, and European and U.S. Responses." Testimony before the U.S. House Committee on Foreign Affairs Subcommittee on Europe and Eurasia, October 27.

Kolanovic, M. and B. Kaplan (2018). "Flash Crash, Flows, and Investment Opportunities—ALERT." JP Morgan market commentary, February 5.

Krinsman, A.N. (2007). "Subprime Mortgage Meltdown: How Did It Happen and How Will It End?" *Journal of Structured Finance* 13 (2): 13–29.

Krishnamurthy, A., S. Nagel, and D. Orlov (2014). "Sizing Up Repo." *Journal of Finance* 69 (6): 2381–2417.

Kroszner, R.S. and R.J. Shiller (2011). *Reforming U.S. Financial Markets*. Cambridge, MA: MIT Press.

Kuhn, B.A., G.J. Kuserk, and P. Locke (1991). "Do Circuit Breakers Moderate Volatility? Evidence from October 1989." *Review of Futures Markets* 10 (1): 136–175.

Kyle, A.S. and A.A. Obizhaeva (2016). "Large Bets and Stock Market Crashes." University of Maryland Working Paper, January 31.

Lea, M. (2010). "Alternative Forms of Mortgage Finance: What Can We Learn From Other Countries?" Paper prepared for Harvard Joint Center for Housing Studies National Symposium, April.

Leland, H.E. (1980). "Who Should Buy Portfolio Insurance?" *Journal of Finance* 35 (2): 581–594.

——— (1984). "Portfolio Insurance Performance, 1928–1983." Leland O'Brien Rubinstein Associates.

——— (1987). "On the Stock Market Crash and Portfolio Insurance." University of California, Berkeley.

——— (2011). "Leverage, Forced Asset Sales, and Market Stability: Lessons from Past Market Crises and the Flash Crash." The Future of Computer Trading in Financial Markets—Foresight Driver Review—DR9. London: Government Office for Science.

Leland, H.E. and M. Rubinstein (1988). "Comments on the Market Crash: Six Months After." *Journal of Economic Perspectives* 2 (3): 45–50.

Lewis, M. (1999). "How the Eggheads Cracked." *New York Times Magazine*, January 24.

——— (2010). *The Big Short: Inside the Doomsday Machine*. New York: W.W. Norton & Co.

Lindsey, R.R. and A.P. Pecora (1998). "10 Years After: Regulatory Developments in the Securities Markets Since the 1987 Market Break." *Journal of Financial Services Research* 13 (3): 283–314.

Lowenstein, R. (1997). "Why Stock Options Are Really Dynamite." *Wall Street Journal*, November 6.

——— (2000). *When Genius Failed: The Rise and Fall of Long-Term Capital Management*. New York: Random House.

——— (2001). "Exuberance Is Rational." *New York Times Magazine*, February 11.

——— (2004). *Origins of the Crash: The Great Bubble and Its Undoing*. New York: The Penguin Press.

MacKenzie, D. (2006). *An Engine, Not a Camera*. Cambridge, MA: MIT Press.

Markose, S., S. Giansante, M. Gatkowski, and A.R. Shaghaghi (2010). "Too Interconnected to Fail: Financial Contagion and Systematic Risk in Network Model of CDS and Other Credit Enhancement Obligations of US Banks." University of Essex Discussion Paper Series 683, February.

Markose, S., S. Giansante, and A.R. Saghaghi (2012). "'Too Interconnected to Fail' Financial Network of US CDS Market: Topological Fragility and Systemic Risk." *Journal of Economic Behavior and Organizations* 83: 627–646.

Markowitz, H.M. (1952). "Portfolio Selection." *Journal of Finance* 7 (1): 77–91.

——— (1959). *Portfolio Selection: Efficient Diversification of Investments*. New Haven: Yale University Press.

——— (1999). "Foreword." In B.I. Jacobs, *Capital Ideas and Market Realities: Option Replication, Investor Behavior, and Stock Market Crashes* (Malden, MA: Blackwell, 1999).

Martin, F.M. and C.J. Waller (2012). "Sovereign Debt: A Modern Greek Tragedy." *Federal Reserve Bank of St. Louis Annual Report 2011*: 4–17.

Mason, J.R. and J. Rosner (2007). "Where Did the Risk Go? How Misapplied Bond Ratings Cause Mortgage Backed Securities and Collateralized Debt Obligation Market Disruption." Working Paper, May 14.

Masood, O. (2009). "Balance Sheet Exposures Leading toward the Credit Crunch in Global Investment Banks." *Journal of Credit Risk* 5 (2): 57–75.

Mattera, P. (2016). *The $160 Billion Bank Fee: What Violation Tracker 2.0 Shows about Penalties Imposed on Major Financial Offenders*. Washington, DC: GoodJobsFirst.Org.

Mayer, C., K. Pence, and S.M. Sherlund (2009). "The Rise in Mortgage Defaults." *Journal of Economic Perspectives* 23 (1): 27–50.

Mayer, M. (2009). Presentation to the American Institute for Economic Research, June 25.

McBride, B. (2017). "Black Knight: Mortgage 'Origination Volumes in 2016 Highest Level Seen in Nine Years.'" Calculated Risk blog, March 9. Available at: www.calculatedriskblog.com/2017/03/black-knight-mortgage-origination.html.

McDonald, R. and A. Paulson (2015). "AIG in Hindsight." *Journal of Economic Perspectives* 29 (2): 81–106.

McDonough, W.J. (1998). "Statement before the US House of Representatives Committee on Banking and Finance Services," Washington, DC, October 1.

McGuire, P. and G. von Peter (2012). "The Dollar Shortage in Global Banking and the International Policy Response." *International Finance* 15 (2): 155–178.

Mehra, R. and E.C. Prescott (1985). "The Equity Premium: A Puzzle." *Journal of Monetary Economics* 15 (2): 145–161.

Merton, R.C. (1973). "Theory of Rational Option Pricing." *Bell Journal of Economics and Management Science* 4 (1): 141–183.

Mian, A. and A. Sufi (2009). "The Consequences of Mortgage Credit Expansion: Evidence from the U.S. Mortgage Default Crisis." *Quarterly Journal of Economics* 124 (4): 1446–1496.

——— (2010). "Household Leverage and the Recession of 2007–09." *IMF Economic Review* 58 (1): 74–117.

Mian, A., A. Sufi, and F. Trebbi (2015). "Foreclosure, House Prices, and the Real Economy." *Journal of Finance* 70 (6): 2587–2633.

Minsky, H.P. (1992). "The Financial Instability Hypothesis." Jerome Levy Economics Institute of Bard College Working Paper 74, May.

Mishkin, F.S. and E.N. White (2002). "U.S. Stock Market Crashes and Their Aftermath: Implications for Monetary Policy." National Bureau of Economic Research Working Paper 8992, June.

Mitchell, M.L. and J.M. Netter (1989). "Triggering the 1987 Stock Market Crash: Anti-Takeover Provisions in the Proposed House Ways and Means Tax Bill?" *Journal of Financial Economics* 24 (1): 37–68.

Mittnik, S. and W. Semmler (2014). "Overleveraging, Financial Fragility and the Banking-Macro Link: Theory and Empirical Evidence." Center for European Economic Research Discussion Paper 14–110, November 20.

Modest, D.M. (1999). "Long-Term Capital Management: An Internal Perspective." Presentation to the Institute for Quantitative Research in Finance, Palm Springs, CA, October 18.

Mody, A. and D. Sandri (2012). "The Eurozone Crisis: How Banks and Sovereigns Came to Be Joined at the Hip." *Economic Policy* 27 (70): 199–230.

Moyer, L. (2007). "Citigroup Goes It Alone to Rescue SIVs." *Forbes*. December 13.

Murphy, D. (2009). *Unravelling the Credit Crunch*. Boca Raton, FL: CRC Press.

Nelson, R.M., P. Belkin, and D.E. Mix (2011). "Greece's Debt Crisis: Overview, Policy Responses, and Implications." Library of Congress Congressional Research Service Report 7–5700, Washington, DC, August 18.

Nothaft, F. (2011). "The Boom, the Bubble, and the Bust Abroad." Freddie Mac Executive Perspectives blog, February 14. Available at: http://www.freddiemac.com/news/blog/frank_nothaft/20110214_boom_bubble_and_bust_abroad.html.

——— (2016). "Single-Family Mortgage Default Rate Falls to Pre-Recession Level." CoreLogic Insights blog, June 2. Available at: http://www.corelogic.com/blog/authors/frank-nothaft/2016/06/single-family-mortgage-default-rate-falls-to-pre-recession-level.aspx#.WjrCwlWnGM8.

O'Brien, J.W. (1983). "Research Questioned" (letter). *Pensions & Investment Age*, September 19.

Ofek, E. and M. Richardson (2003). "DotCom Mania: The Rise and Fall of Internet Stock Prices." *Journal of Finance* 58 (3): 1113–1137.

Office of Federal Housing Enterprise Oversight (2008). "Mortgage Markets and the Enterprises in 2007," July. Available at: www.ofheo.gov/media/research/MME2007.pdf.

Office of Financial Research (2012). *2012 Annual Report*. Washington, DC: Department of the Treasury.

Office of the Comptroller of the Currency, Federal Reserve System, and Federal Deposit Insurance Corporation (2014). "Regulatory Capital Rules: Regulatory Capital, Enhanced Supplementary Leverage Ratio Standards for Certain Bank Holding Companies and Their Subsidiary Insured Depository Institutions Final Rule." *Federal Register* 79 (84).

Overdahl, J. and B. Schachter (1995). "Derivatives Regulation and Financial Management: Lessons from Gibson Greetings." *Financial Management* 24 (1): 68–78.

Partnoy, F. (1999). *F.I.A.S.C.O. The Inside Story of a Wall Street Trader*. New York: Penguin Books.

——— (2003). *Infectious Greed: How Deceit and Risk Corrupted the Financial Markets*. New York: Times Books.

Pendley, D., G. Costello, and M. Kelsch (2007). "The Impact of Poor Underwriting Practices and Fraud in Subprime RMBS Performance." Fitch Ratings Structured Finance US Mortgage Special Report.

Pérez-Caldentey, E. and M. Vernengo (2012). "The Euro Imbalances and Financial Deregulation: A Post-Keynesian Interpretation of the European Debt Crisis." Levy Economics Institute of Bard College Working Paper 702, January.

Perold, A.F. (1999). "Long-Term Capital Management L.P." Harvard Business School Case 9-200-007.

Poundstone, W. (2005). *Fortune's Formula: The Untold Story of the Scientific Betting System That Beat the Casinos and Wall Street.* New York: Hill and Wang.

President's Working Group on Financial Markets (1999). "Hedge Funds, Leverage, and the Lessons of Long-Term Capital Management." Washington, DC, April.

Ranieri, L.S. (2017). "I Blew Up the World: War Stories" (video interview with Lewis S. Ranieri), *Institutional Investor*, November 9. Available at: https://www.institutionalinvestor.com/article/b160qlmj90f9g7/i-blew-up-the-world-war-stories?utm_medium=email&utm_campaign=The%20Essential%20II%20Daily%2012132017&utm_content=The%20Essential%20II%20Daily%2012132017%20CID_582a28f5e8089b5ad239195686ddb504&utm_source=CampaignMonitorEmail&utm_term=I%20Blew%20Up%20the%20World%20War%20Stories.

Reinhart, C.M. and K.S. Rogoff (2009). *This Time Is Different: Eight Centuries of Financial Folly.* Princeton, NJ: Princeton University Press.

Richard, C.S. (2010). *Confidence Game: How Hedge Fund Manager Bill Ackman Called Wall Street's Bluff.* Hoboken, NJ: Wiley.

Ring, T. (1986). Portfolio Insurance's Merits Spur Debate. *Pensions & Investment Age*, July 7.

——— (1988). "66 Percent Drop in Portfolio Insurance." *Pensions & Investment Age*, January 25.

Roll, R. (1988). "The International Crash of October 1987." *Financial Analysts Journal* 44 (5): 19–35.

Romer, C.D. (2003). "Great Depression." In: *Encyclopaedia Britannica.* Chicago: Encyclopaedia Britannica.

Rosenberg, J. (2009). "Toward a Clear Understanding of the Systemic Risks of Large Institutions." *Journal of Credit Risk* 5 (2): 77–85.

Rosengren, E.S. (2010). "Asset Bubbles and Systemic Risk." Presentation to the Global Interdependence Center Conference on Financial Interdependence in the World's Post-Crisis Capital Markets, Philadelphia, March 3.

Rubinstein, M. (1988). "Portfolio Insurance and the Market Crash." *Financial Analysts Journal* 44 (1): 38–47.

——— (2000). Correspondence to Michael Brennan, February 14 (shared with the editor of *Derivatives Strategy* at its 2000 Hall of Fame Roundtable, "Portfolio Insurance Revisited," New York, April 14, 2000).

Rubinstein, M. and H.E. Leland (1981). "Replicating Options with Positions in Stock and Cash." *Financial Analysts Journal* 37 (4): 63–72.

Salmon, F. (2009). "Recipe for Disaster: The Formula That Killed Wall Street." *Wired*, February 23. Available at: https://www.wired.com/2009/02/wp-quant/.

Schapiro, M.L. (2010). "Testimony Concerning the Severe Market Disruption on May 6, 2010." Testimony before the Subcommittee on Capital Markets, Insurance and Government-Sponsored Enterprises of the United States House of Representatives Committee on Financial Services, May 11.

Scholes, M.S. (2000). "The Near Crash of 1998: Crisis and Risk Management." *American Economic Review Papers and Proceedings* 90 (2): 17–21.

Schumpeter, J.A. (1942). *Capitalism, Socialism and Democracy.* New York: Harper and Brothers.

Securities and Exchange Commission v. Capital Gains Research Bureau, Inc., et al., Supreme Court of the United States 375 U.S. 180 (1963).

Securities and Exchange Commission (1987). "The Role of Index-Related Trading in the Market Decline on September 11 and 12, 1986." Washington, DC: Division of Market Regulation, SEC.

——— (1988). "The October 1987 Market Break." Washington, DC: Division of Market Regulation, SEC.

——— (1990). "Market Analysis of October 13 and 16, 1989." Washington, DC: Division of Market Regulation, SEC.

——— (1990). "Trading Analysis of October 13 and 16, 1989." Washington, DC: Division of Market Regulation, SEC.

——— (1991). "Market Decline on November 15, 1991" (memorandum from William H. Hayman, Director, Division of Market Regulation, to SEC Chairman Richard C. Breeden). Washington, DC: Division of Market Regulation, SEC, December 24.

——— (1992). "Trading Analysis of November 15, 1991." Staff Report, Division of Market Regulation, SEC.

——— (1995). "In the Matter of Gibson Greetings, Inc., Ward A. Cavanaugh, and James H. Johnsen." Accounting and Auditing Enforcement Release 730, October 11.

——— (2008). "Summary Report of Issues Identified in the Commission Staff's Examinations of Select Credit Rating Agencies." Office of Compliance Inspections and Examinations, Division of Trading and Markets and Office of Economic Analysis, SEC, July.

Securities Industry and Financial Markets Association (2010). Global CDO Issuance–Quarterly Data From 2000 to 2010. Available at: http://www.sifma.org/research/statistics.aspx.

Sharpe, W.F. (1963). "A Simplified Model for Portfolio Analysis," *Management Science* 9 (2): 277–293.

——— (1964). "Capital Asset Prices: A Theory of Market Equilibrium Under Conditions of Risk." *Journal of Finance* 19 (3): 425–442.

Shefrin, H. (2000). *Beyond Greed and Fear: Understanding Behavioral Finance and the Psychology of Investing.* Boston: Harvard Business School Press.

——— (2009). "How Psychological Pitfalls Generated the Global Financial Crisis." In L.B. Siegel (ed.), *Insights Into the Global Financial Crisis*. Charlottesville, VA: Research Foundation of the CFA Institute.

Shiller, R.J. (1988). "Portfolio Insurance and Other Investor Fashions as Factors in the 1987 Stock Market Crash." In S. Fischer (ed.), *NBER Macroeconomics Annual 1988*. Cambridge, MA: MIT Press.

——— (1989). "Investor Behavior in the October 1987 Stock Market Crash: Survey Evidence." In R.J. Shiller, *Market Volatility*. Cambridge, MA: MIT Press.

——— (2000): *Irrational Exuberance*. Princeton, NJ: Princeton University Press.

——— (2005). *Irrational Exuberance* (2nd ed.). Princeton, NJ: Princeton University Press.

Shin, H.S. (2009). "Reflections on Northern Rock: The Bank Run That Heralded the Global Financial Crisis." *Journal of Economic Perspectives* 23 (1): 101–119.

——— (2009). "Securitisation and Financial Stability." *Economic Journal* 119 (536): 309–332.

Shirreff, D. (2004). *Dealing with Financial Risk*. New York: Bloomberg Press.

Shleifer, A. and R.W. Vishny (1997). "The Limits of Arbitrage." *Journal of Finance* 52 (1): 35–55.

Siconolfi, M., A. Raghavan, and M. Pacelle (1998). "How Salesmanship and Brainpower Failed to Save Long-Term Capital." *Wall Street Journal*, November 16.

Siegel, J.J. (1994). *Stocks for the Long Run: The Definitive Guide to Financial Market Returns & Long-Term Investment Strategies*. Burr Ridge, IL: Irwin Professional Publishing.

Sorkin, A.R. (2012). "At JP Morgan, 'Perfect Hedge' Still Elusive." *New York Times*, May 15.

Stanton, R. and N. Wallace (2011). "The Bear's Lair: Indexed Credit Default Swaps and the Subprime Mortgage Crisis." *Review of Financial Studies* 24: 3250–3280.

Stulz, R.M. (2010). "Credit Default Swaps and the Credit Crisis." *Journal of Economic Perspectives* 24 (1): 73–92.

Sullivan, A. (2008). "AIG's Failure Is So Much Bigger Than Enron." *The Motley Fool*, September 17.

Syz, J.M. and P. Vanini (2009). "Property Derivatives and the Subprime Crisis." *Wilmott Journal* 1 (3): 163–166.

Tabe, H. (2010). *The Unravelling of Structured Investment Vehicles: How Liquidity Leaked Through SIVs. Lessons in Risk Management and Regulatory Oversight*. Chatham, Kent, UK: Thoth Capital.

Taleb, N.N. (2007). *The Black Swan: The Impact of the Highly Improbable*. New York: Random House.

Tate, R. (1988). "The Insurance Company Guarantee." In D. Luskin (ed.), *Portfolio Insurance: A Guide to Dynamic Hedging*, 182–185. New York: John Wiley.

Tavakoli, J.M. (*2008*). *Structured Finance & Collateralized Debt Obligations* (2nd ed.). Hoboken, NJ: Wiley.

——— (2009). "Beware of Geeks Bearing Grifts." *Risk Professional*, December.

Tett, G. (2009). *Fool's Gold: How the Bold Dream of a Small Tribe at J. P. Morgan Was Corrupted.* New York: Simon & Schuster.

Thurner, S., J.D. Farmer, and J. Geanakoplos (2012). "Leverage Causes Fat Tails and Clustered Volatility." *Quantitative Finance* 12 (5): 695–707.

Tichy, G. (2012). "The Sovereign Debt Crisis: Causes and Consequences." *Austrian Economic Quarterly* 17 (2): 95–107.

Treynor, J.L. (1988). "Portfolio Insurance and Market Volatility." *Financial Analysts Journal* 44 (6): 71–73.

Tudball, D. (2009). "Whodunit?" (interview with Robert C. Merton). *Wilmott Magazine*, May.

Turner, A. (2016). *Between Debt and the Devil: Money, Credit, and Fixing Global Finance*. Princeton, NJ: Princeton University Press.

Tversky, A. and D. Kahneman (1974). "Judgment under Uncertainty: Heuristics and Biases." *Science* 185 (4157): 1124–1131.

Twain, M. (2010). *Pudd'nhead Wilson*, Ch. 13. New York: Simon & Schuster.

UBS (2008). "Shareholder Report on UBS's Write-Downs." Available at: www.ubs.com/1/ShowMedia/investors/shareholderreport?contentId=140333&name=080418ShareholderReport.pdf.

Valukas, A.R. (2010). "Report of Examiner Anton R. Valukas in re Lehman Brothers Holdings Inc., et al." United States Bankruptcy Court Southern District of New York, Chapter 11 Case 08-13555 (JPM).

Varadarajan, T. (2010)."Wall Street's Fortune Teller." *Daily Beast*, May 13. Available at www.thedailybeast.com/wall-streets-fortune-teller.

Vaughan, L. (2017). "How the Flash Crash Trader's $50 Million Fortune Vanished." *Bloomberg Markets*, February 9. Available at: www.bloomberg.com/news/features/2017-02-10/how-the-flash-crash-trader-s-50-million-fortune-vanished.

Véron, N. (2011). "The European Debt and Financial Crisis: Origins, Options, and Implications for the U.S. and Global Economy." Testimony before the US Senate Committee on Banking, Housing, and Urban Affairs Subcommittee on Security and International Trade and Finance, September 22.

——— (2015). "Europe's Radical Banking Union." Bruegel Essay and Lecture Series, May.

Wallison, P.J. (2009). "Everything You Wanted to Know about Credit Default Swaps: But Were Never Told." *Journal of Structured Finance* 15 (2).

Welch, I. (2000). "Herding Among Security Analysts." *Journal of Financial Economics* 58 (3): 369–396.

Wells, S. and G. Taylor (eds.) (1988). *William Shakespeare: The Complete Works* (Oxford, UK: Oxford University Press).

Wiggins, R.Z. and A. Metrick (2015). "The Lehman Brothers Bankruptcy G: The Special Case of Derivatives." Yale Program on Financial Stability Case Study 2014-3G-V1, Yale School of Management, New Haven, CT, April 7.

Wiggins, R.Z., T. Piontek, and A. Metrick (2014). "The Lehman Brothers Bankruptcy A: Overview." Yale Program on Financial Stability Case Study 2014-3A-V1, Yale School of Management, New Haven, CT, October 1.

Yorulmazer, T. (2014). "Case Studies on Disruptions during the Crisis." *FBRNY Economic Policy Review* 20 (1): 17–28.

Zettelmeyer, J., C. Trebesch, and M. Gulati (2013). "The Greek Debt Restructuring: An Autopsy." *Economic Policy* 28 (75): 513–563.

Zuckerman, G. (2000). "Long-Term Capital Chief Acknowledges Flawed Tactics." *Wall Street Journal*, August 21.

——— (2009). *The Greatest Trade Ever: The Behind-the-Scenes Story of How John Paulson Defied Wall Street and Made Financial History.* New York: Broadway Books.

# INDEX

## ABOUT THE AUTHOR

**BRUCE I. JACOBS** is co-founder, co-chief investment officer, and co-director of research at Jacobs Levy Equity Management. For 35 years, he has been a major voice for financial transparency. Jacobs has written investment books and articles on equity management and financial crises for leading journals.

Bruce Jacobs is author of *Capital Ideas and Market Realities: Option Replication, Investor Behavior, and Stock Market Crashes* and co-author with Ken Levy of *Equity Management: The Art and Science of Modern Quantitative Investing,* 2nd ed., co-editor of *Market Neutral Strategies,* and co-editor of *The Bernstein Fabozzi/Jacobs Levy Awards: Five Years of Award-Winning Articles from the Journal of Portfolio Management,* Volumes One through Three. He was a featured contributor to *How I Became a Quant: Insights from 25 of Wall Street's Elite.*

Jacobs's articles have appeared in the *Financial Analysts Journal, Journal of Portfolio Management, Journal of Investing, Journal of Financial Perspectives, Japanese Security Analysts Journal*, and *Operations Research.* He has received several Graham and Dodd Awards from the *Financial Analysts Journal*, a Bernstein Fabozzi/Jacobs Levy Award from the *Journal of Portfolio Management*, and an Outstanding Article Award from the *Journal of Investing.*

He has spoken at many forums, including the Jacobs Levy Equity Management Center for Quantitative Financial Research at the Wharton School, the Institute for Quantitative Research in Finance, Berkeley Program in Finance, CFA Institute, Society of Quantitative Analysts, and New York Society of Security Analysts, and he has given a *Financial Analysts Journal* Media Seminar and presented at conferences for Goldman Sachs and Morgan Stanley.

Prior to founding Jacobs Levy Equity Management, he was First Vice President of the Prudential Insurance Company of America, where he served as Senior Managing Director of a quantitative equity management affiliate of the Prudential Asset Management Company and Managing Director of the Pension Asset Management Group. Prior to that, he was on the finance faculty of the University of Pennsylvania's Wharton School and consulted to the Rand Corporation.

Dr. Jacobs has a B.A. from Columbia College, an M.S. in Operations Research and Computer Science from Columbia University's School of Engineering and Applied Science, an M.S.I.A. from Carnegie Mellon University's Graduate School of Industrial Administration, and an M.A. in Applied Economics and a Ph.D. in Finance from the Wharton School.

He serves on the *Journal of Portfolio Management* Advisory Board, is an Associate Editor of the *Journal of Trading*, and has served on the *Financial Analysts Journal* Advisory Council. Jacobs also served on the Committee to Establish the National Institute of Finance and was a member of its successor, the Office of Financial Research Discussion Forum. He is Chair of the Advisory Board of the Jacobs Levy Equity Management Center for Quantitative Financial Research at the Wharton School and Chair of the Prize Selection Committee for the Wharton-Jacobs Levy Prize for Quantitative Financial Innovation.